PÉNÉLOPE BAGIEU

CALIFORNIA DREAMIN'

:01

First Second

New York

This is dedicated to the one I love

First Second

English translation by Nanette McGuinness
English translation © 2017 by Roaring Brook Press,
a division of Holtzbrinck Publishing Holdings Limited Partnership

Published by First Second
First Second is an imprint of Roaring Brook Press,
a division of Holtzbrinck Publishing Holdings Limited Partnership
175 Fifth Avenue, New York, New York 10010
All rights reserved

Library of Congress Control Number: 2012951851

ISBN 978-1-62672-546-1

Our books may be purchased in bulk for promotional, educational, or business use.
Please contact your local bookseller or the Macmillan Corporate and Premium Sales Department
at (800) 221-7945 ext. 5442 or by e-mail at MacmillanSpecialMarkets@macmillan.com.

Drawn on Canson Montval paper with Faber Castell H, 2B, and 4B graphite pencils.

FIRST
EDITION

Originally published in 2015 in French by Gallimard
French edition © 2015 by Gallimard
First American edition 2017
Book design by Chris Dickey

Printed in the United States of America

10 9 8 7 6 5 4 3 2 1

PROLOGUE

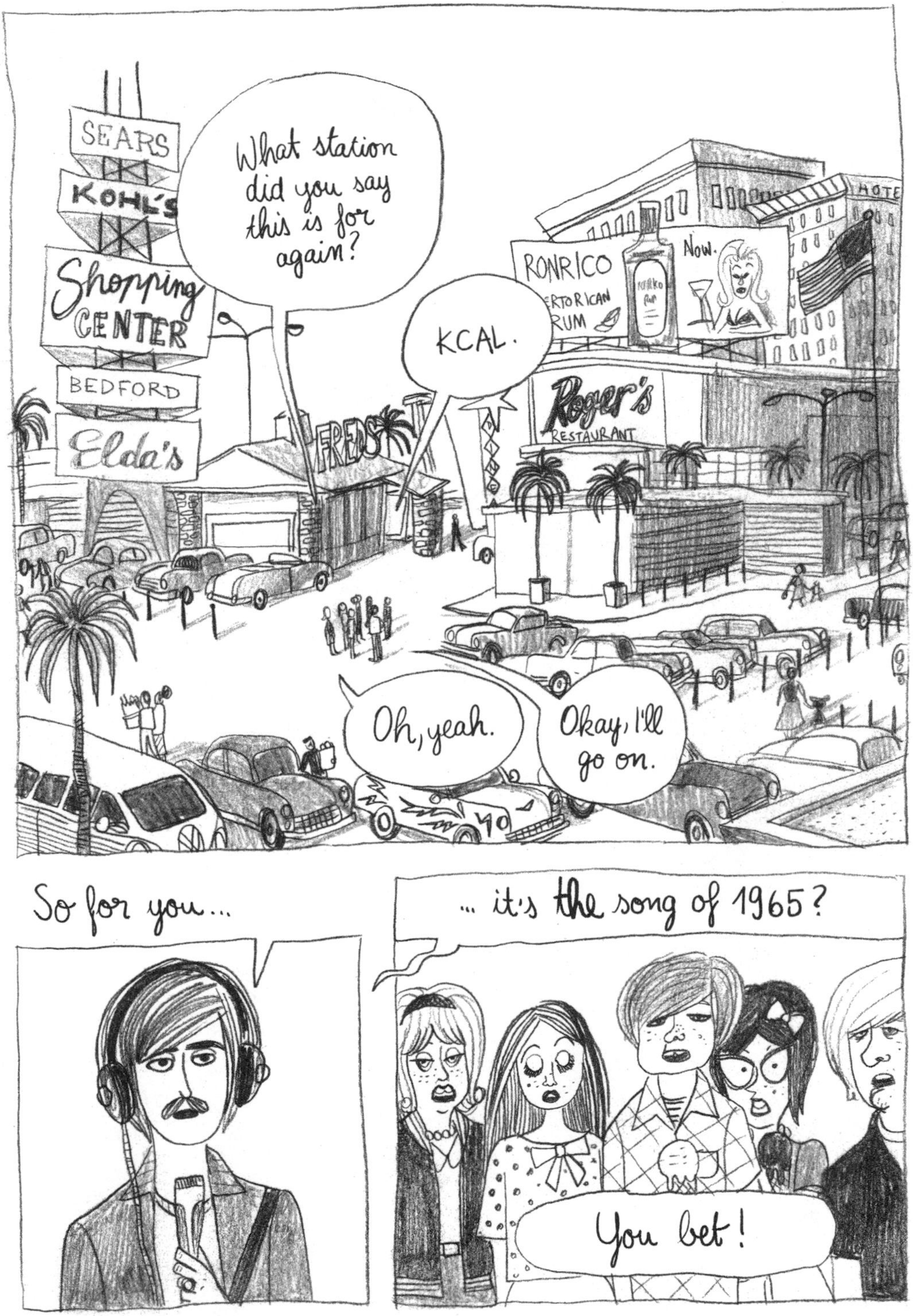
SEARS
KOHL'S
Shopping CENTER
BEDFORD
Elda's
What station did you say this is for again?
KCAL.
FREDS
RONRICO
RUM
Now.
Roger's RESTAURANT
Oh, yeah.
Okay, I'll go on.
So for you...
... it's the song of 1965?
You bet!

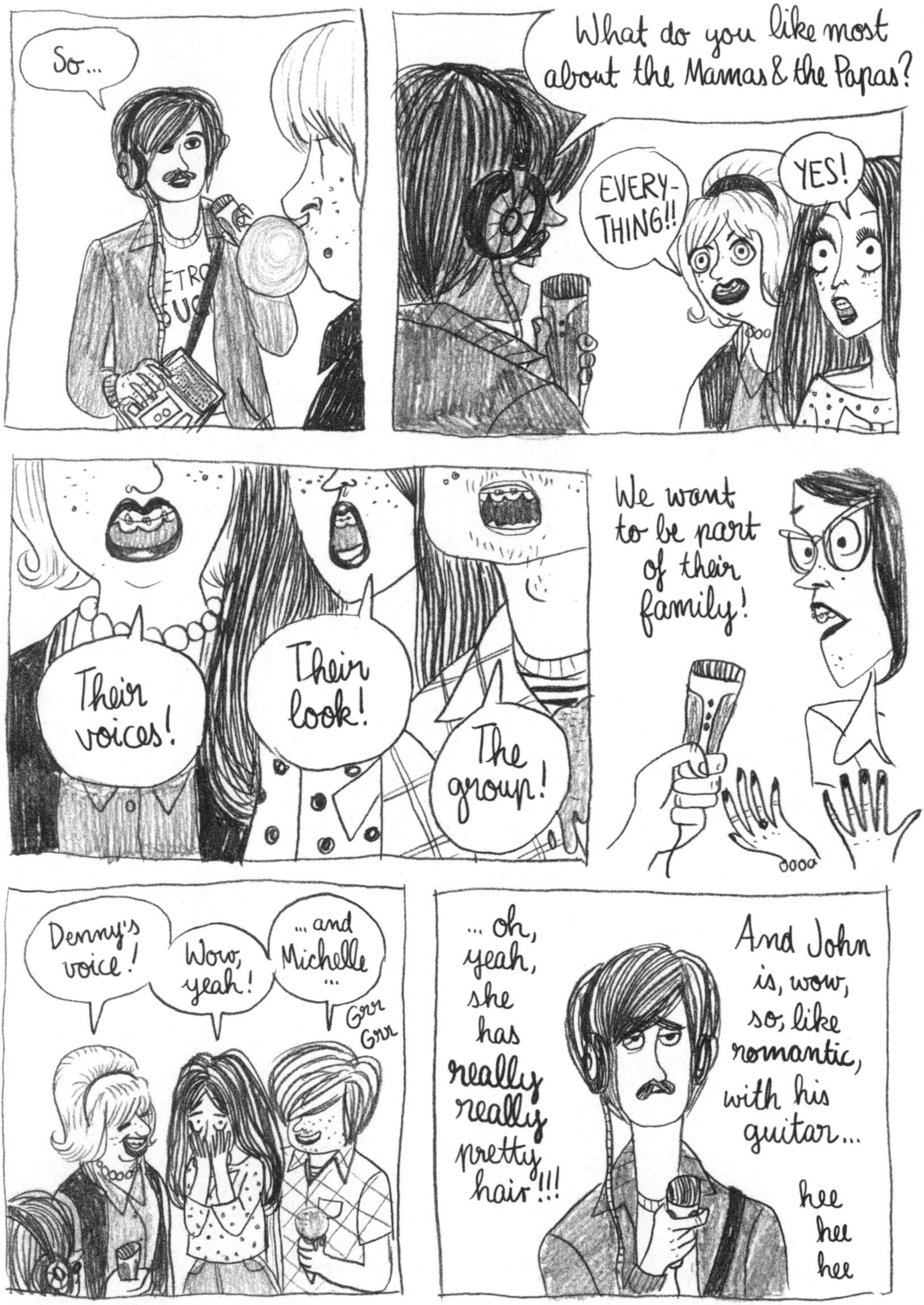

So...
RETRO SUC
What do you like most about the Mamas & the Papas?
EVERY-THING!!
YES!
Their voices!
Their look!
The group!
We want to be part of their family!
Denny's voice!
Wow, yeah!
...and Michelle ...
Grr Grr
... oh, yeah, she has really really pretty hair!!!
And John is, wow, so, like romantic, with his guitar...
hee hee hee

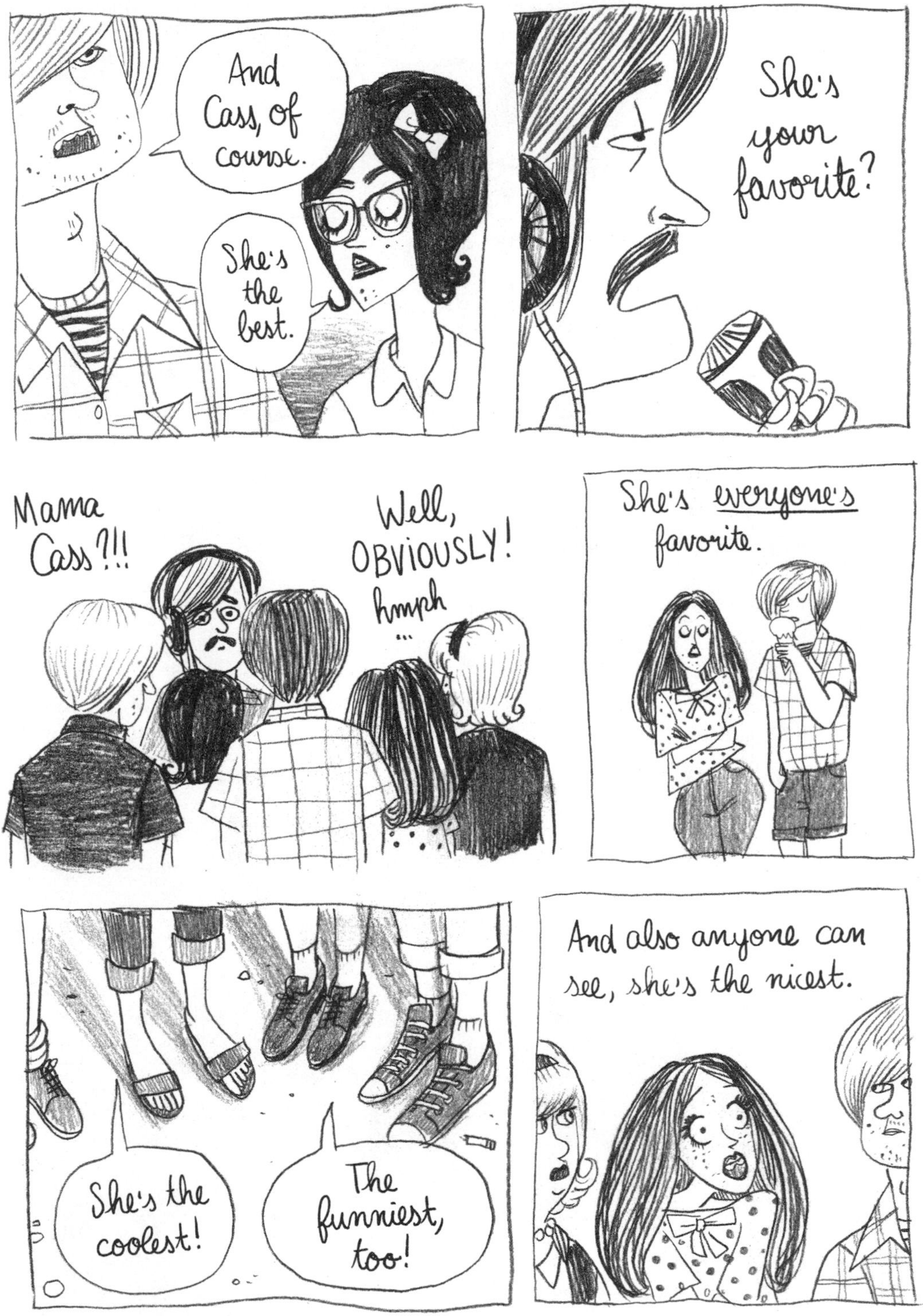
And Cass, of course.
She's the best.
She's your favorite?
Mama Cass?!!
Well, OBVIOUSLY!
hmph ...
She's everyone's favorite.
She's the coolest!
The funniest, too!
And also anyone can see, she's the nicest.

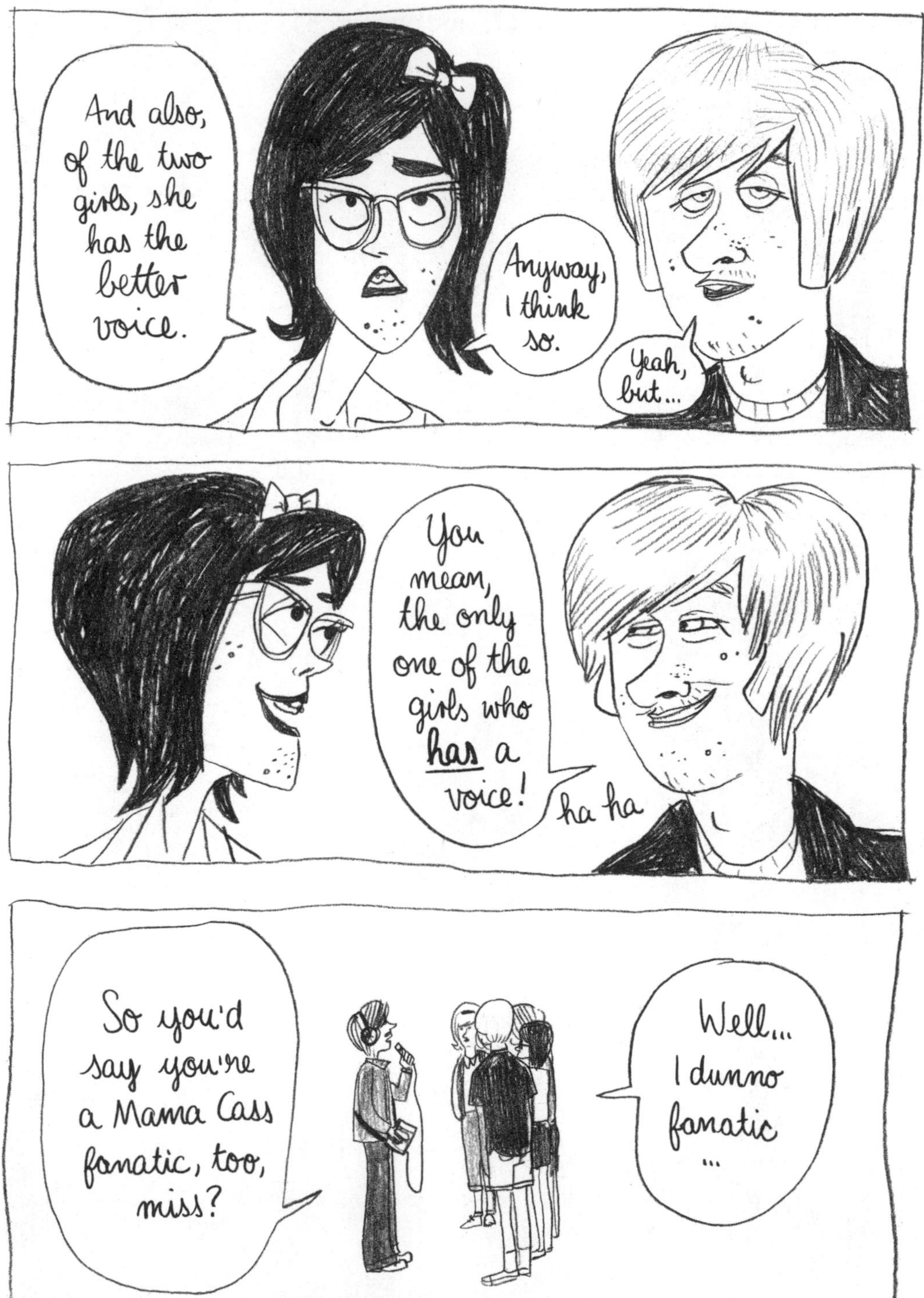
And also, of the two girls, she has the better voice.
Anyway, I think so.
Yeah, but...
You mean, the only one of the girls who **has** a voice!
ha ha
So you'd say you're a Mama Cass fanatic, too, miss?
Well... I dunno fanatic ...

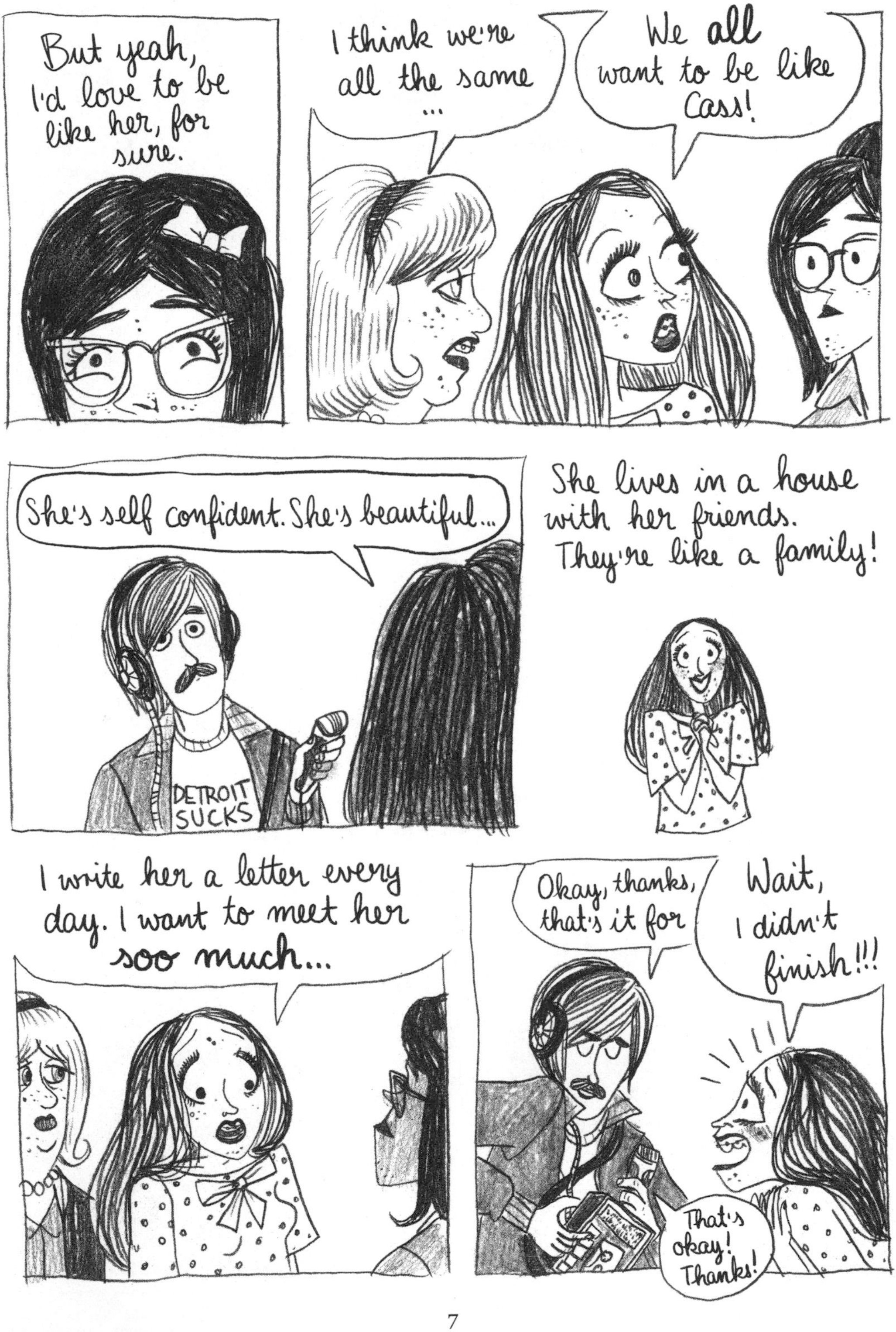
But yeah, I'd love to be like her, for sure.
I think we're all the same ...
We all want to be like Cass!
She's self confident. She's beautiful...
DETROIT SUCKS
She lives in a house with her friends. They're like a family!
I write her a letter every day. I want to meet her soo much...
Okay, thanks, that's it for
Wait, I didn't finish!!!
That's okay! Thanks!

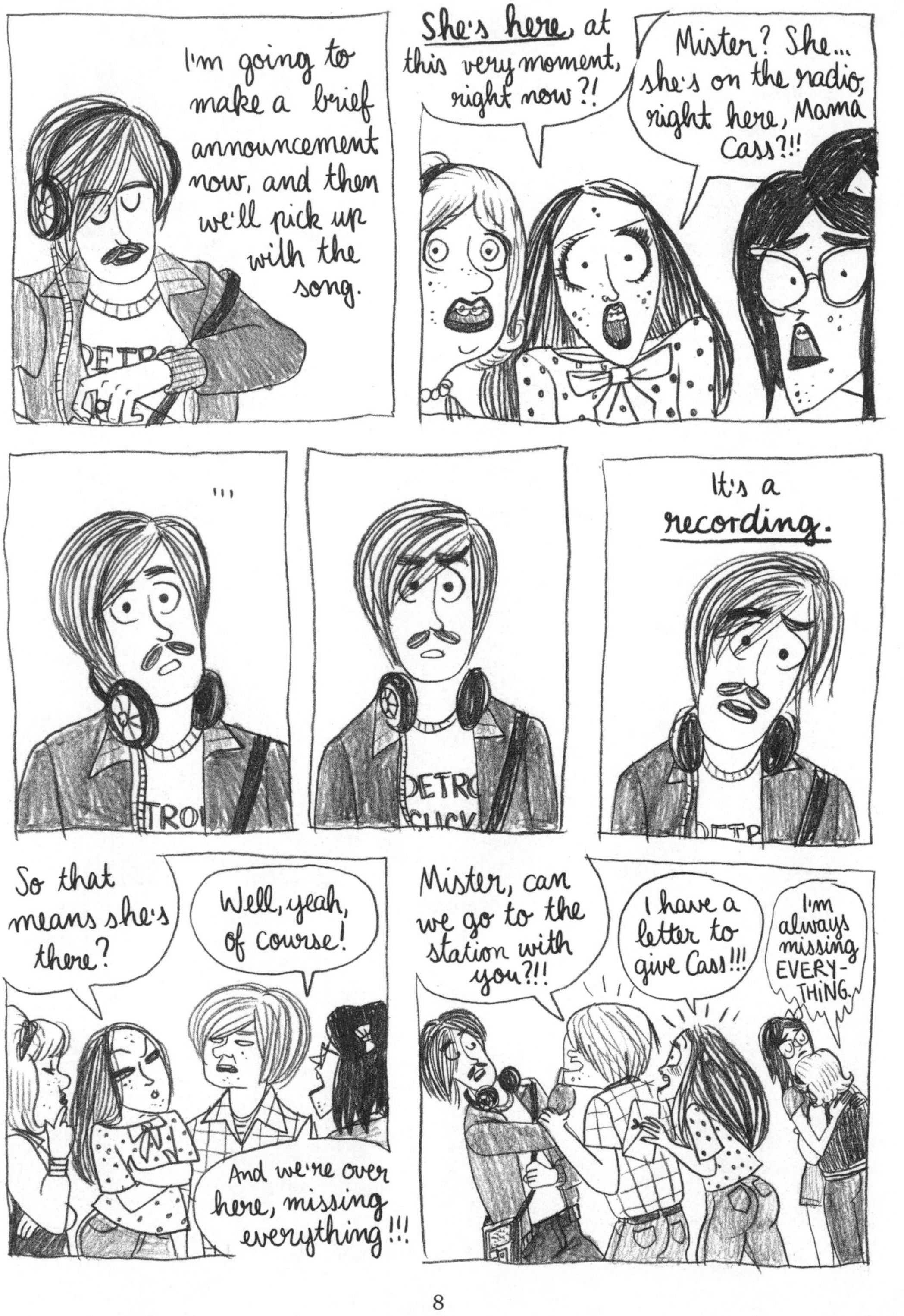
I'm going to make a brief announcement now, and then we'll pick up with the song.
She's here, at this very moment, right now?!
Mister? She... she's on the radio, right here, Mama Cass?!!
...
It's a recording.
So that means she's there?
Well, yeah, of course!
And we're over here, missing everything!!!
Mister, can we go to the station with you?!!
I have a letter to give Cass!!!
I'm always missing EVERY-THING.

1 - Leah

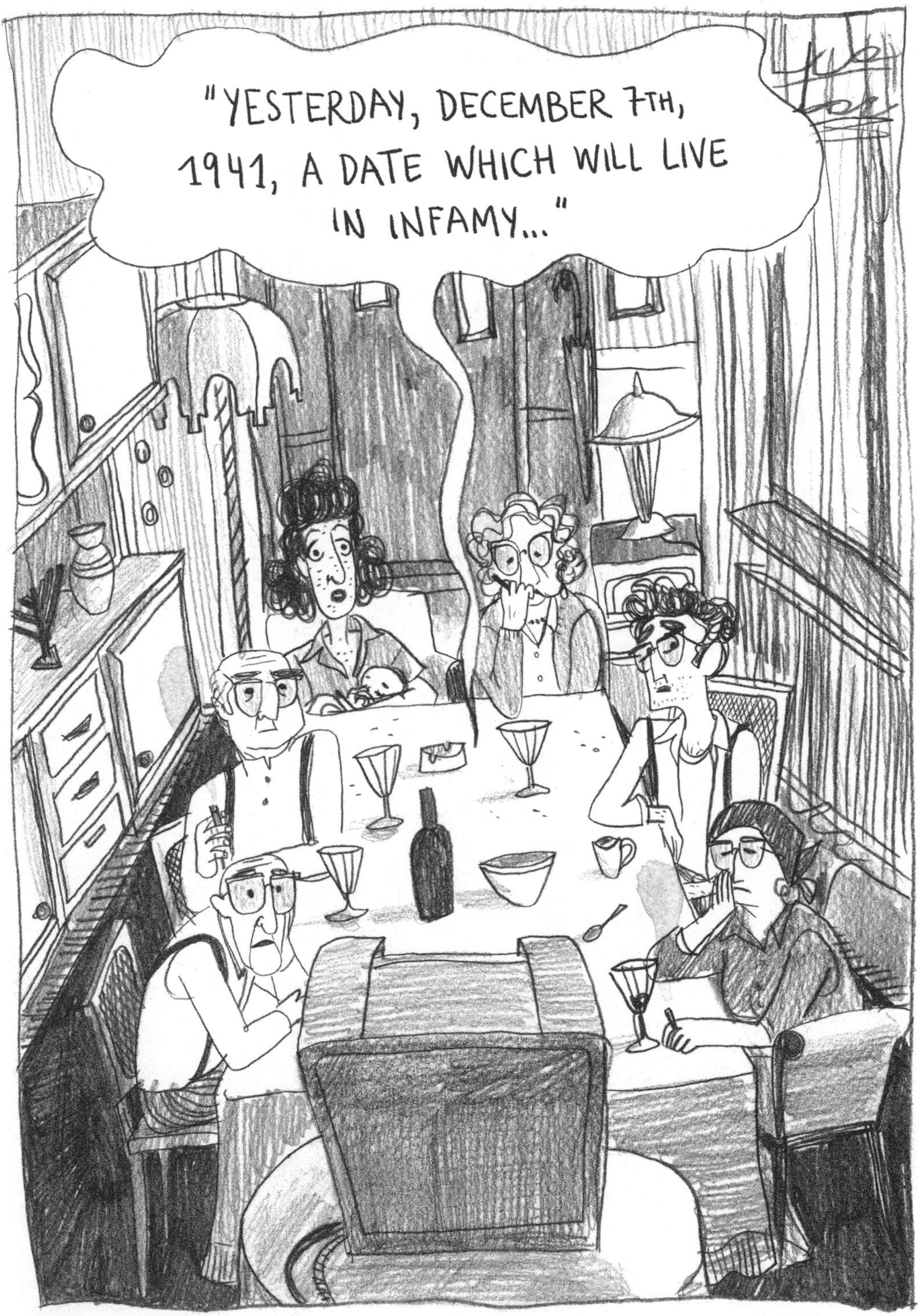
"YESTERDAY, DECEMBER 7TH, 1941, A DATE WHICH WILL LIVE IN INFAMY..."

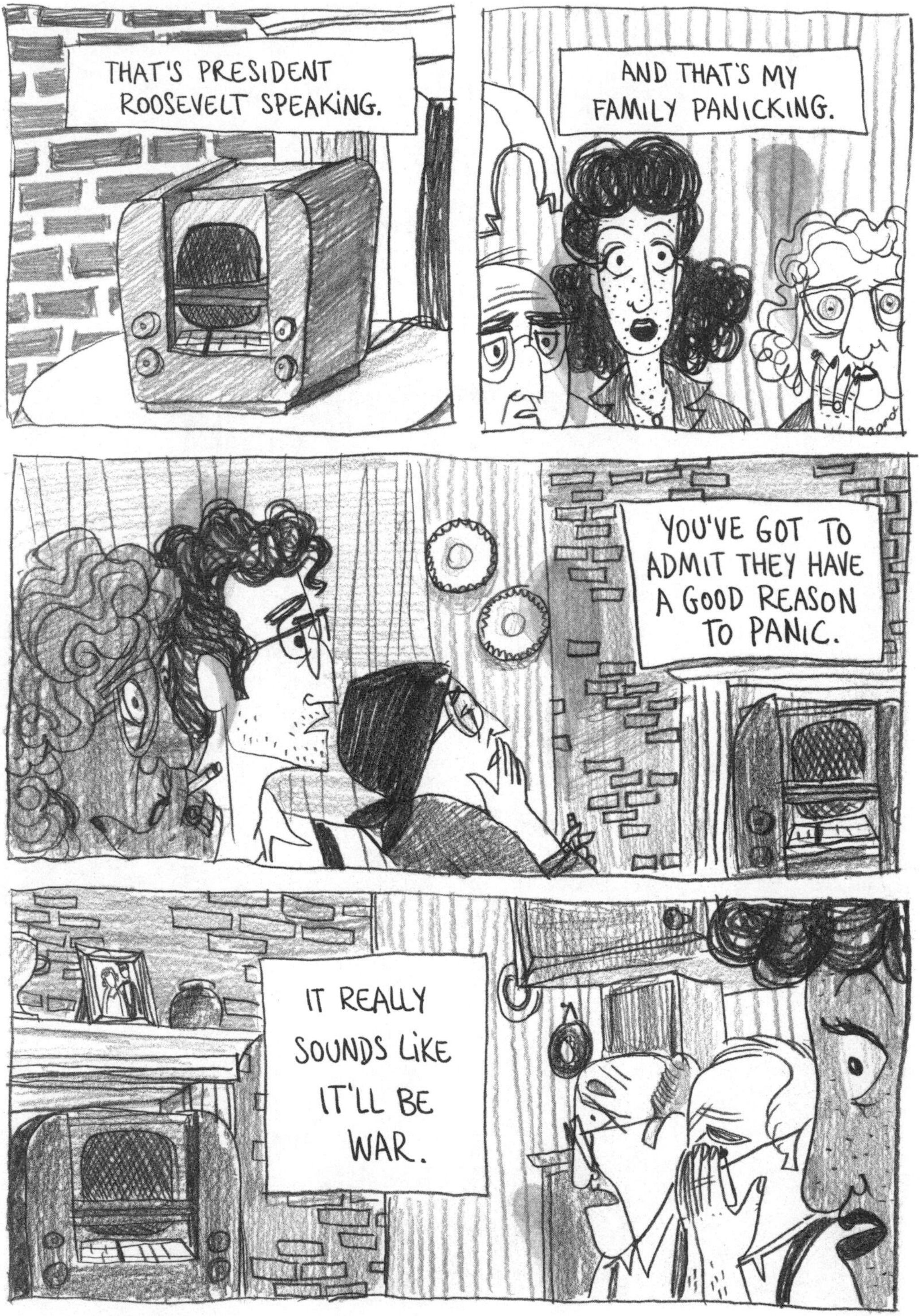
THAT'S PRESIDENT ROOSEVELT SPEAKING.
AND THAT'S MY FAMILY PANICKING.
YOU'VE GOT TO ADMIT THEY HAVE A GOOD REASON TO PANIC.
IT REALLY SOUNDS LIKE IT'LL BE WAR.

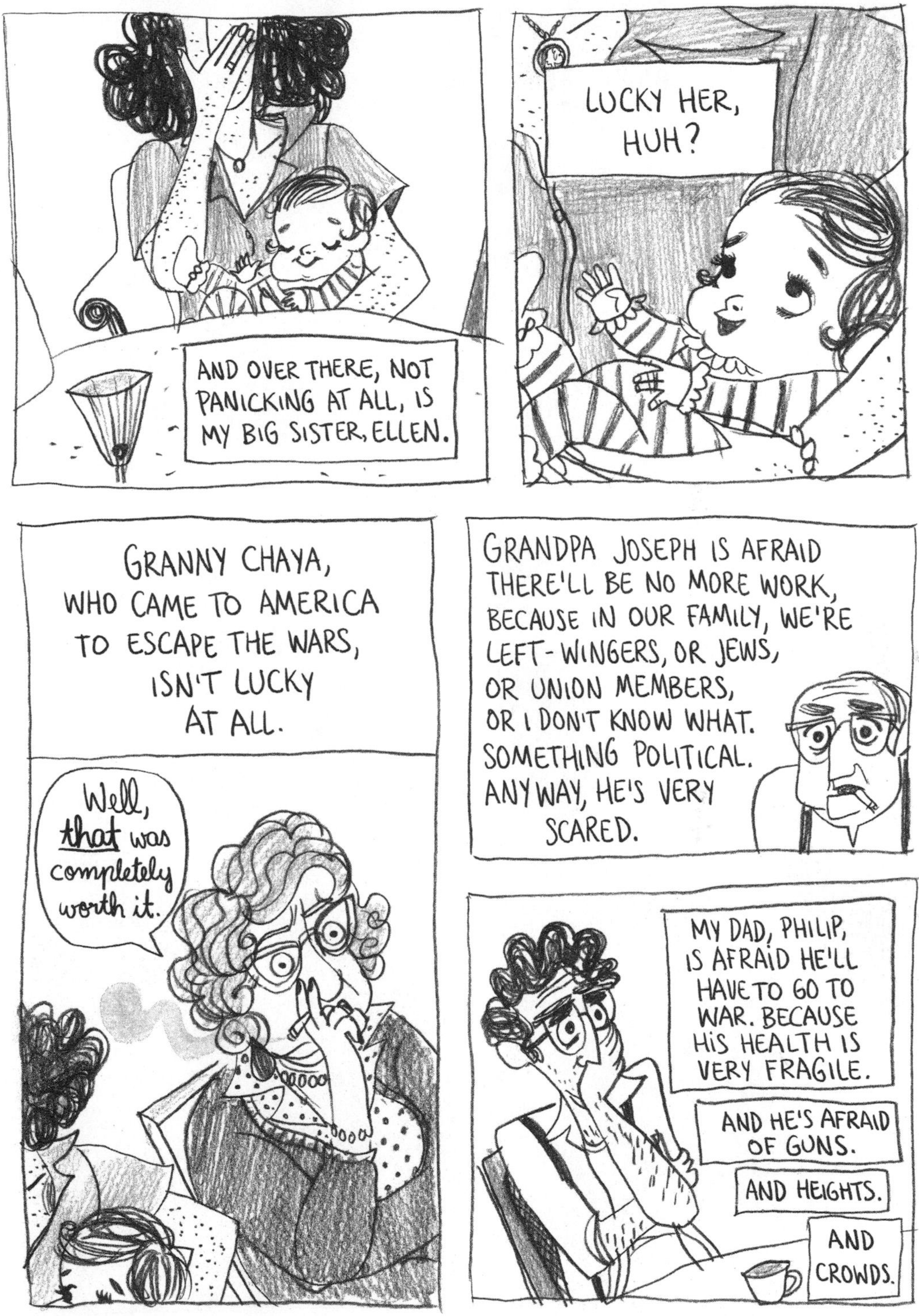
AND OVER THERE, NOT PANICKING AT ALL, IS MY BIG SISTER, ELLEN.
LUCKY HER, HUH?
GRANNY CHAYA, WHO CAME TO AMERICA TO ESCAPE THE WARS, ISN'T LUCKY AT ALL.
Well, that was completely worth it.
GRANDPA JOSEPH IS AFRAID THERE'LL BE NO MORE WORK, BECAUSE IN OUR FAMILY, WE'RE LEFT-WINGERS, OR JEWS, OR UNION MEMBERS, OR I DON'T KNOW WHAT. SOMETHING POLITICAL. ANYWAY, HE'S VERY SCARED.
MY DAD, PHILIP, IS AFRAID HE'LL HAVE TO GO TO WAR. BECAUSE HIS HEALTH IS VERY FRAGILE.
AND HE'S AFRAID OF GUNS.
AND HEIGHTS.
AND CROWDS.

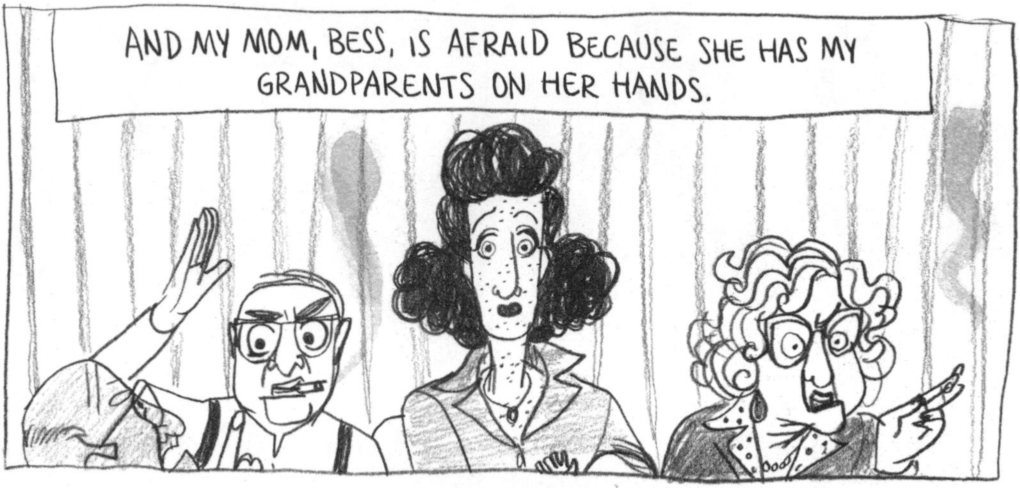
AND MY MOM, BESS, IS AFRAID BECAUSE SHE HAS MY GRANDPARENTS ON HER HANDS.

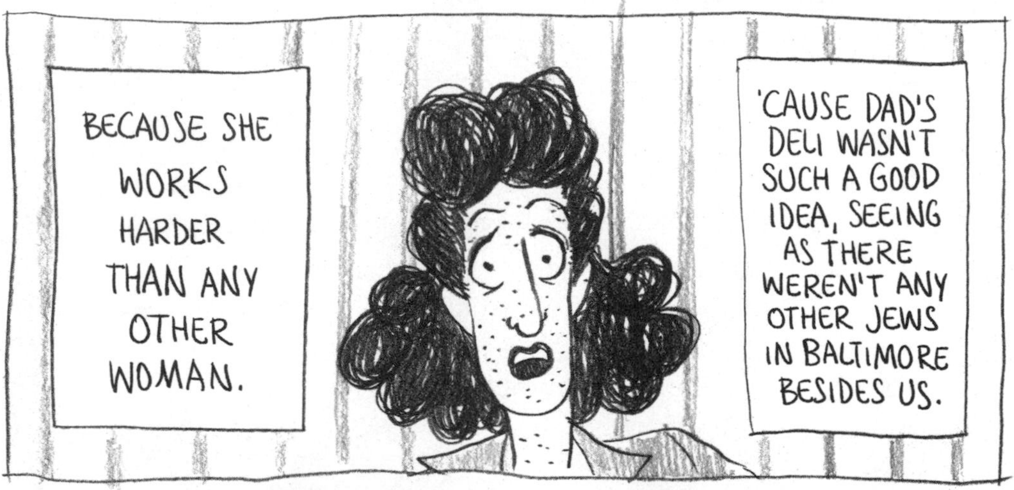
BECAUSE SHE WORKS HARDER THAN ANY OTHER WOMAN.
'CAUSE DAD'S DELI WASN'T SUCH A GOOD IDEA, SEEING AS THERE WEREN'T ANY OTHER JEWS IN BALTIMORE BESIDES US.

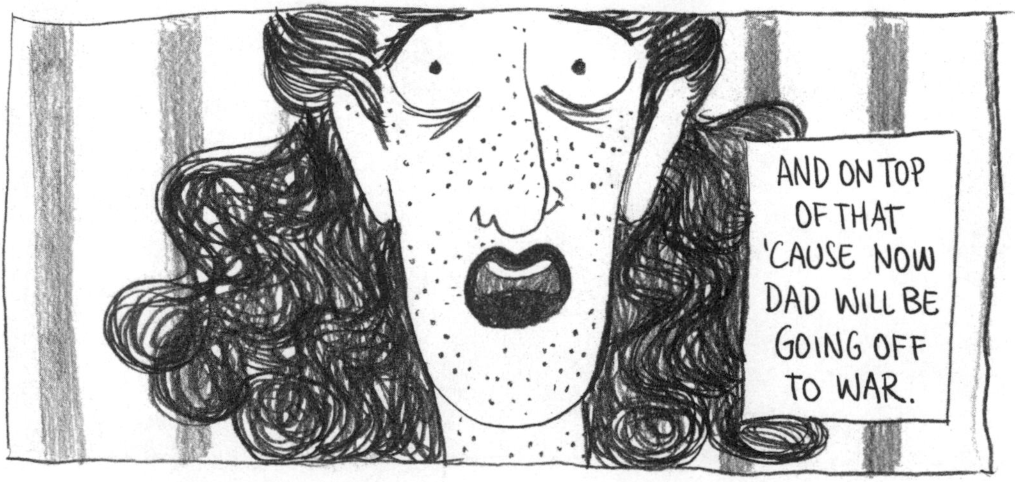
AND ON TOP OF THAT 'CAUSE NOW DAD WILL BE GOING OFF TO WAR.

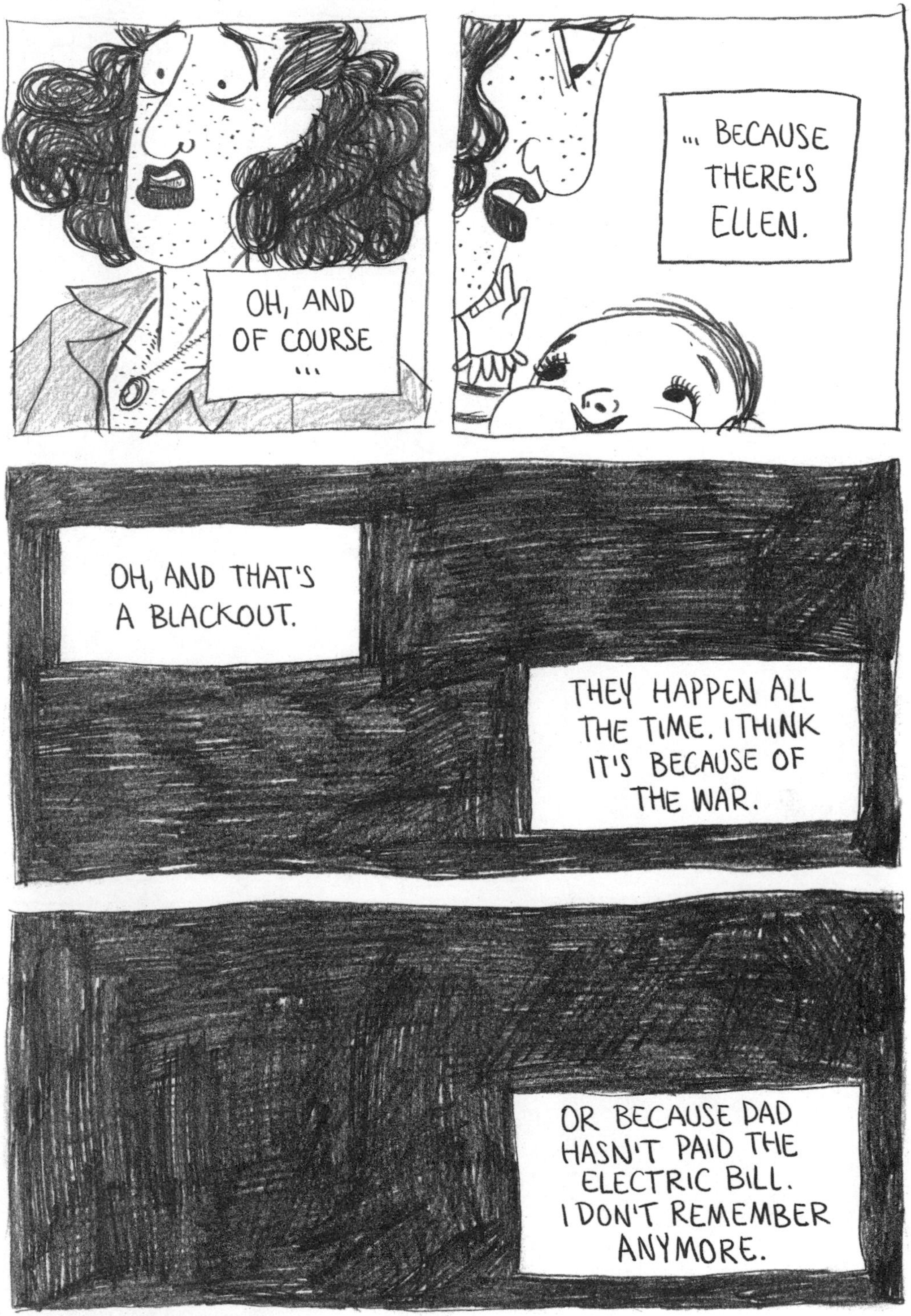
OH, AND OF COURSE ...
... BECAUSE THERE'S ELLEN.
OH, AND THAT'S A BLACKOUT.
THEY HAPPEN ALL THE TIME. I THINK IT'S BECAUSE OF THE WAR.
OR BECAUSE DAD HASN'T PAID THE ELECTRIC BILL. I DON'T REMEMBER ANYMORE.

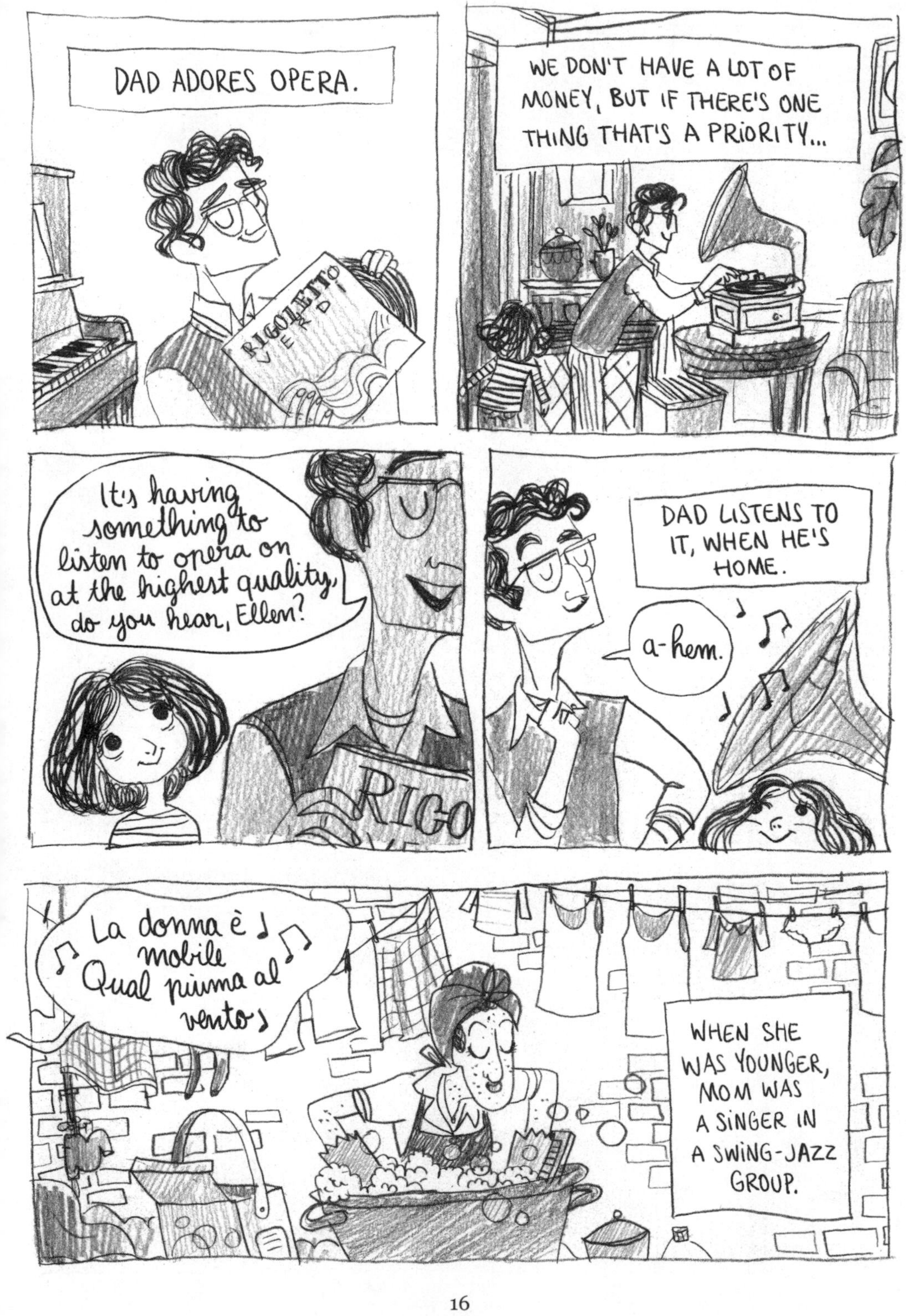
DAD ADORES OPERA.
RIGOLETTO VERDI
WE DON'T HAVE A LOT OF MONEY, BUT IF THERE'S ONE THING THAT'S A PRIORITY...
It's having something to listen to opera on at the highest quality, do you hear, Ellen?
RIGO
DAD LISTENS TO IT, WHEN HE'S HOME.
a-hem.
La donna è mobile Qual piuma al vento
WHEN SHE WAS YOUNGER, MOM WAS A SINGER IN A SWING-JAZZ GROUP.

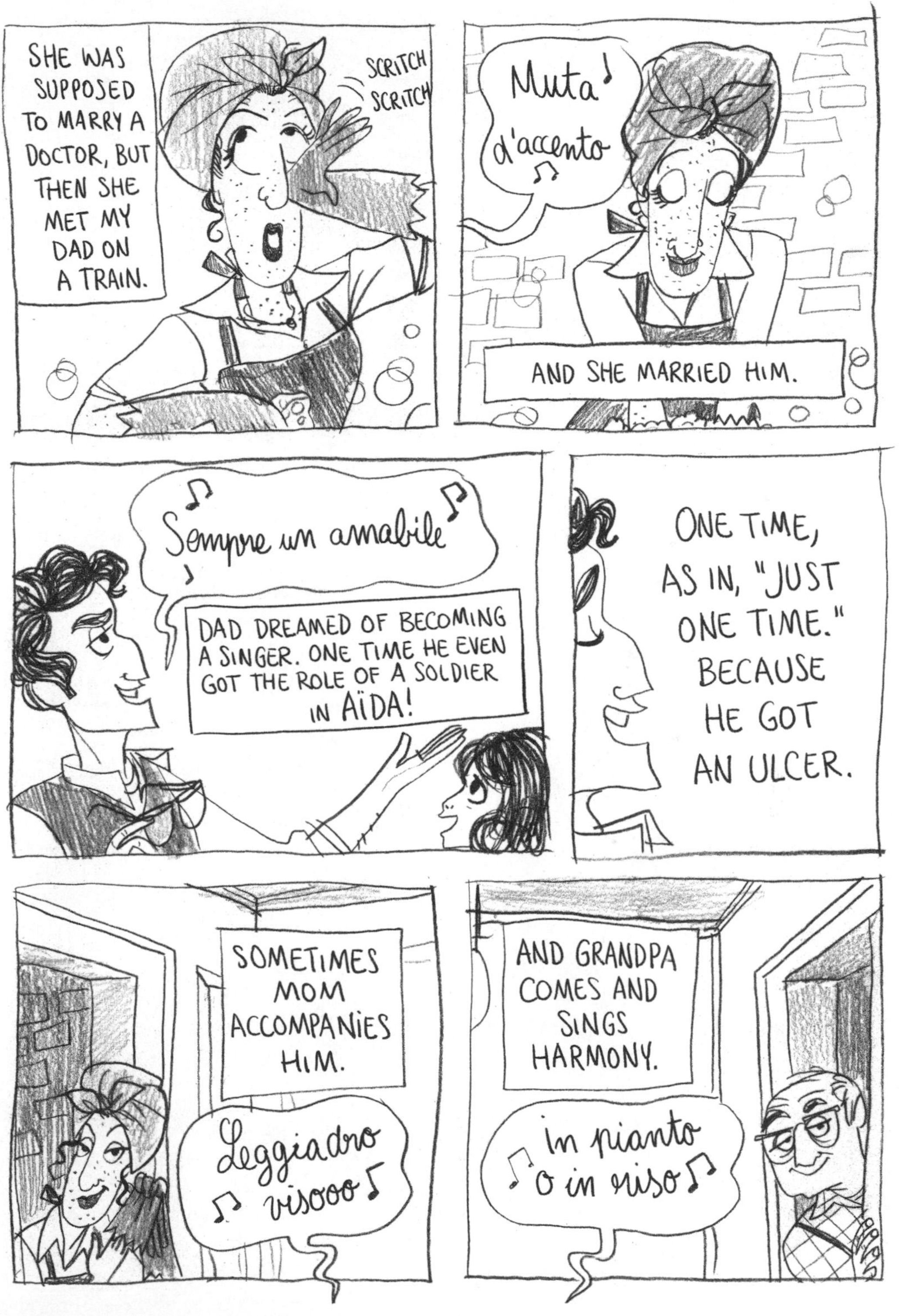
SHE WAS SUPPOSED TO MARRY A DOCTOR, BUT THEN SHE MET MY DAD ON A TRAIN.
SCRITCH SCRITCH
Muta d'accento
AND SHE MARRIED HIM.
Sempre un amabile
DAD DREAMED OF BECOMING A SINGER. ONE TIME HE EVEN GOT THE ROLE OF A SOLDIER IN AÏDA!
ONE TIME, AS IN, "JUST ONE TIME." BECAUSE HE GOT AN ULCER.
SOMETIMES MOM ACCOMPANIES HIM.
Leggiadro visooo
AND GRANDPA COMES AND SINGS HARMONY.
In pianto o in riso

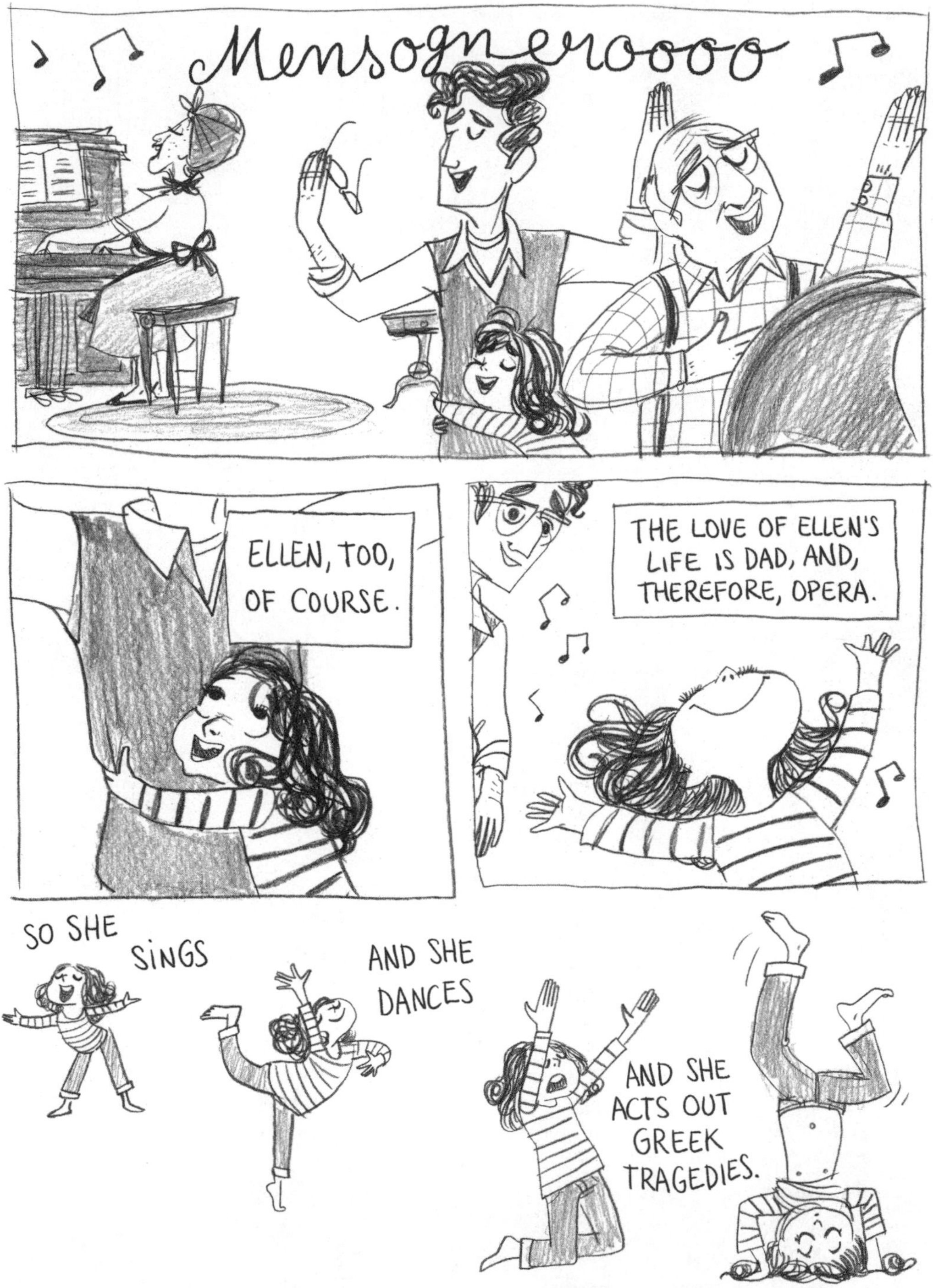
Mensognerooooo
ELLEN, TOO, OF COURSE.
THE LOVE OF ELLEN'S LIFE IS DAD, AND, THEREFORE, OPERA.
SO SHE SINGS
AND SHE DANCES
AND SHE ACTS OUT GREEK TRAGEDIES.
AND SHE WALKS ON HER HEAD.

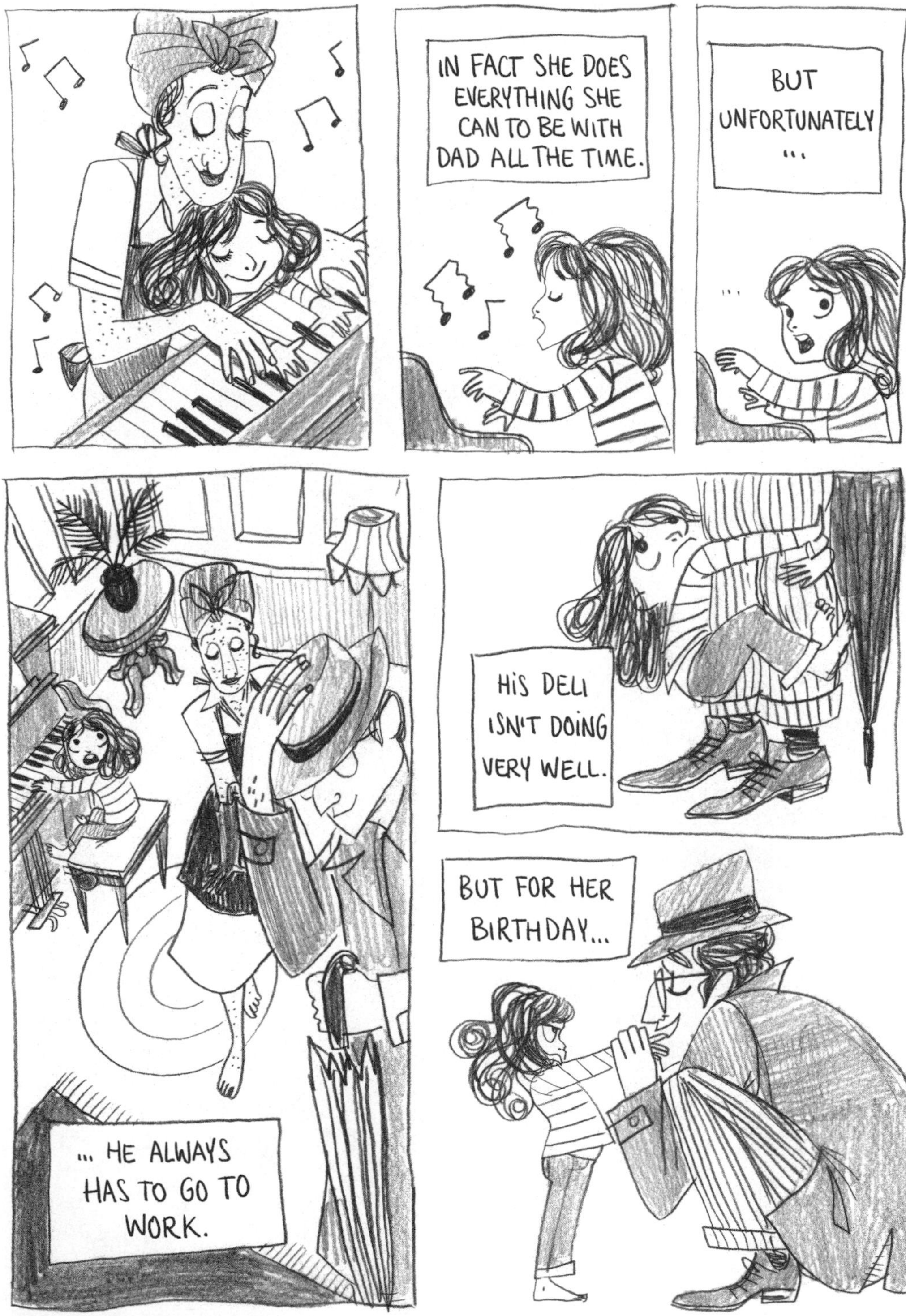

IN FACT SHE DOES EVERYTHING SHE CAN TO BE WITH DAD ALL THE TIME.
BUT UNFORTUNATELY ...
...
... HE ALWAYS HAS TO GO TO WORK.
HIS DELI ISN'T DOING VERY WELL.
BUT FOR HER BIRTHDAY...

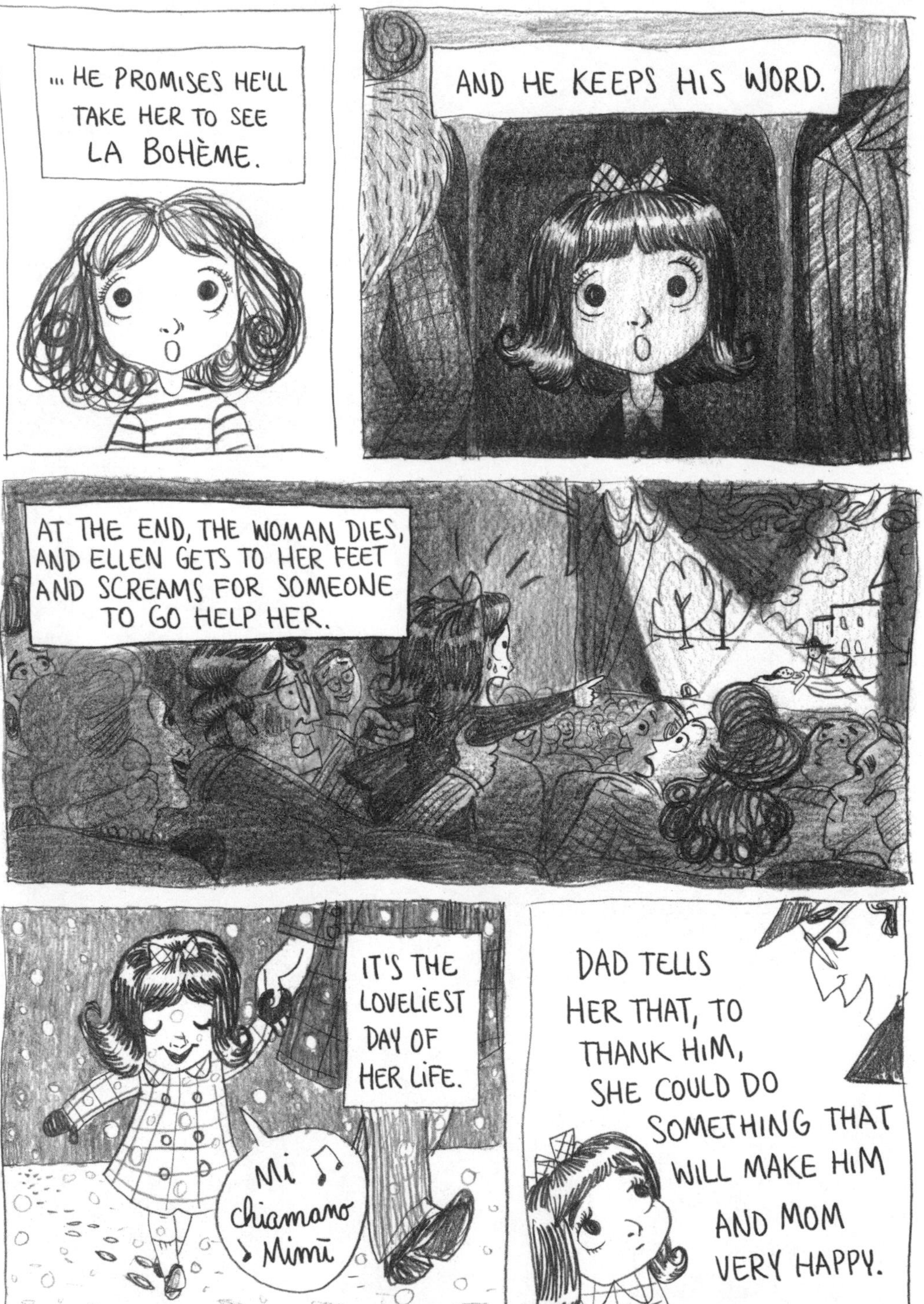
... HE PROMISES HE'LL TAKE HER TO SEE LA BOHÈME.
AND HE KEEPS HIS WORD.
AT THE END, THE WOMAN DIES, AND ELLEN GETS TO HER FEET AND SCREAMS FOR SOMEONE TO GO HELP HER.
IT'S THE LOVELIEST DAY OF HER LIFE.
Mi chiamano Mimì
DAD TELLS HER THAT, TO THANK HIM, SHE COULD DO SOMETHING THAT WILL MAKE HIM AND MOM VERY HAPPY.

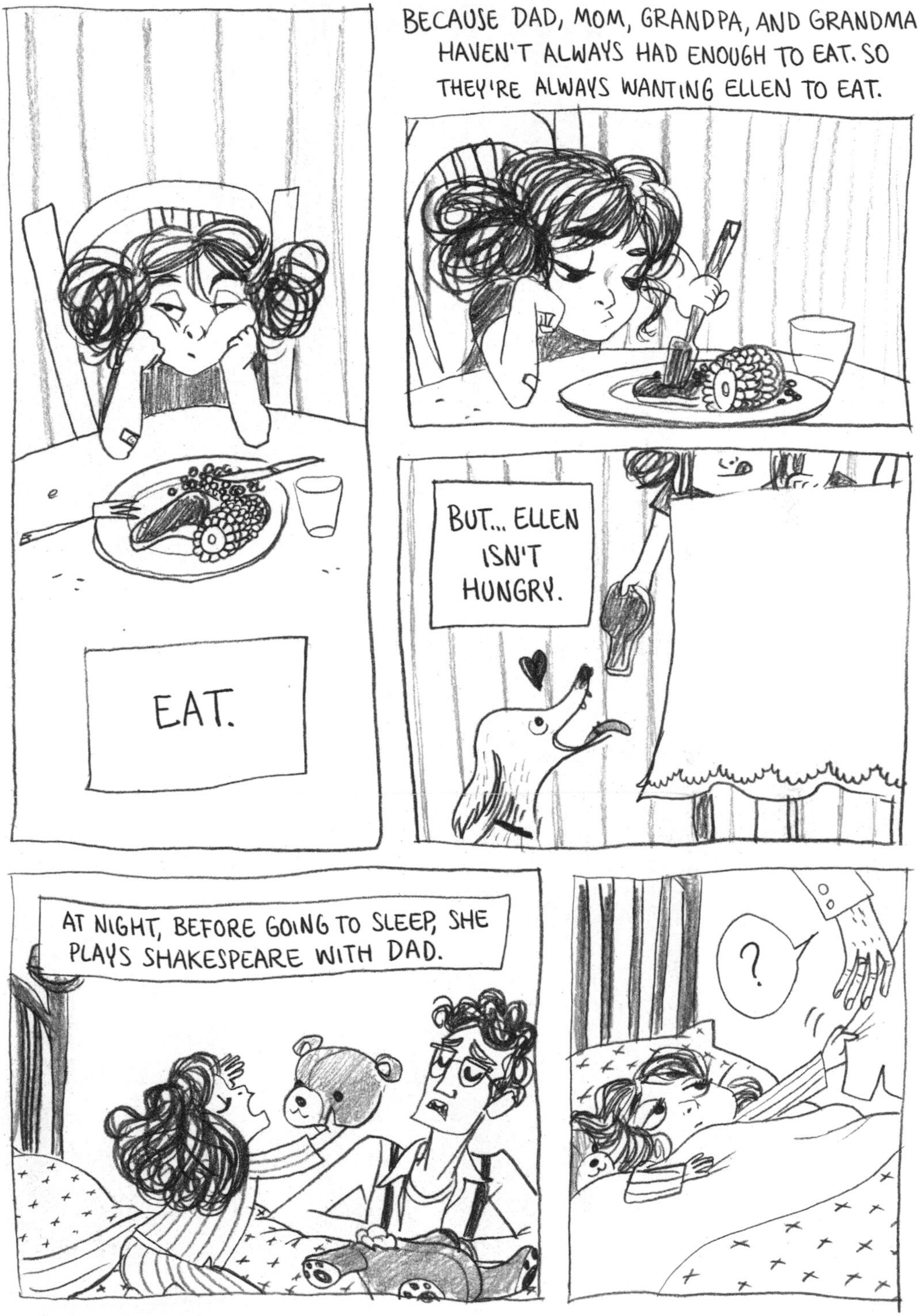

EAT.
BECAUSE DAD, MOM, GRANDPA, AND GRANDMA HAVEN'T ALWAYS HAD ENOUGH TO EAT. SO THEY'RE ALWAYS WANTING ELLEN TO EAT.
BUT... ELLEN ISN'T HUNGRY.
AT NIGHT, BEFORE GOING TO SLEEP, SHE PLAYS SHAKESPEARE WITH DAD.
?

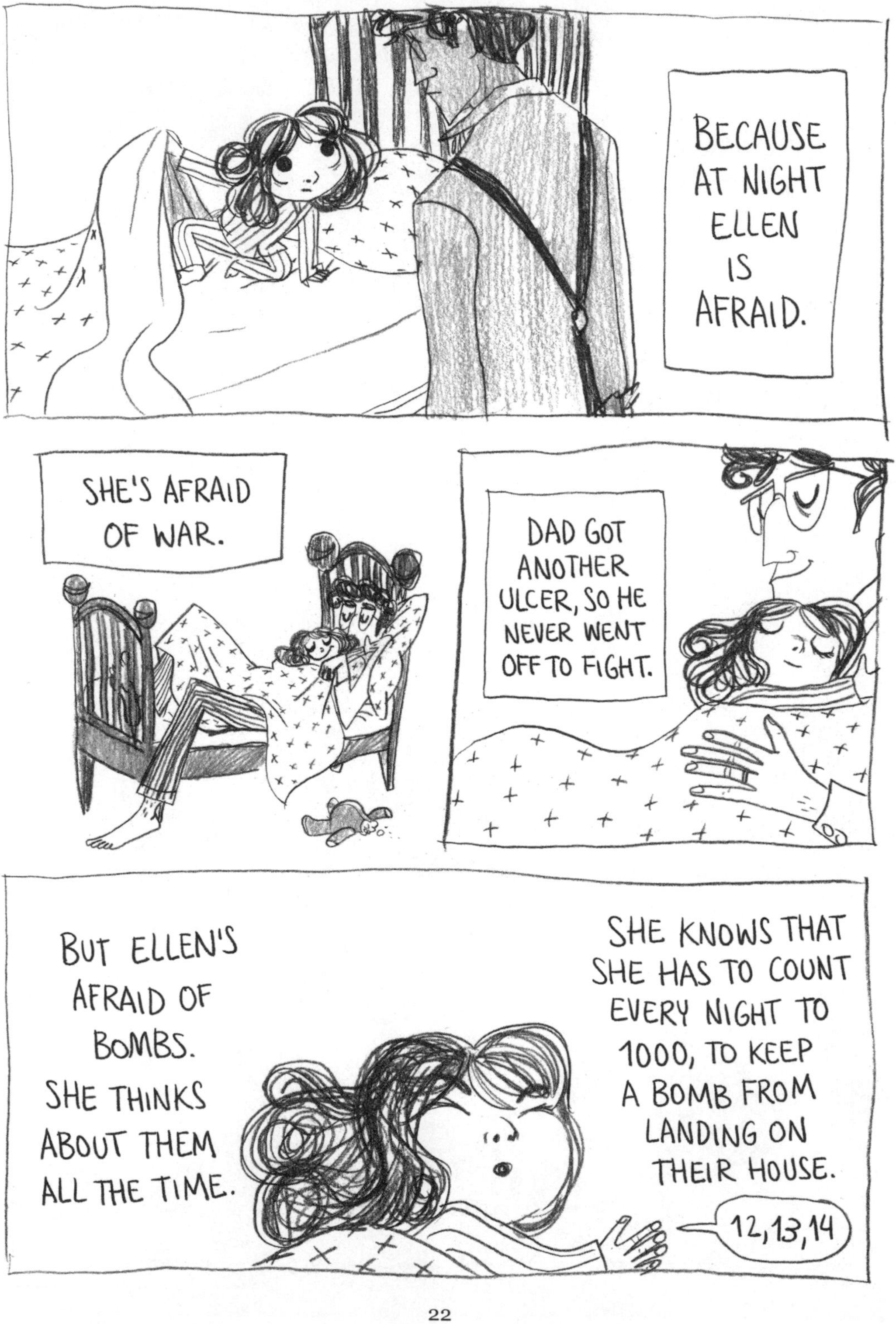

BECAUSE AT NIGHT ELLEN IS AFRAID.
SHE'S AFRAID OF WAR.
DAD GOT ANOTHER ULCER, SO HE NEVER WENT OFF TO FIGHT.
BUT ELLEN'S AFRAID OF BOMBS. SHE THINKS ABOUT THEM ALL THE TIME.
SHE KNOWS THAT SHE HAS TO COUNT EVERY NIGHT TO 1000, TO KEEP A BOMB FROM LANDING ON THEIR HOUSE.
12, 13, 14

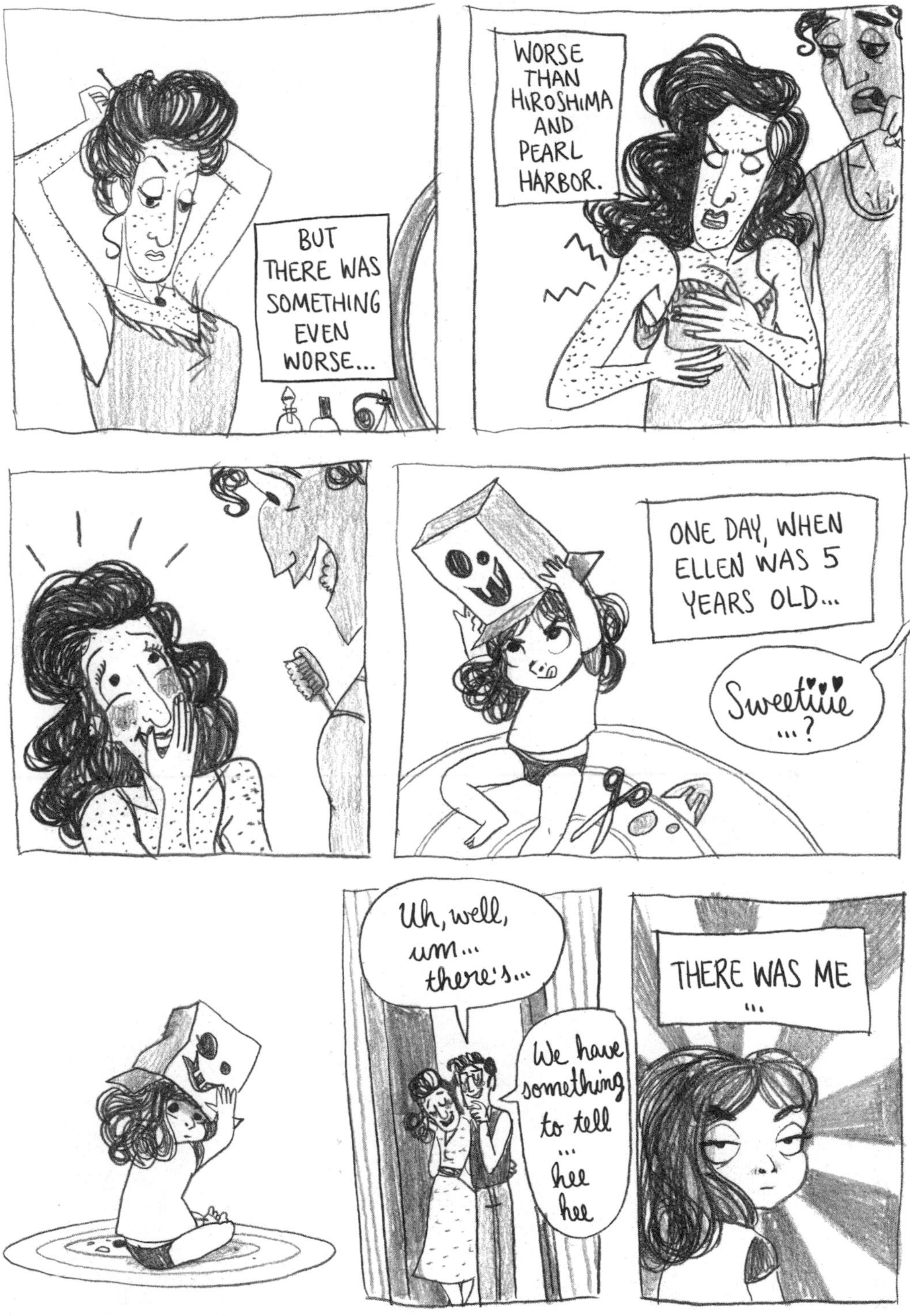
BUT THERE WAS SOMETHING EVEN WORSE...
WORSE THAN HIROSHIMA AND PEARL HARBOR.
ONE DAY, WHEN ELLEN WAS 5 YEARS OLD...
Sweetiiie ...?
Uh, well, um... there's...
We have something to tell ... hee hee
THERE WAS ME ...

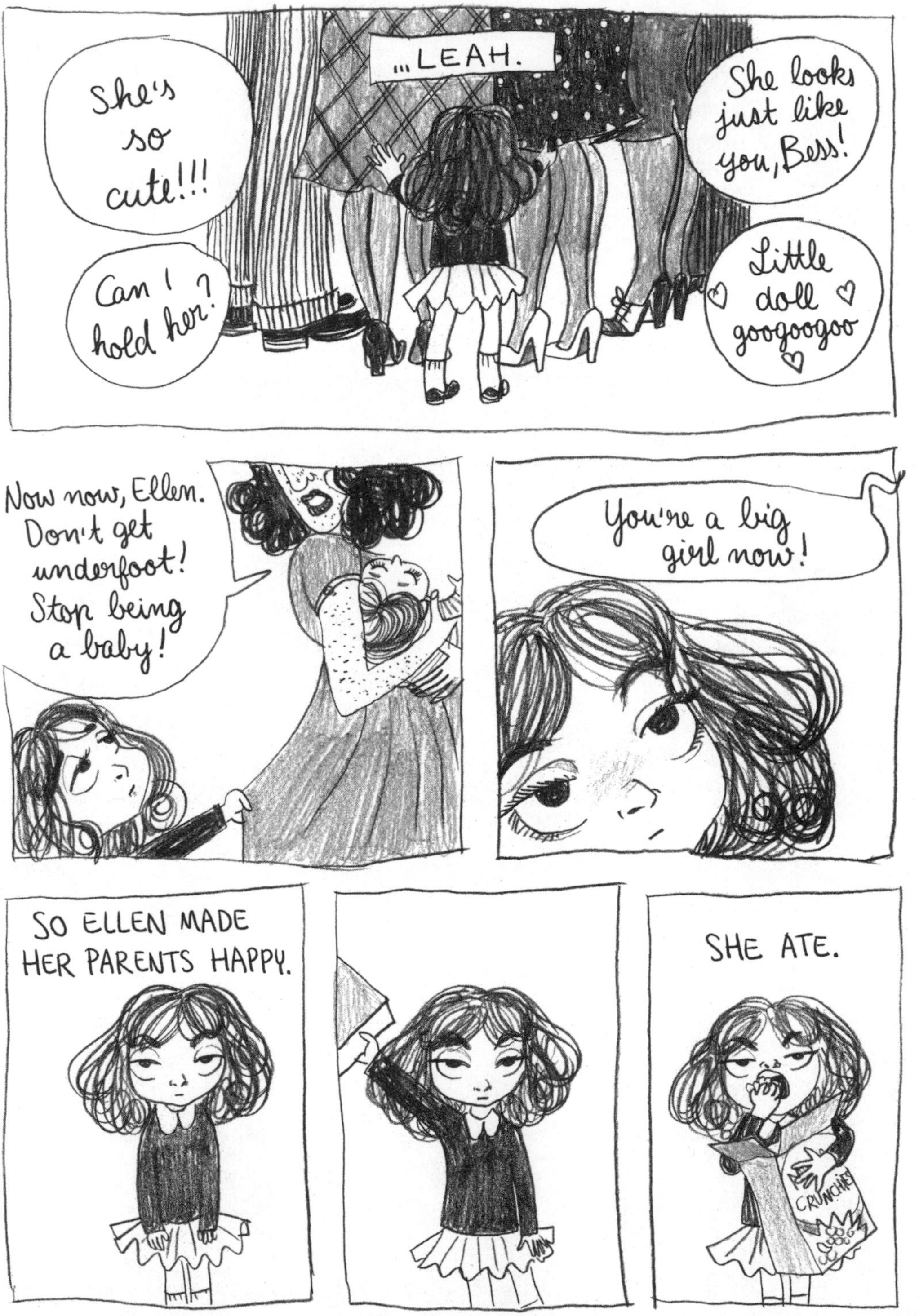
...LEAH.
She's so cute!!!
She looks just like you, Bess!
Can I hold her?
Little doll googoogoo
Now now, Ellen. Don't get underfoot! Stop being a baby!
You're a big girl now!
SO ELLEN MADE HER PARENTS HAPPY.
SHE ATE.
CRUNCHIES

2 - Joey

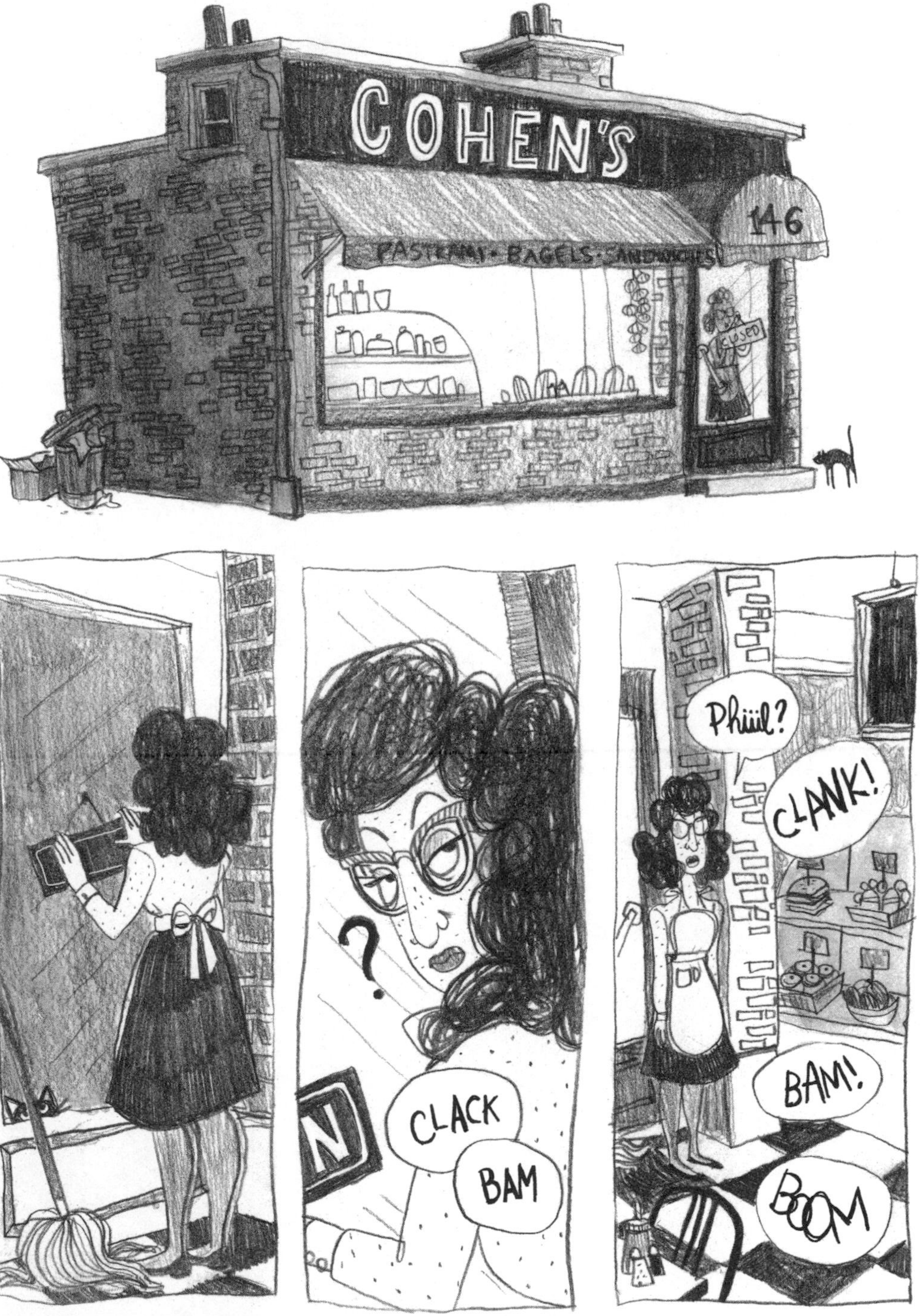
COHEN'S
146
PASTRAMI • BAGELS • SANDWICHES
CLOSED
CLACK
BAM
Phiiil?
CLANK!
BAM!
BOOM

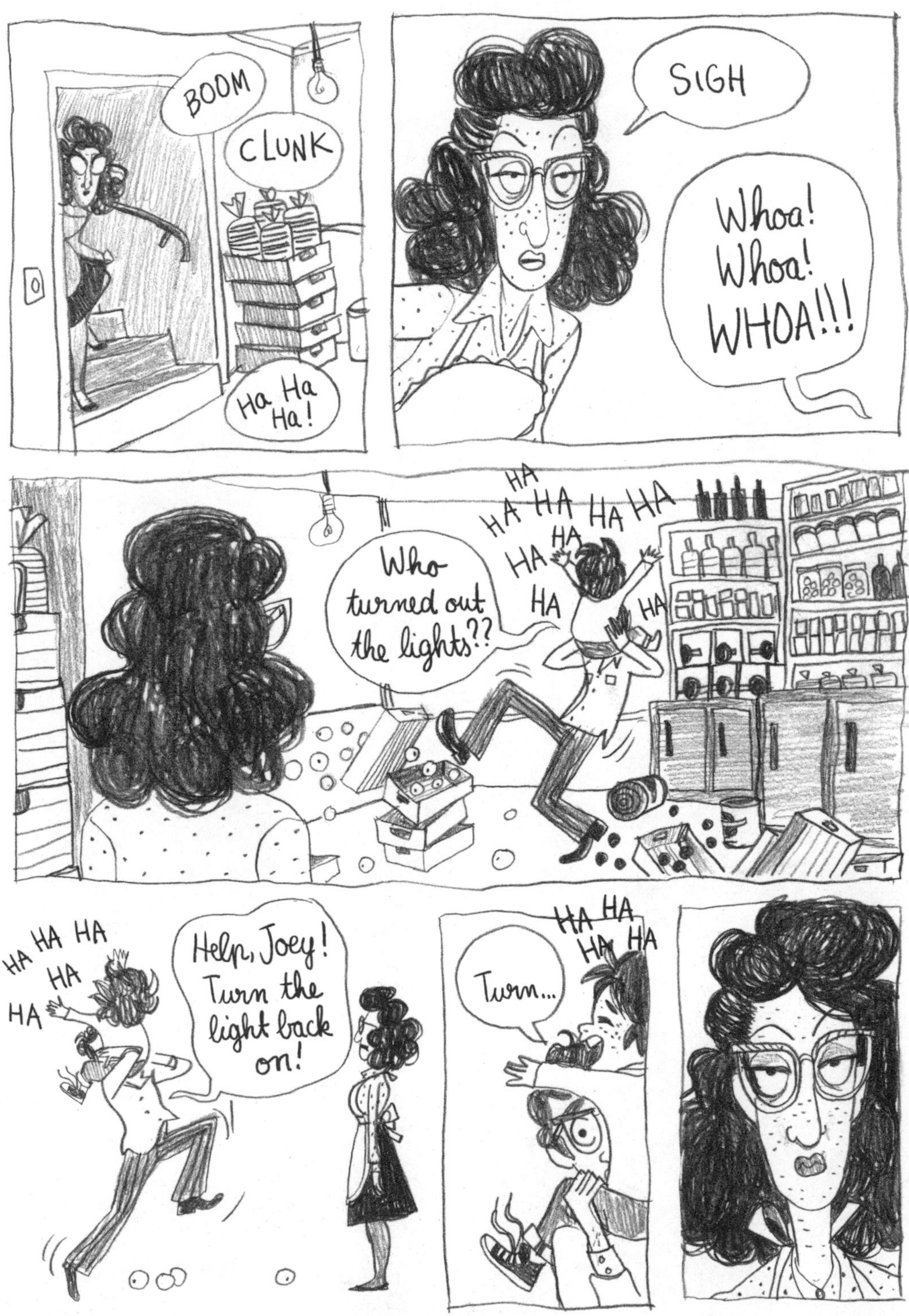

BOOM
CLUNK
Ha Ha Ha!
SIGH
Whoa! Whoa! WHOA!!!
HA HA HA HA HA HA HA HA HA
Who turned out the lights??
HA HA HA HA HA
Help, Joey! Turn the light back on!
HA HA HA HA
Turn...

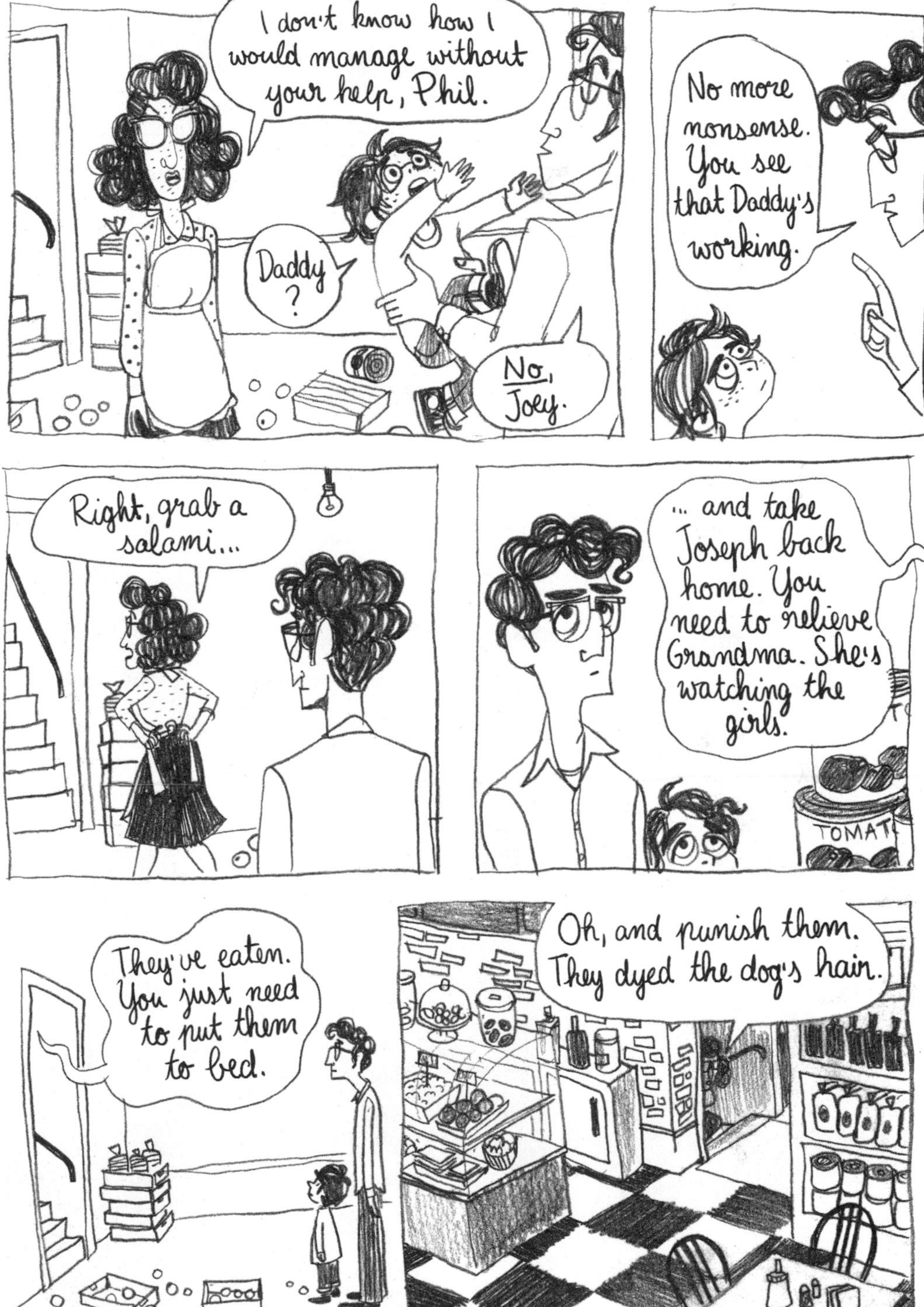
I don't know how I would manage without your help, Phil.
Daddy?
No, Joey.
No more nonsense. You see that Daddy's working.
Right, grab a salami...
... and take Joseph back home. You need to relieve Grandma. She's watching the girls.
TOMAT
They've eaten. You just need to put them to bed.
Oh, and punish them. They dyed the dog's hair.

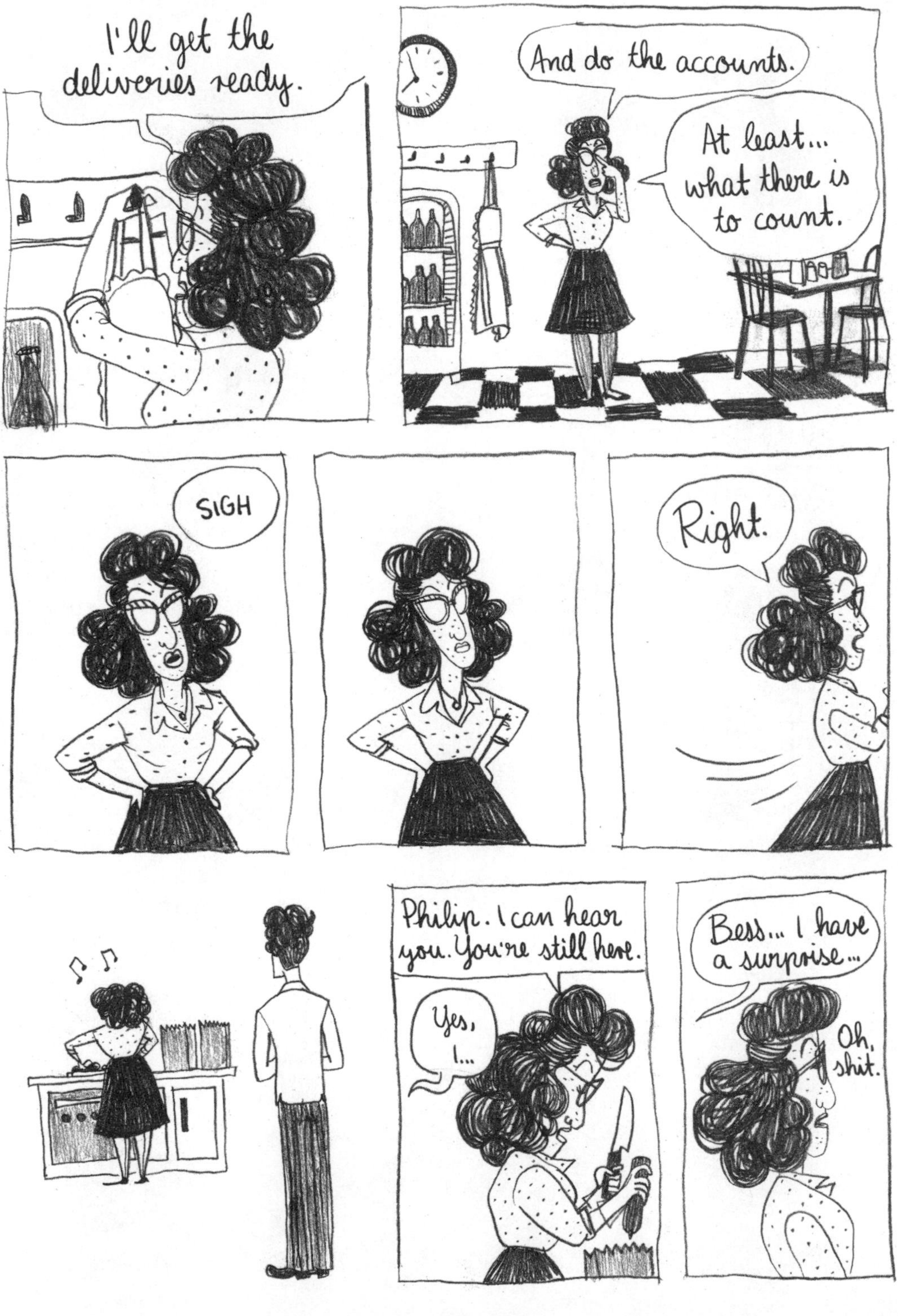

I'll get the deliveries ready.
And do the accounts.
At least... what there is to count.
SIGH
Right.
Philip. I can hear you. You're still here.
Yes, I...
Bess... I have a surprise...
Oh, shit.

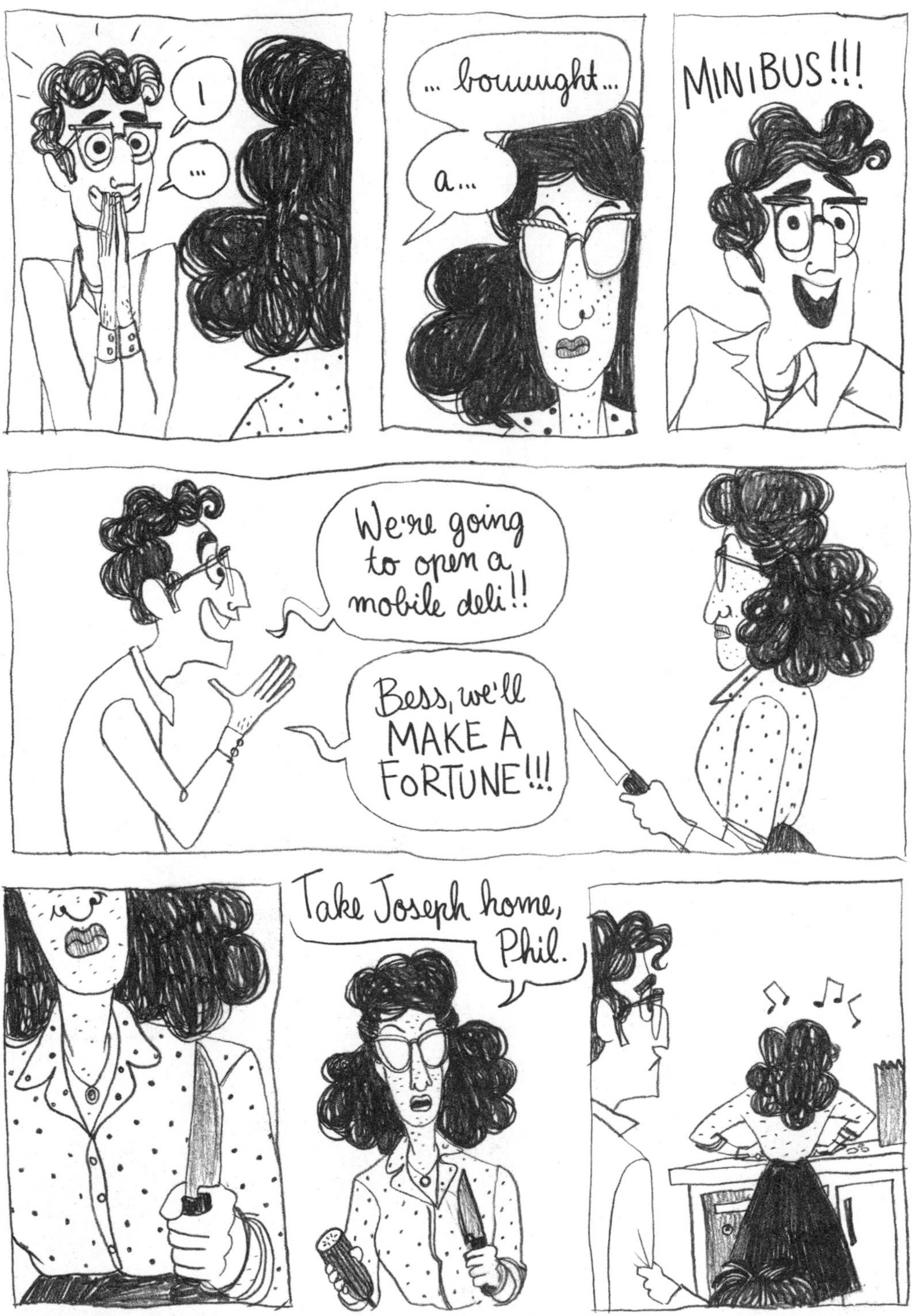
I
...
... bouuught...
a...
MINIBUS!!!
We're going to open a mobile deli!!
Bess, we'll MAKE A FORTUNE!!!
Take Joseph home, Phil.

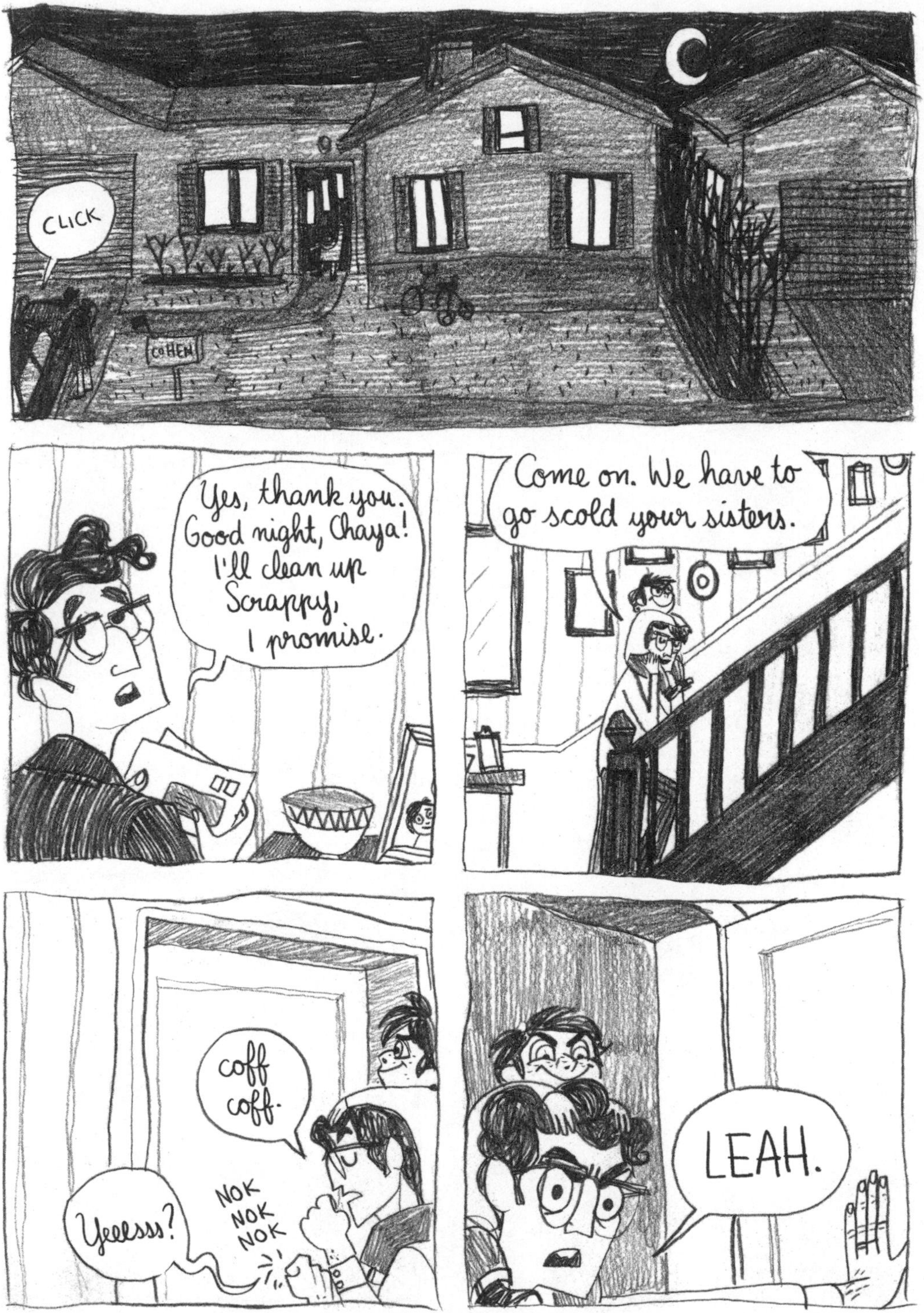
CLICK
COHEN
Yes, thank you. Good night, Chaya! I'll clean up Scrappy, I promise.
Come on. We have to go scold your sisters.
coff coff.
Yeeesss?
NOK NOK NOK
LEAH.

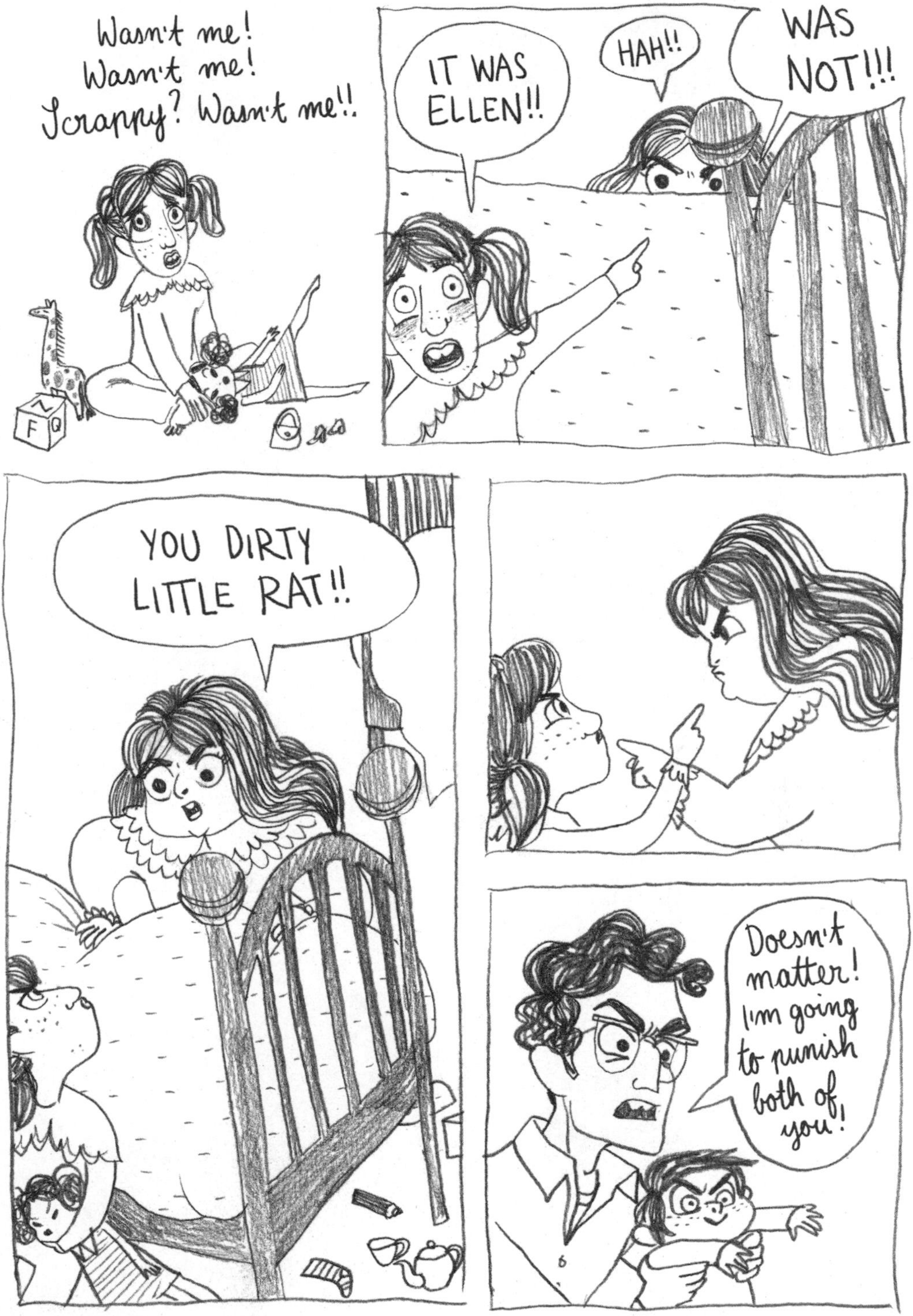
Wasn't me!
Wasn't me!
Scrappy? Wasn't me!!
IT WAS ELLEN!!
HAH!!
WAS NOT!!!
YOU DIRTY LITTLE RAT!!
Doesn't matter! I'm going to punish both of you!

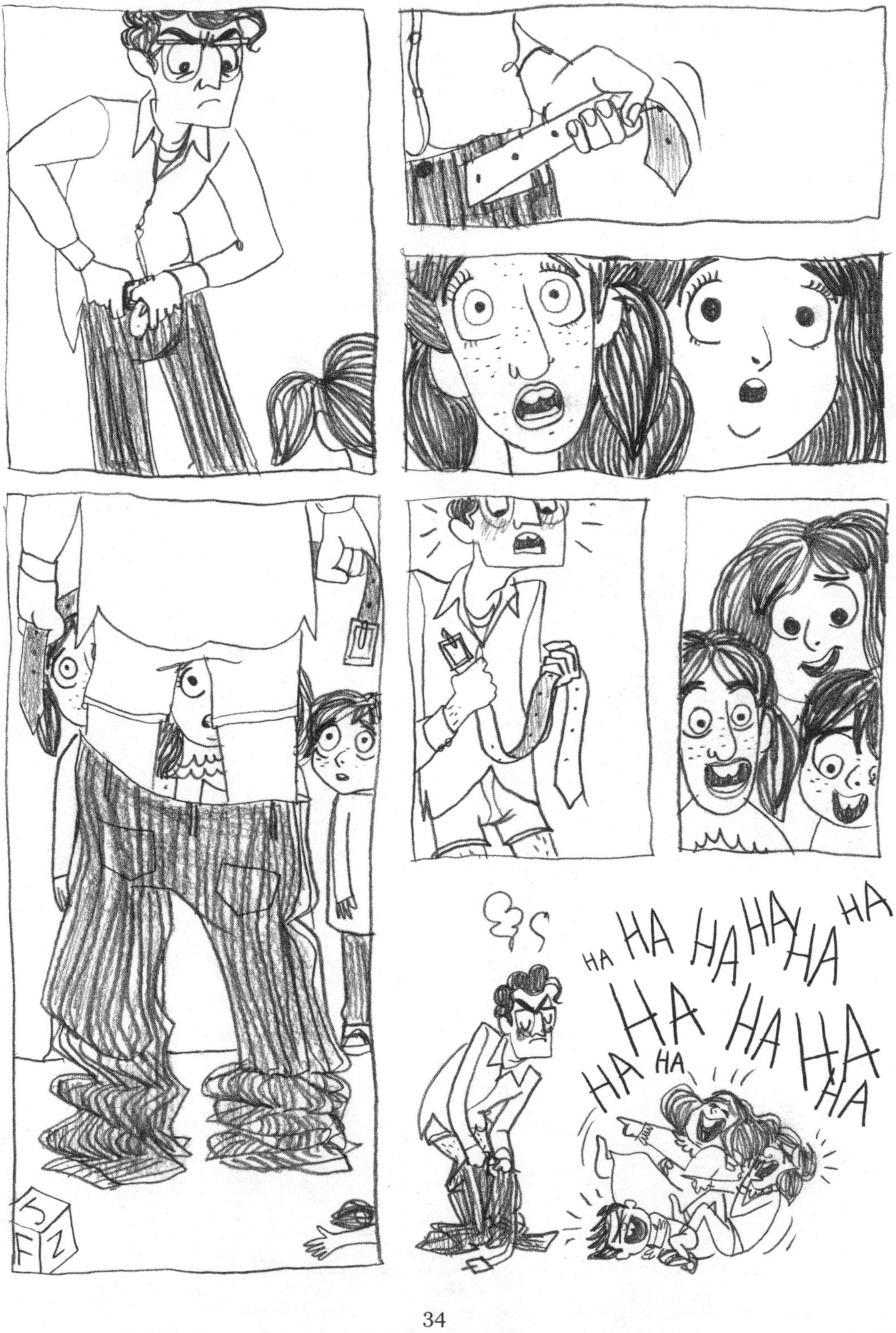
HA HA HA HA HA HA
HA HA
HA HA HA HA HA HA

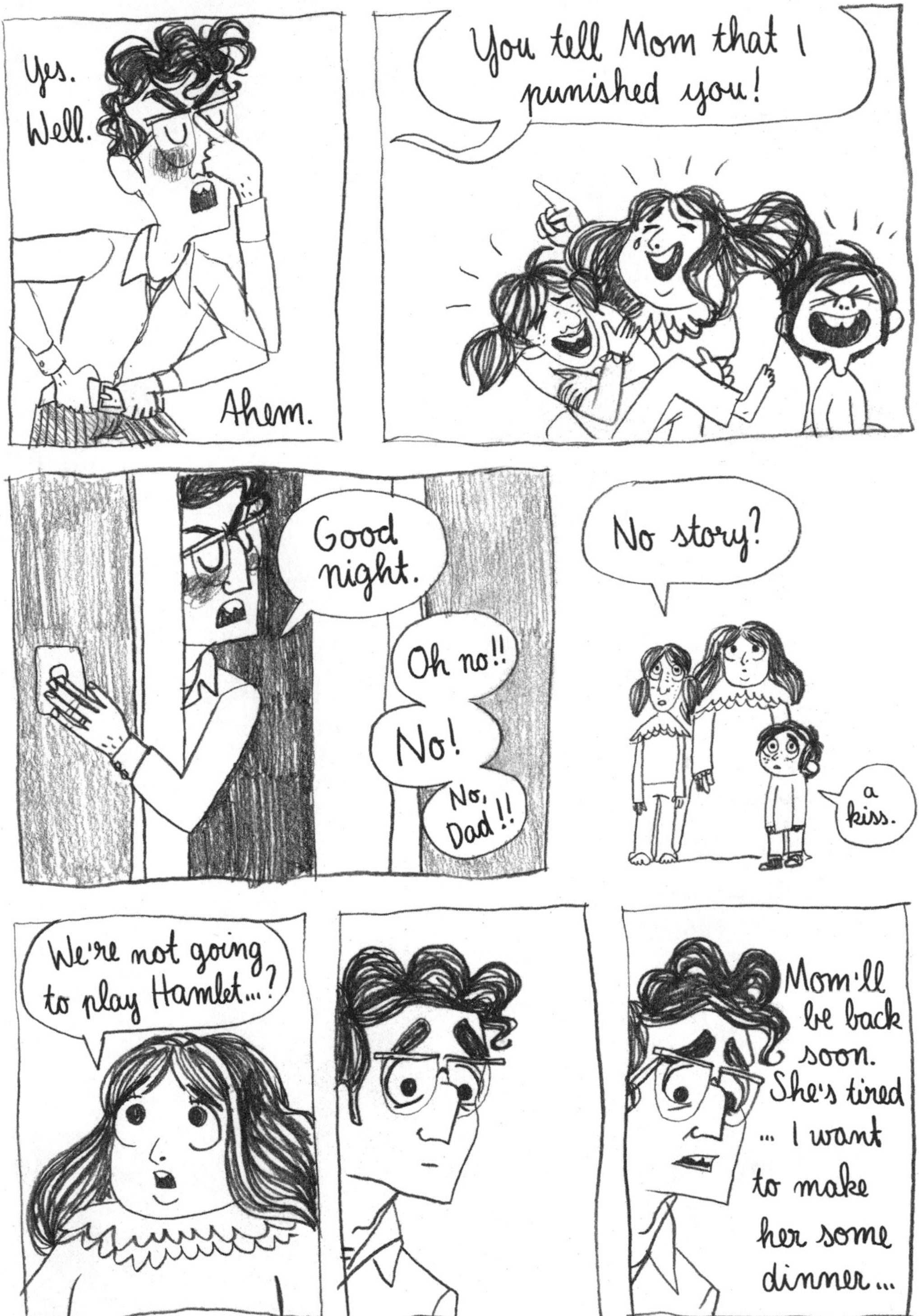
Yes.
Well.
Ahem.
You tell Mom that I punished you!
Good night.
Oh no!!
No!
No, Dad!!
No story?
a kiss.
We're not going to play Hamlet...?
Mom'll be back soon. She's tired ... I want to make her some dinner...

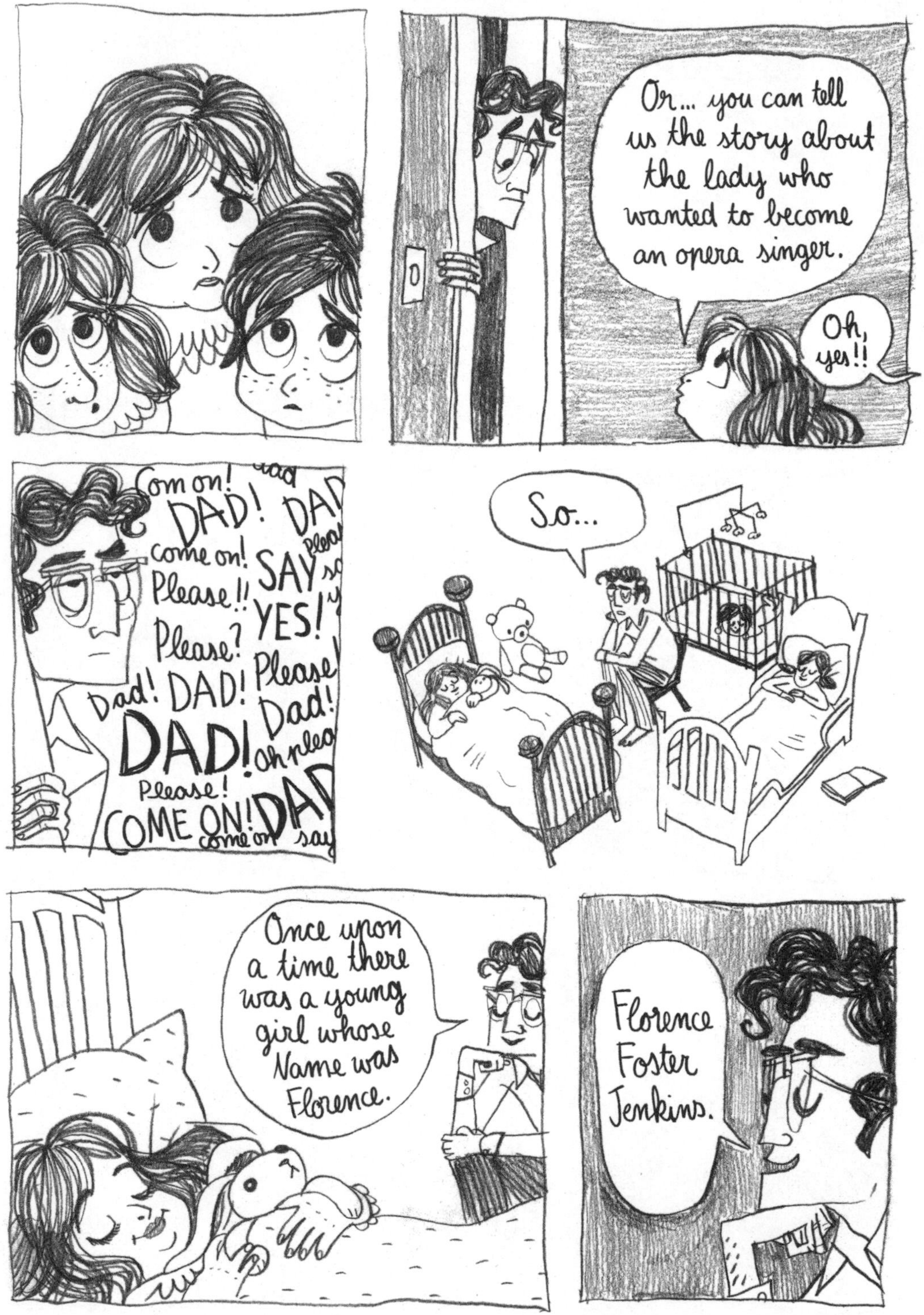

Or... you can tell us the story about the lady who wanted to become an opera singer.
Oh, yes!!
Com on!
DAD!
come on!
Please!!
Please?
Dad! DAD!
DAD!
Please!
COME ON!
come on
SAY
YES!
Please!
Dad!
So...
Once upon a time there was a young girl whose Name was Florence.
Florence Foster Jenkins.

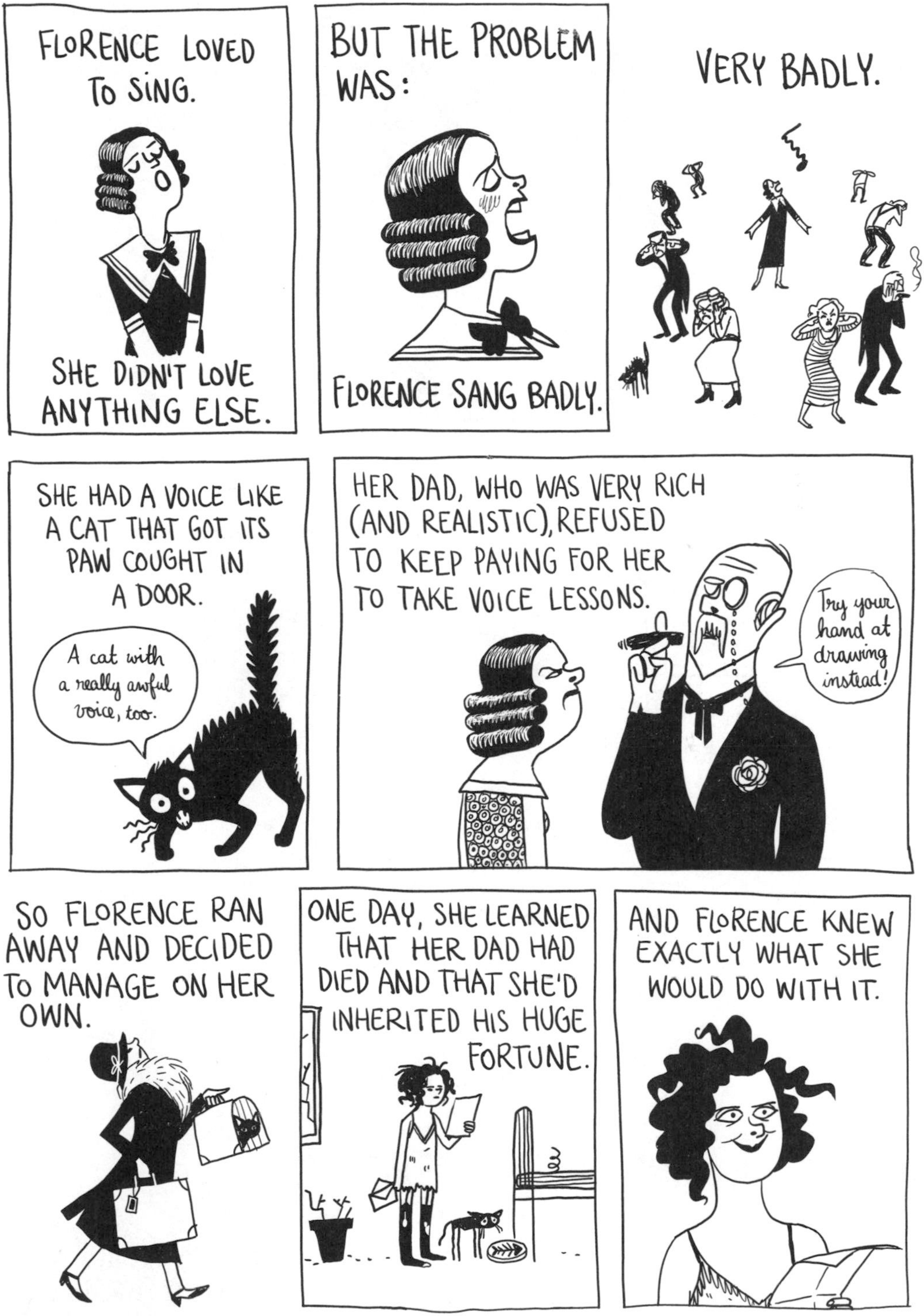
FLORENCE LOVED TO SING.
SHE DIDN'T LOVE ANYTHING ELSE.
BUT THE PROBLEM WAS:
FLORENCE SANG BADLY.
VERY BADLY.
SHE HAD A VOICE LIKE A CAT THAT GOT ITS PAW COUGHT IN A DOOR.
A cat with a really awful voice, too.
HER DAD, WHO WAS VERY RICH (AND REALISTIC), REFUSED TO KEEP PAYING FOR HER TO TAKE VOICE LESSONS.
Try your hand at drawing instead!
SO FLORENCE RAN AWAY AND DECIDED TO MANAGE ON HER OWN.
ONE DAY, SHE LEARNED THAT HER DAD HAD DIED AND THAT SHE'D INHERITED HIS HUGE FORTUNE.
AND FLORENCE KNEW EXACTLY WHAT SHE WOULD DO WITH IT.

SHE DECIDED TO GET A PIANIST

RECORDINGS

"Like a Bird"
(Words by Mme. Jenkins)

RECORDING
MELO TONE
25 CENTRAL PARK WEST
Telephone CIRCLE-3SS
NEW YORK
sung by
FLORENCE FOSTER JENKINS
(Cosme McMoon, PIANO)

EXTRAVAGANT THEATRICAL COSTUMES

INTEREST FROM THE PRESS

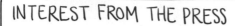

"You can say that I can't sing, but you can't say that I didn't sing."
F.F. Jenkins

AN AUDIENCE

Bravo! Bravo! What a talent!

AND ONE FINE DAY, SHE EVEN PAID FOR

PLAYBILL
FLORENCE FOSTER JENKINS
QUEEN OF THE NIGHT

A RECITAL AT CARNEGIE HALL.

(FILLED WITH A CROWD THAT SHE'D INVITED.)

AT CARNEGIE HALL, PEOPLE LAUGHED, BUT FLORENCE DIDN'T CARE.

Oh, la. Dreadful, such jealousy.

SHE DIED VERY OLD AND VERY HAPPY.

AND TO THIS DAY, EVEN IF IT'S TO MAKE FUN OF "THE WORST SOPRANO IN THE WORLD," OPERA LOVERS COLLECT HER RECORDS.

AND SO FLORENCE FULLFILLED HER DREAM.

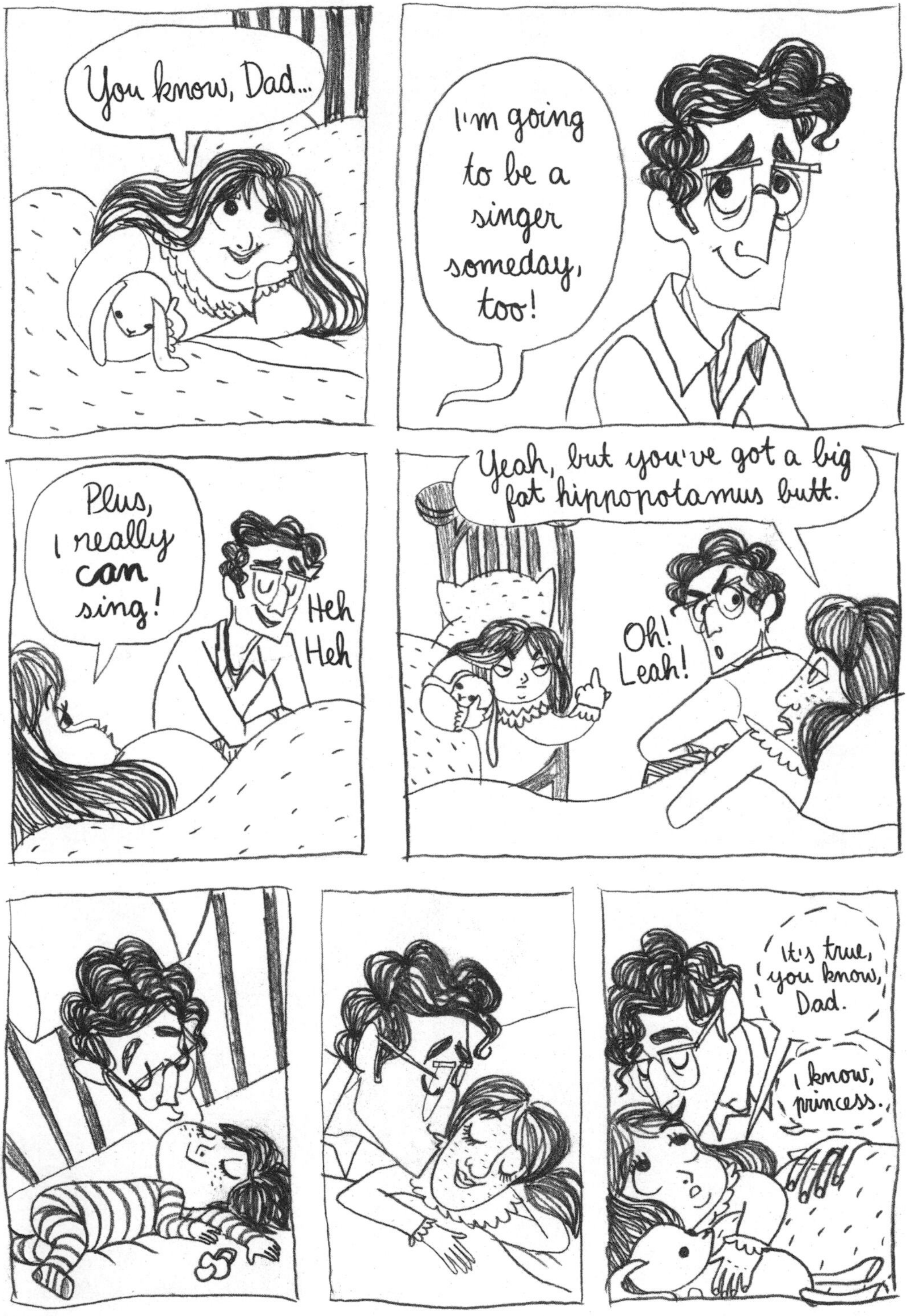
You know, Dad...
I'm going to be a singer someday, too!
Plus, I really **can** sing!
Heh Heh
Yeah, but you've got a big fat hippopotamus butt.
Oh! Leah!
It's true, you know, Dad.
I know, princess.

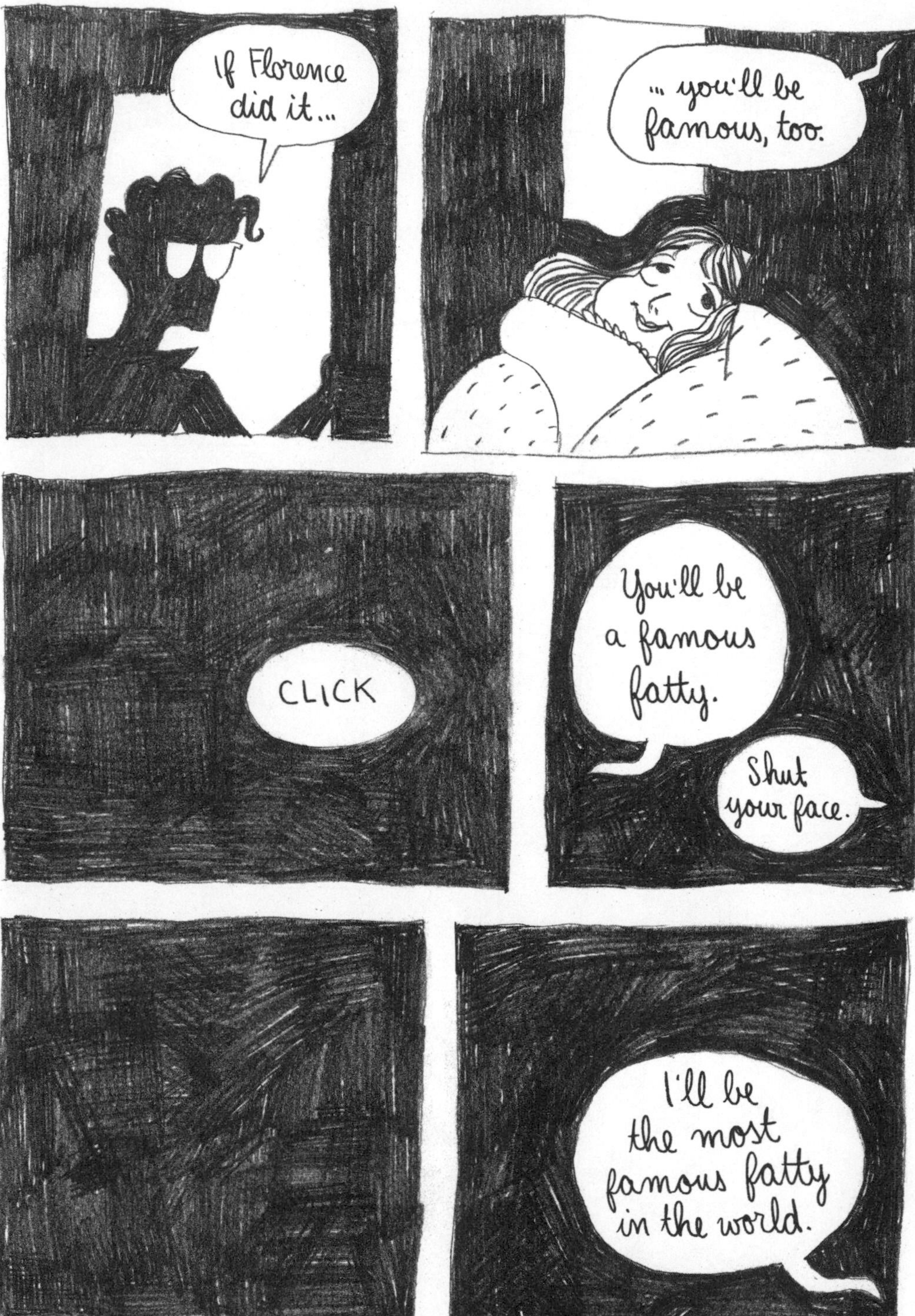
If Florence did it...
... you'll be famous, too.
CLICK
You'll be a famous fatty.
Shut your face.
I'll be the most famous fatty in the world.

3-Ken

MY NAME IS KEN WAISSMAN. THAT'S MY HIGH SCHOOL.

FOREST PARK
HIGH
TODAY'S STUDENTS
TOMORROW'S LEADERS

AND THAT'S ME.

NO, NOT THE BIG GUY WITH THE FLASHING PEARLY WHITES.

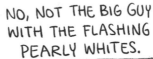

Theater Club!

THE OTHER GUY.

THWAP.

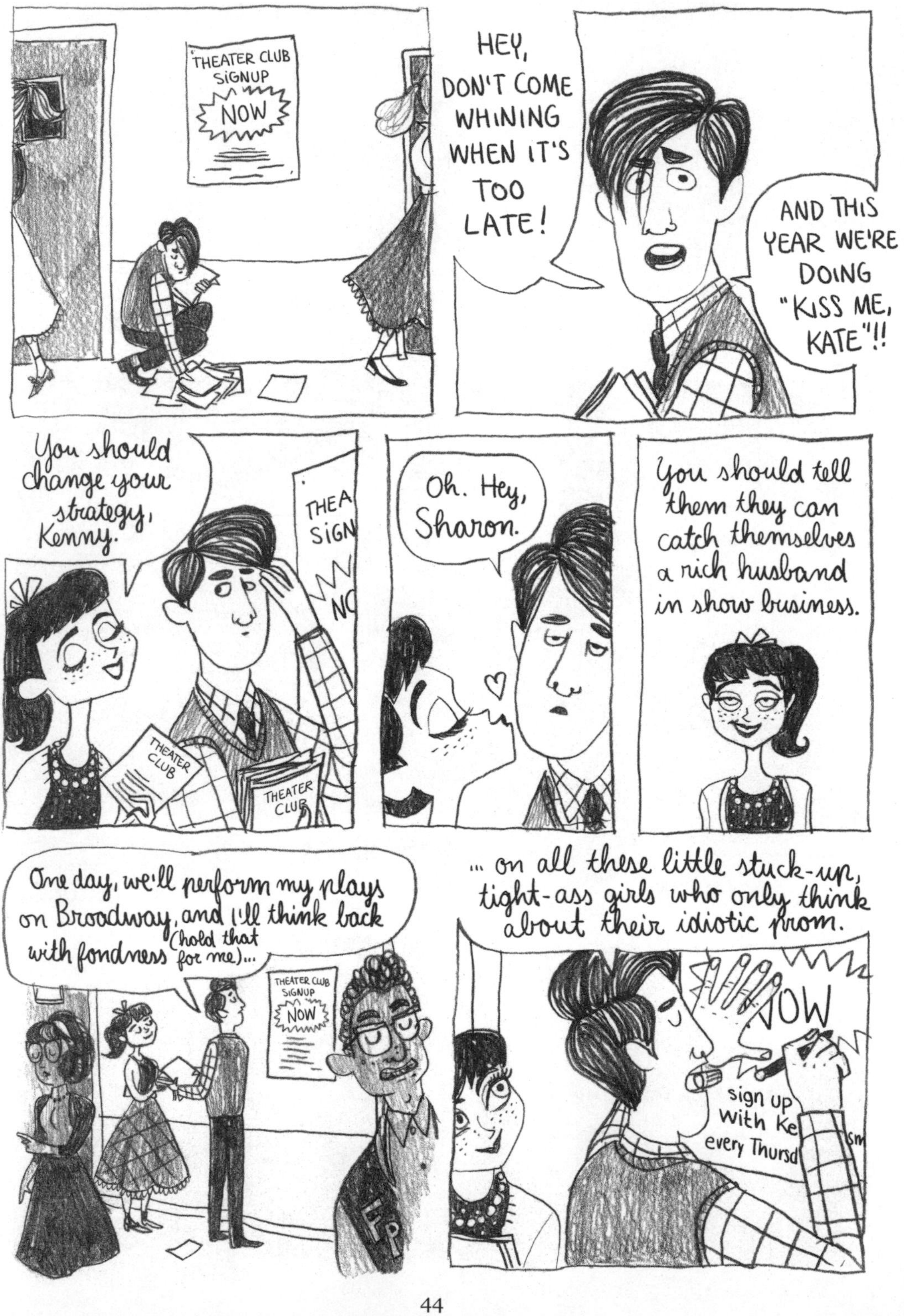
THEATER CLUB SIGNUP NOW
HEY, DON'T COME WHINING WHEN IT'S TOO LATE!
AND THIS YEAR WE'RE DOING "KISS ME, KATE"!!
You should change your strategy, Kenny.
THEATER CLUB
THEATER CLUB
Oh. Hey, Sharon.
You should tell them they can catch themselves a rich husband in show business.
One day, we'll perform my plays on Broadway, and I'll think back with fondness (hold that for me)...
THEATER CLUB SIGNUP NOW
... on all these little stuck-up, tight-ass girls who only think about their idiotic prom.
NOW
sign up with Ke
every Thursd

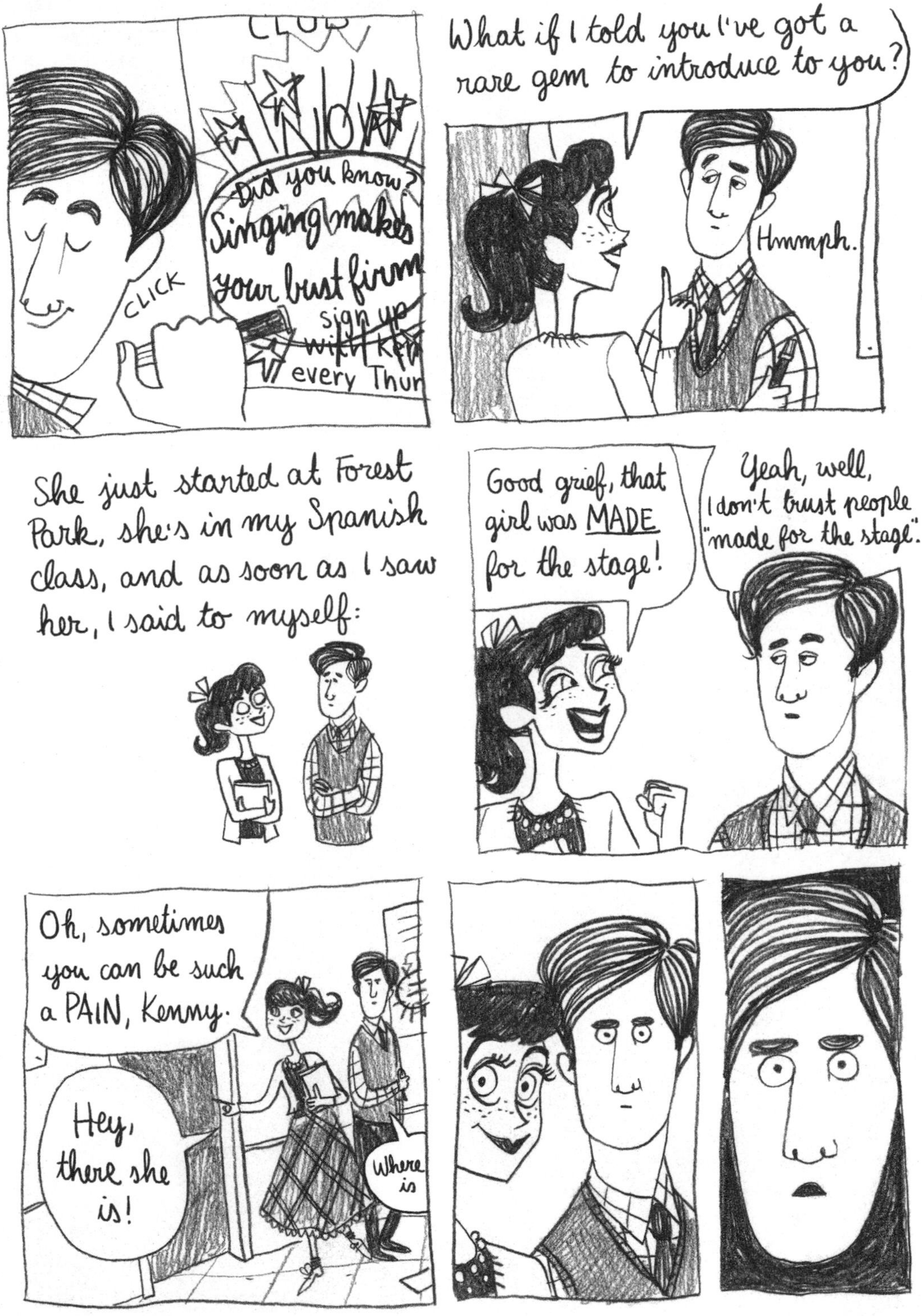
CLUB
NOW
Did you know?
Singing makes your bust firm
sign up with KF
every Thur
CLICK
What if I told you I've got a rare gem to introduce to you?
Hmmph.
She just started at Forest Park, she's in my Spanish class, and as soon as I saw her, I said to myself:
Good grief, that girl was MADE for the stage!
Yeah, well, I don't trust people "made for the stage".
Oh, sometimes you can be such a PAIN, Kenny.
Hey, there she is!
Where is

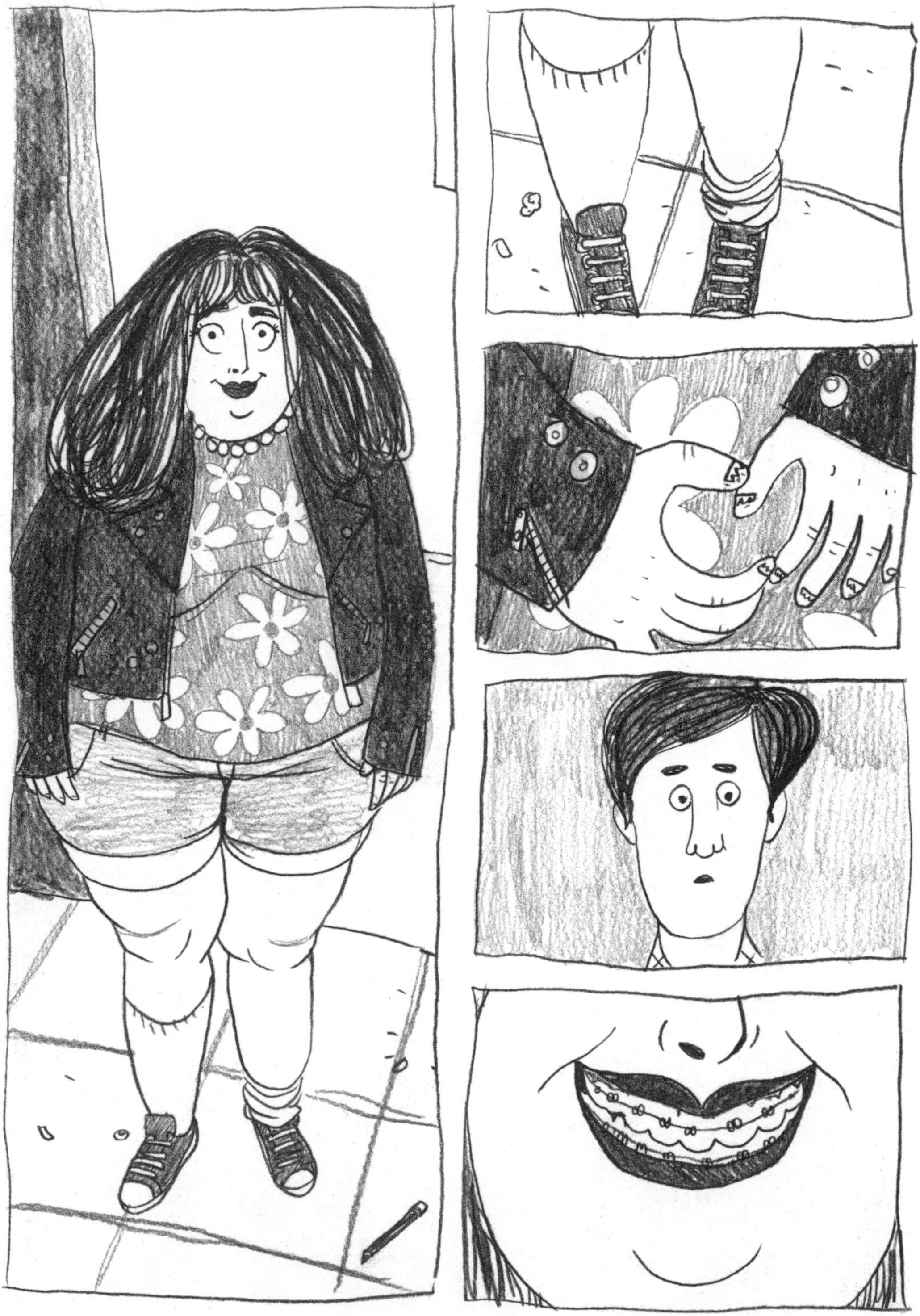

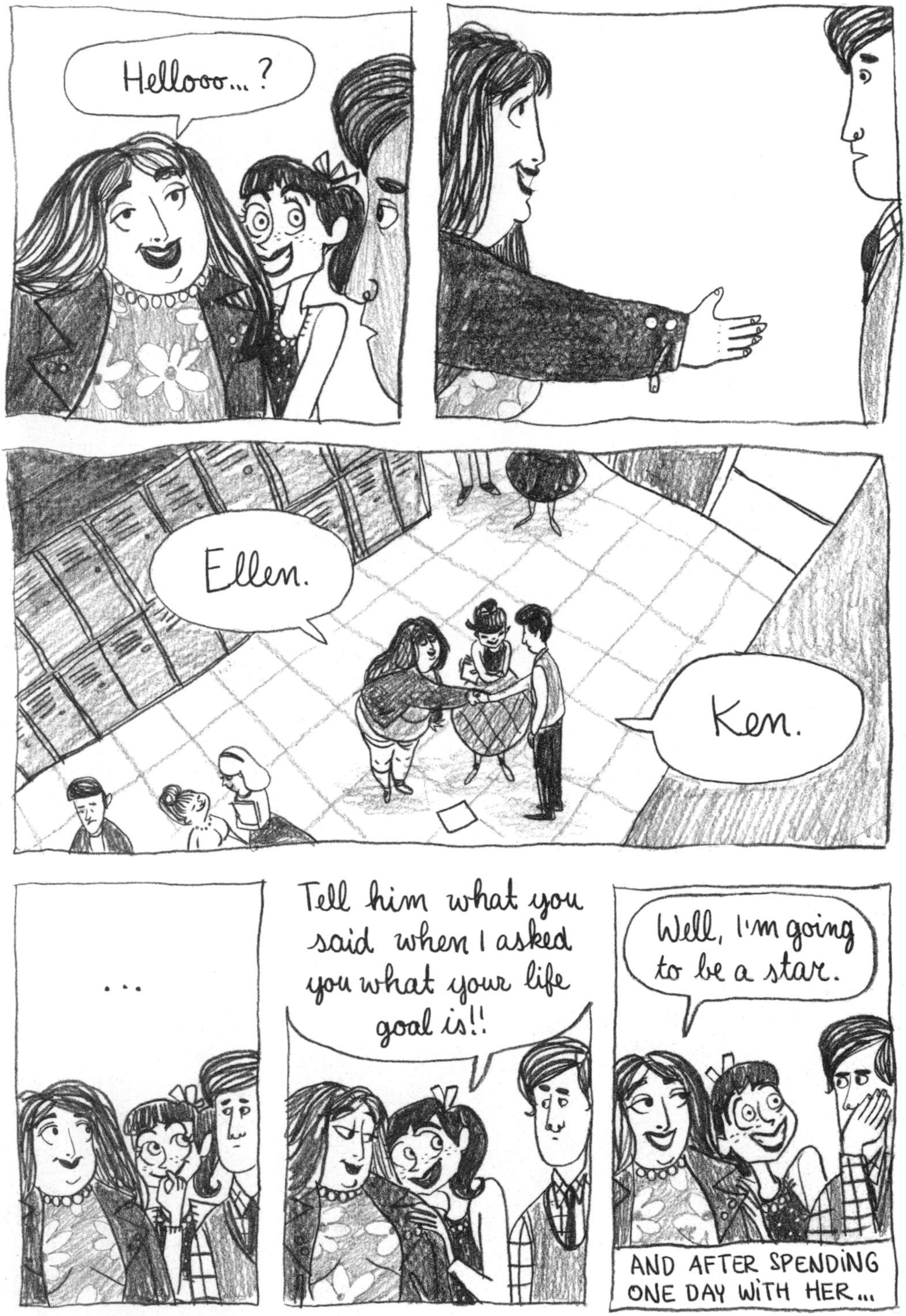
Hellooo...?
Ellen.
Ken.
...
Tell him what you said when I asked you what your life goal is!!
Well, I'm going to be a star.
AND AFTER SPENDING ONE DAY WITH HER...

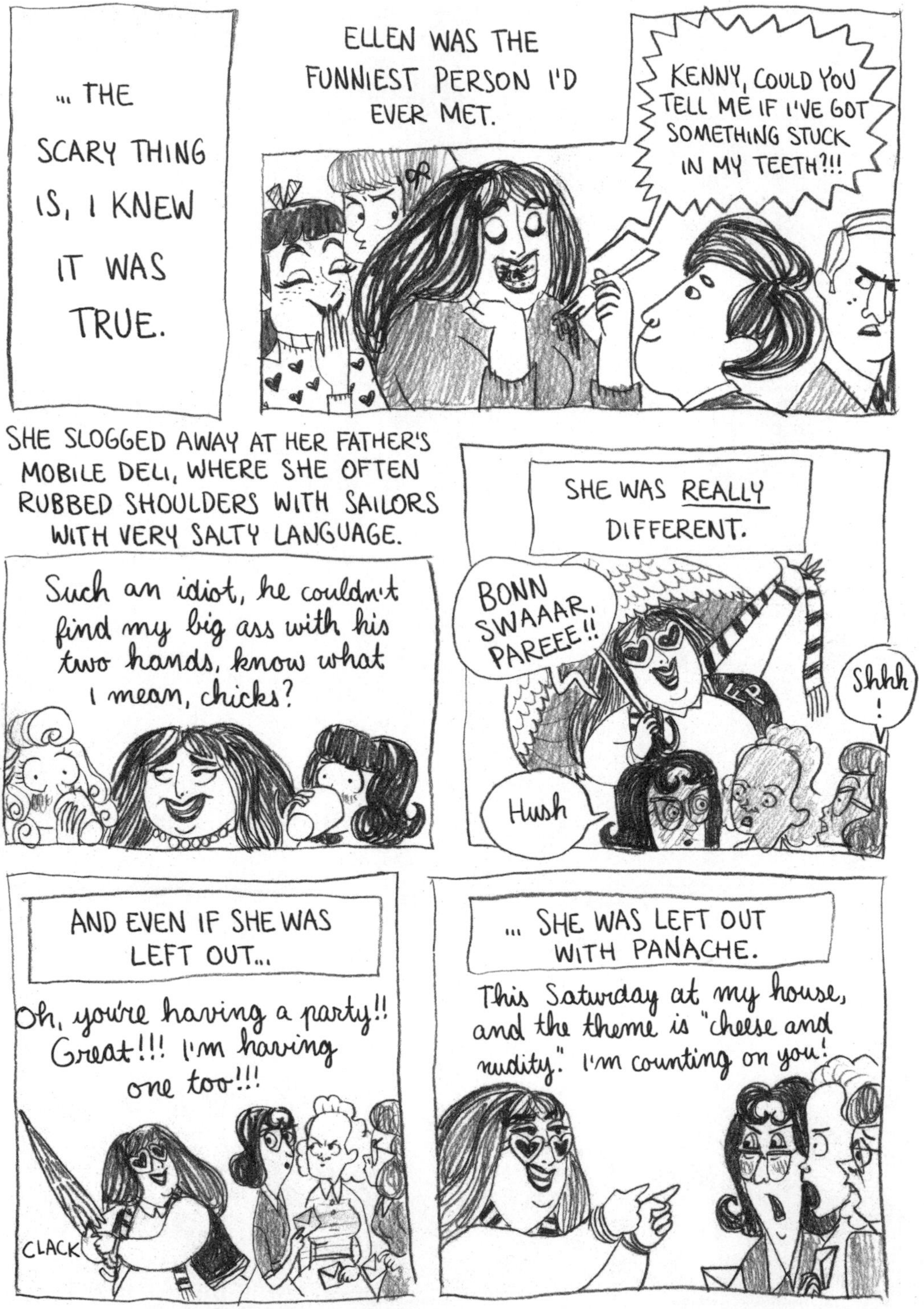
... THE SCARY THING IS, I KNEW IT WAS TRUE.
ELLEN WAS THE FUNNIEST PERSON I'D EVER MET.
KENNY, COULD YOU TELL ME IF I'VE GOT SOMETHING STUCK IN MY TEETH?!!
SHE SLOGGED AWAY AT HER FATHER'S MOBILE DELI, WHERE SHE OFTEN RUBBED SHOULDERS WITH SAILORS WITH VERY SALTY LANGUAGE.
Such an idiot, he couldn't find my big ass with his two hands, know what I mean, chicks?
SHE WAS REALLY DIFFERENT.
BONN SWAAAR, PAREEE!!
Shhh!
Hush
AND EVEN IF SHE WAS LEFT OUT...
Oh, you're having a party!! Great!!! I'm having one too!!!
CLACK
... SHE WAS LEFT OUT WITH PANACHE.
This Saturday at my house, and the theme is "cheese and nudity." I'm counting on you!

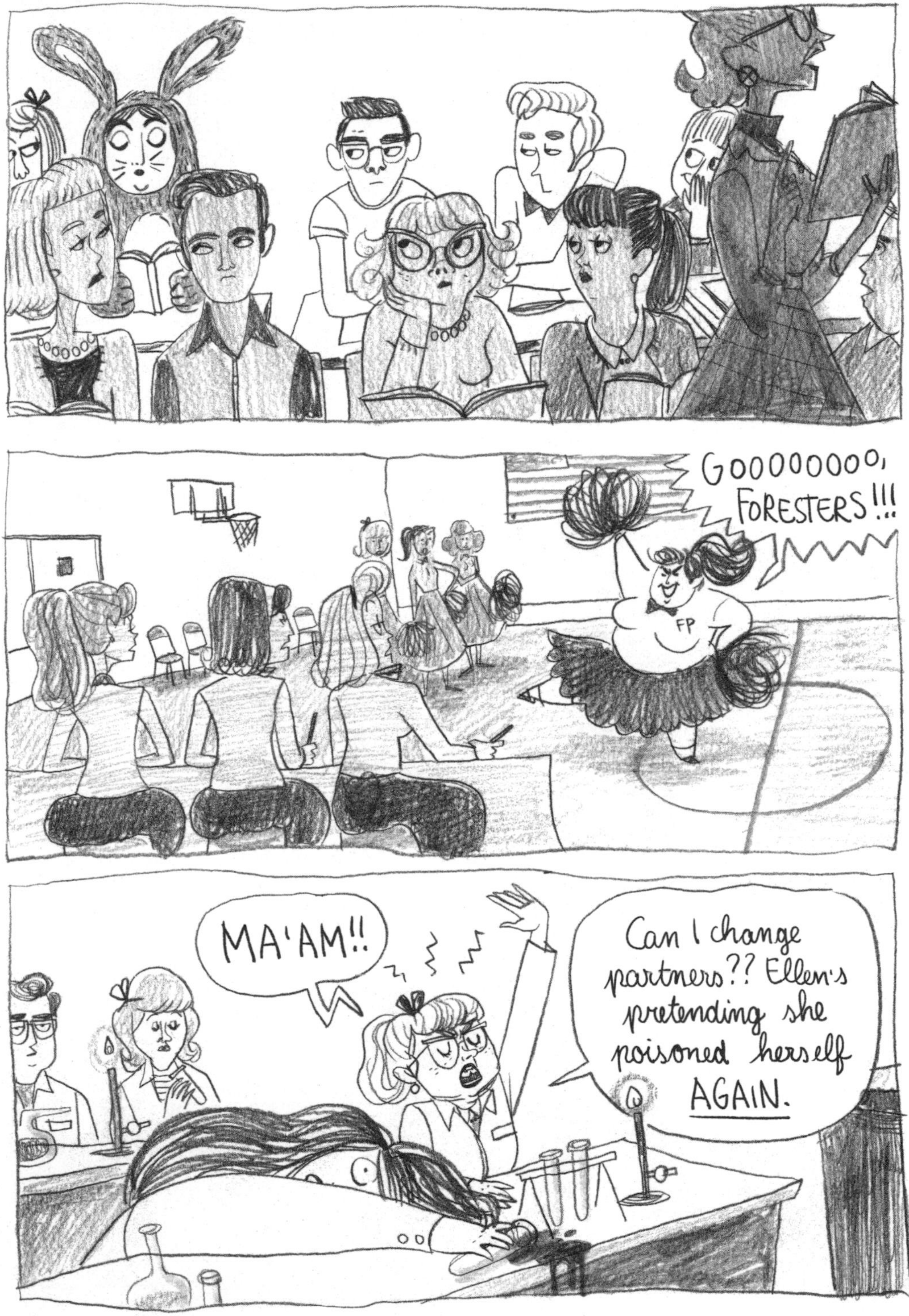
GOOOOOOOO, FORESTERS!!!
FP
MA'AM!!
Can I change partners?? Ellen's pretending she poisoned herself AGAIN.

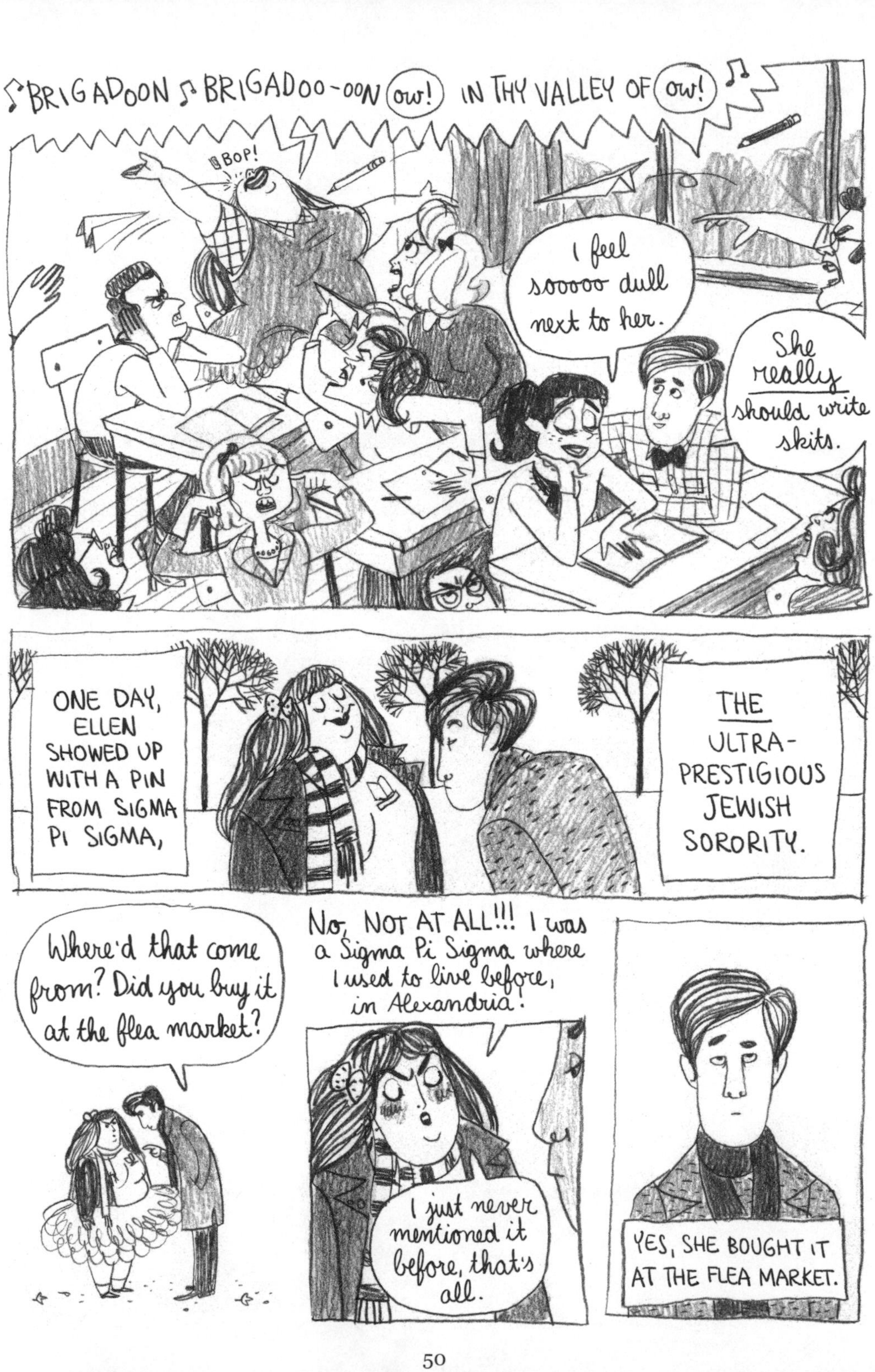
BRIGADOON BRIGADOO-OON ow! IN THY VALLEY OF ow!
BOP!
I feel sooooo dull next to her.
She really should write skits.
ONE DAY, ELLEN SHOWED UP WITH A PIN FROM SIGMA PI SIGMA,
THE ULTRA-PRESTIGIOUS JEWISH SORORITY.
Where'd that come from? Did you buy it at the flea market?
No, NOT AT ALL!!! I was a Sigma Pi Sigma where I used to live before, in Alexandria!
I just never mentioned it before, that's all.
YES, SHE BOUGHT IT AT THE FLEA MARKET.

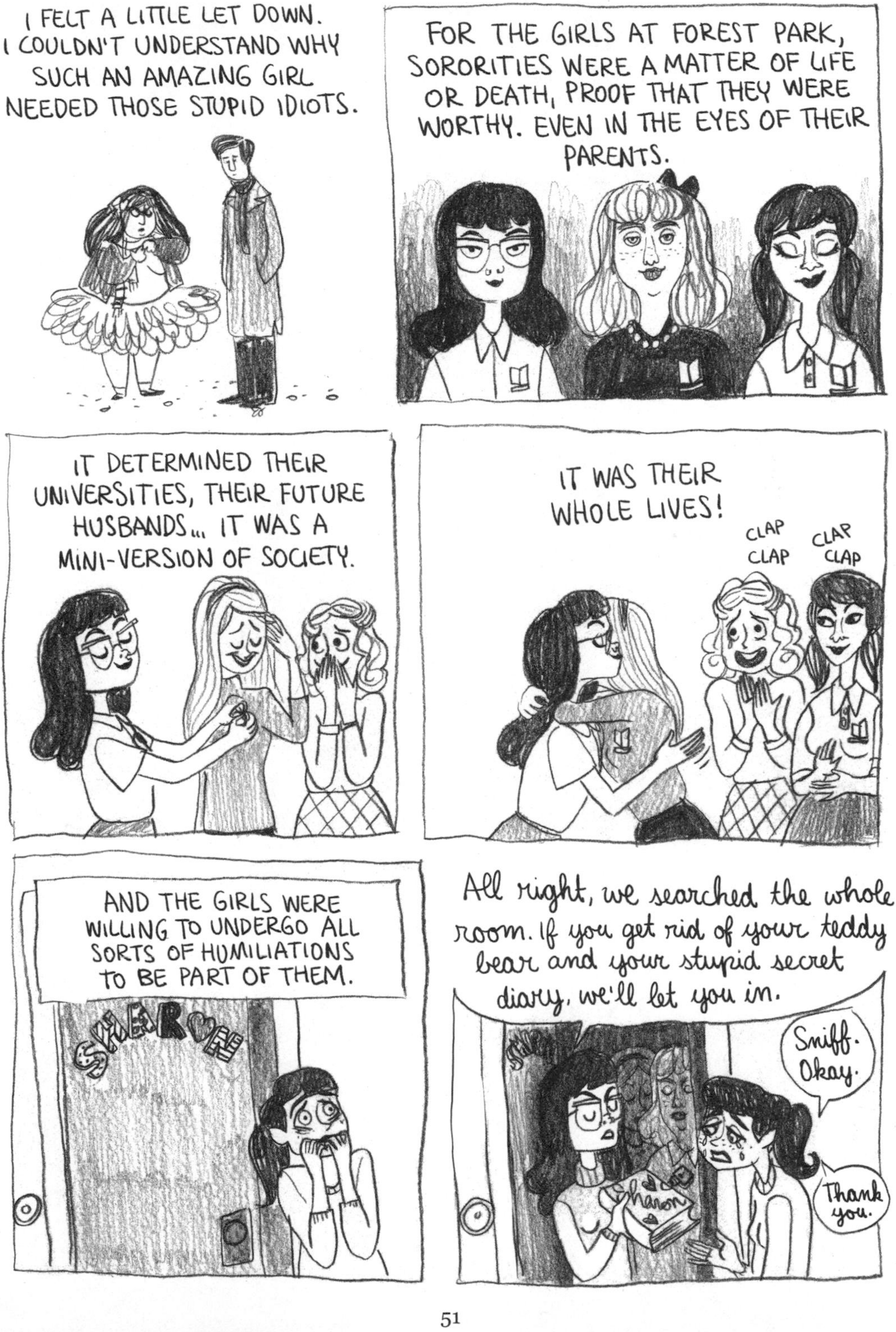
I FELT A LITTLE LET DOWN. I COULDN'T UNDERSTAND WHY SUCH AN AMAZING GIRL NEEDED THOSE STUPID IDIOTS.
FOR THE GIRLS AT FOREST PARK, SORORITIES WERE A MATTER OF LIFE OR DEATH, PROOF THAT THEY WERE WORTHY. EVEN IN THE EYES OF THEIR PARENTS.
IT DETERMINED THEIR UNIVERSITIES, THEIR FUTURE HUSBANDS... IT WAS A MINI-VERSION OF SOCIETY.
IT WAS THEIR WHOLE LIVES!
CLAP CLAP
CLAP CLAP
AND THE GIRLS WERE WILLING TO UNDERGO ALL SORTS OF HUMILIATIONS TO BE PART OF THEM.
SHARON
All right, we searched the whole room. If you get rid of your teddy bear and your stupid secret diary, we'll let you in.
Sniff. Okay.
Thank you.

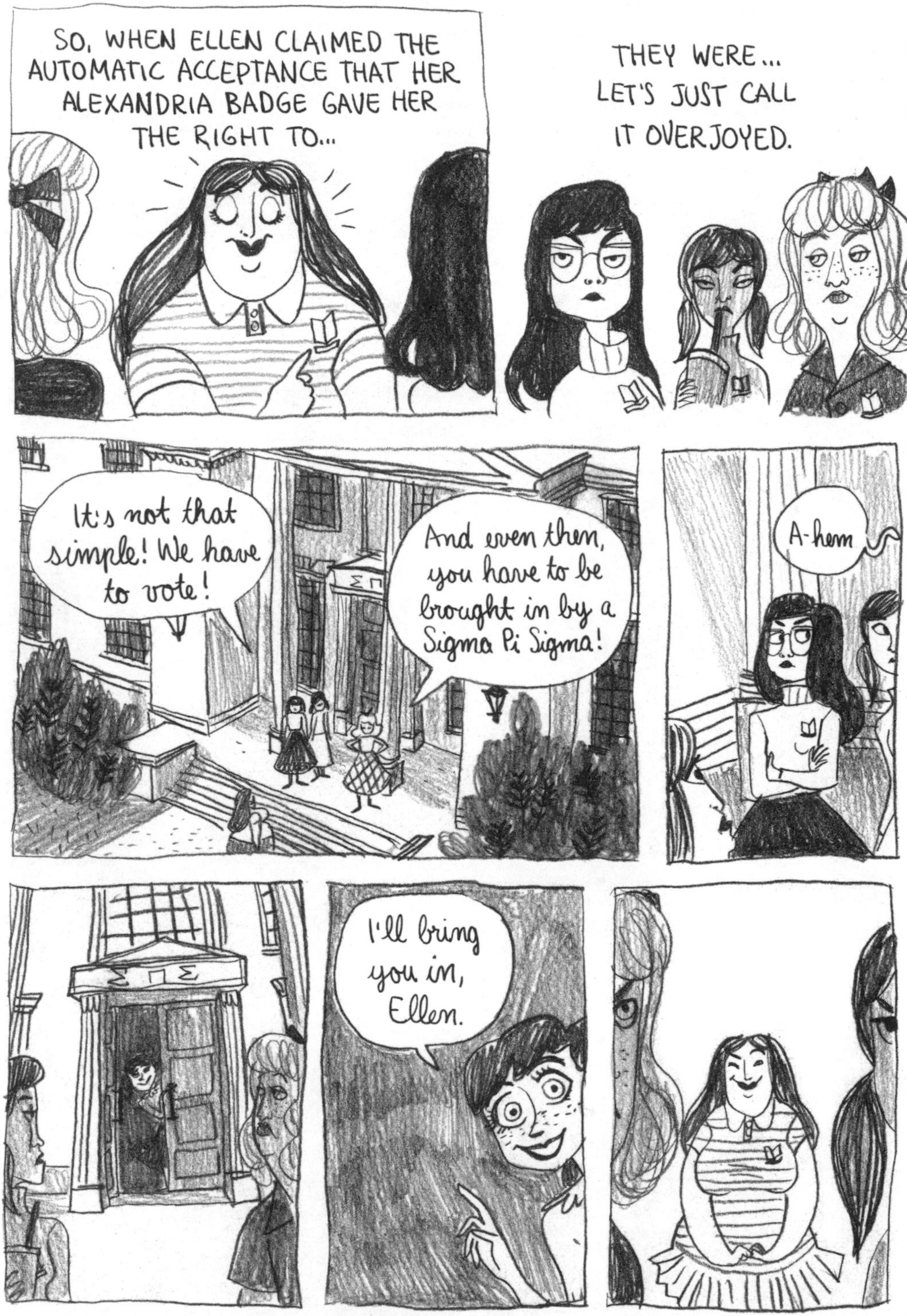
SO, WHEN ELLEN CLAIMED THE AUTOMATIC ACCEPTANCE THAT HER ALEXANDRIA BADGE GAVE HER THE RIGHT TO...
THEY WERE... LET'S JUST CALL IT OVERJOYED.
It's not that simple! We have to vote!
And even then, you have to be brought in by a Sigma Pi Sigma!
A-hem
Σ Π Σ
I'll bring you in, Ellen.

4-Sharon

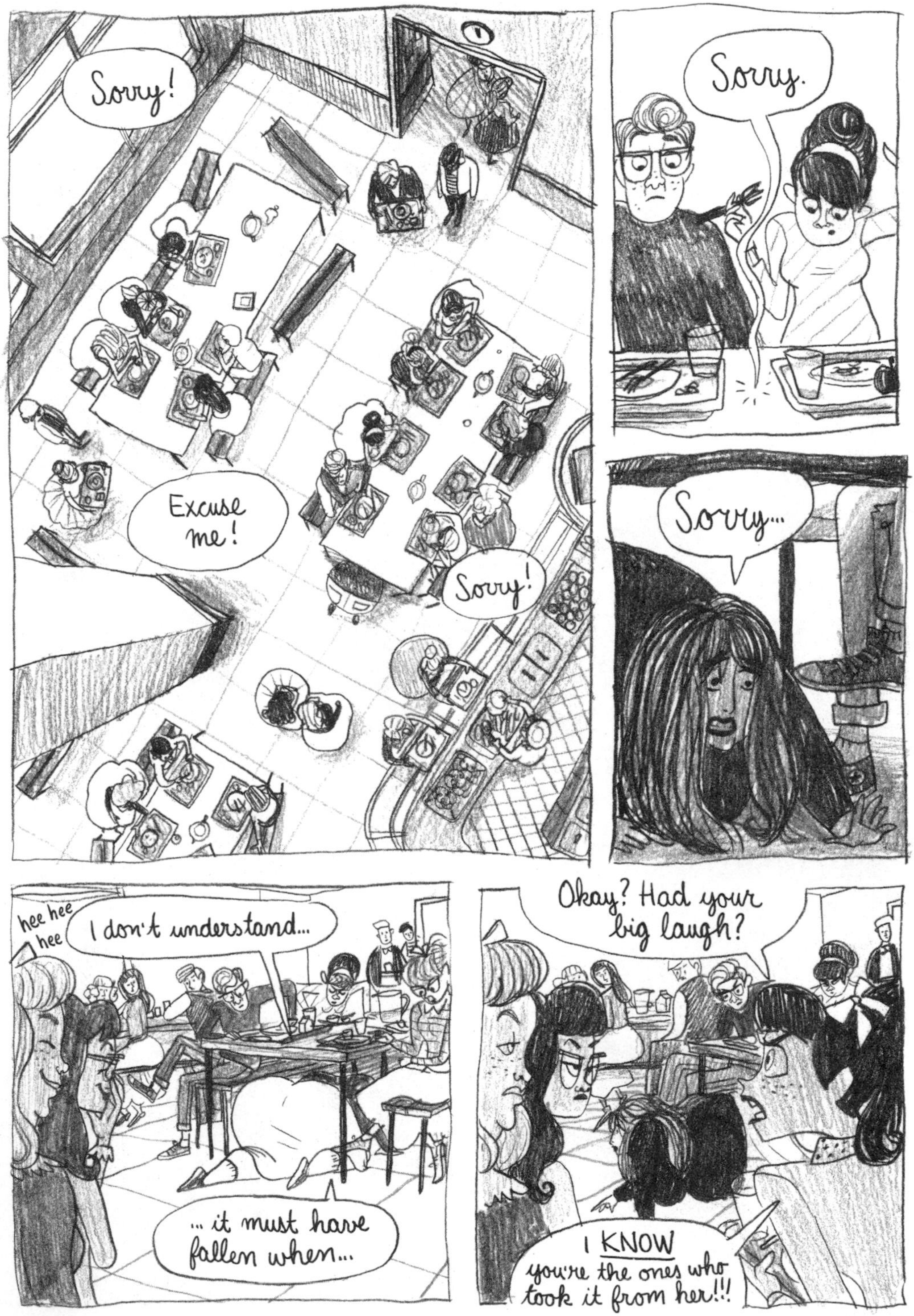
Sorry!
Excuse me!
Sorry!
Sorry.
Sorry...
hee hee hee
I don't understand...
... it must have fallen when...
Okay? Had your big laugh?
I KNOW you're the ones who took it from her!!!

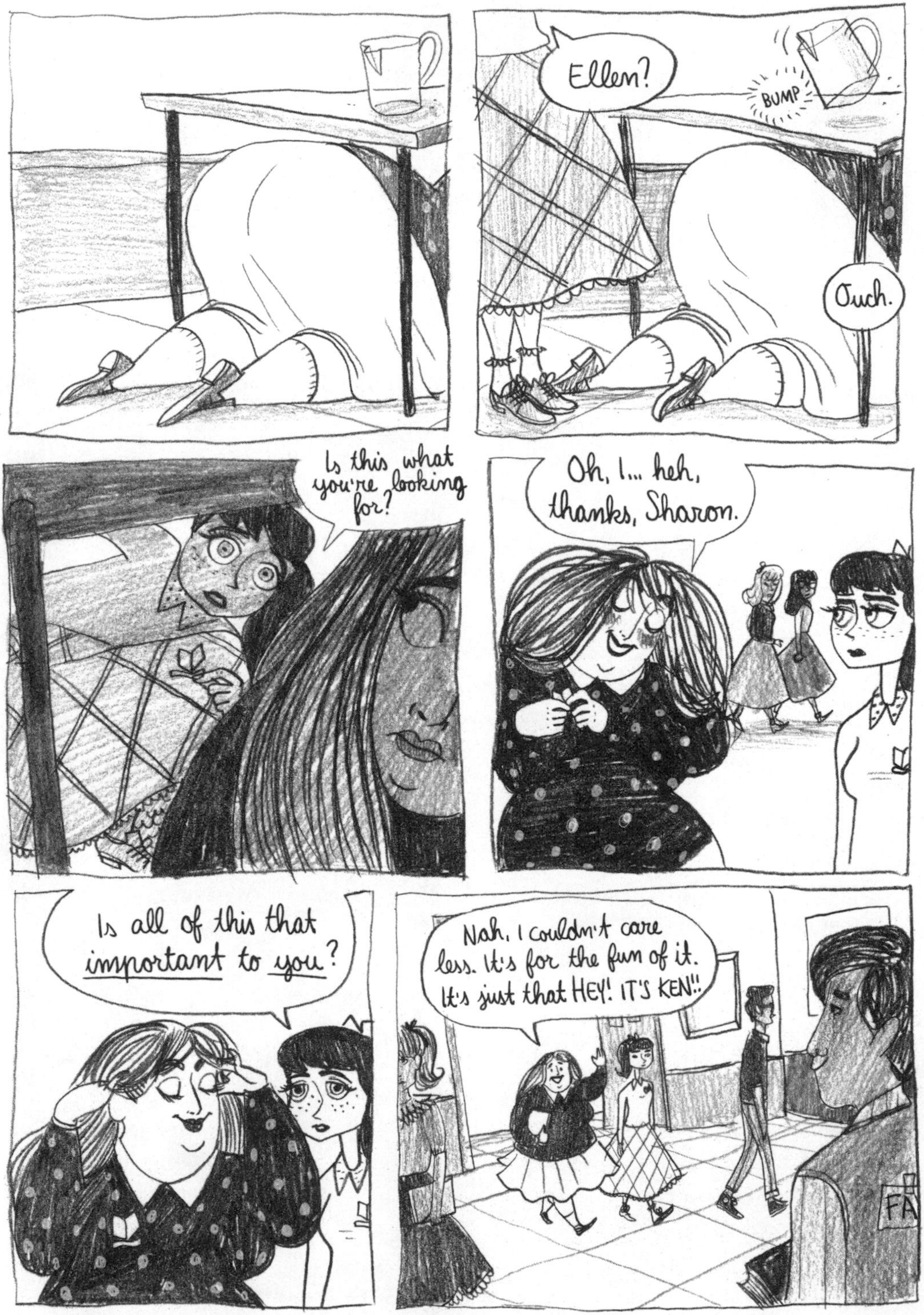
Ellen?
BUMP
Ouch.
Is this what you're looking for?
Oh, I... heh, thanks, Sharon.
Is all of this that important to you?
Nah, I couldn't care less. It's for the fun of it. It's just that HEY! IT'S KEN!!

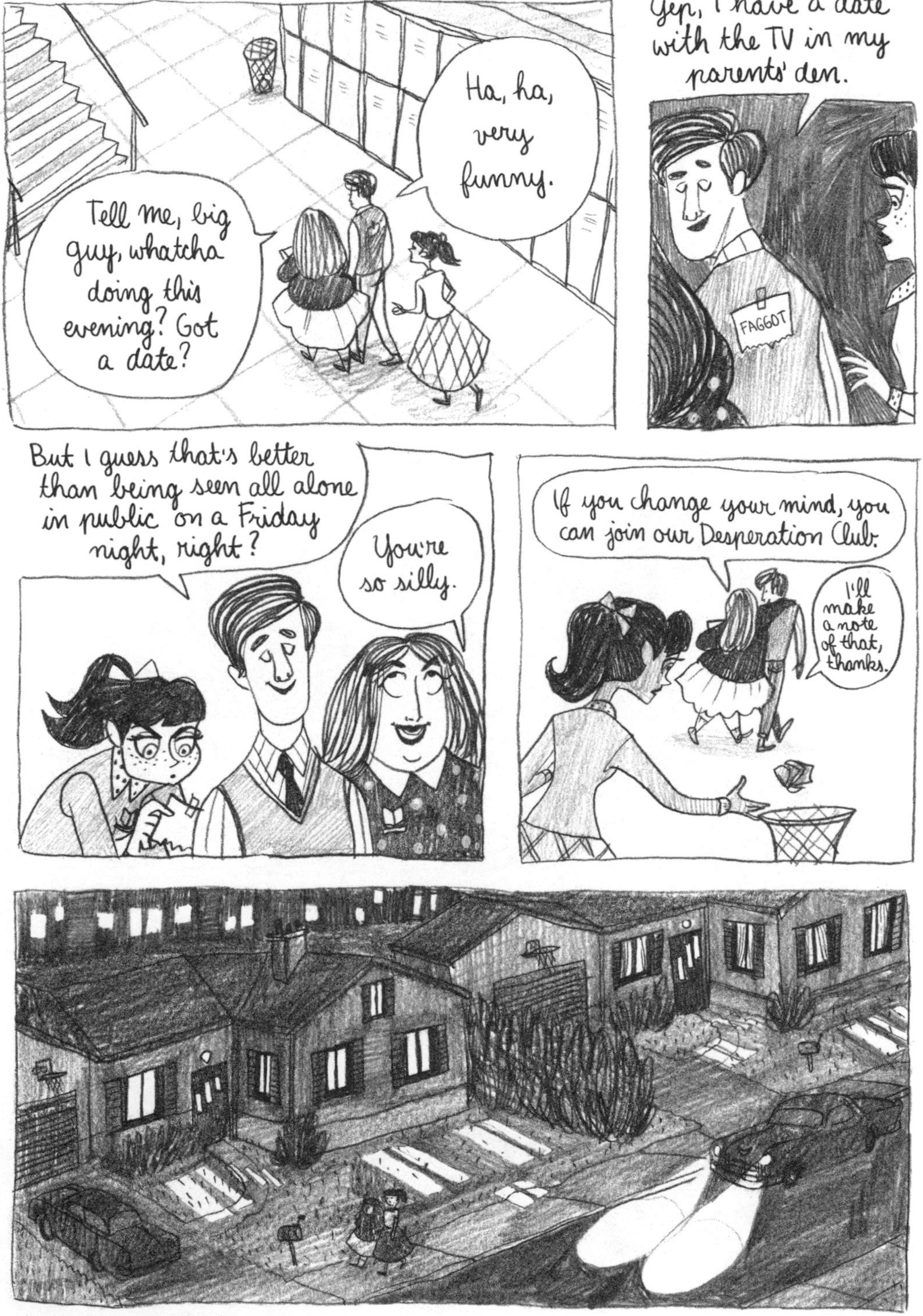
Tell me, big guy, whatcha doing this evening? Got a date?
Ha, ha, very funny.
Yep, I have a date with the TV in my parents' den.
FAGGOT
But I guess that's better than being seen all alone in public on a Friday night, right?
You're so silly.
If you change your mind, you can join our Desperation Club.
I'll make a note of that, thanks.

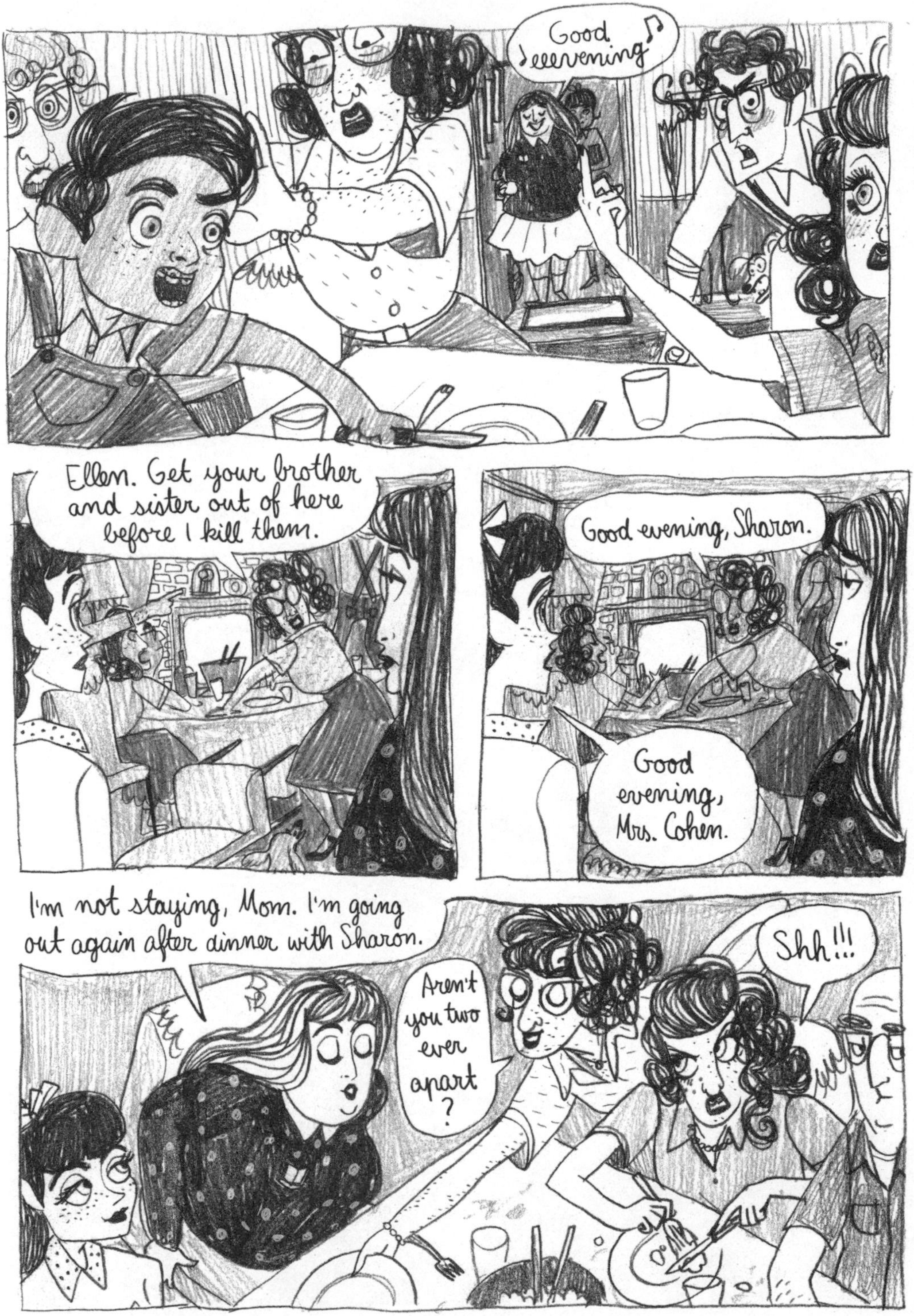
Good eeeevening
Ellen. Get your brother and sister out of here before I kill them.
Good evening, Sharon.
Good evening, Mrs. Cohen.
I'm not staying, Mom. I'm going out again after dinner with Sharon.
Aren't you two ever apart?
Shh!!!

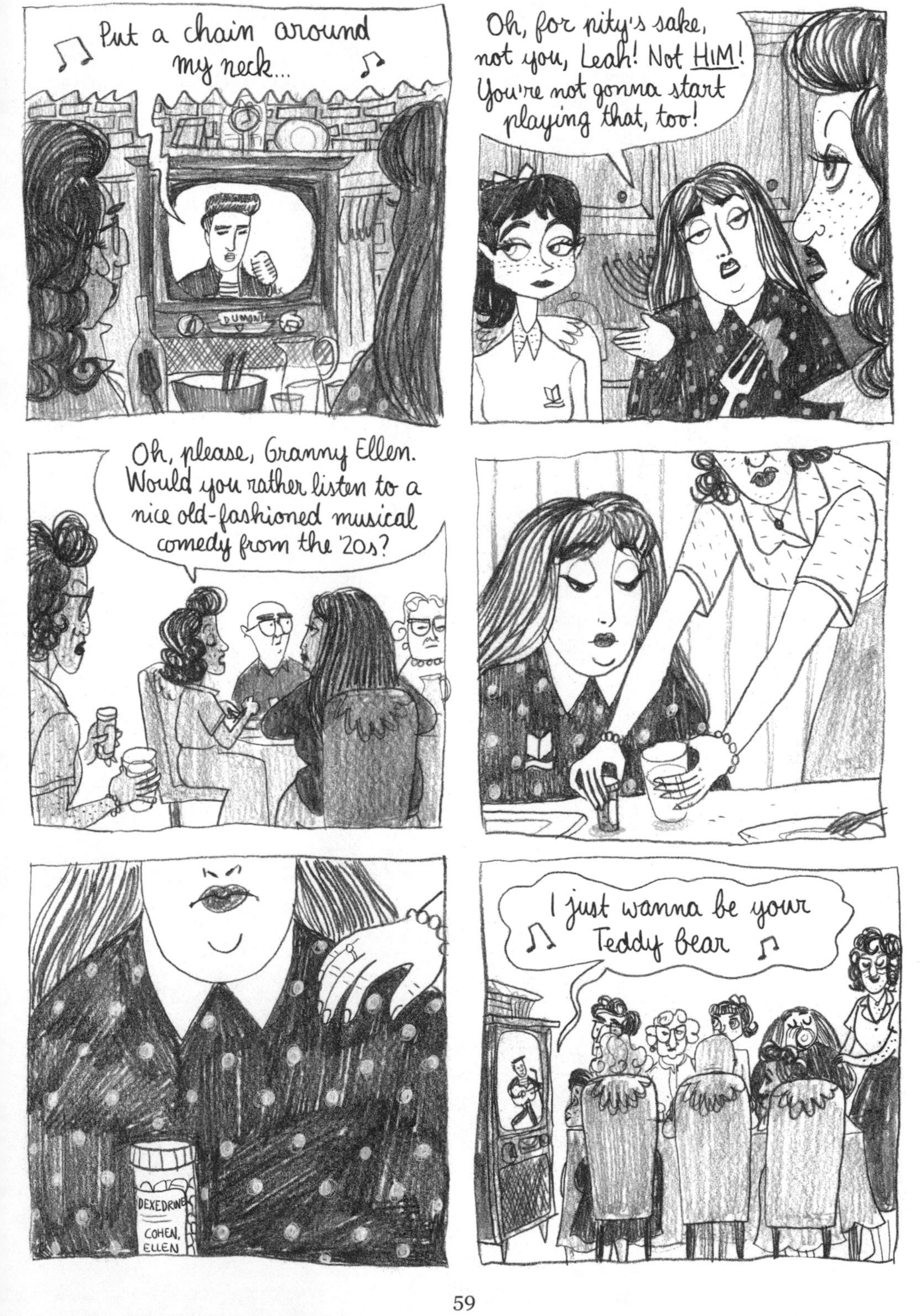
♫ Put a chain around my neck... ♫
DUMONT
Oh, for pity's sake, not you, Leah! Not HIM! You're not gonna start playing that, too!
Oh, please, Granny Ellen. Would you rather listen to a nice old-fashioned musical comedy from the '20s?
DEXEDRINE
COHEN, ELLEN
♫ I just wanna be your Teddy bear ♫

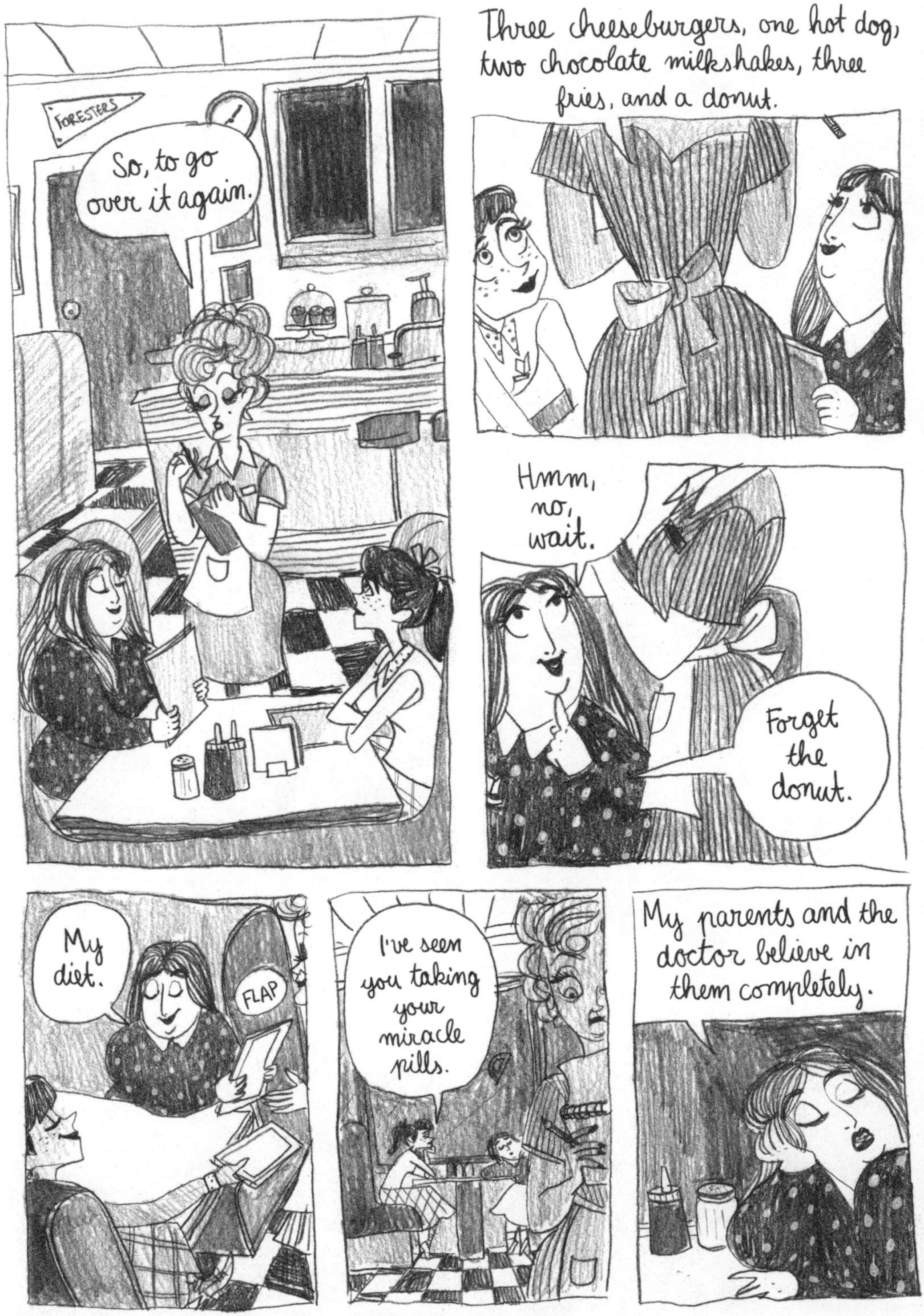
So, to go over it again.
FORESTERS
Three cheeseburgers, one hot dog, two chocolate milkshakes, three fries, and a donut.
Hmm, no, wait.
Forget the donut.
My diet.
FLAP
I've seen you taking your miracle pills.
My parents and the doctor believe in them completely.

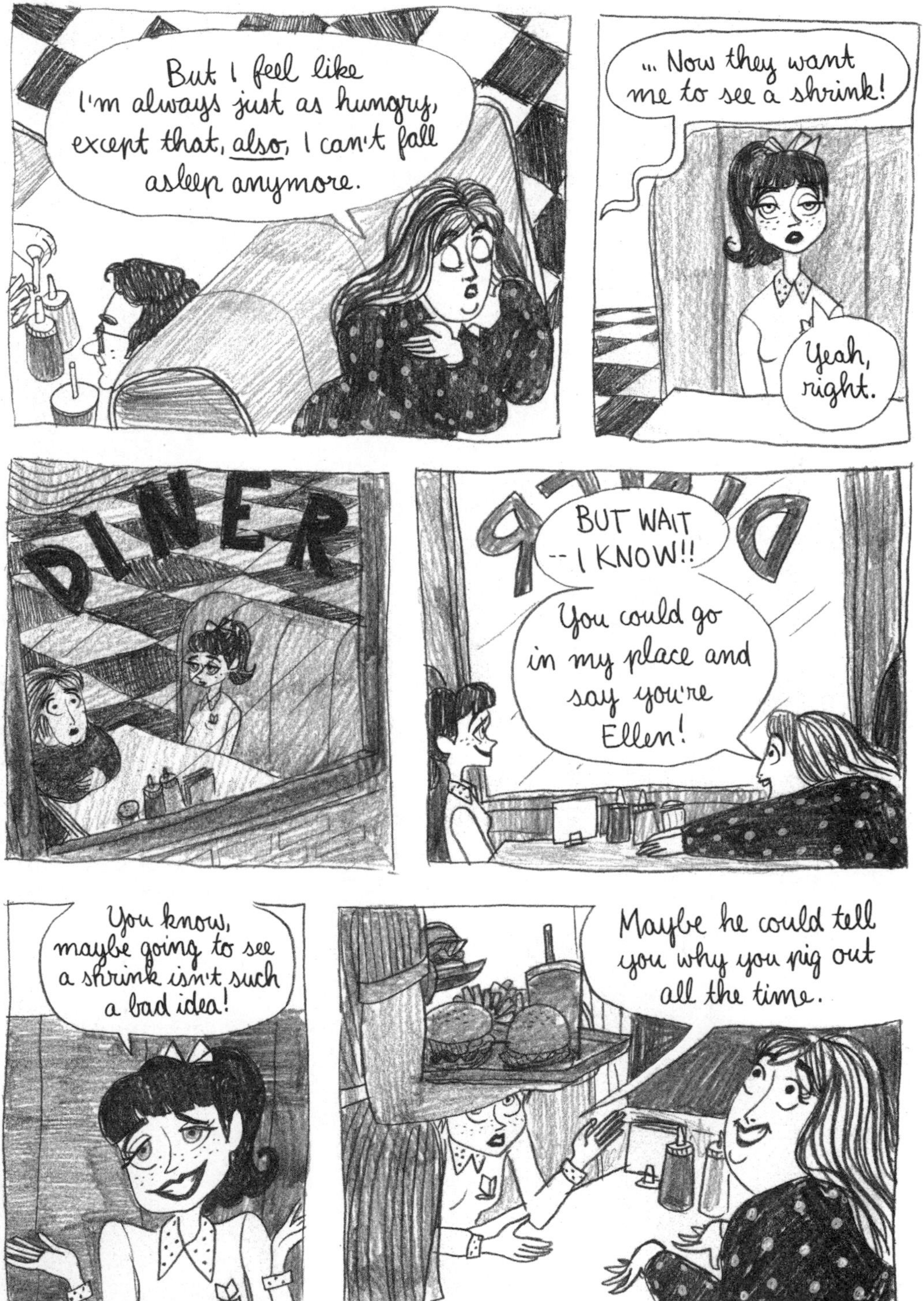

But I feel like I'm always just as hungry, except that, also, I can't fall asleep anymore.
... Now they want me to see a shrink!
Yeah, right.
DINER
BUT WAIT -- I KNOW!!
You could go in my place and say you're Ellen!
You know, maybe going to see a shrink isn't such a bad idea!
Maybe he could tell you why you pig out all the time.

When I lived in Alexandria, I was super skinny. I was a cheerleader and all that.

I had lots of dates. Guys were lining up to go out with me.

I had a boyfriend, an Italian, super sexy. Older than me. Roberto. We made love all the time, and he NEVER had enough.

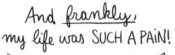

And *frankly,* my life was SUCH A PAIN!

I swear it!

I think things are a lot easier the way I am now.

Wait, I should have a picture of me from back than ...

SLURP

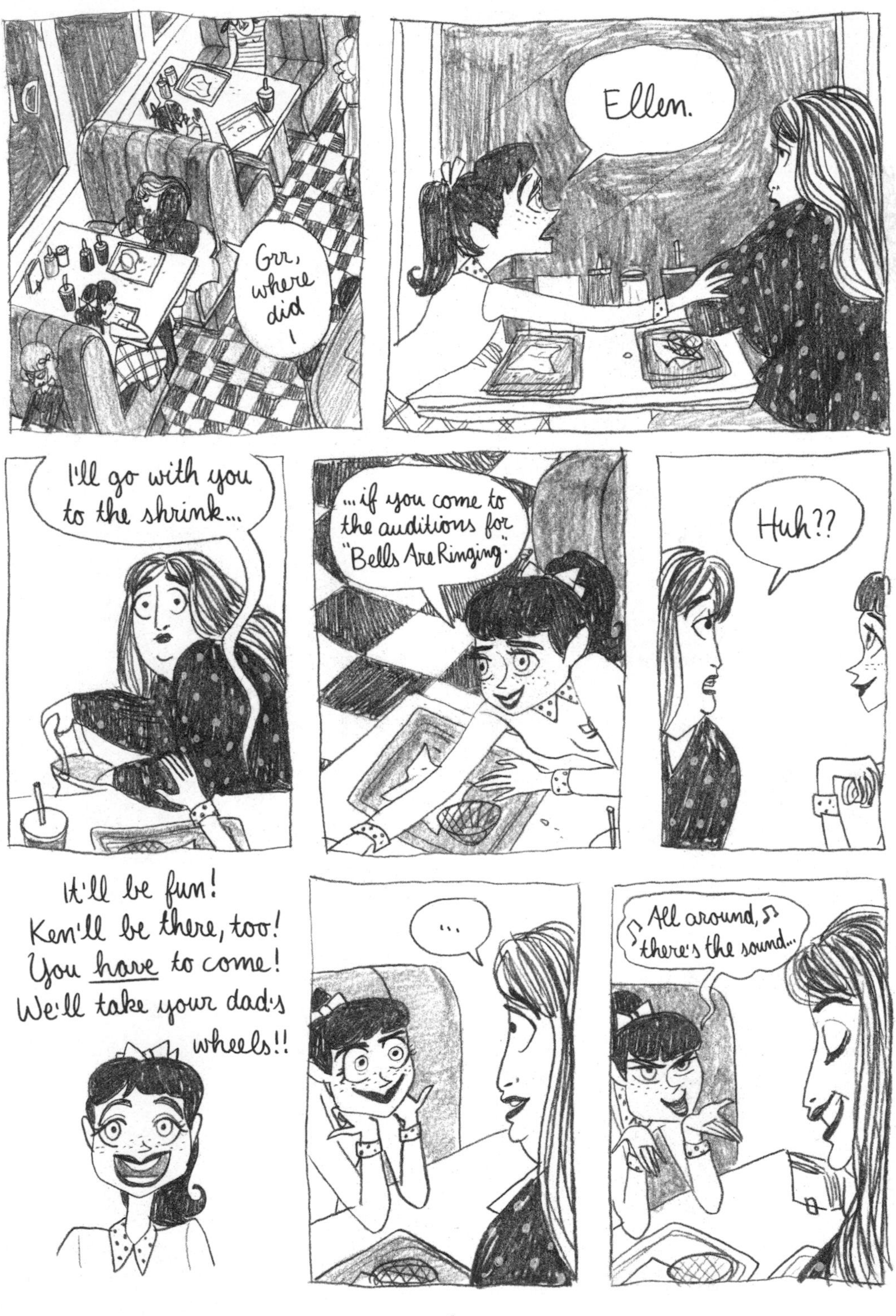
Grr, where did I
Ellen.
I'll go with you to the shrink...
...if you come to the auditions for "Bells Are Ringing."
Huh??
It'll be fun! Ken'll be there, too! You have to come! We'll take your dad's wheels!!
...
♫ All around, ♫ there's the sound...

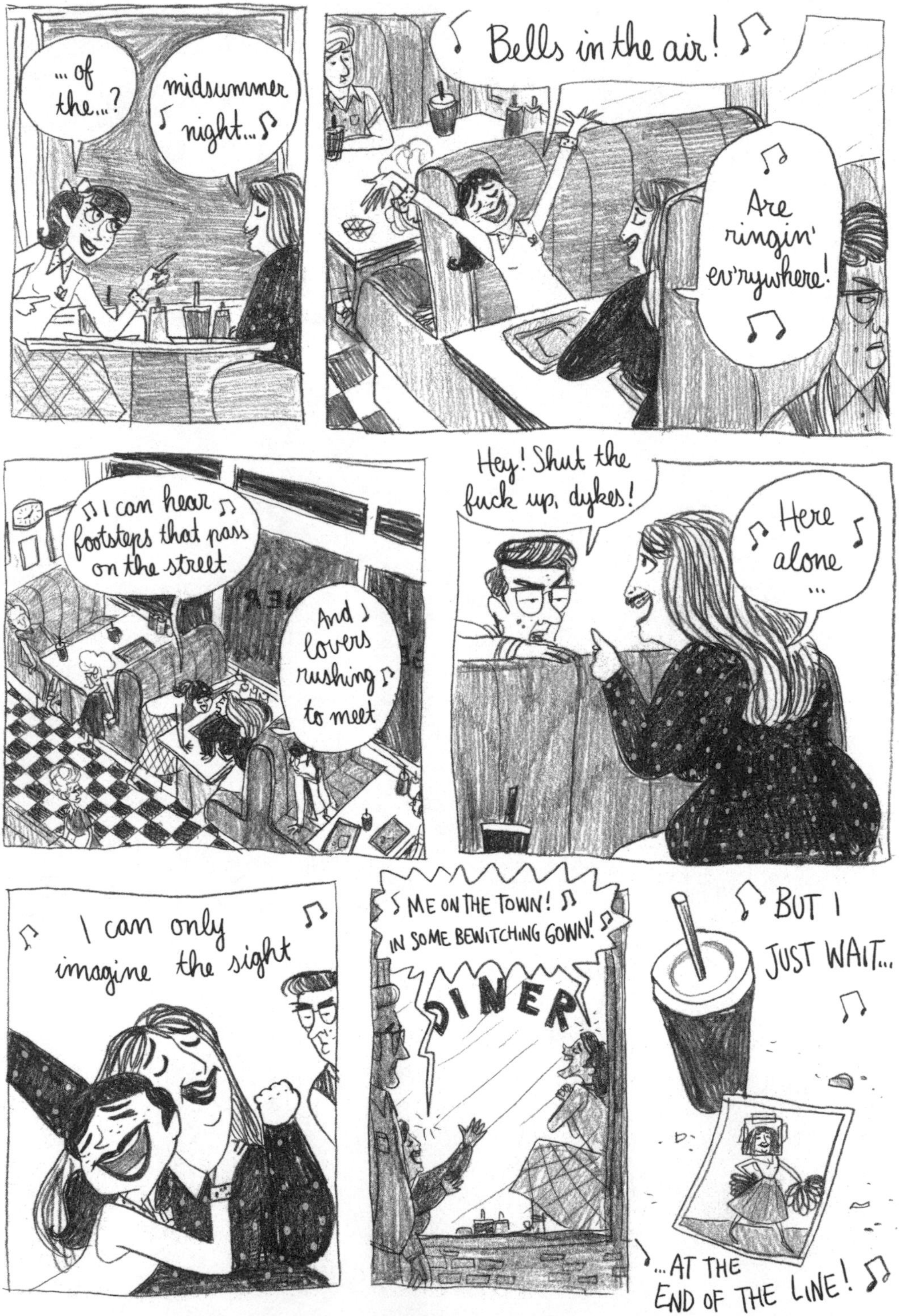
... of the...?
midsummer night...
Bells in the air!
Are ringin' ev'rywhere!
I can hear footsteps that pass on the street
And lovers rushing to meet
Hey! Shut the fuck up, dykes!
Here alone ...
I can only imagine the sight
ME ON THE TOWN!
IN SOME BEWITCHING GOWN!
DINER
BUT I JUST WAIT...
...AT THE END OF THE LINE!

5-Shirley

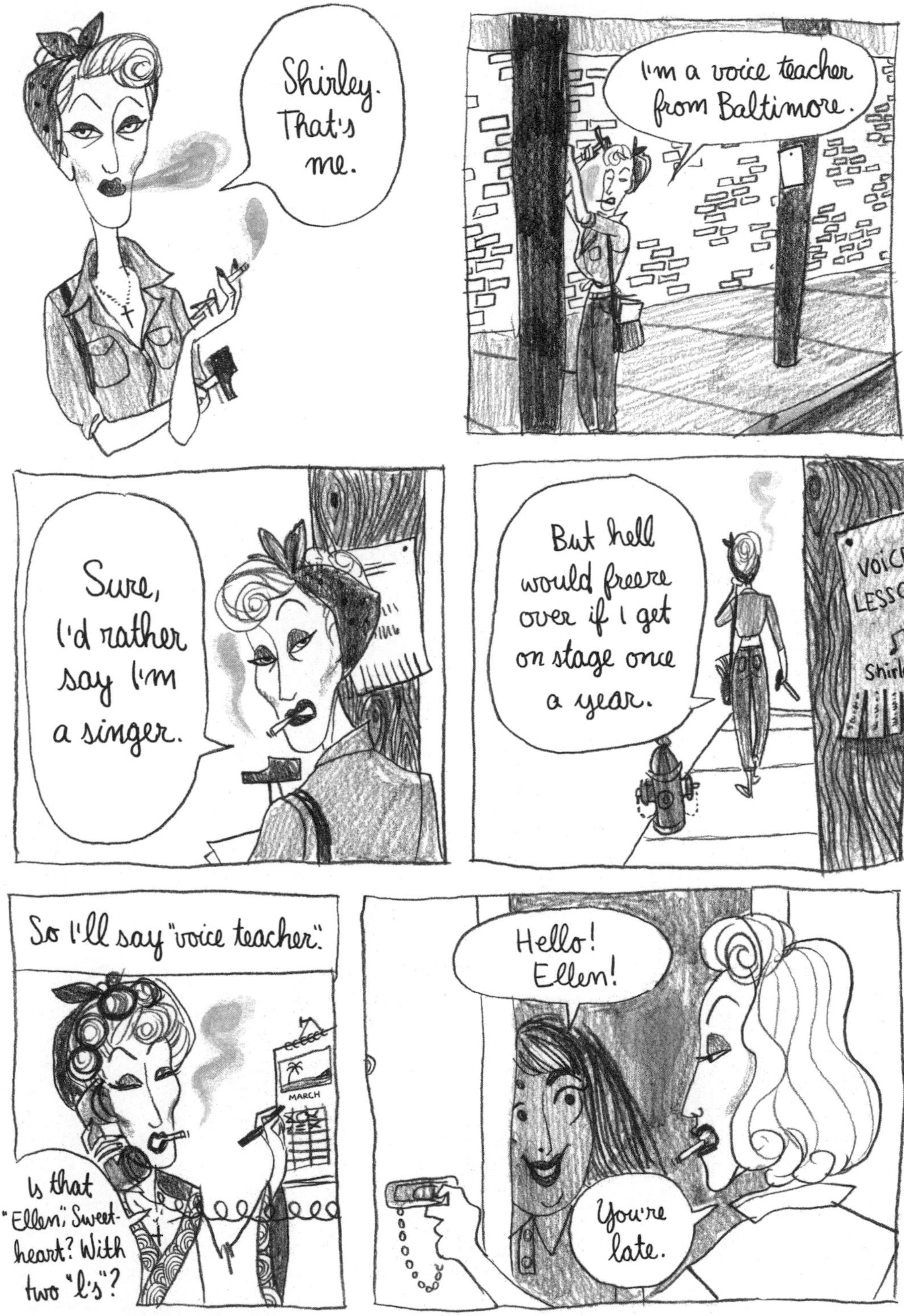
Shirley. That's me.
I'm a voice teacher from Baltimore.
Sure, I'd rather say I'm a singer.
But hell would freeze over if I get on stage once a year.
VOICE LESSO
Shirle
So I'll say "voice teacher."
MARCH
Is that "Ellen," Sweetheart? With two "l's"?
Hello! Ellen!
You're late.

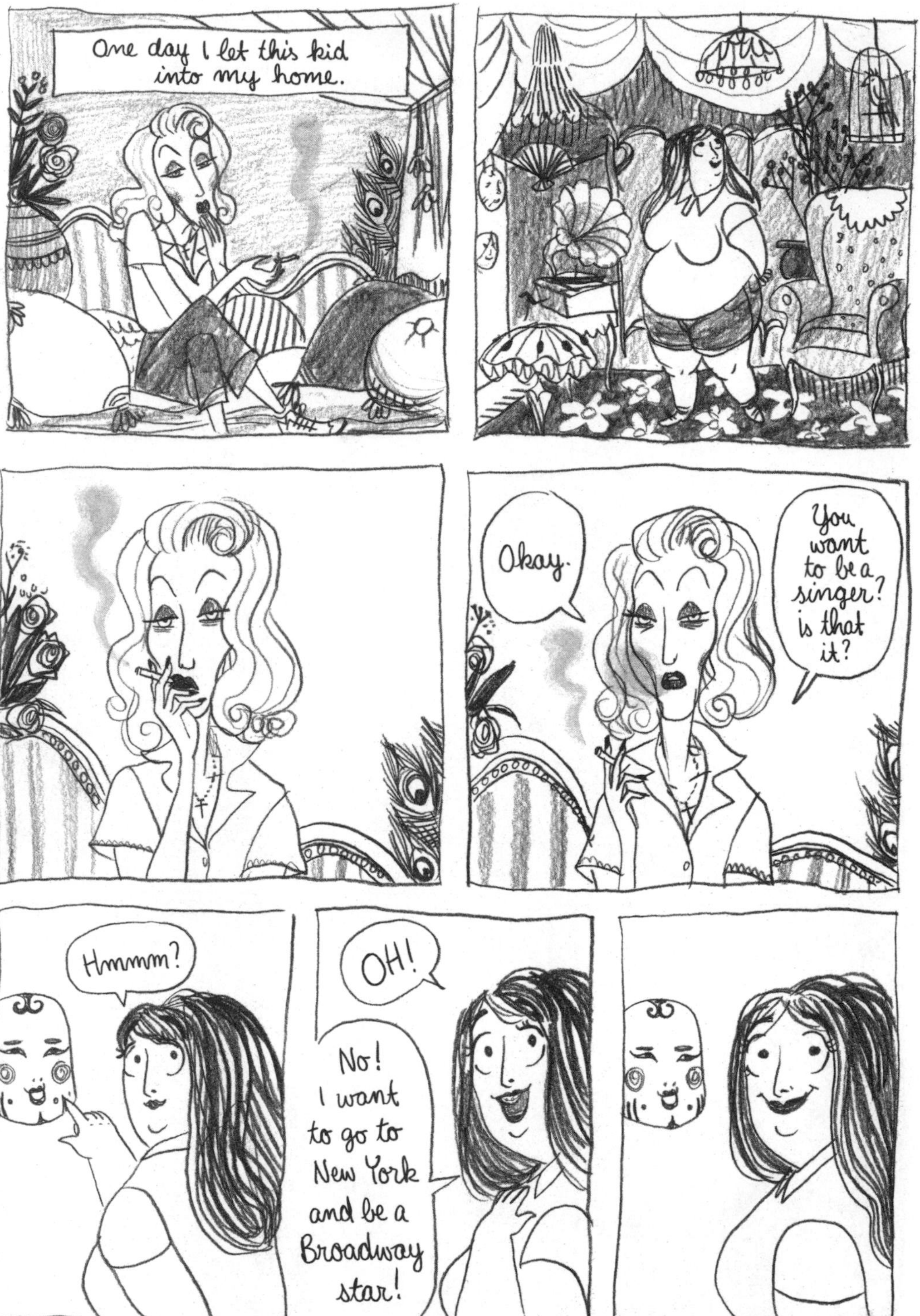
One day I let this kid into my home.
Okay.
You want to be a singer? is that it?
Hmmm?
OH!
No! I want to go to New York and be a Broadway star!

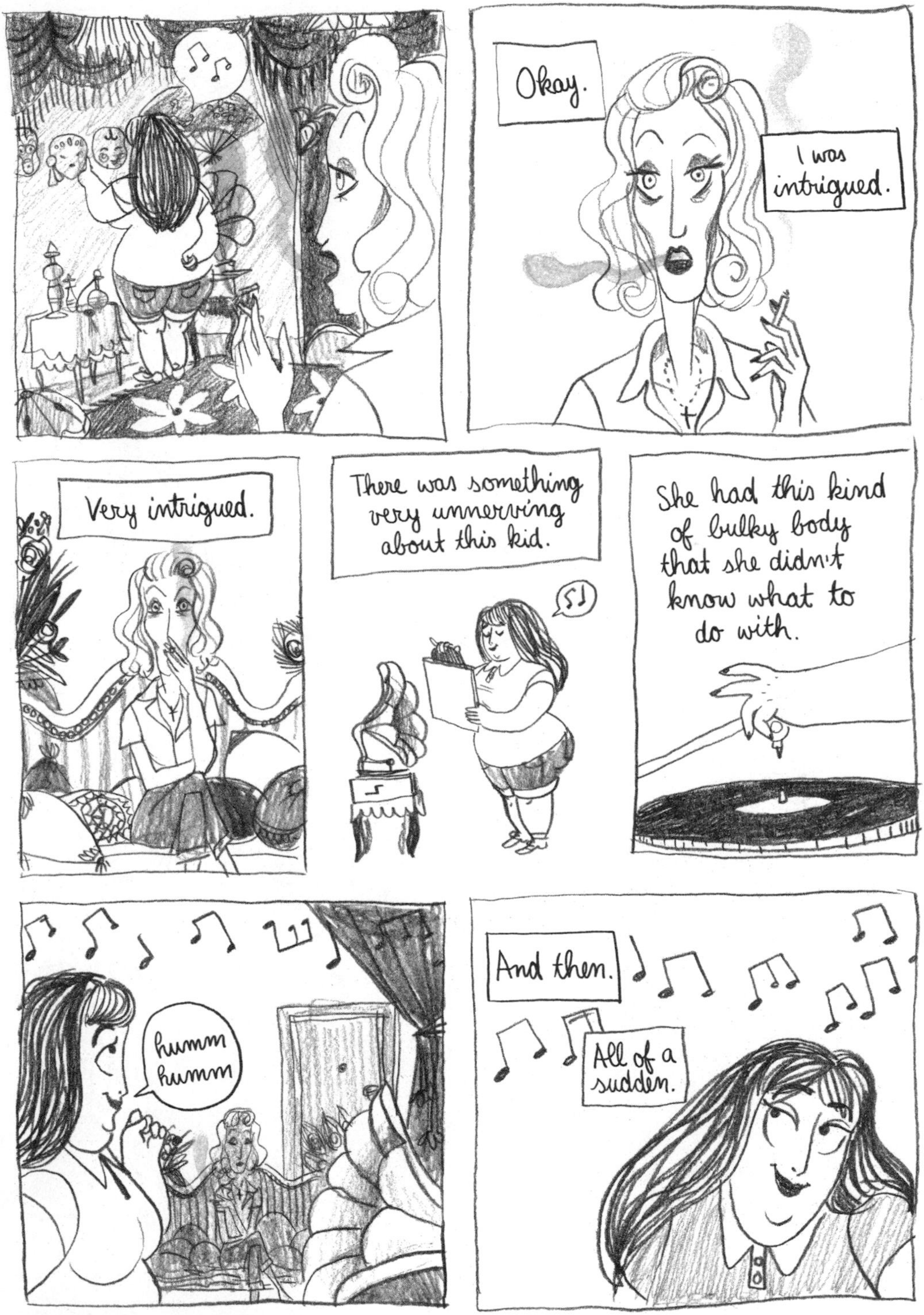
Okay.
I was intrigued.
Very intrigued.
There was something very unnerving about this kid.
She had this kind of bulky body that she didn't know what to do with.
humm humm
And then.
All of a sudden.

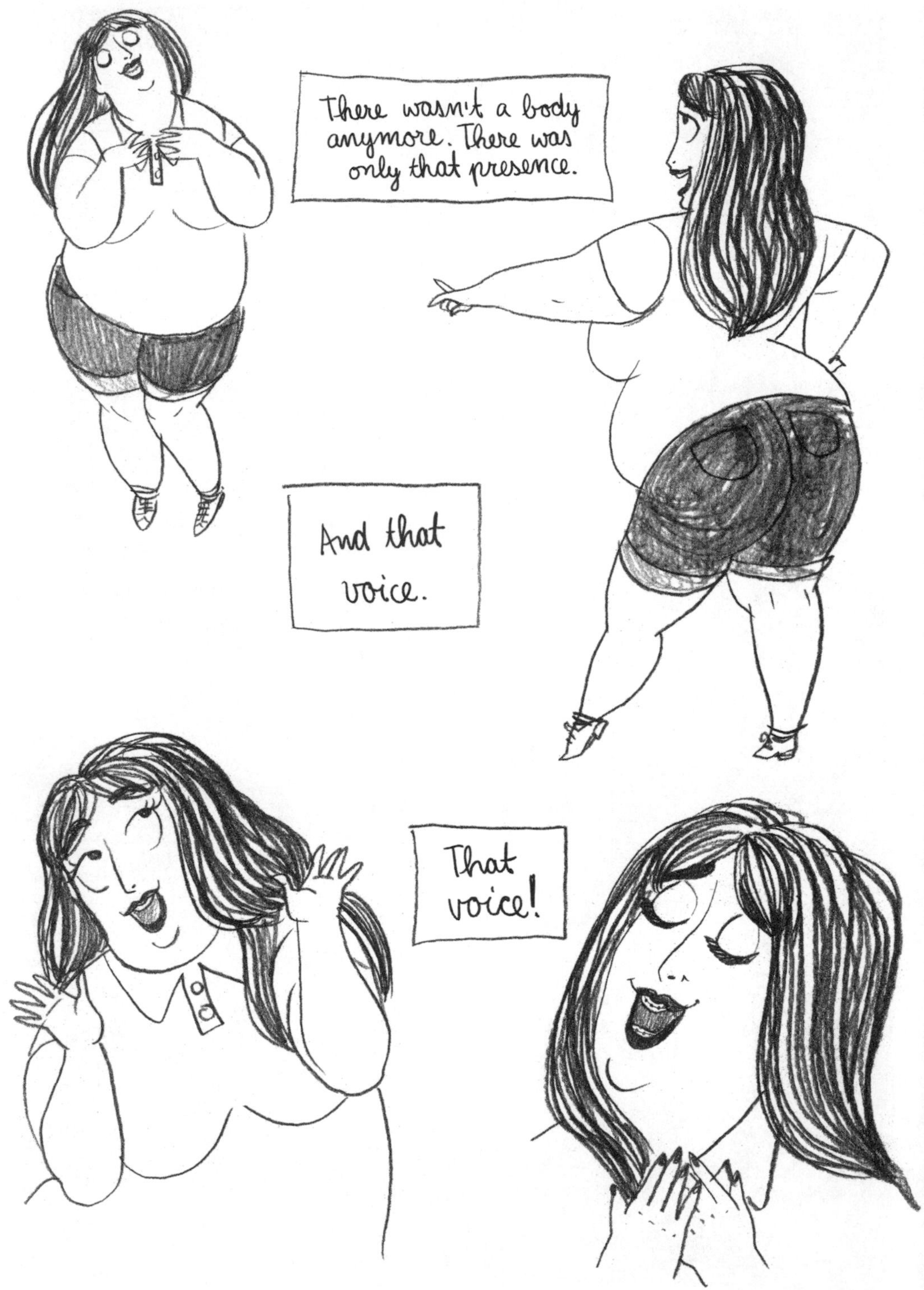
There wasn't a body anymore. There was only that presence.
And that voice.
That voice!

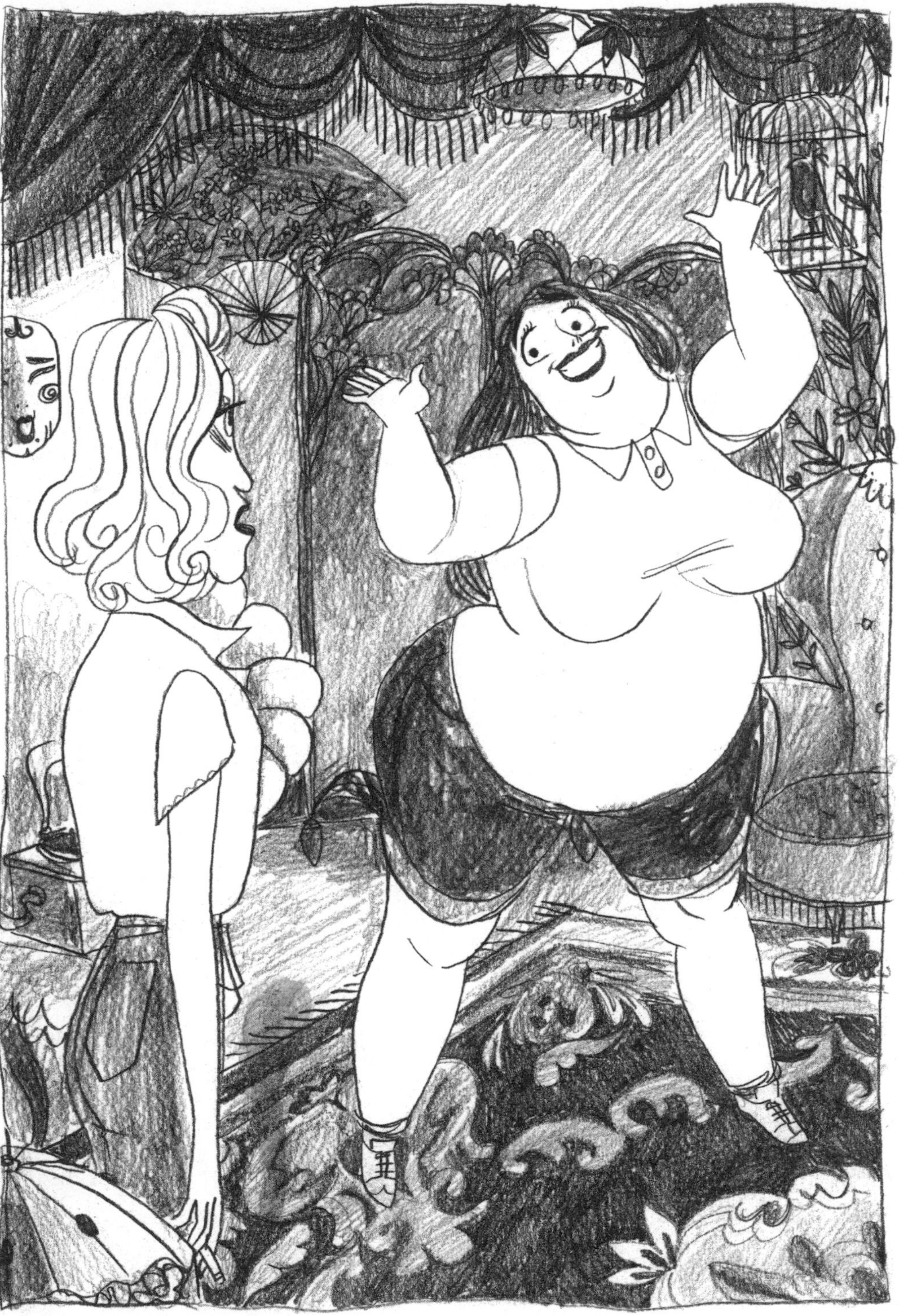

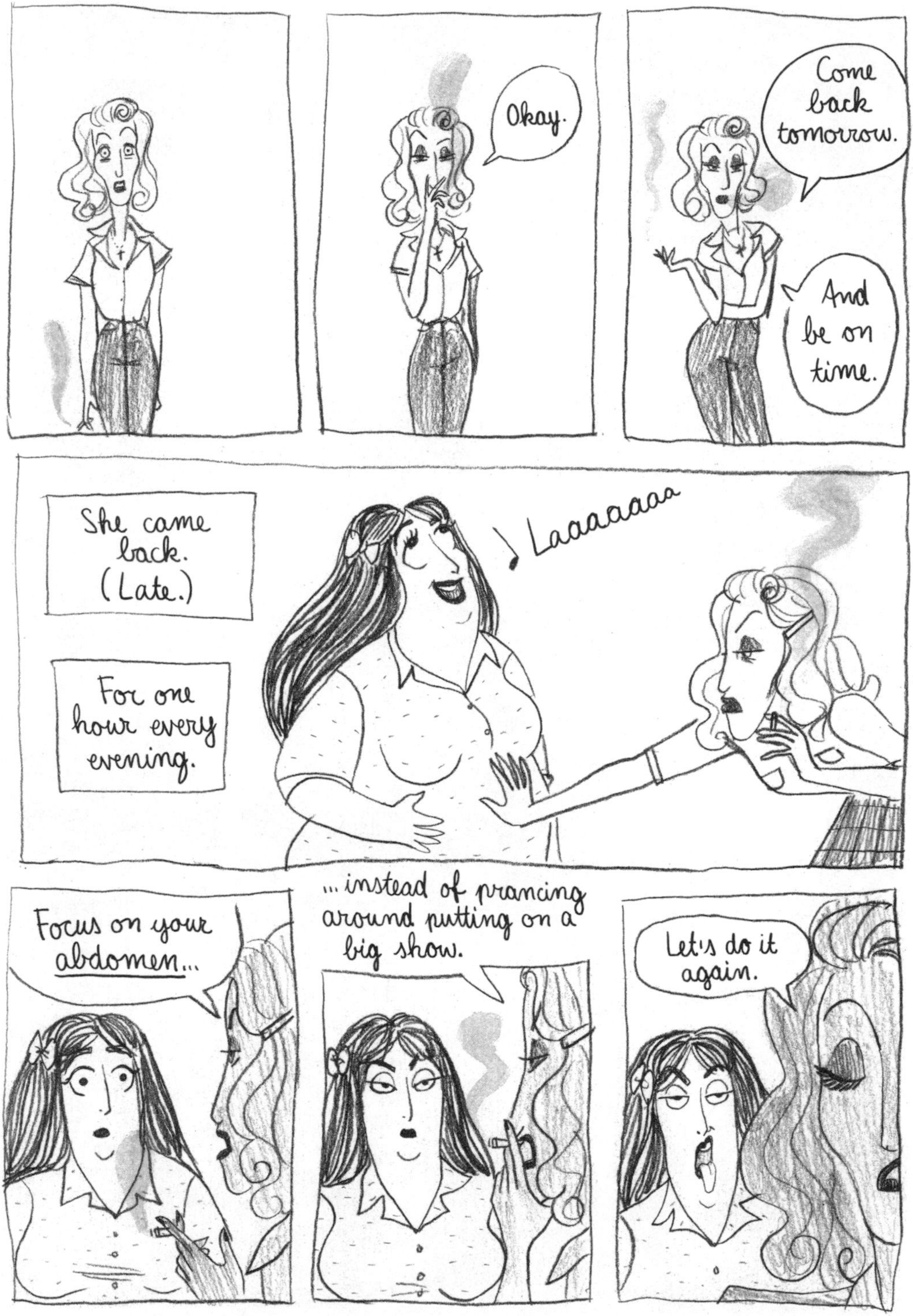
Okay.
Come back tomorrow.
And be on time.
She came back. (Late.)
For one hour every evening.
Laaaaaaa
Focus on your abdomen...
...instead of prancing around putting on a big show.
Let's do it again.

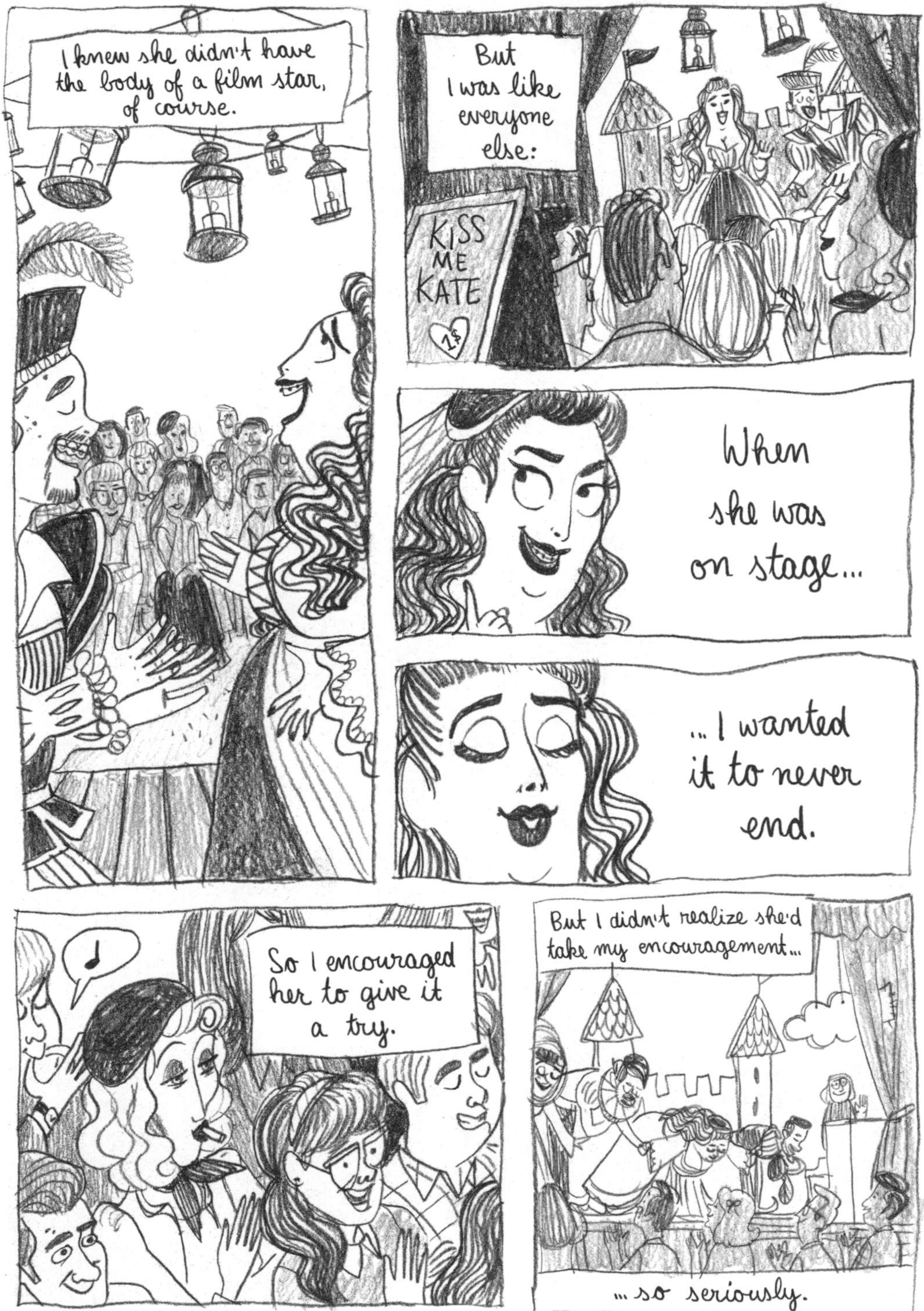
I knew she didn't have the body of a film star, of course.
But I was like everyone else:
KISS ME KATE
1$
When she was on stage...
...I wanted it to never end.
So I encouraged her to give it a try.
But I didn't realize she'd take my encouragement...
...so seriously.

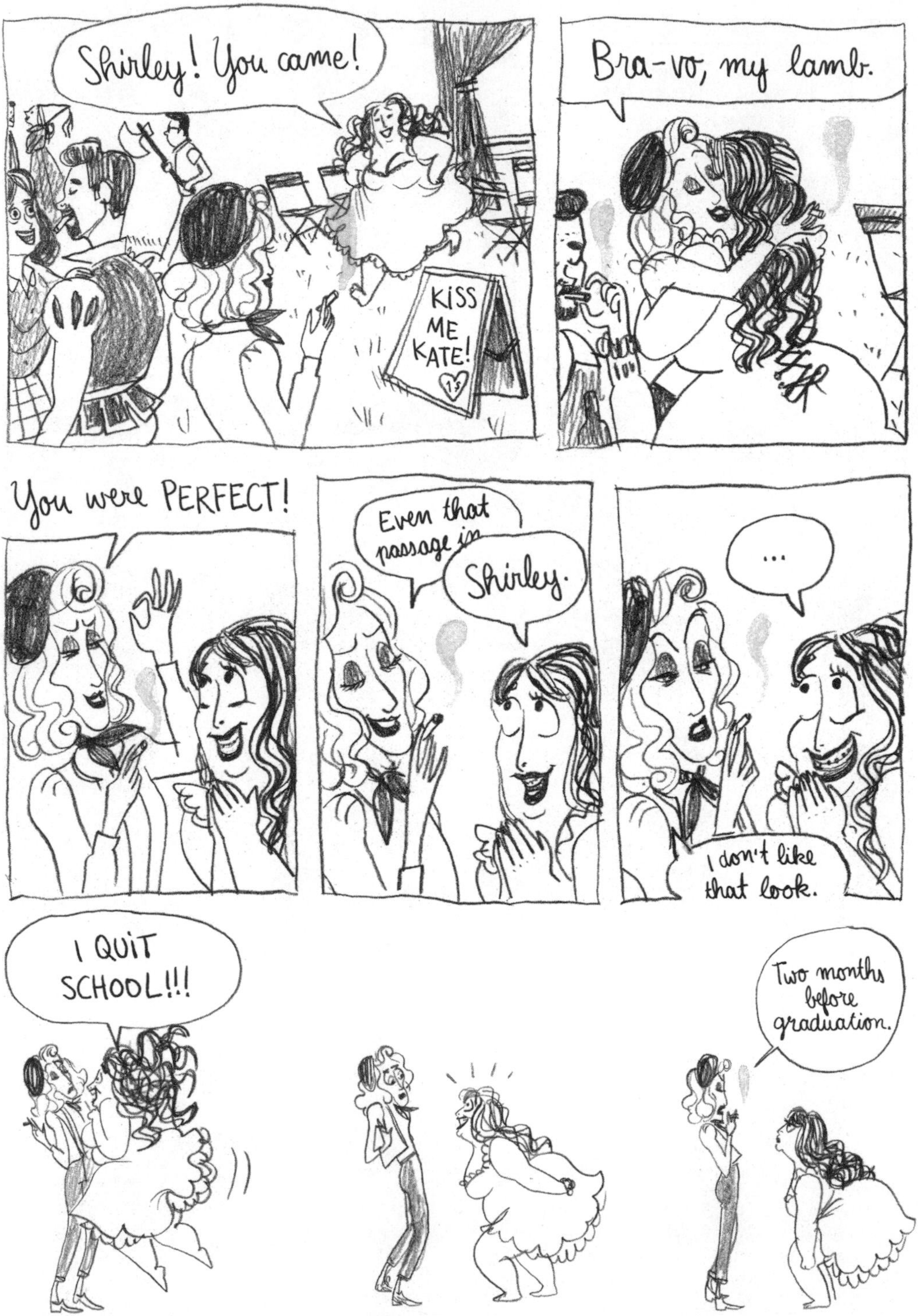
Shirley! You came!
KISS ME KATE!
Bra-vo, my lamb.
You were PERFECT!
Even that passage in
Shirley.
...
I don't like that look.
I QUIT SCHOOL!!!
Two months before graduation.

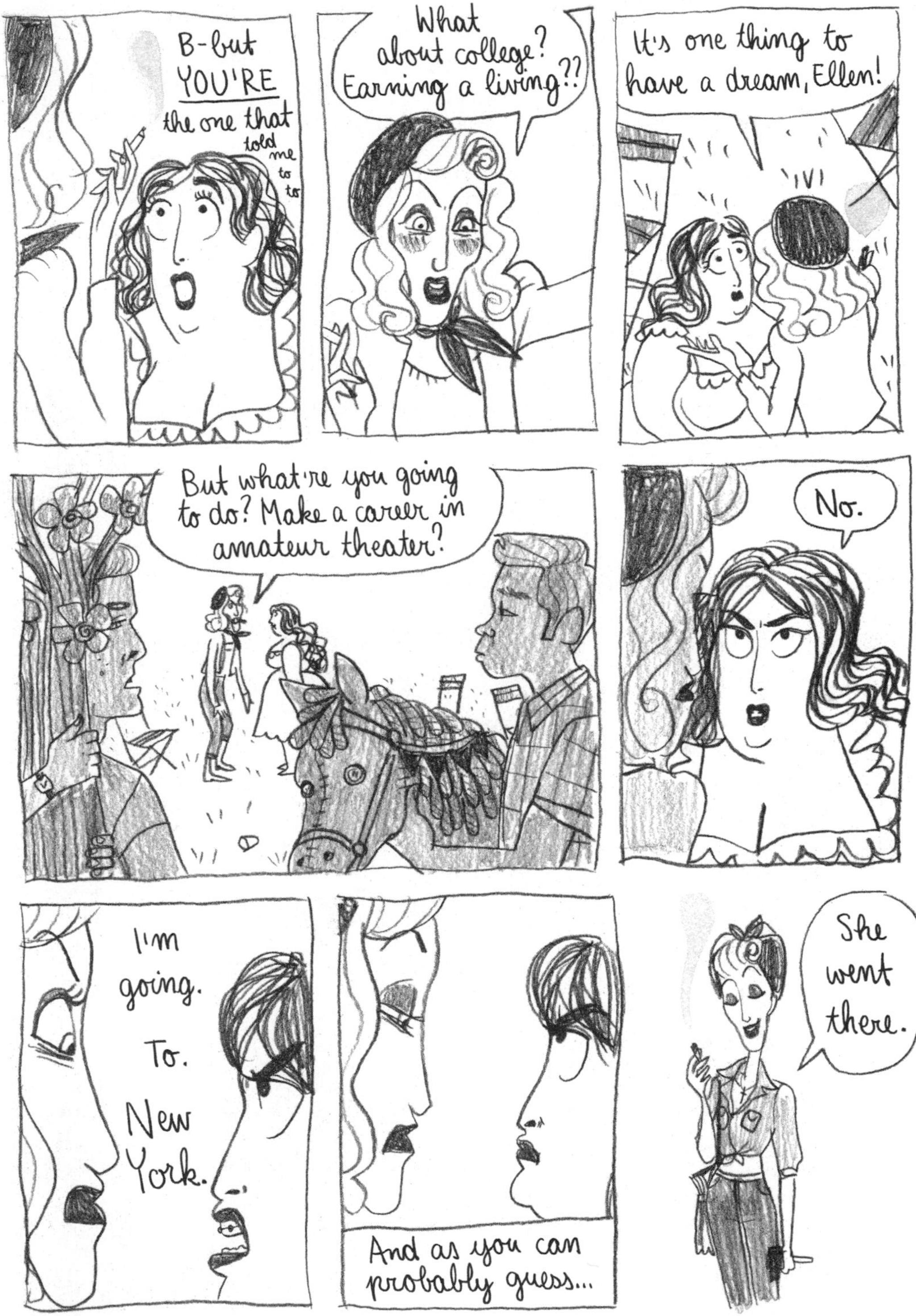
B-but YOU'RE the one that told me to to
What about college? Earning a living??
It's one thing to have a dream, Ellen!
But what're you going to do? Make a career in amateur theater?
No.
I'm going. To. New York.
And as you can probably guess...
She went there.

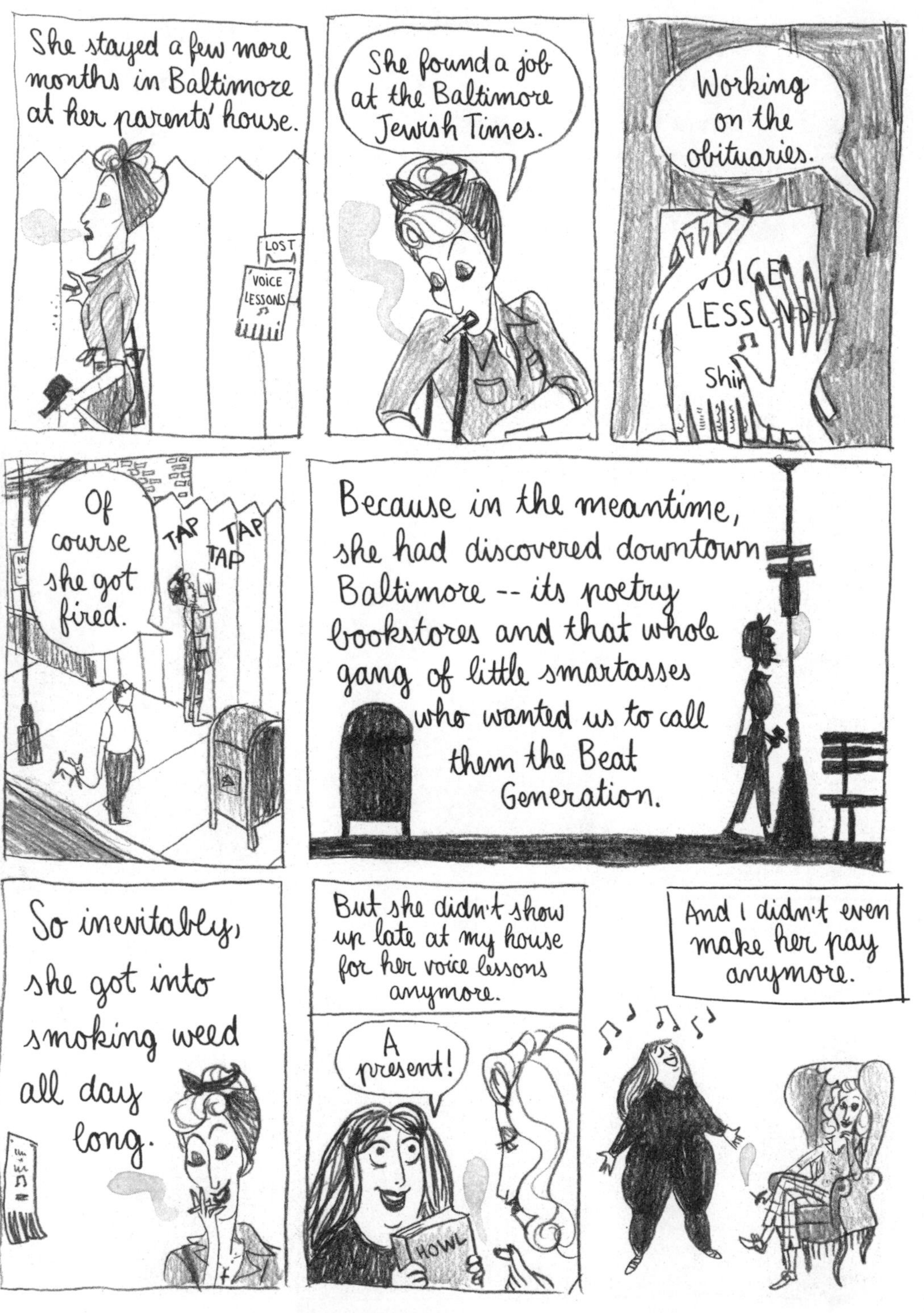
She stayed a few more months in Baltimore at her parents' house.
LOST
VOICE LESSONS
She found a job at the Baltimore Jewish Times.
Working on the obituaries.
VOICE LESSONS
Shir
Of course she got fired.
TAP TAP TAP
Because in the meantime, she had discovered downtown Baltimore -- its poetry bookstores and that whole gang of little smartasses who wanted us to call them the Beat Generation.
So inevitably, she got into smoking weed all day long.
But she didn't show up late at my house for her voice lessons anymore.
A present!
HOWL
And I didn't even make her pay anymore.

Hey, don't light up that garbage in here!

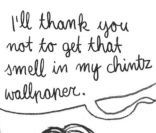

I'll thank you not to get that smell in my chintz wallpaper.

You know, Shirley, you were right.

I'm not going to New York. I won't become a star. Well, only a pastrami sandwich star at my father's deli.

I mean, look! I don't even have a job! I don't even have a way to GO to New York!

And then, because I'm an idiot, I said,

What if, say, I gave you my car to get there?

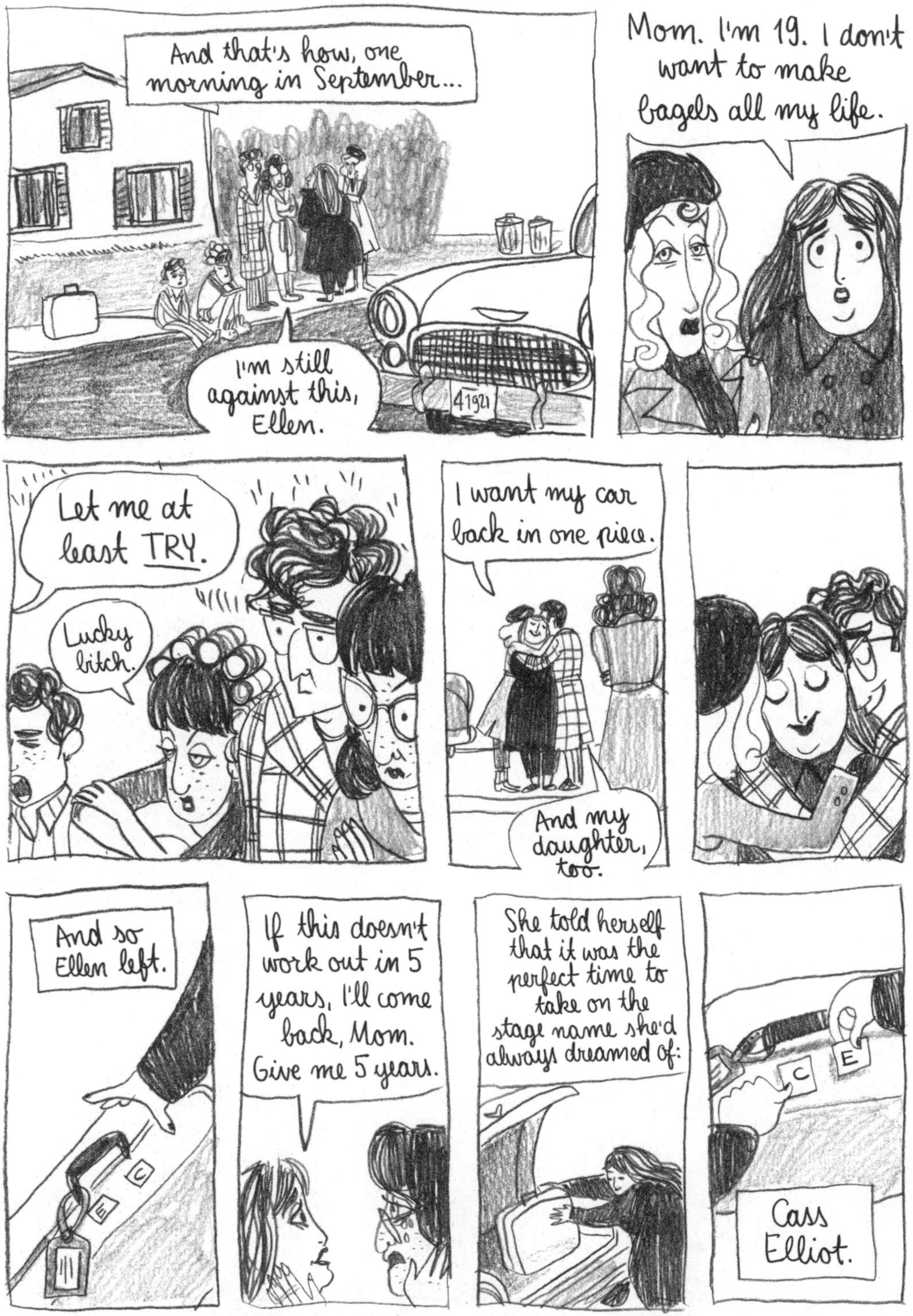
And that's how, one morning in September...
I'm still against this, Ellen.
Mom. I'm 19. I don't want to make bagels all my life.
Let me at least TRY.
Lucky bitch.
I want my car back in one piece.
And my daughter, too.
And so Ellen left.
If this doesn't work out in 5 years, I'll come back, Mom. Give me 5 years.
She told herself that it was the perfect time to take on the stage name she'd always dreamed of:
C
E
Cass Elliot.
4 1921

6-Philip

My name is
Philip Cohen.

I'm 42 years old.

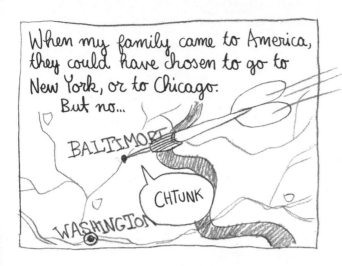

When my family came to America, they could have chosen to go to New York, or to Chicago. But no...

BALTIMORE

CHTUNK

WASHINGTON

I've never understood why.

<u>Baltimore.</u>

Always in Washington's shadow, Baltimore has two big points of pride:

Its football team

COLTS

and its steamed crab.

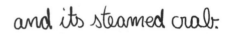

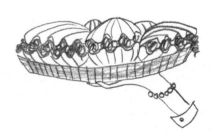

But we Cohens...

...opened up delis.

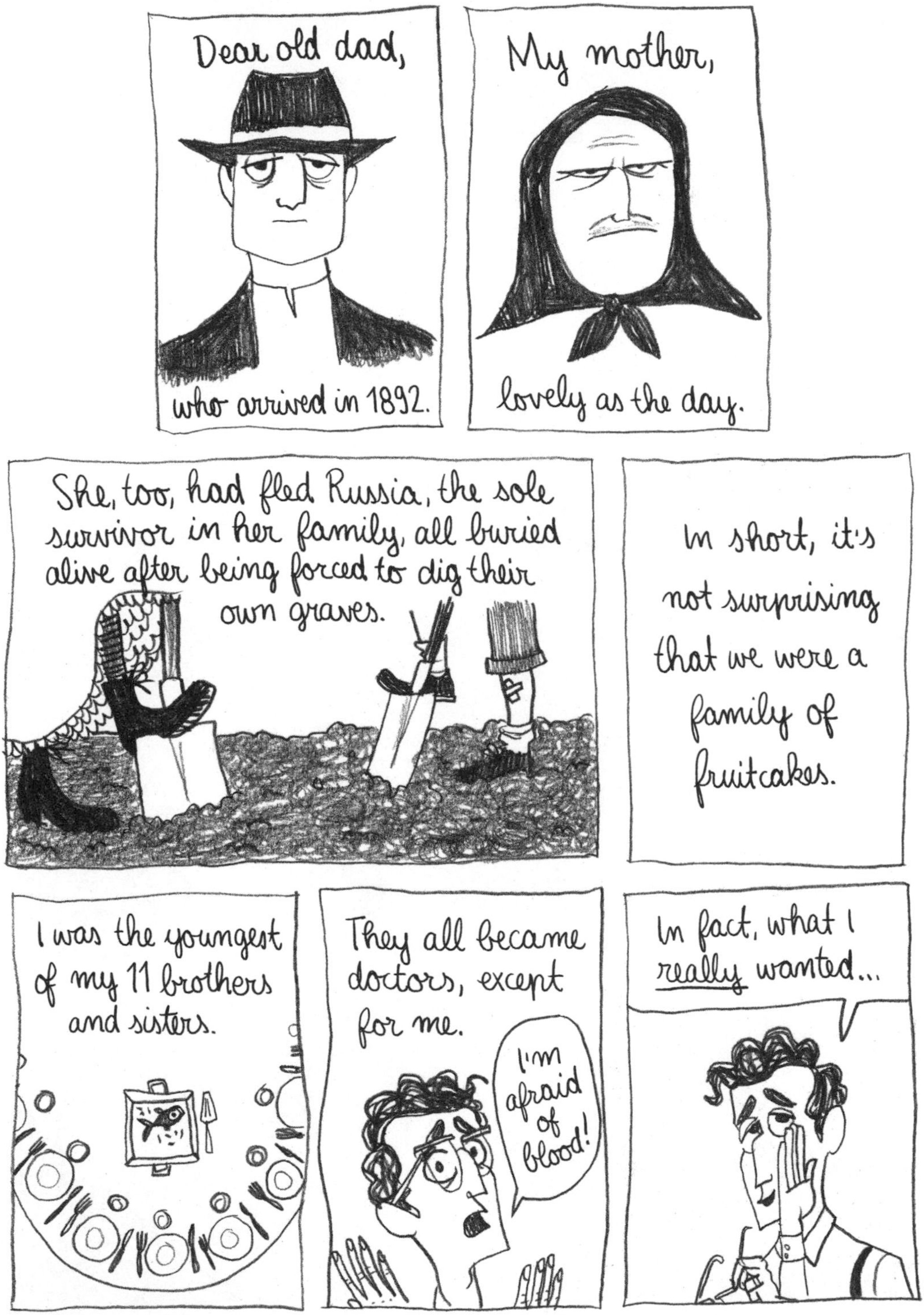
Dear old dad,
who arrived in 1892.
My mother,
lovely as the day.
She, too, had fled Russia, the sole survivor in her family, all buried alive after being forced to dig their own graves.
In short, it's not surprising that we were a family of fruitcakes.
I was the youngest of my 11 brothers and sisters.
They all became doctors, except for me.
I'm afraid of blood!
In fact, what I really wanted...

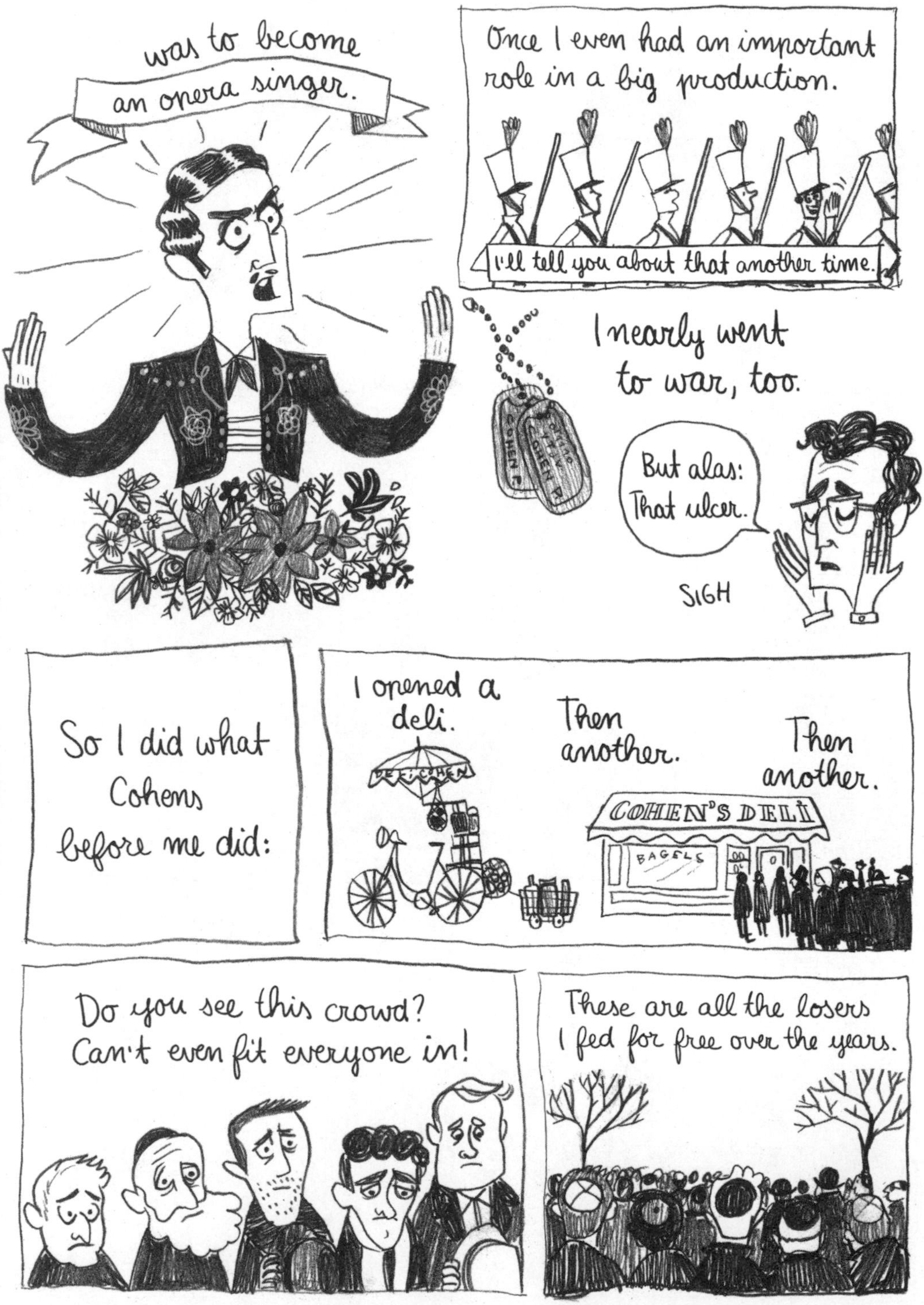
was to become
an opera singer.
Once I even had an important role in a big production.
I'll tell you about that another time.
I nearly went to war, too.
COHEN P.
But alas: That ulcer.
SIGH
So I did what Cohens before me did:
I opened a deli.
DELI-COHEN
Then another.
Then another.
COHEN'S DELI
BAGELS
Do you see this crowd? Can't even fit everyone in!
These are all the losers I fed for free over the years.

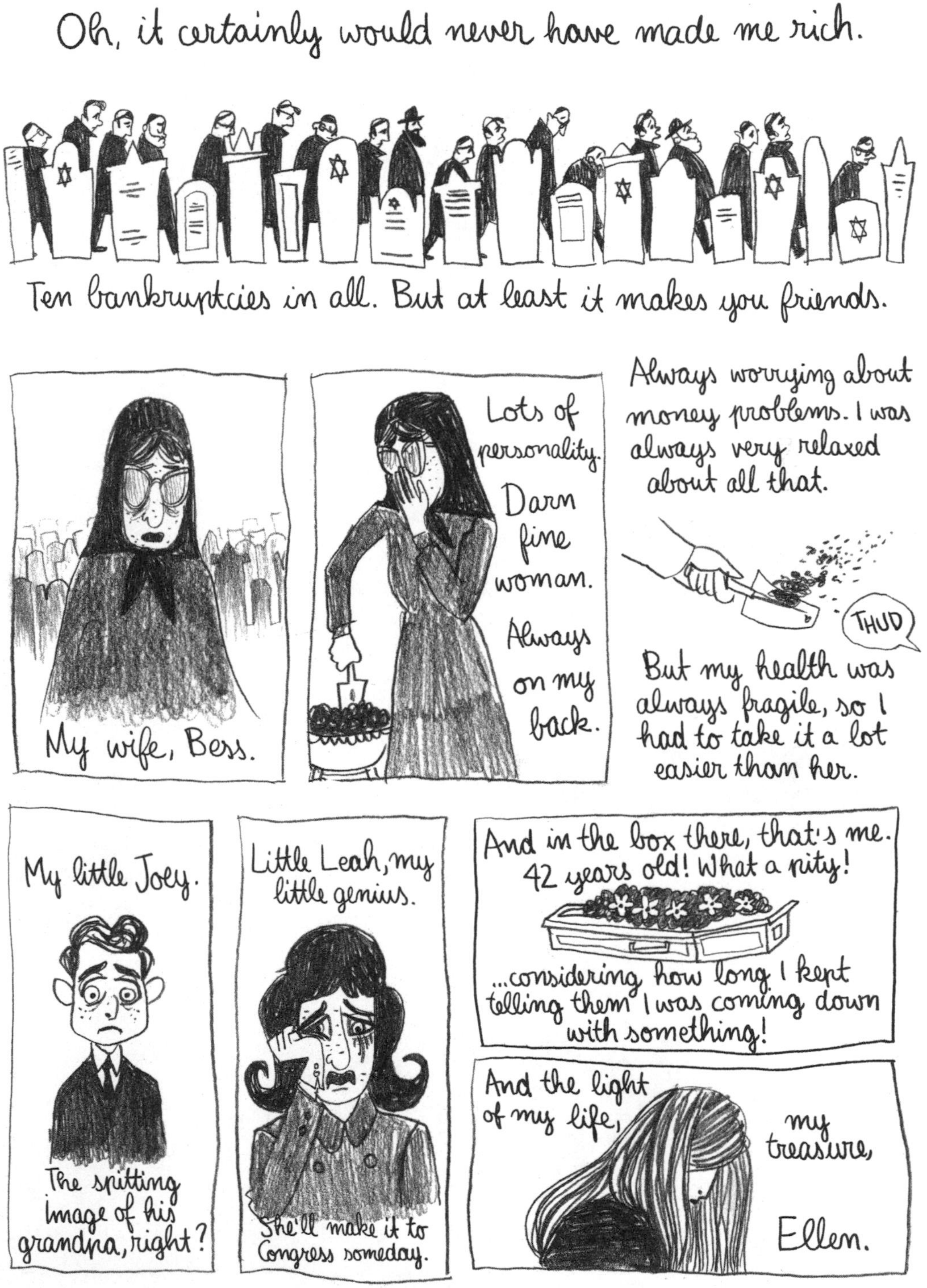
Oh, it certainly would never have made me rich.
Ten bankruptcies in all. But at least it makes you friends.
My wife, Bess.
Lots of personality.
Darn fine woman.
Always on my back.
Always worrying about money problems. I was always very relaxed about all that.
THUD
But my health was always fragile, so I had to take it a lot easier than her.
My little Joey.
The spitting image of his grandpa, right?
Little Leah, my little genius.
She'll make it to Congress someday.
And in the box there, that's me. 42 years old! What a pity!
...considering how long I kept telling them I was coming down with something!
And the light of my life,
my treasure,
Ellen.

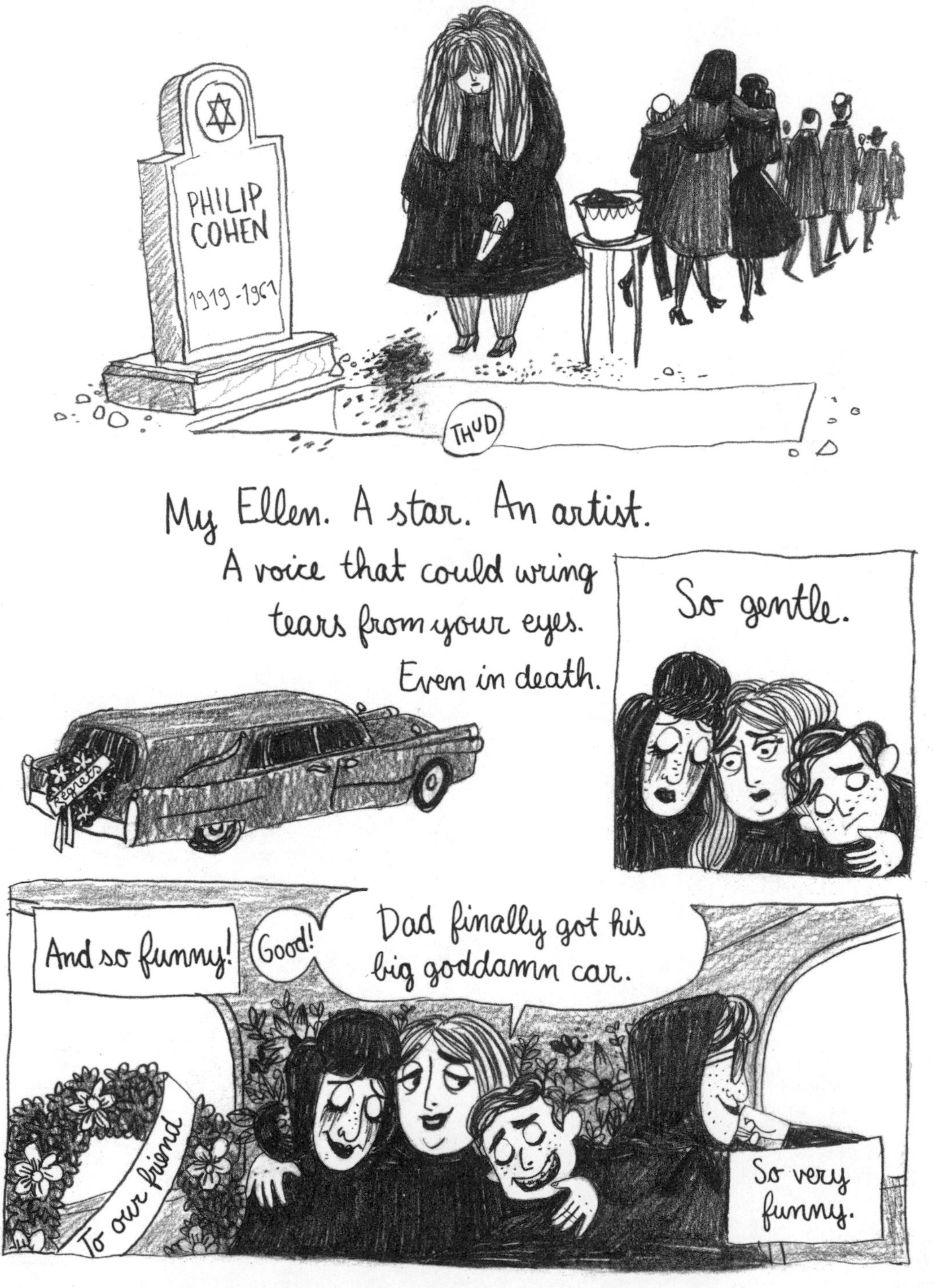
PHILIP
COHEN
1919 - 1967
THUD
My Ellen. A star. An artist.
A voice that could wring
tears from your eyes.
Even in death.
Regrets
So gentle.
And so funny!
Good!
Dad finally got his
big goddamn car.
To our friend
So very
funny.

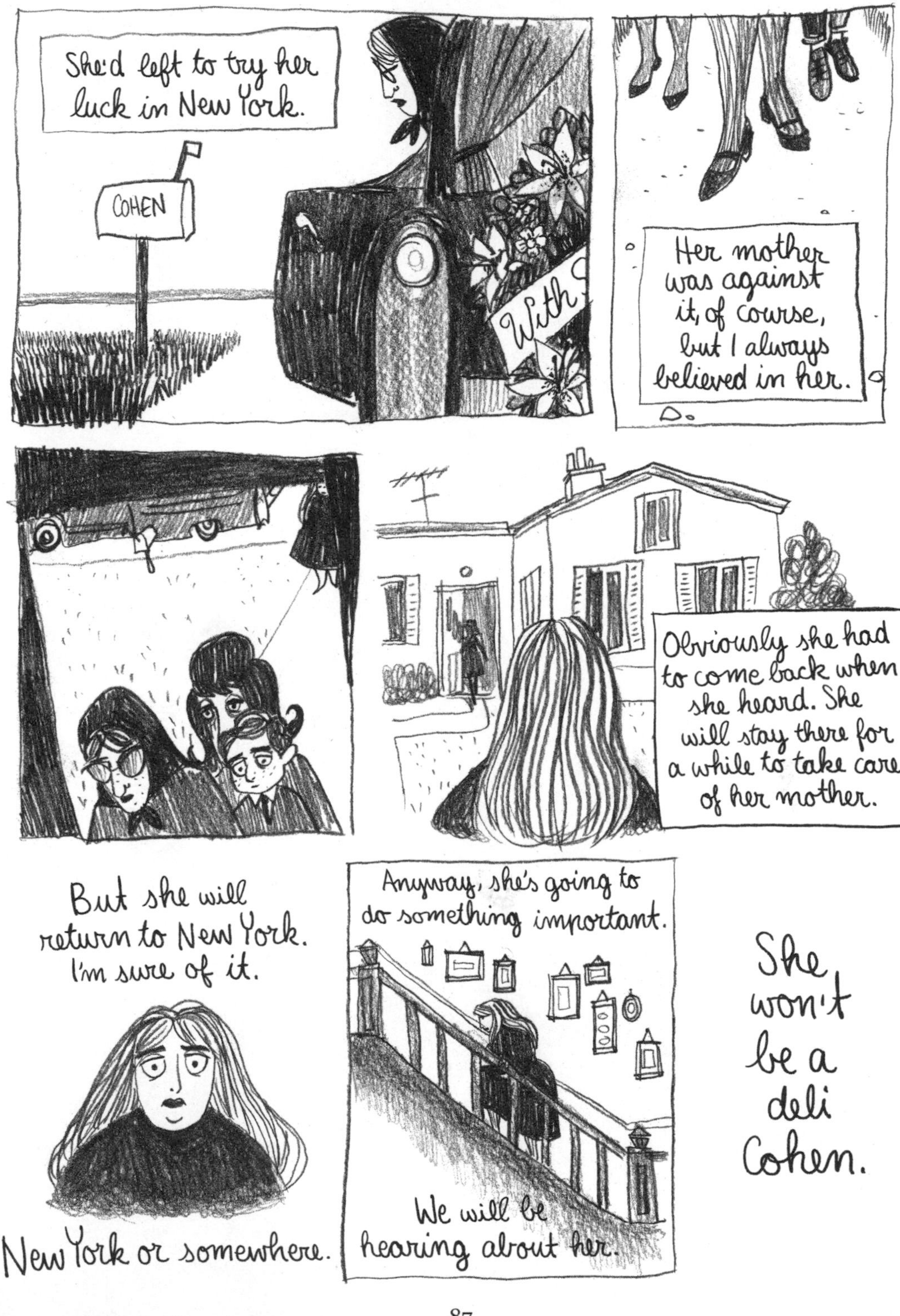
She'd left to try her luck in New York.
COHEN
With
Her mother was against it, of course, but I always believed in her.
Obviously she had to come back when she heard. She will stay there for a while to take care of her mother.
But she will return to New York. I'm sure of it.
New York or somewhere.
Anyway, she's going to do something important.
We will be hearing about her.
She won't be a deli Cohen.

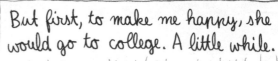

But first, to make me happy, she would go to college. A little while.

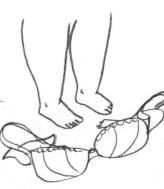

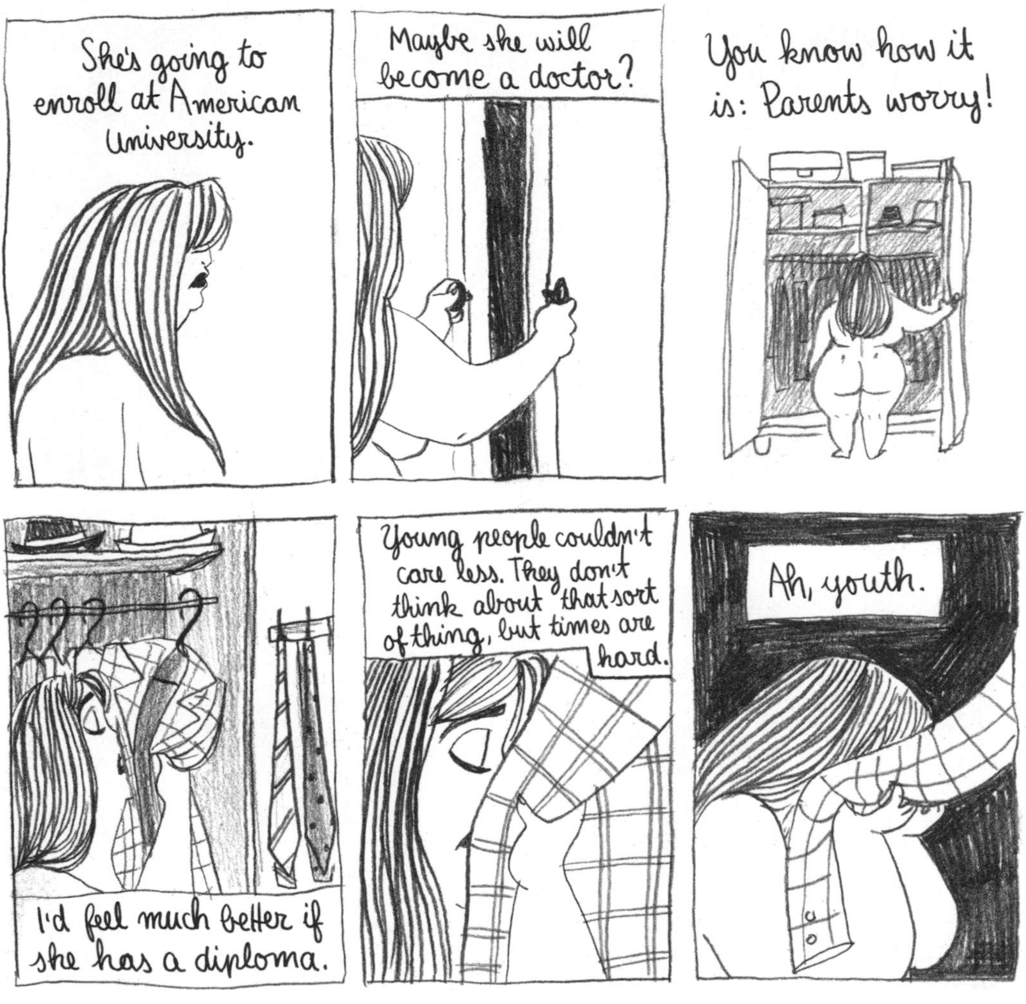
She's going to enroll at American University.
Maybe she will become a doctor?
You know how it is: Parents worry!
I'd feel much better if she has a diploma.
Young people couldn't care less. They don't think about that sort of thing, but times are hard.
Ah, youth.

Yesterday evening, Ellen didn't sit shiva with the rest of the family.

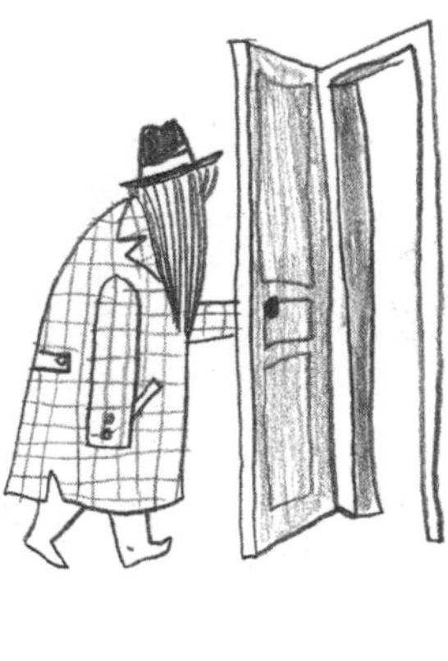

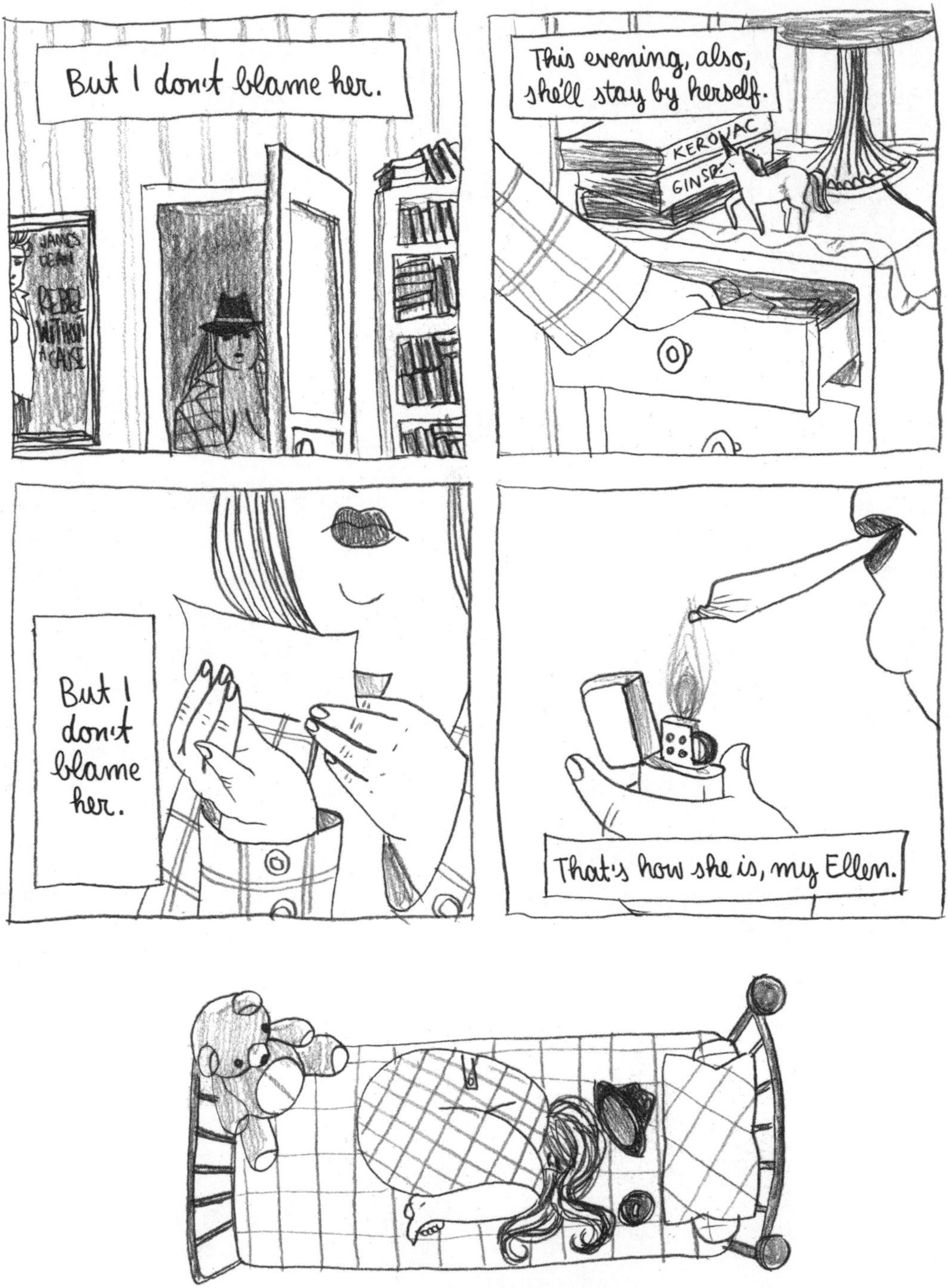
But I don't blame her.
JAMES DEAN
This evening, also, she'll stay by herself.
KEROUAC
But I don't blame her.
That's how she is, my Ellen.
She's untamed.

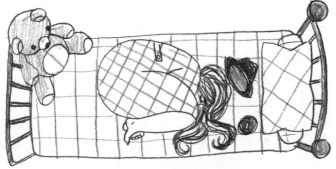

7-Alan

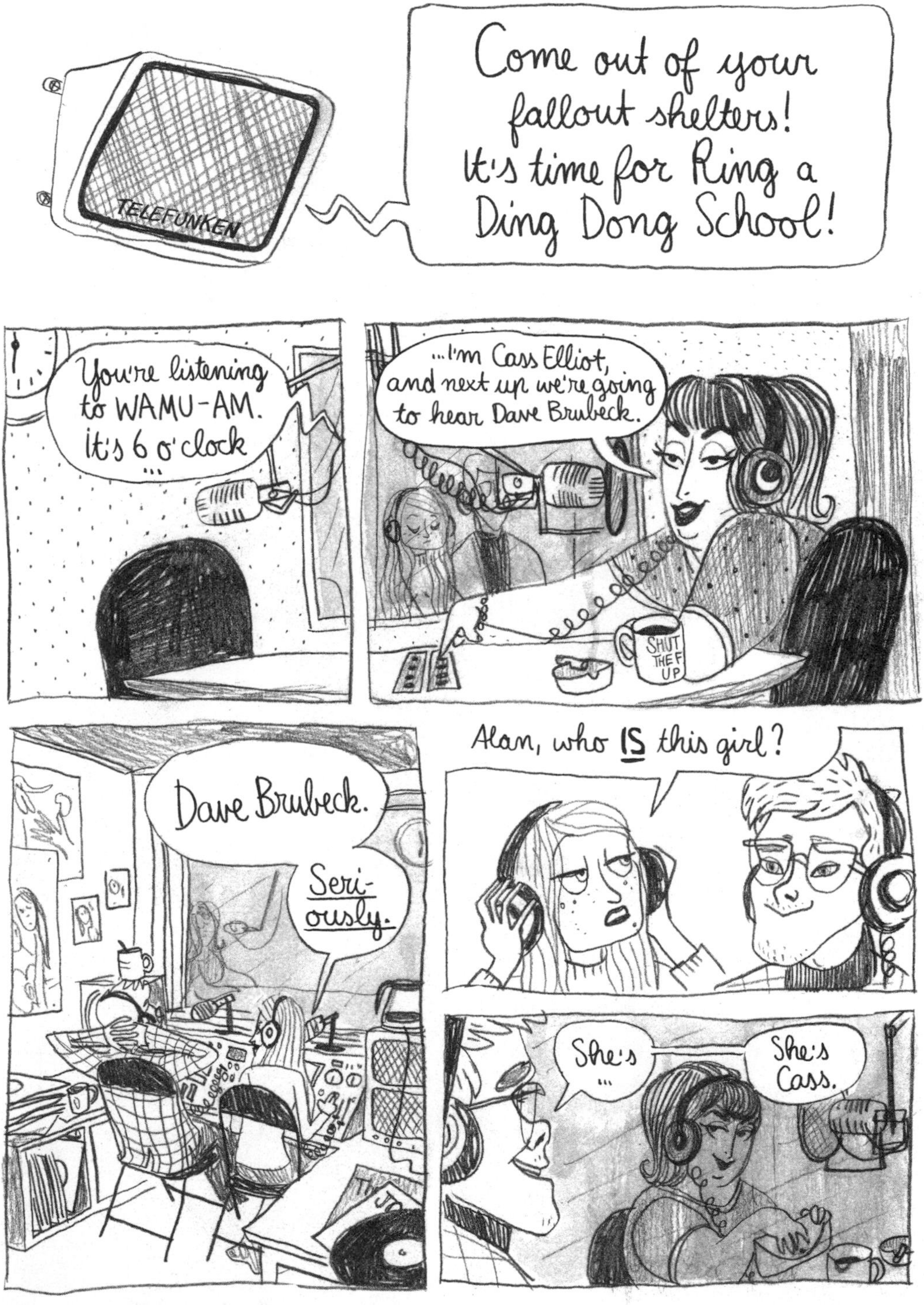
TELEFUNKEN
Come out of your fallout shelters! It's time for Ring a Ding Dong School!
You're listening to WAMU-AM. It's 6 o'clock ...
...I'm Cass Elliot, and next up we're going to hear Dave Brubeck.
SHUT THE F UP
Dave Brubeck.
Seri-ously.
Alan, who IS this girl?
She's ...
She's Cass.

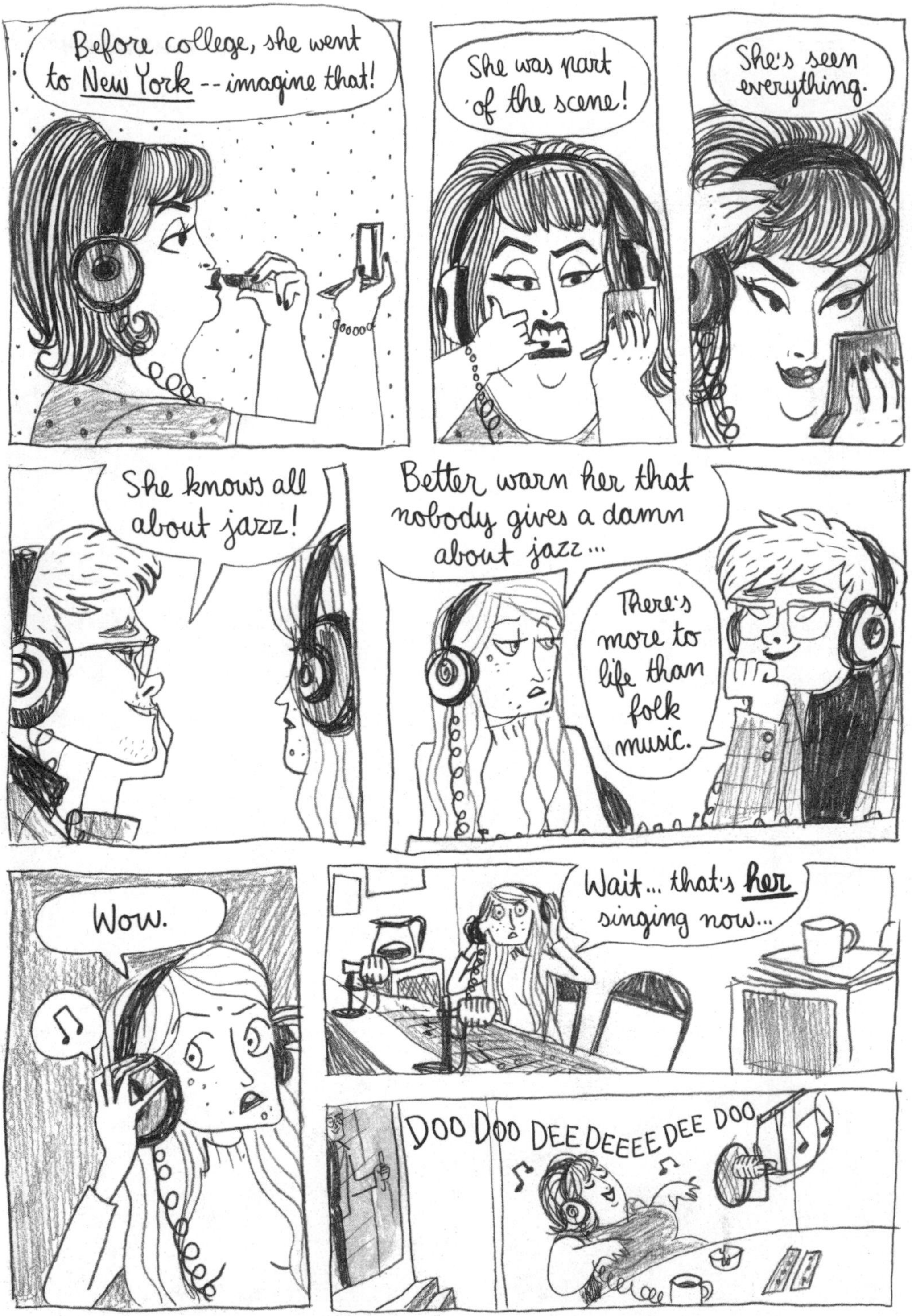
Before college, she went to New York -- imagine that!
She was part of the scene!
She's seen everything.
She knows all about jazz!
Better warn her that nobody gives a damn about jazz...
There's more to life than folk music.
Wow.
♫
Wait... that's her singing now...
DOO DOO DEE DEEEE DEE DOO

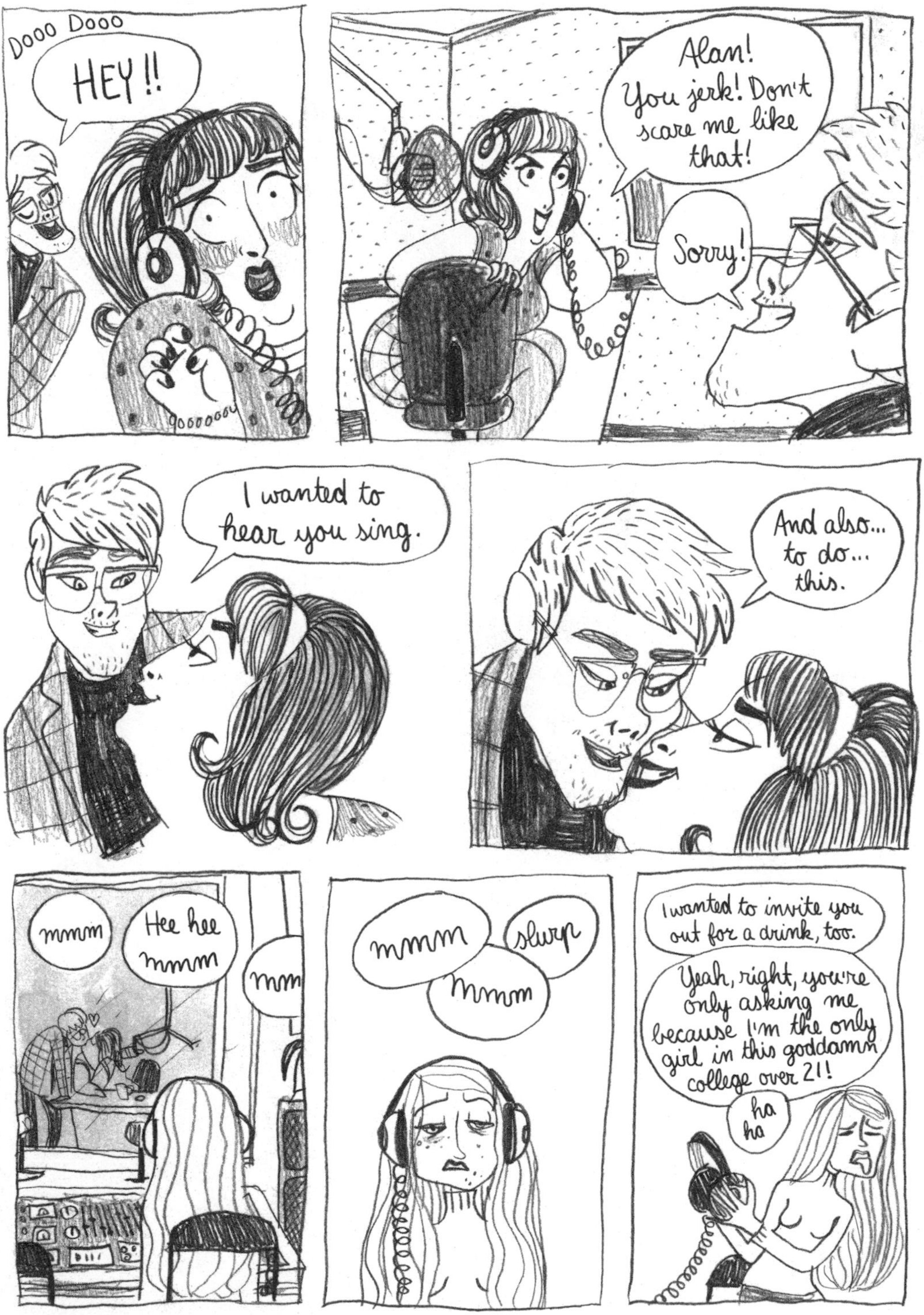

Dooo Dooo
HEY!!
gooooooo
Alan! You jerk! Don't scare me like that!
Sorry!
I wanted to hear you sing.
And also... to do... this.
mmm
Hee hee mmm
mm
mmm
slurp
Mmm
I wanted to invite you out for a drink, too.
Yeah, right, you're only asking me because I'm the only girl in this goddamn college over 21!
ha ha

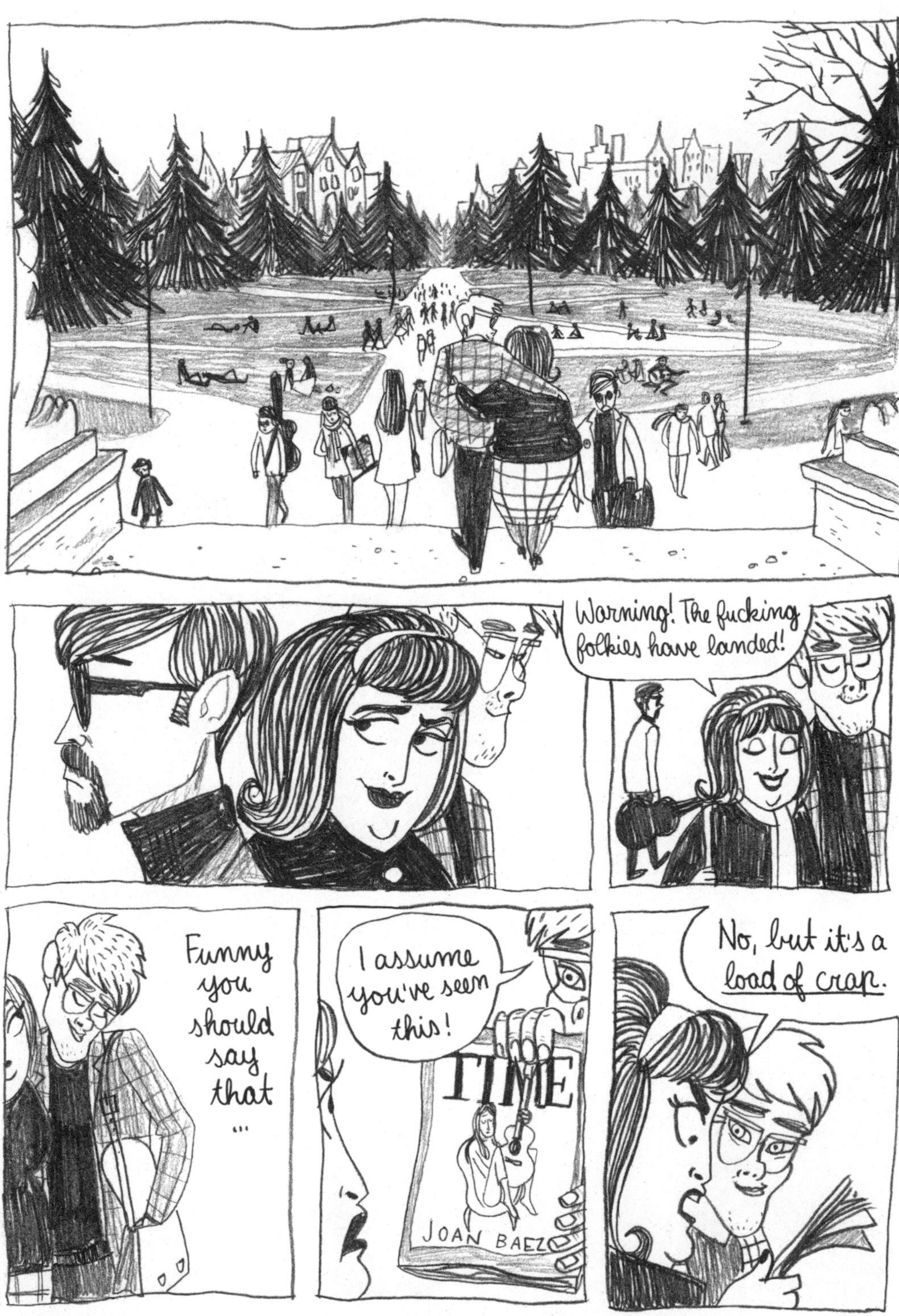
Warning! The fucking folkies have landed!
Funny you should say that ...
I assume you've seen this!
TIME
JOAN BAEZ
No, but it's a load of crap.

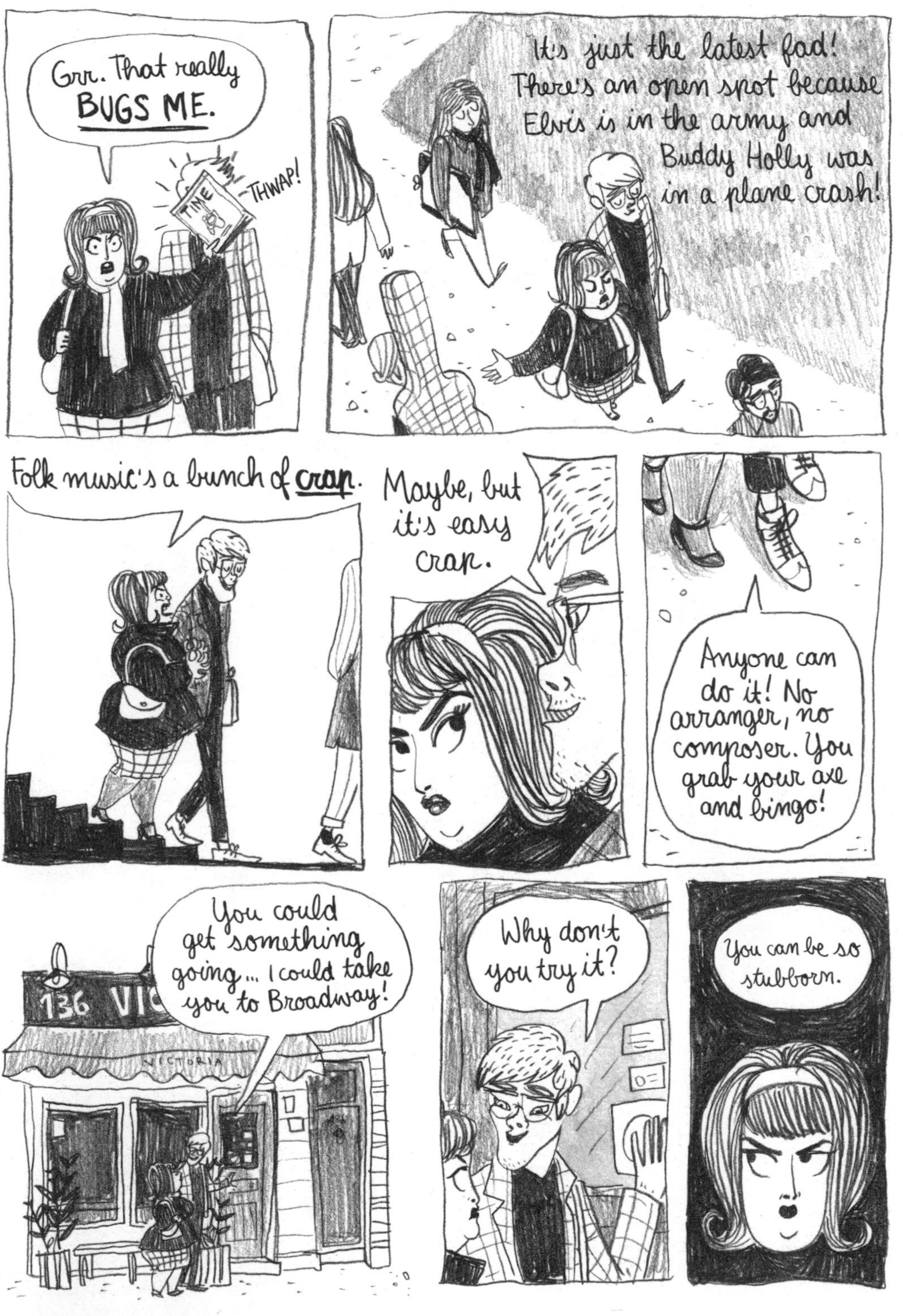
Grr. That really **BUGS ME.**
TIME
THWAP!
It's just the latest fad! There's an open spot because Elvis is in the army and Buddy Holly was in a plane crash!
Folk music's a bunch of crap.
Maybe, but it's easy crap.
Anyone can do it! No arranger, no composer. You grab your axe and bingo!
136 VIC
VICTORIA
You could get something going... I could take you to Broadway!
Why don't you try it?
You can be so stubborn.

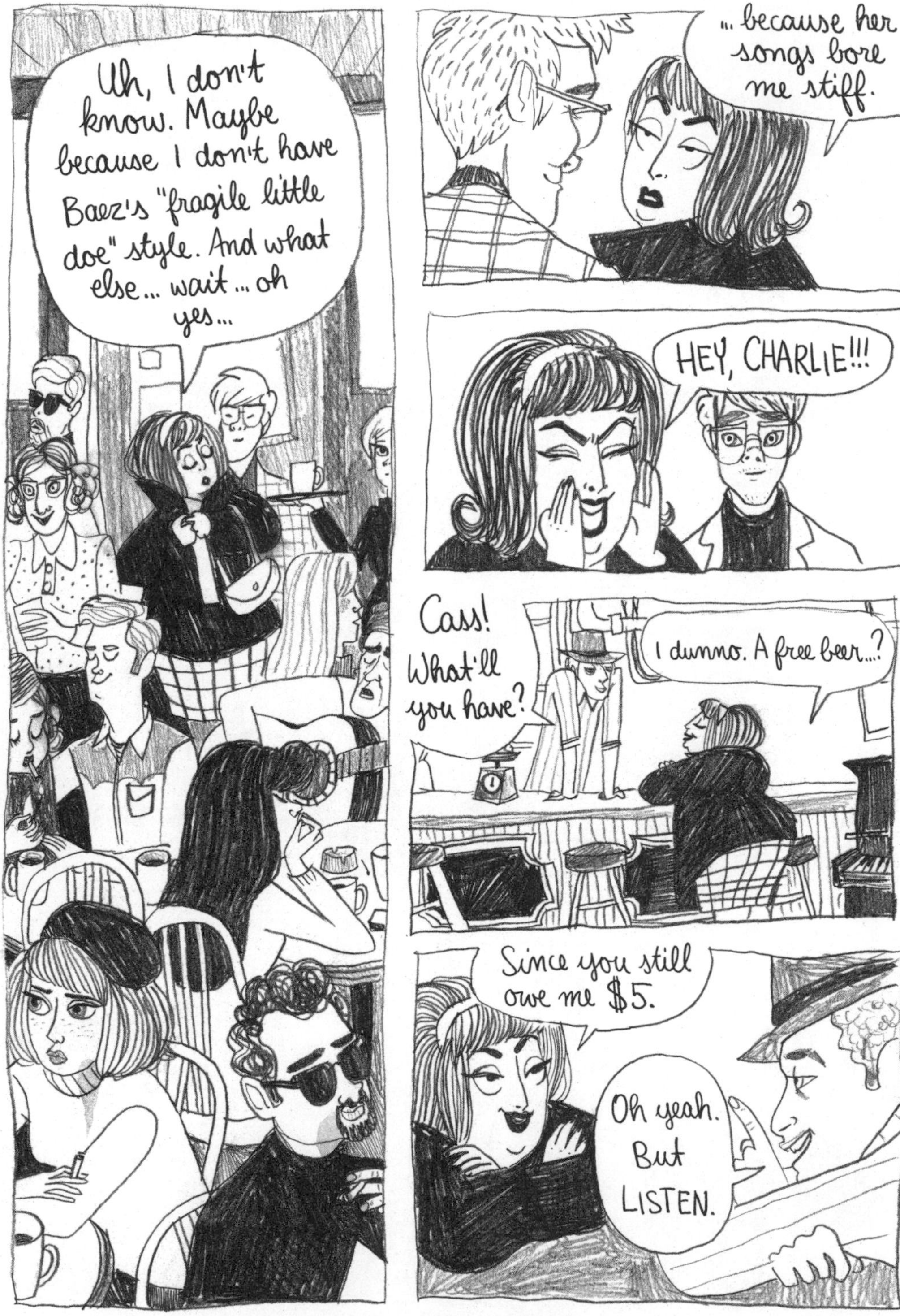
Uh, I don't know. Maybe because I don't have Baez's "fragile little doe" style. And what else... wait... oh yes...
... because her songs bore me stiff.
HEY, CHARLIE!!!
Cass! What'll you have?
I dunno. A free beer...?
Since you still owe me $5.
Oh yeah. But LISTEN.

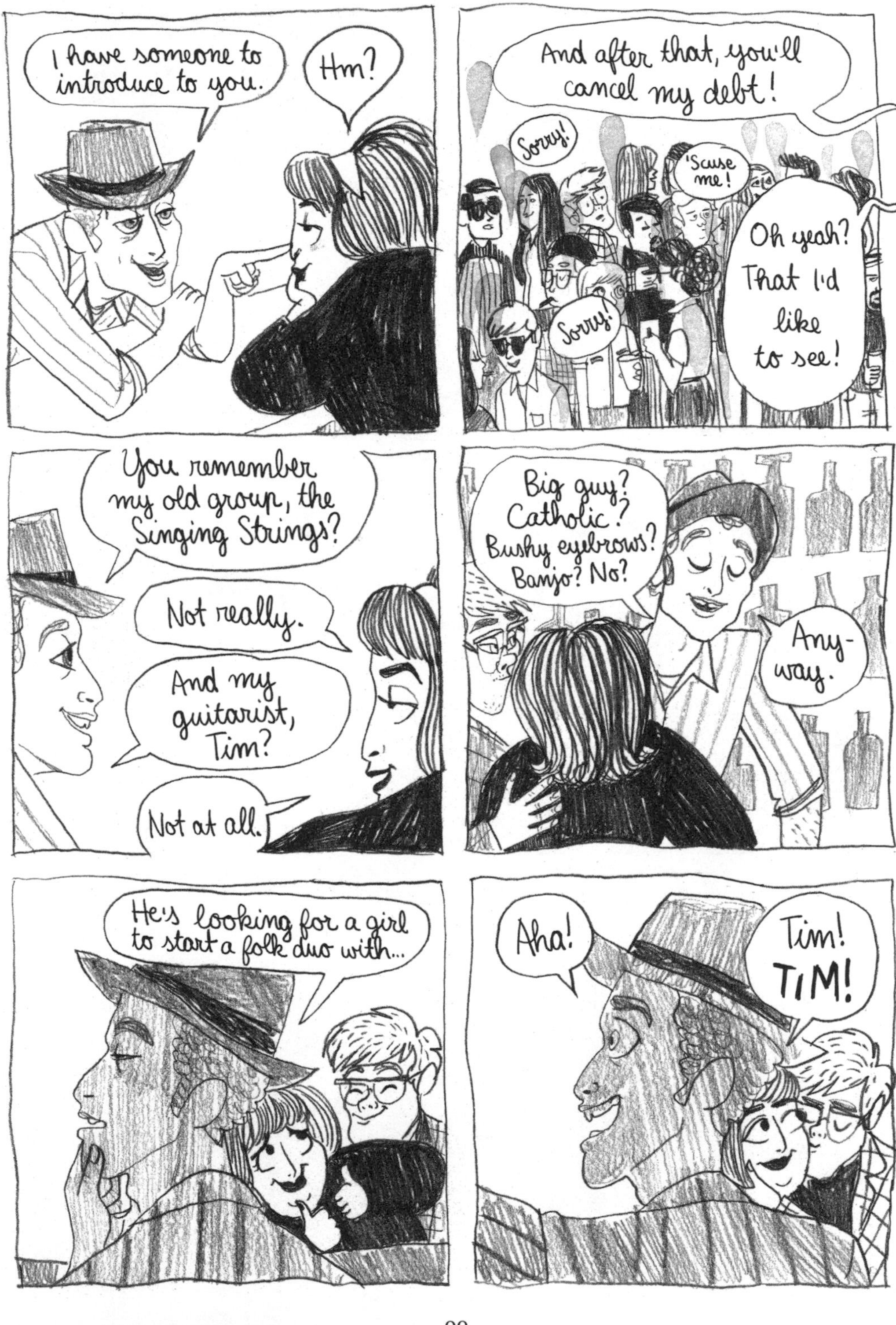
I have someone to introduce to you.
Hm?
And after that, you'll cancel my debt!
Sorry!
'Scuse me!
Sorry!
Oh yeah? That I'd like to see!
You remember my old group, the Singing Strings?
Not really.
And my guitarist, Tim?
Not at all.
Big guy? Catholic? Bushy eyebrows? Banjo? No?
Any-way.
He's looking for a girl to start a folk duo with...
Aha!
Tim! TIM!

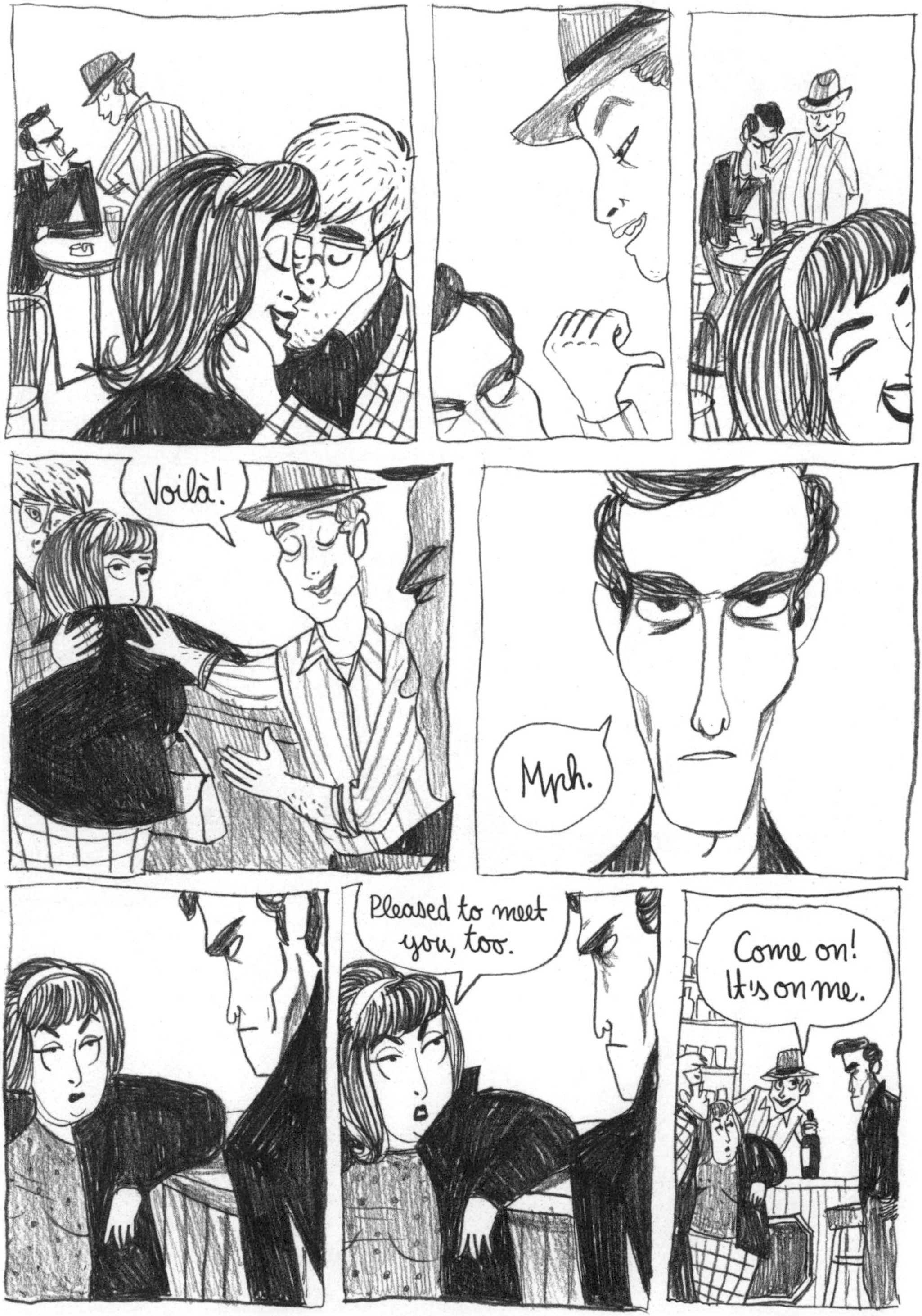
Voilà!
Mph.
Pleased to meet you, too.
Come on! It's on me.

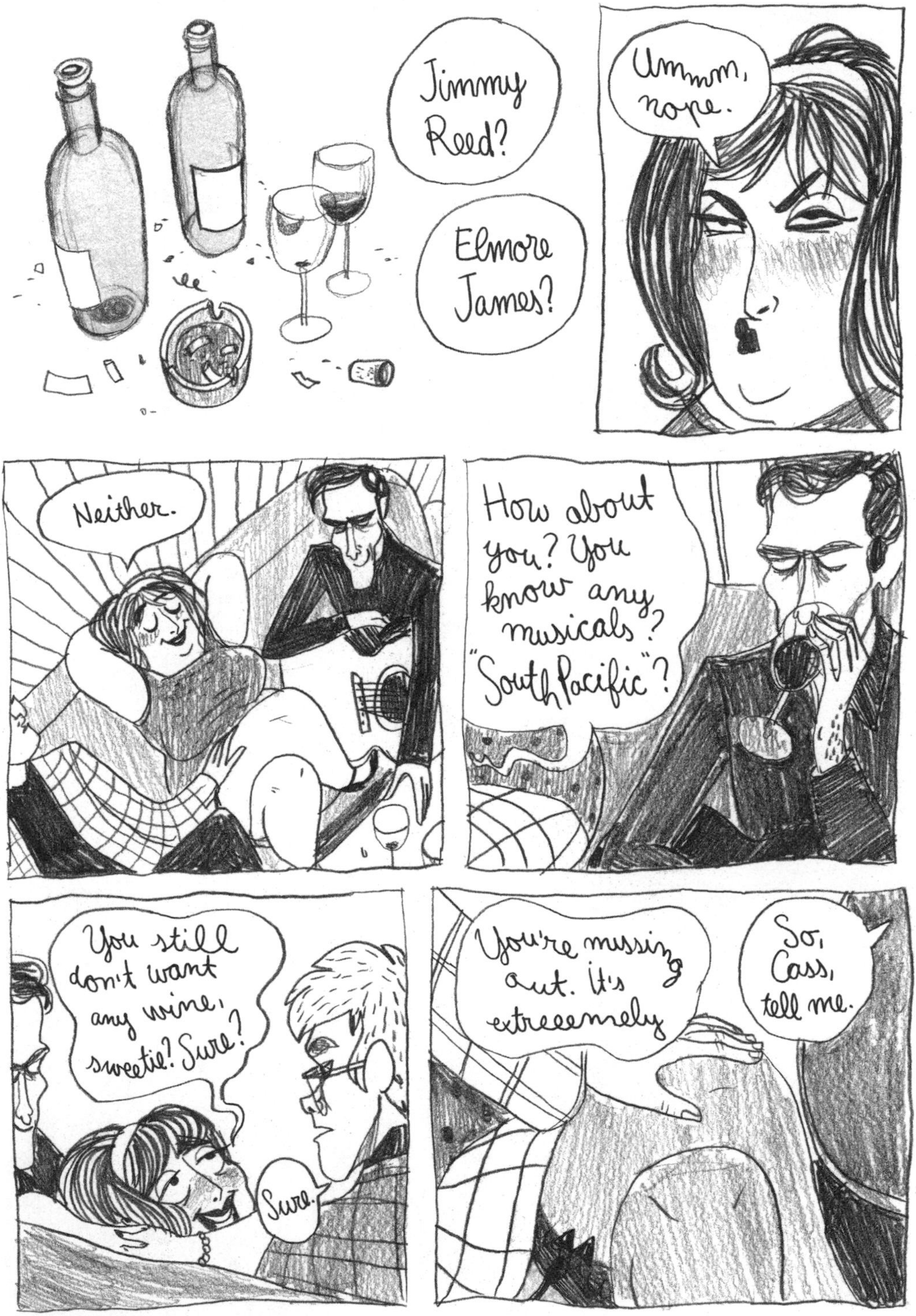
Jimmy Reed?
Elmore James?
Ummm, nope.
Neither.
How about you? You know any musicals? "South Pacific"?
You still don't want any wine, sweetie? Sure?
Sure.
You're missing out. It's extreeemely
So, Cass, tell me.

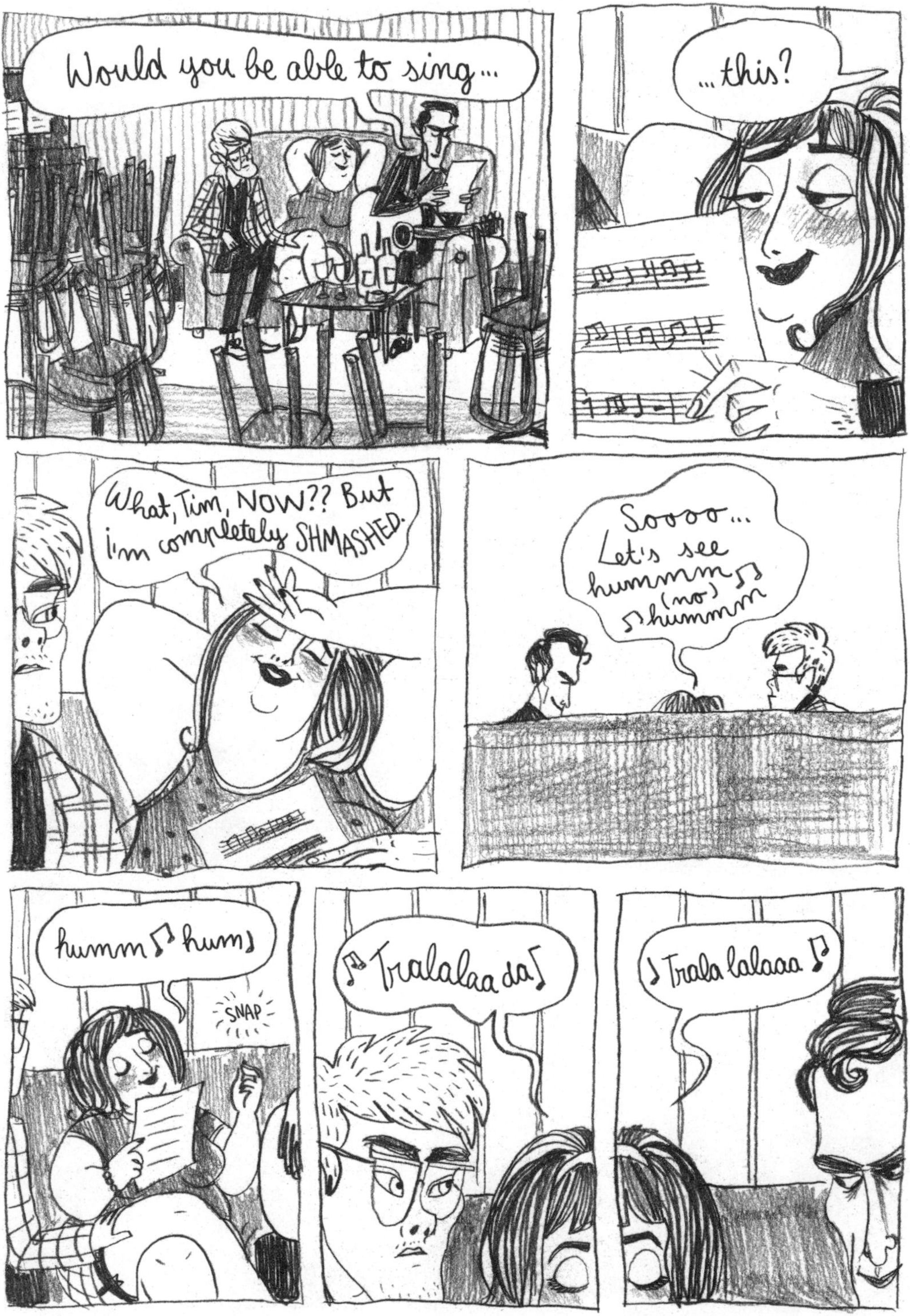
Would you be able to sing...
...this?
What, Tim, NOW?? But i'm completely SHMASHED.
Soooo... Let's see hummm (no) hummm
humm hum
SNAP
Tralalaa da
Trala lalaaa

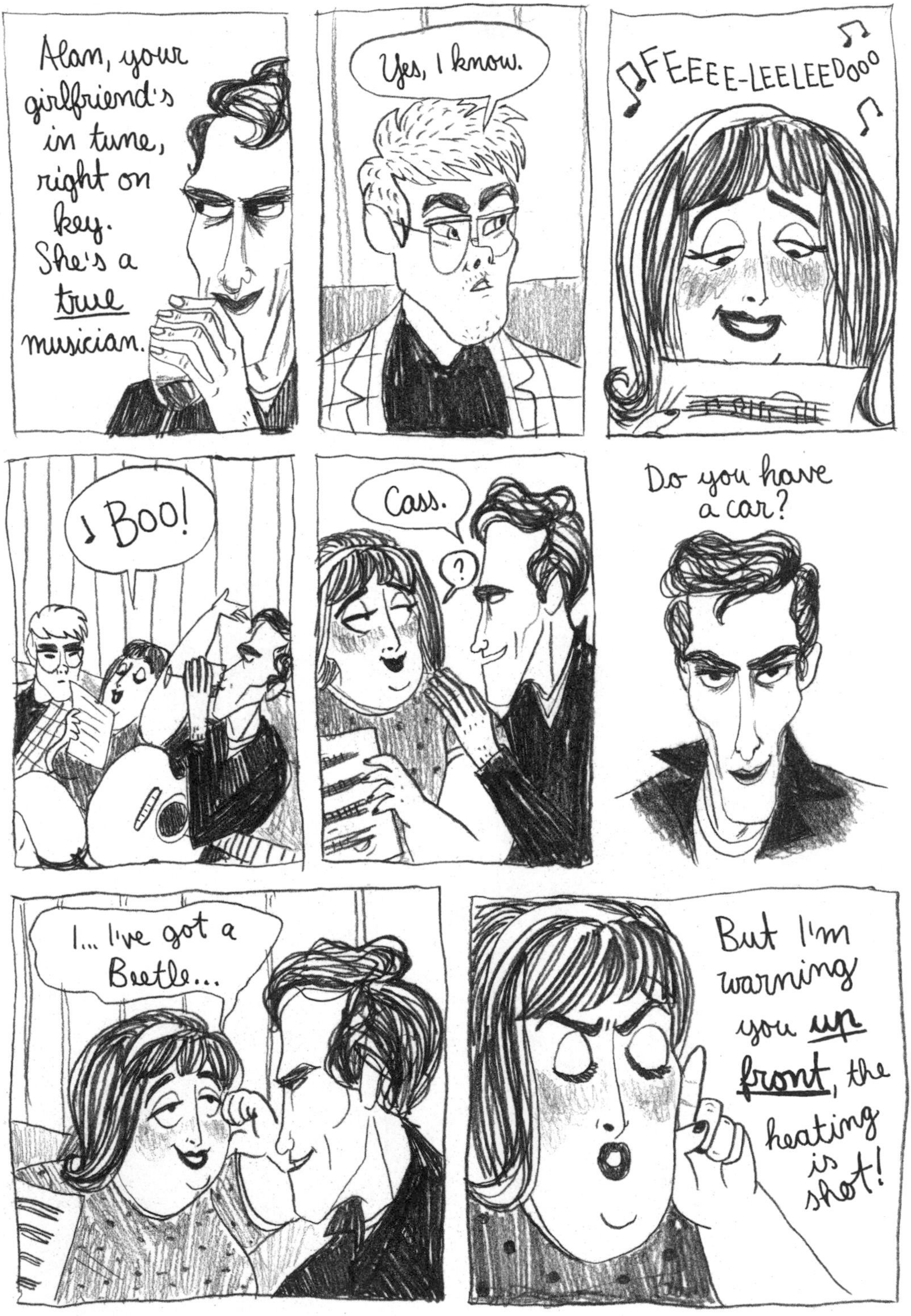
Alan, your girlfriend's in tune, right on key. She's a true musician.
Yes, I know.
FEEEE-LEELEEDOOO
Boo!
Cass.
?
Do you have a car?
I... I've got a Beetle...
But I'm warning you up front, the heating is shot!

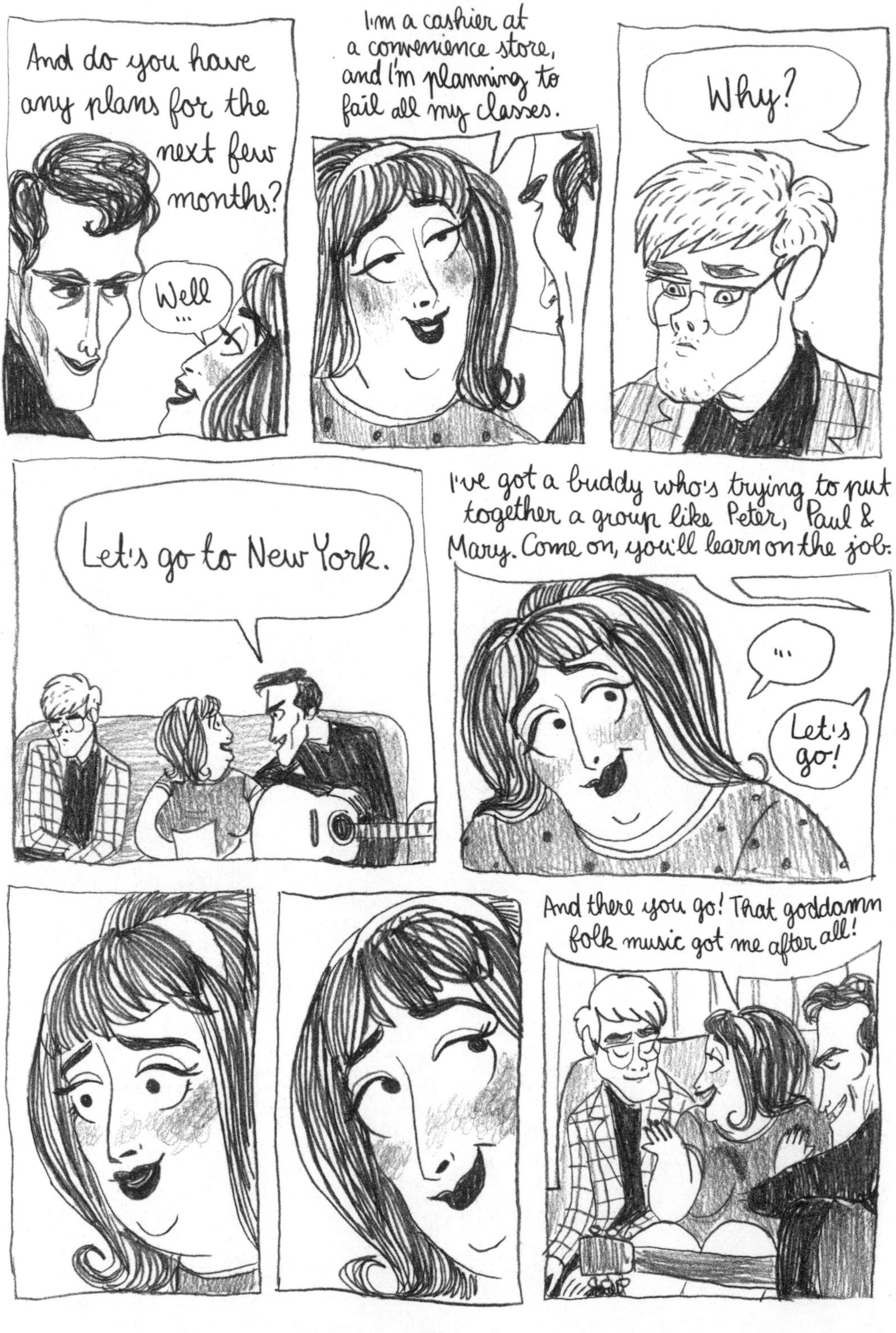

And do you have any plans for the next few months?
Well ...
I'm a cashier at a convenience store, and I'm planning to fail all my classes.
Why?
Let's go to New York.
I've got a buddy who's trying to put together a group like Peter, Paul & Mary. Come on, you'll learn on the job.
...
Let's go!
And there you go! That goddamn folk music got me after all!

8 - Tim

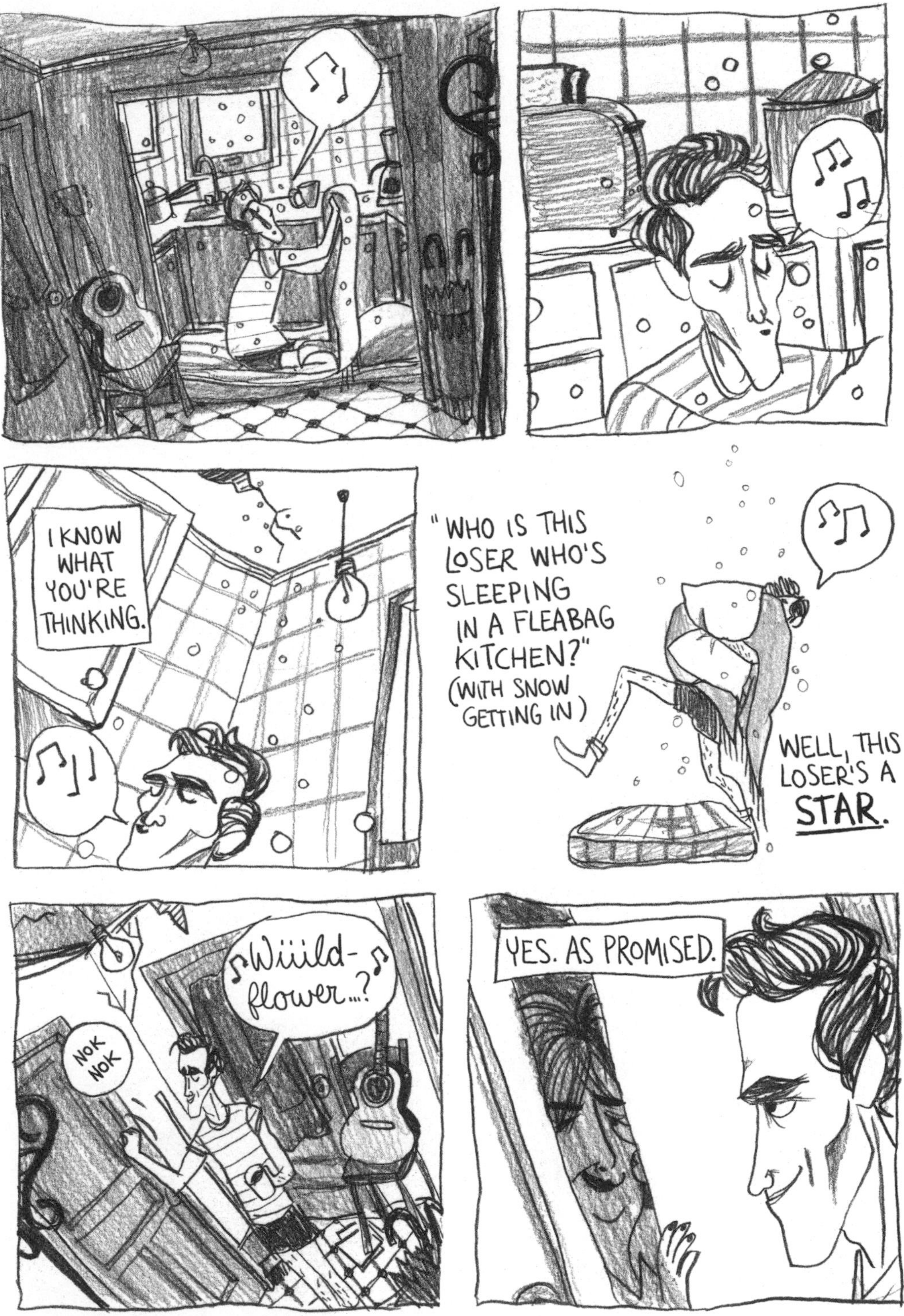
I KNOW WHAT YOU'RE THINKING.
"WHO IS THIS LOSER WHO'S SLEEPING IN A FLEABAG KITCHEN?" (WITH SNOW GETTING IN)
WELL, THIS LOSER'S A STAR.
NOK NOK
Wiiiild-flower...?
YES. AS PROMISED.

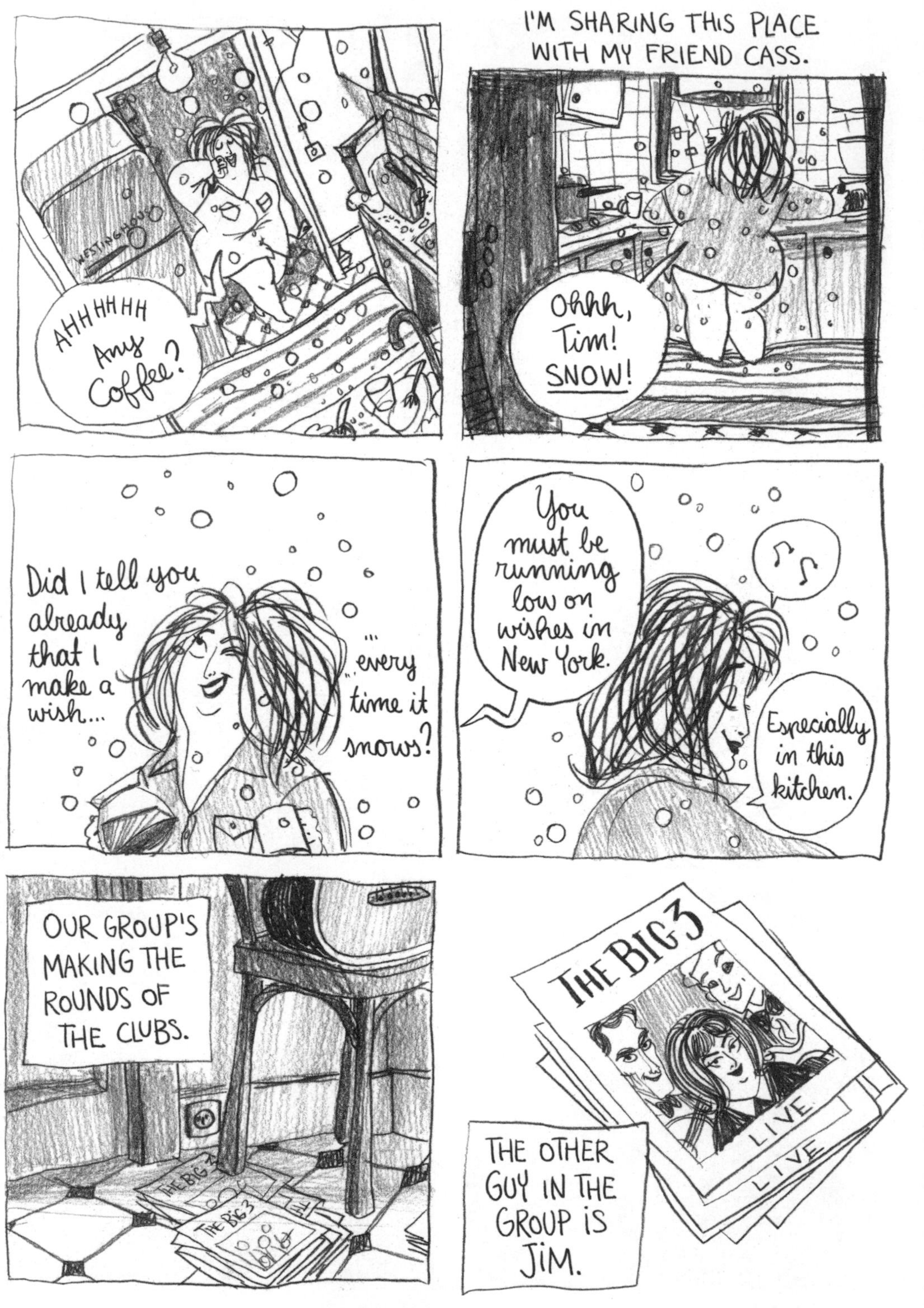
AHHHHHH Any Coffee?
I'M SHARING THIS PLACE WITH MY FRIEND CASS.
Ohhh, Tim! SNOW!
Did I tell you already that I make a wish...
...every time it snows?
You must be running low on wishes in New York.
Especially in this kitchen.
OUR GROUP'S MAKING THE ROUNDS OF THE CLUBS.
THE BIG 3
THE BIG 3
LIVE
LIVE
THE OTHER GUY IN THE GROUP IS JIM.

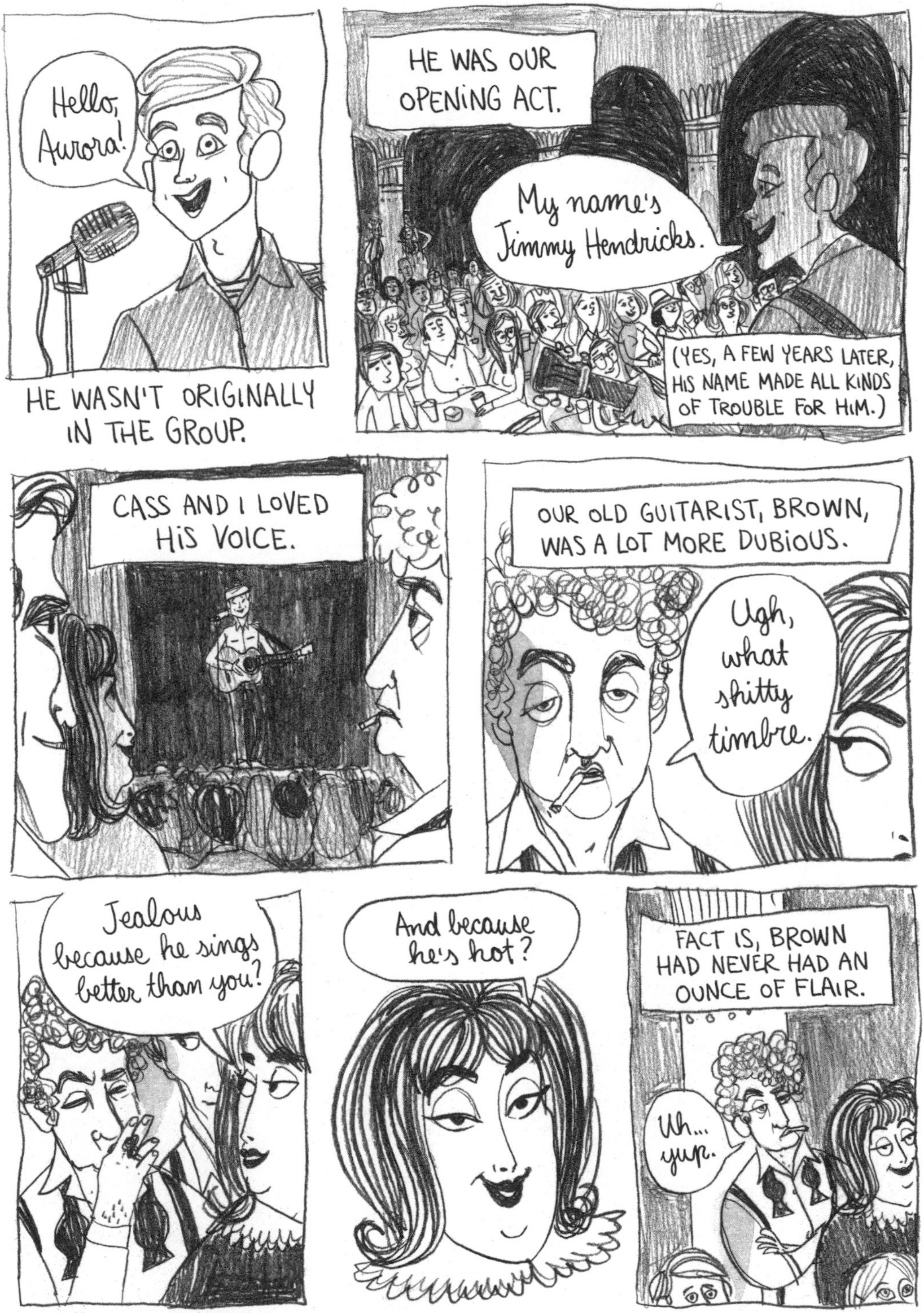
Hello, Aurora!
HE WASN'T ORIGINALLY IN THE GROUP.
HE WAS OUR OPENING ACT.
My name's Jimmy Hendricks.
(YES, A FEW YEARS LATER, HIS NAME MADE ALL KINDS OF TROUBLE FOR HIM.)
CASS AND I LOVED HIS VOICE.
OUR OLD GUITARIST, BROWN, WAS A LOT MORE DUBIOUS.
Ugh, what shitty timbre.
Jealous because he sings better than you?
And because he's hot?
FACT IS, BROWN HAD NEVER HAD AN OUNCE OF FLAIR.
Uh... yup.

LIKE THE TIME WE AUDITIONED THAT GUITARIST IN MINNESOTA...

Your guitar-playing's fine, man.

But you sing like a goat.

Seriously, quit singing.

SO ONE EVENING WE TOOK A VOTE.

AND WE REPLACED BROWN WITH JIM.

Bunch of bastards!

CRACK!

HE DIDN'T TAKE IT VERY WELL.

IT WASN'T A BIG LOSS.

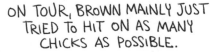

ON TOUR, BROWN MAINLY JUST TRIED TO HIT ON AS MANY CHICKS AS POSSIBLE.

Brown!

(WHILE HIS WIFE MINDED THE KIDS.)

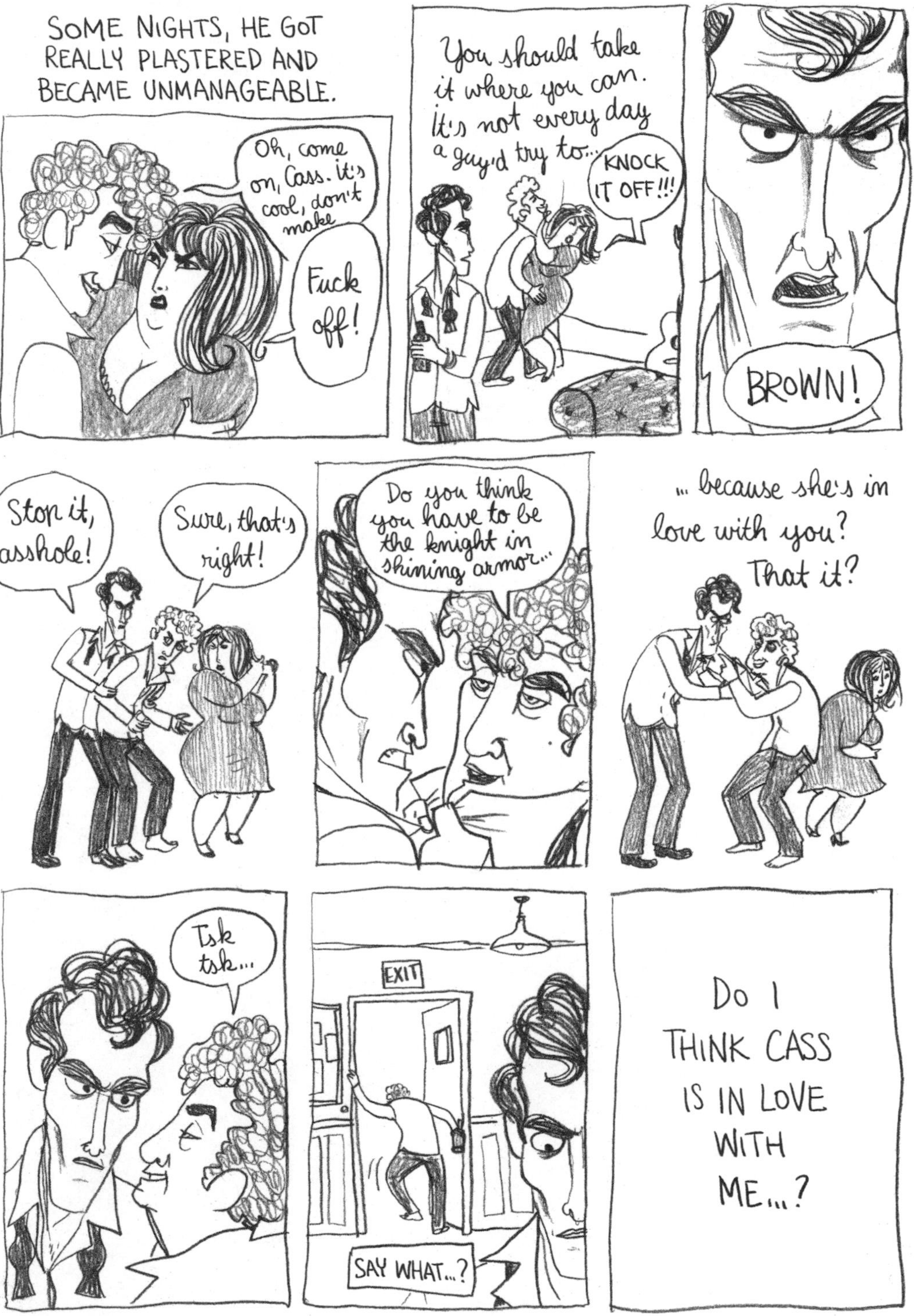

SOME NIGHTS, HE GOT REALLY PLASTERED AND BECAME UNMANAGEABLE.
Oh, come on, Cass. It's cool, don't make
Fuck off!
You should take it where you can. It's not every day a guy'd try to...
KNOCK IT OFF!!!
BROWN!
Stop it, asshole!
Sure, that's right!
Do you think you have to be the knight in shining armor...
... because she's in love with you? That it?
Tsk tsk...
EXIT
SAY WHAT...?
DO I THINK CASS IS IN LOVE WITH ME...?

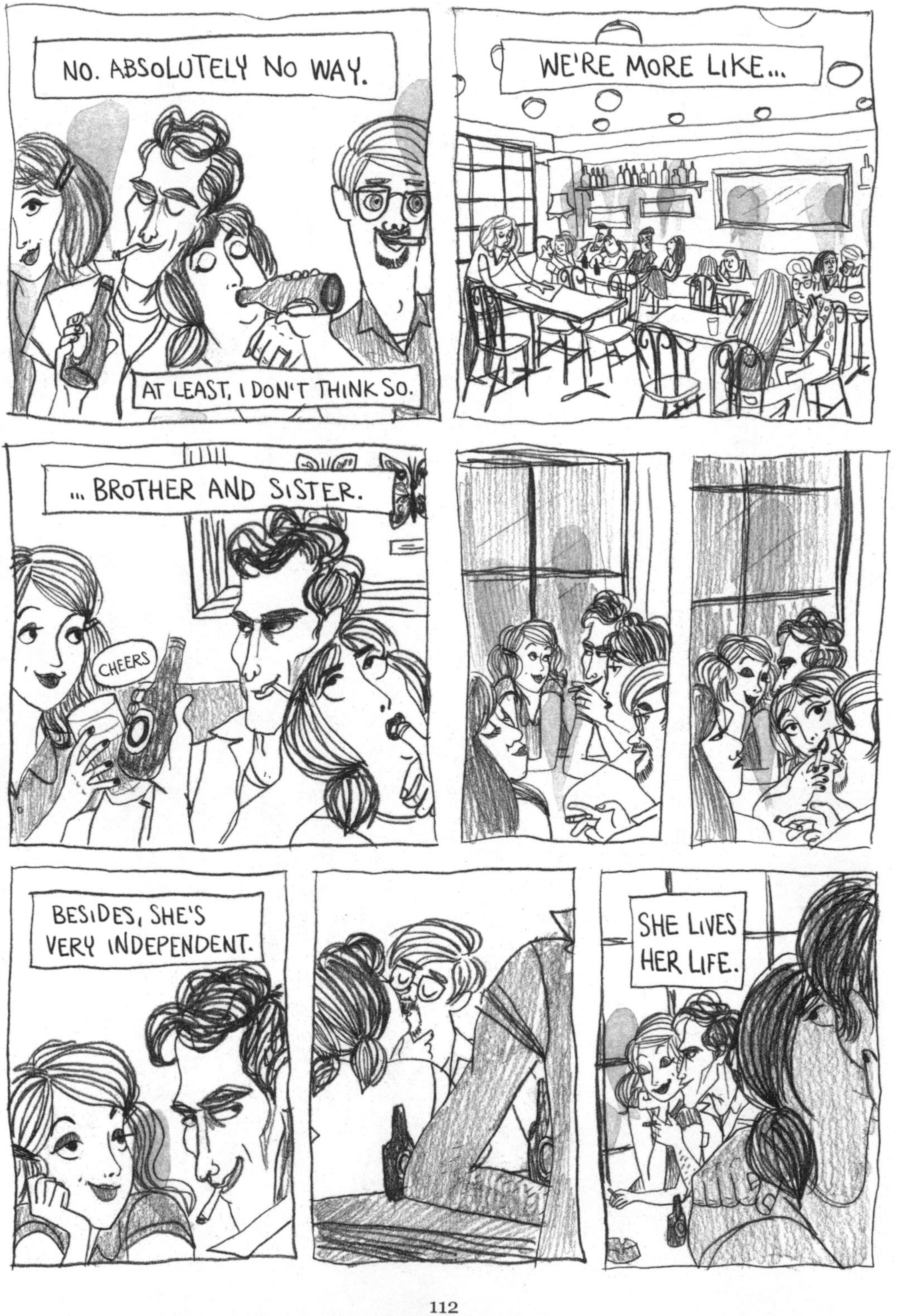
NO. ABSOLUTELY NO WAY.
AT LEAST, I DON'T THINK SO.
WE'RE MORE LIKE...
... BROTHER AND SISTER.
CHEERS
BESIDES, SHE'S VERY INDEPENDENT.
SHE LIVES HER LIFE.

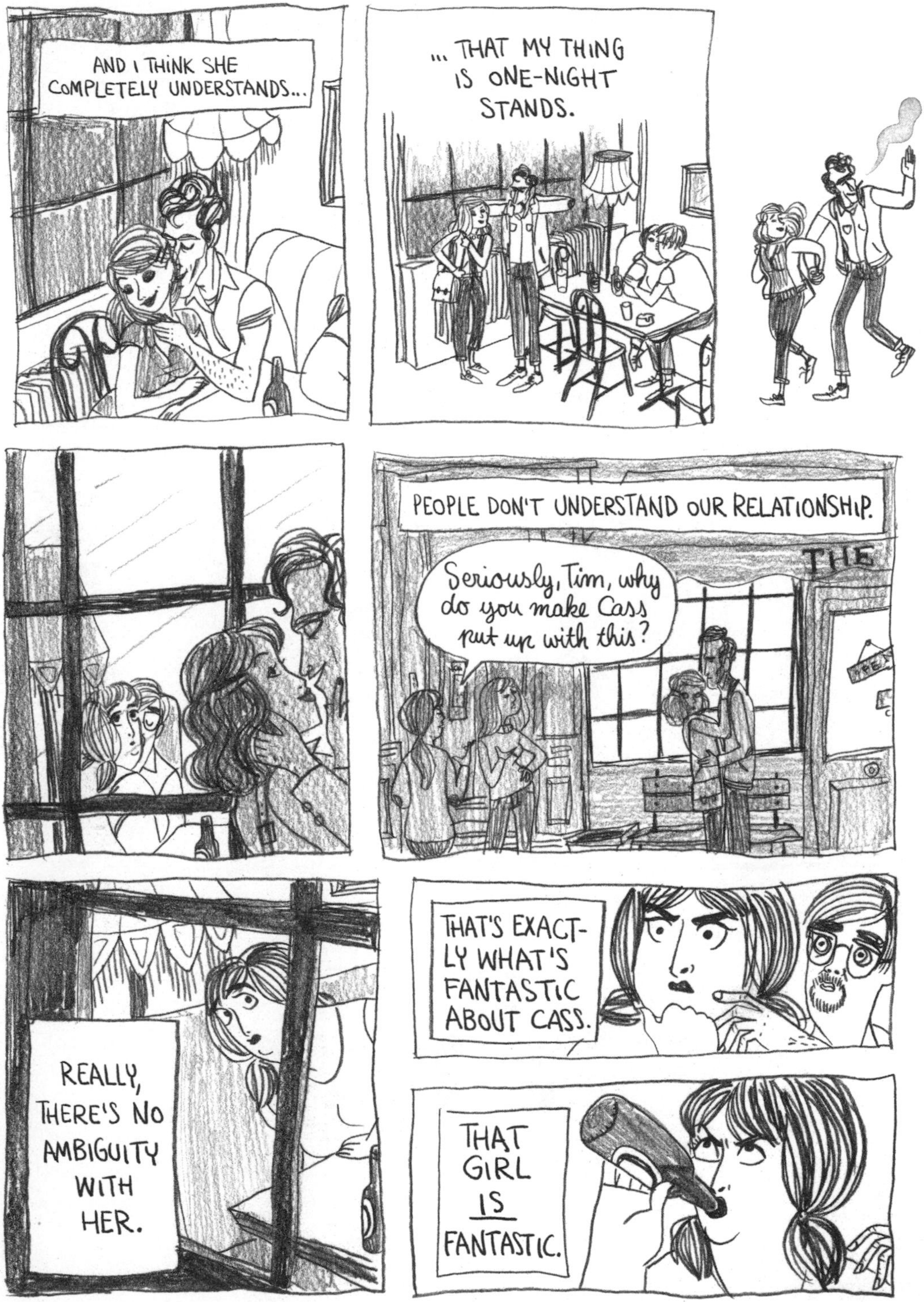
AND I THINK SHE COMPLETELY UNDERSTANDS...
... THAT MY THING IS ONE-NIGHT STANDS.
PEOPLE DON'T UNDERSTAND OUR RELATIONSHIP.
Seriously, Tim, why do you make Cass put up with this?
THE
REALLY, THERE'S NO AMBIGUITY WITH HER.
THAT'S EXACT-LY WHAT'S FANTASTIC ABOUT CASS.
THAT GIRL IS FANTASTIC.

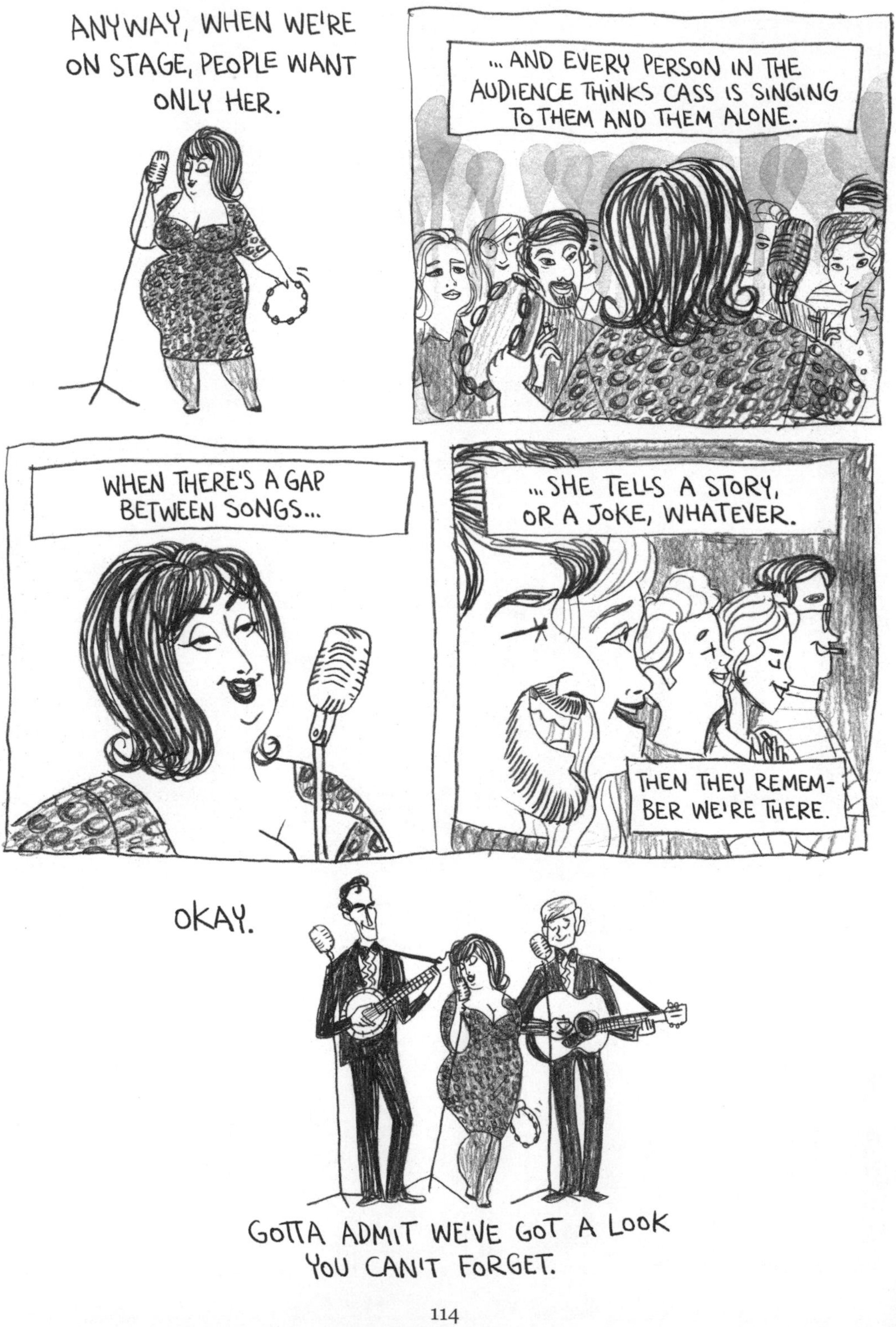
ANYWAY, WHEN WE'RE ON STAGE, PEOPLE WANT ONLY HER.
... AND EVERY PERSON IN THE AUDIENCE THINKS CASS IS SINGING TO THEM AND THEM ALONE.
WHEN THERE'S A GAP BETWEEN SONGS...
... SHE TELLS A STORY, OR A JOKE, WHATEVER.
THEN THEY REMEMBER WE'RE THERE.
OKAY.
GOTTA ADMIT WE'VE GOT A LOOK YOU CAN'T FORGET.

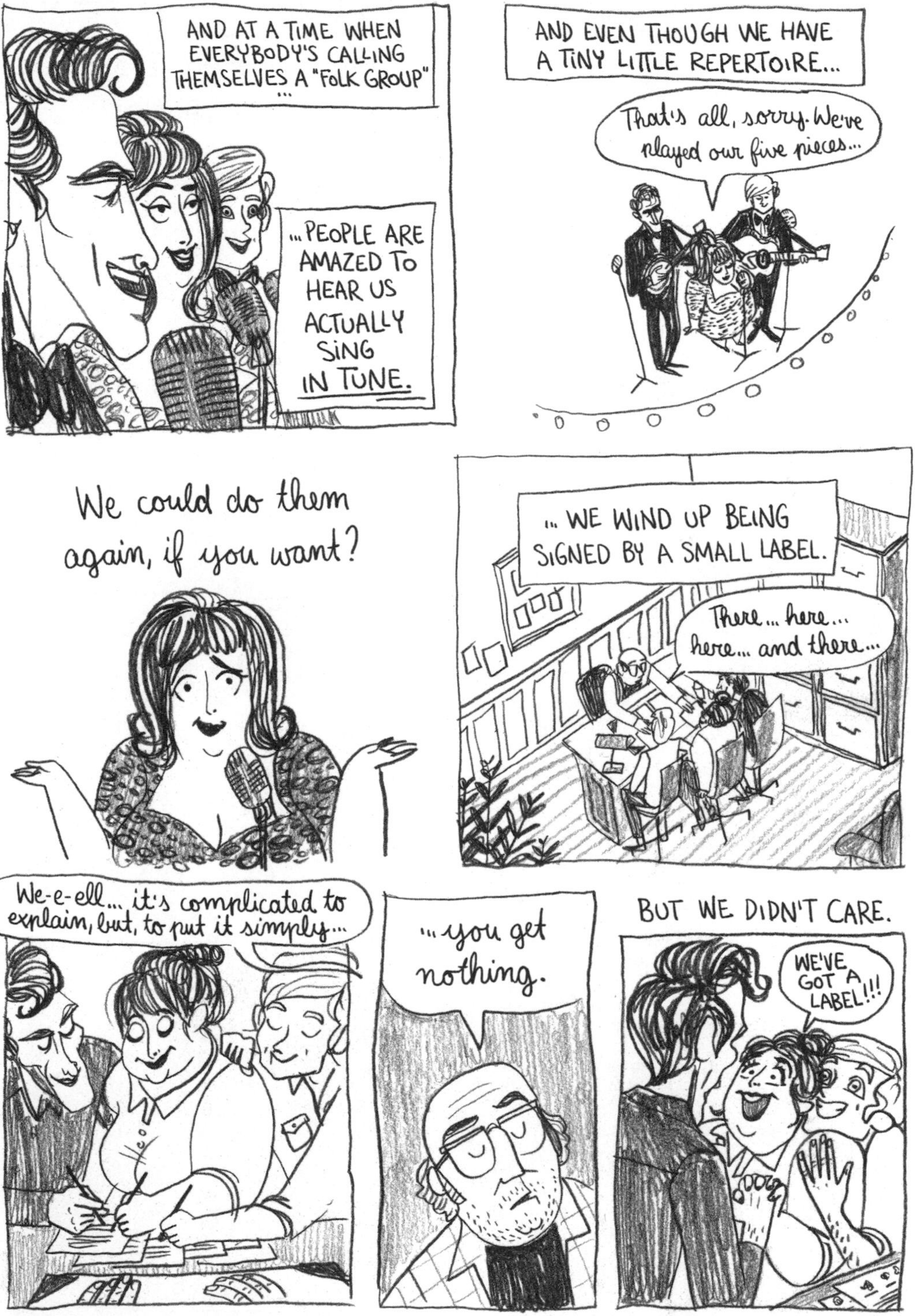
AND AT A TIME WHEN EVERYBODY'S CALLING THEMSELVES A "FOLK GROUP" ...
...PEOPLE ARE AMAZED TO HEAR US ACTUALLY SING IN TUNE.
AND EVEN THOUGH WE HAVE A TINY LITTLE REPERTOIRE...
That's all, sorry. We've played our five pieces...
We could do them again, if you want?
... WE WIND UP BEING SIGNED BY A SMALL LABEL.
There... here... here... and there...
We-e-ell... it's complicated to explain, but, to put it simply...
...you get nothing.
BUT WE DIDN'T CARE.
WE'VE GOT A LABEL!!!

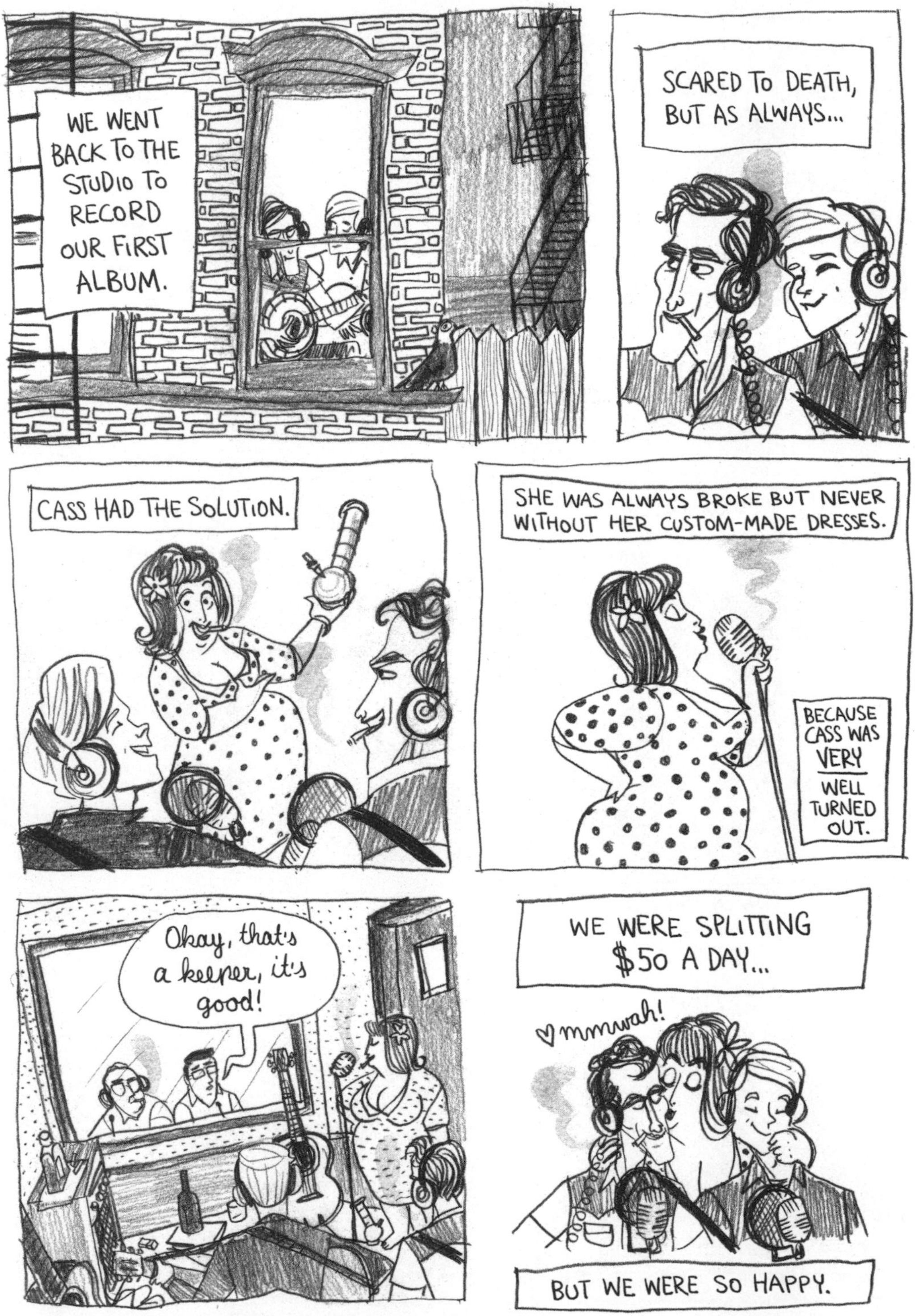

WE WENT BACK TO THE STUDIO TO RECORD OUR FIRST ALBUM.
SCARED TO DEATH, BUT AS ALWAYS...
CASS HAD THE SOLUTION.
SHE WAS ALWAYS BROKE BUT NEVER WITHOUT HER CUSTOM-MADE DRESSES.
BECAUSE CASS WAS VERY WELL TURNED OUT.
Okay, that's a keeper, it's good!
WE WERE SPLITTING $50 A DAY...
♥ mmwah!
BUT WE WERE SO HAPPY.

9 - David

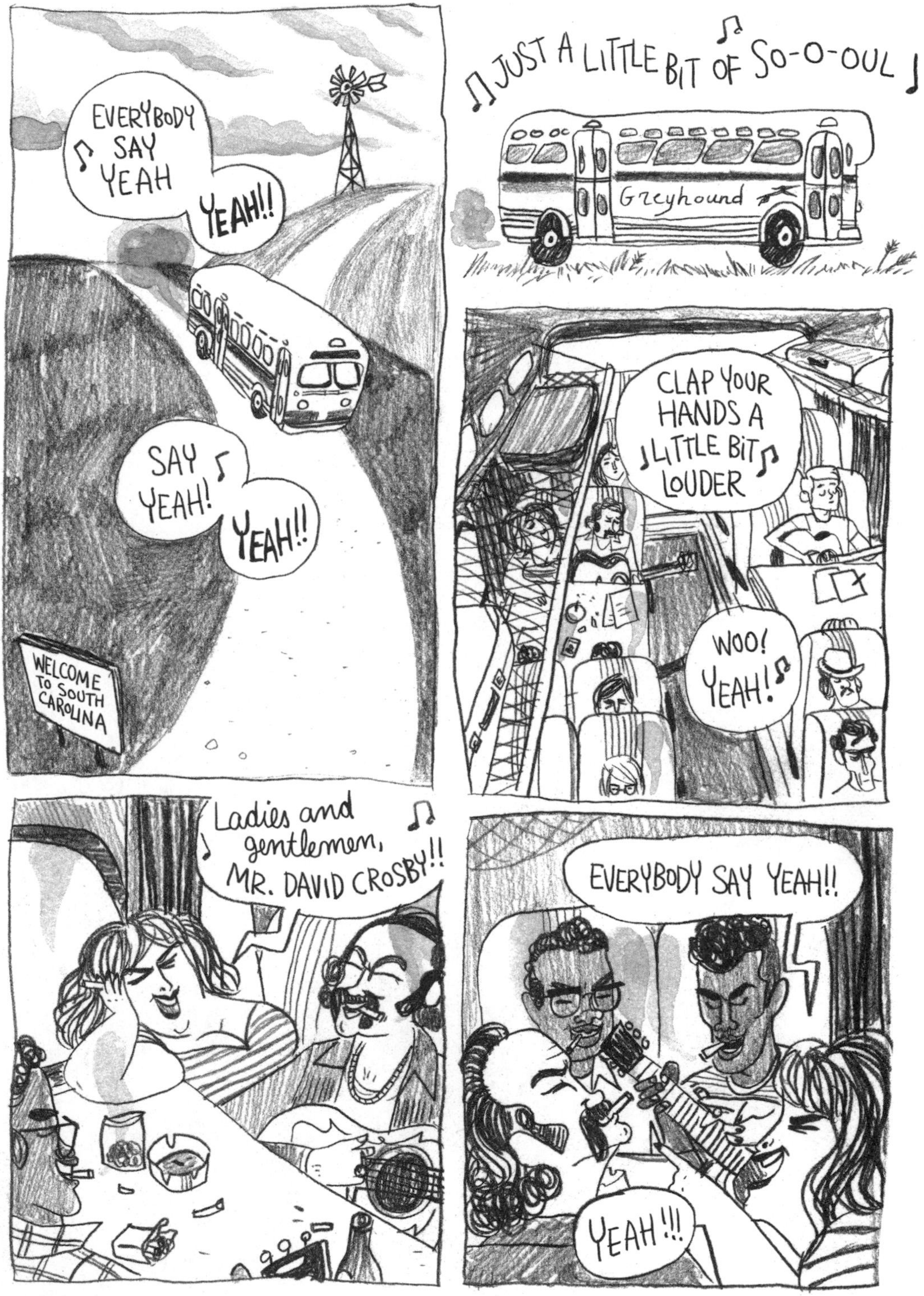
EVERYBODY SAY YEAH
YEAH!!
SAY YEAH!
YEAH!!
WELCOME TO SOUTH CAROLINA
JUST A LITTLE BIT OF SO-O-OUL
Greyhound
CLAP YOUR HANDS A LITTLE BIT LOUDER
WOO! YEAH!
Ladies and gentlemen, MR. DAVID CROSBY!!
EVERYBODY SAY YEAH!!
YEAH!!!

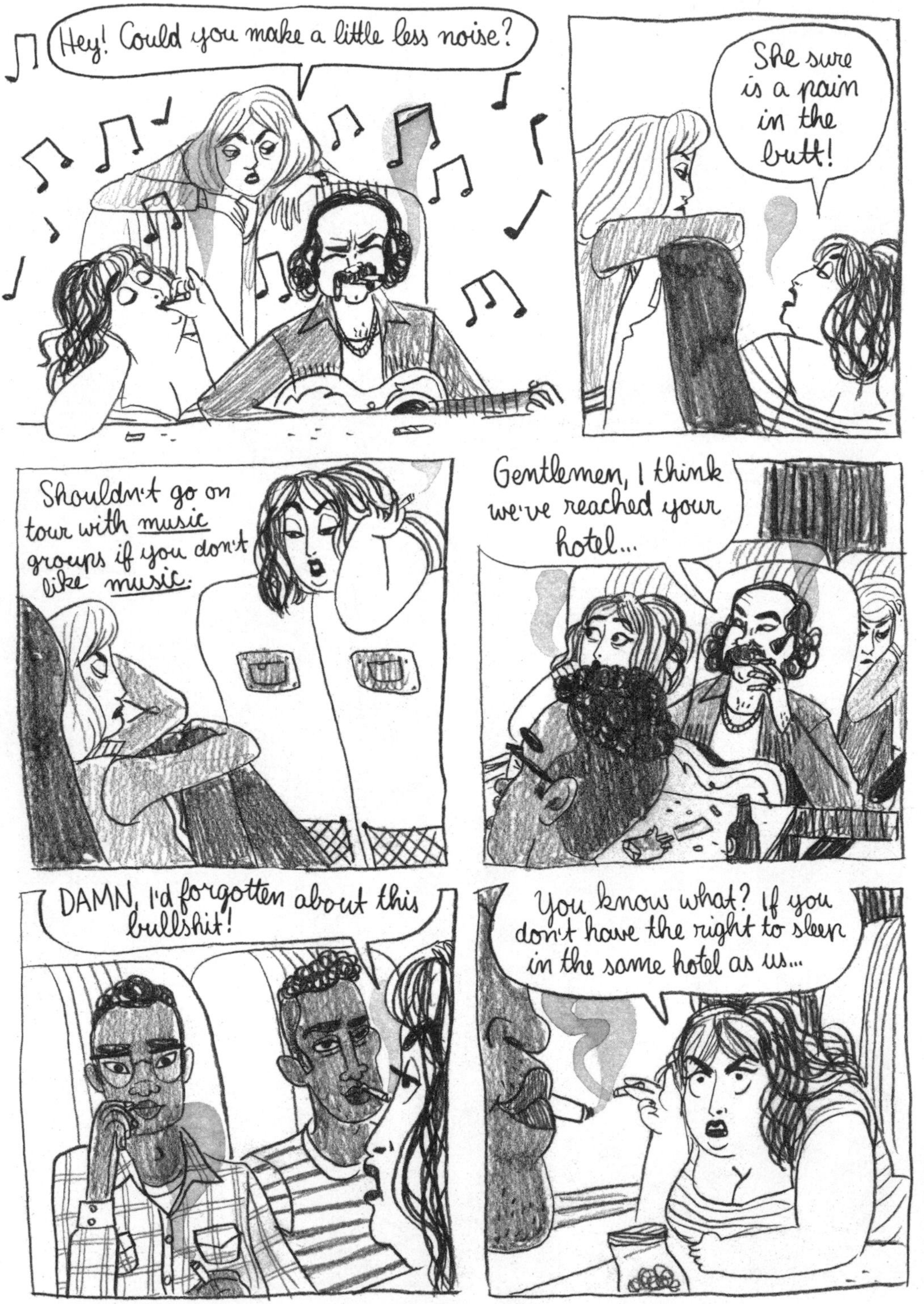
Hey! Could you make a little less noise?
She sure is a pain in the butt!
Shouldn't go on tour with music groups if you don't like music.
Gentlemen, I think we've reached your hotel...
DAMN, I'd forgotten about this bullshit!
You know what? If you don't have the right to sleep in the same hotel as us...

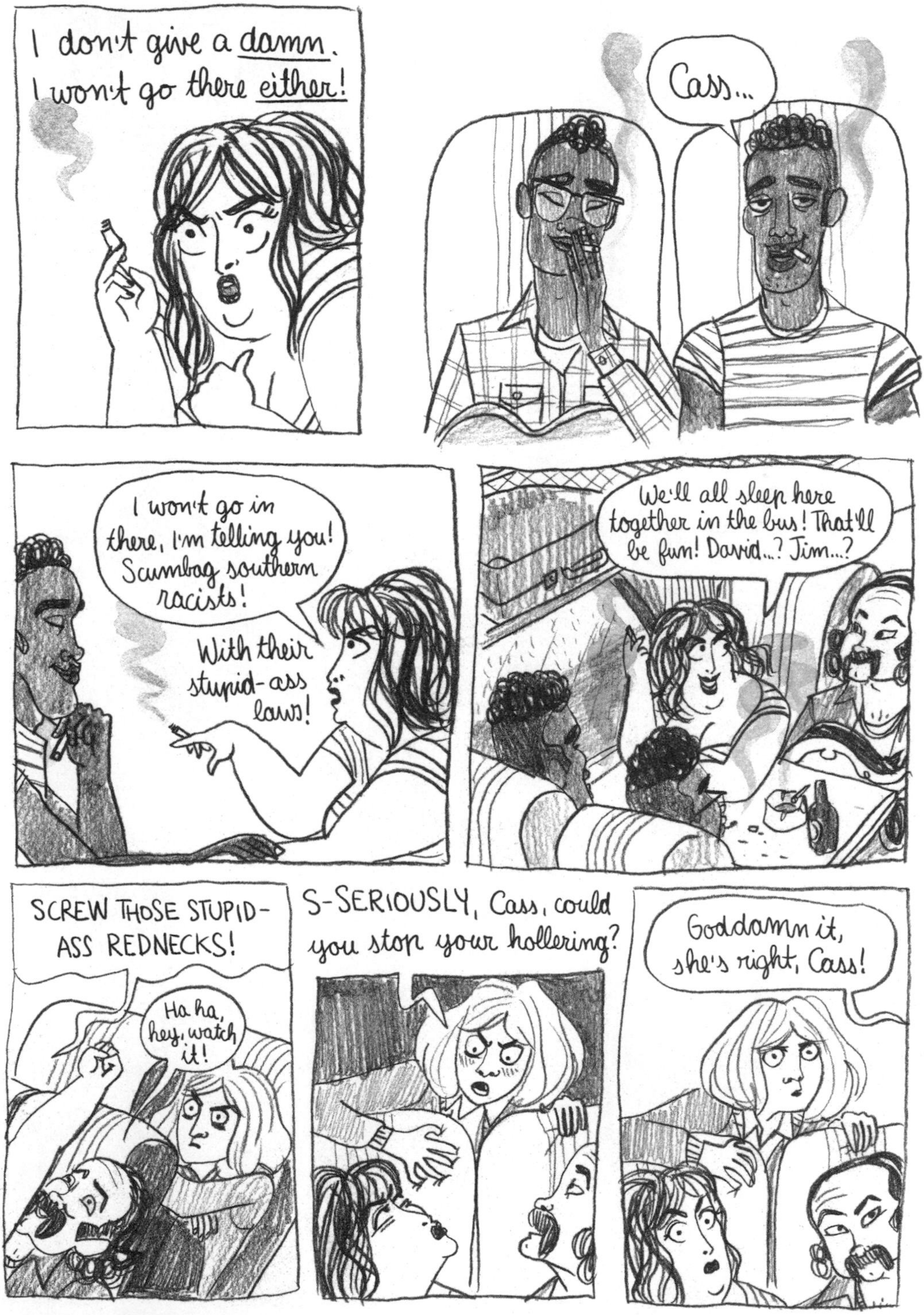
I don't give a damn. I won't go there either!
Cass...
I won't go in there, I'm telling you! Scumbag southern racists!
With their stupid-ass laws!
We'll all sleep here together in the bus! That'll be fun! David...? Jim...?
SCREW THOSE STUPID-ASS REDNECKS!
Ha ha, hey, watch it!
S-SERIOUSLY, Cass, could you stop your hollering?
Goddamn it, she's right, Cass!

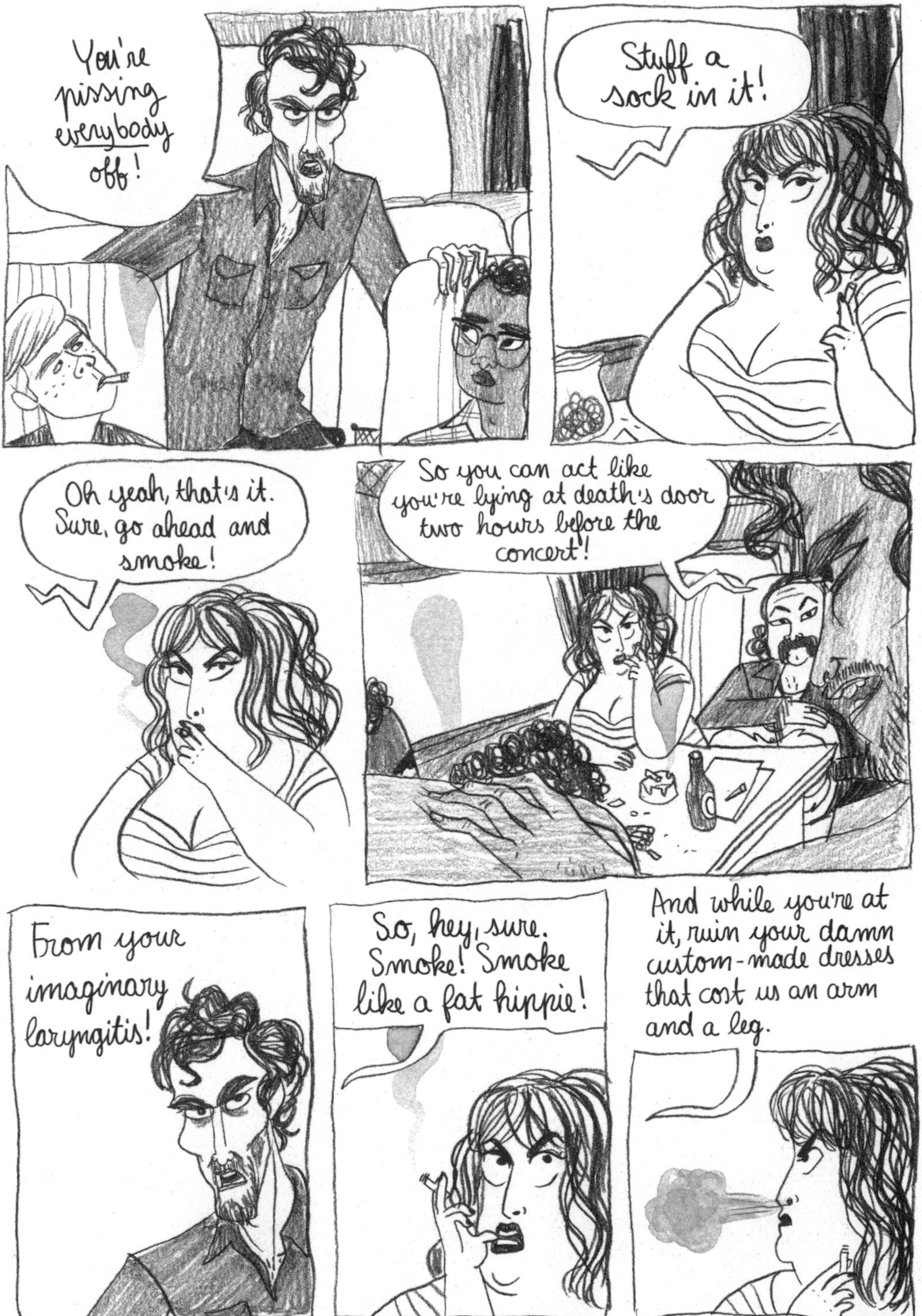
You're pissing everybody off!
Stuff a sock in it!
Oh yeah, that's it. Sure, go ahead and smoke!
So you can act like you're lying at death's door two hours before the concert!
From your imaginary laryngitis!
So, hey, sure. Smoke! Smoke like a fat hippie!
And while you're at it, ruin your damn custom-made dresses that cost us an arm and a leg.

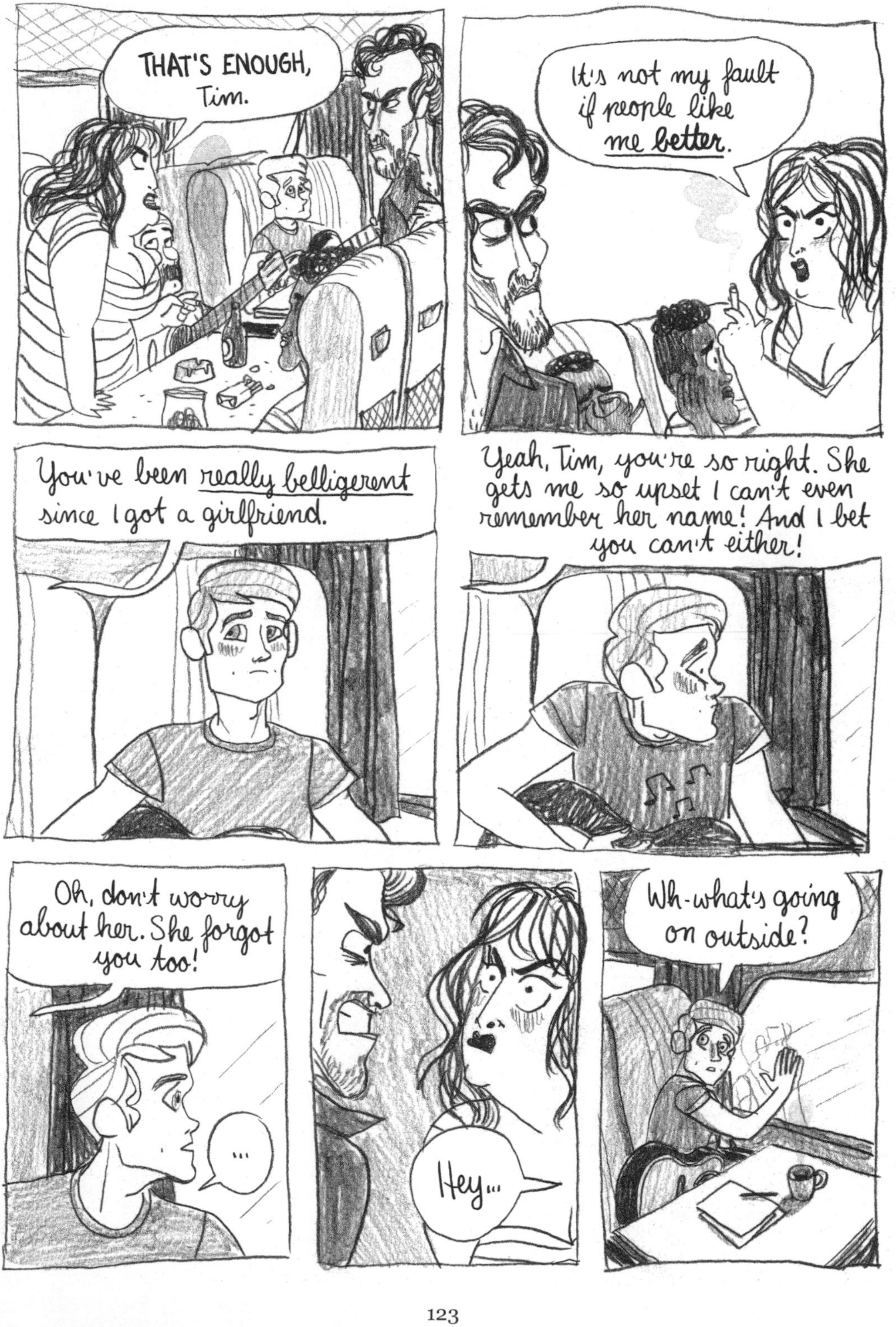
THAT'S ENOUGH, Tim.
It's not my fault if people like me better.
You've been really belligerent since I got a girlfriend.
Yeah, Tim, you're so right. She gets me so upset I can't even remember her name! And I bet you can't either!
Oh, don't worry about her. She forgot you too!
...
Hey...
Wh-what's going on outside?

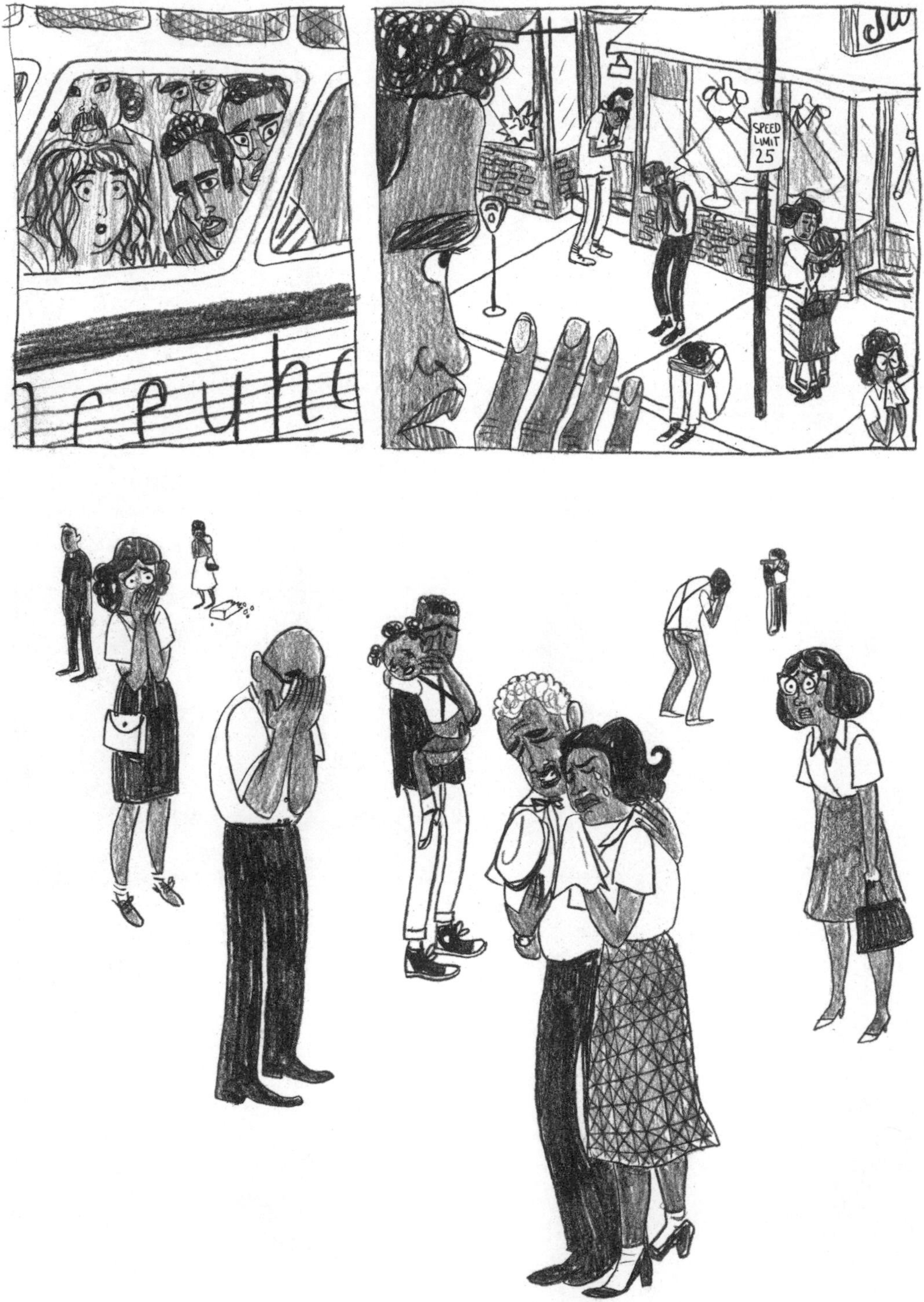
SPEED LIMIT 25

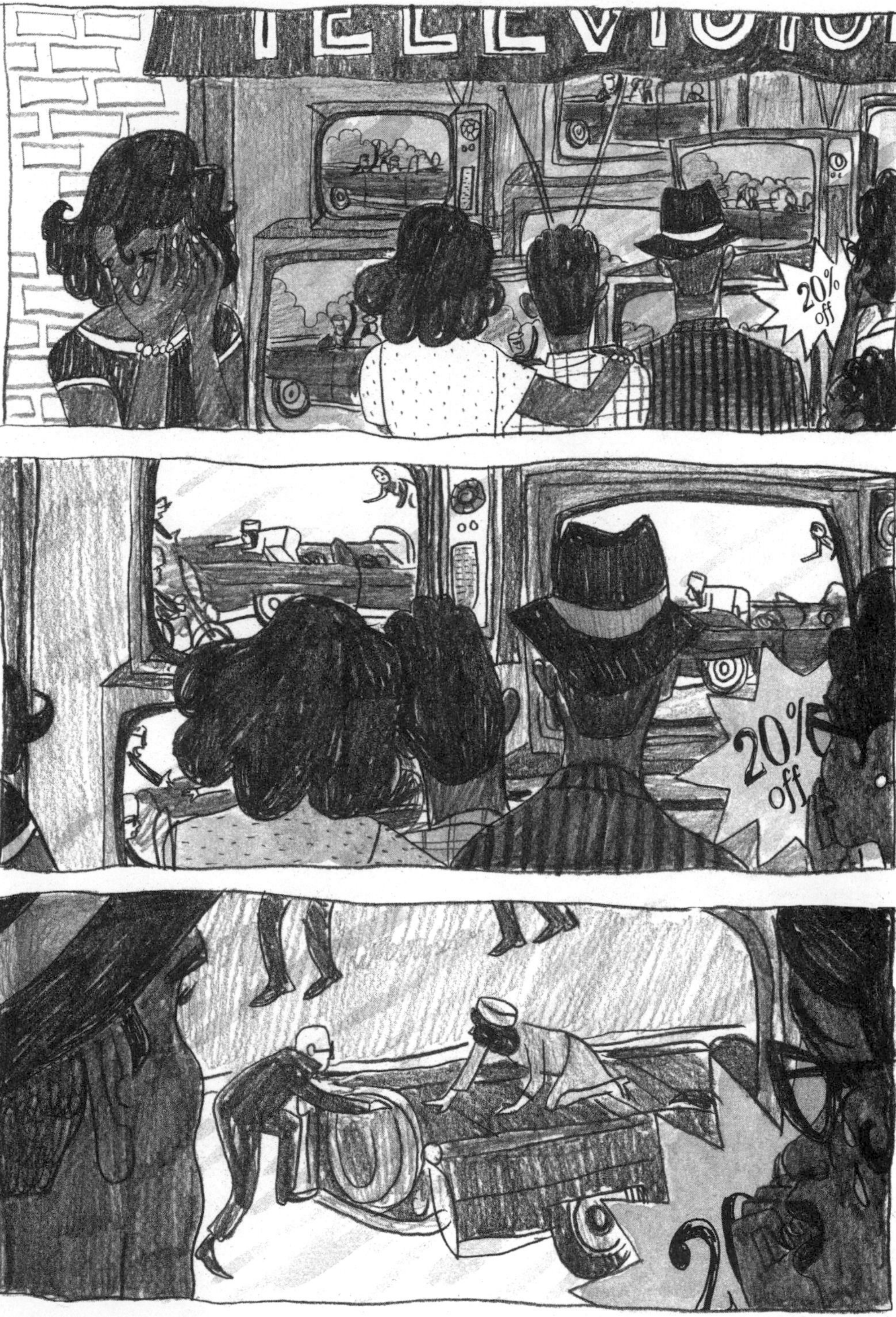
20% off
20% off

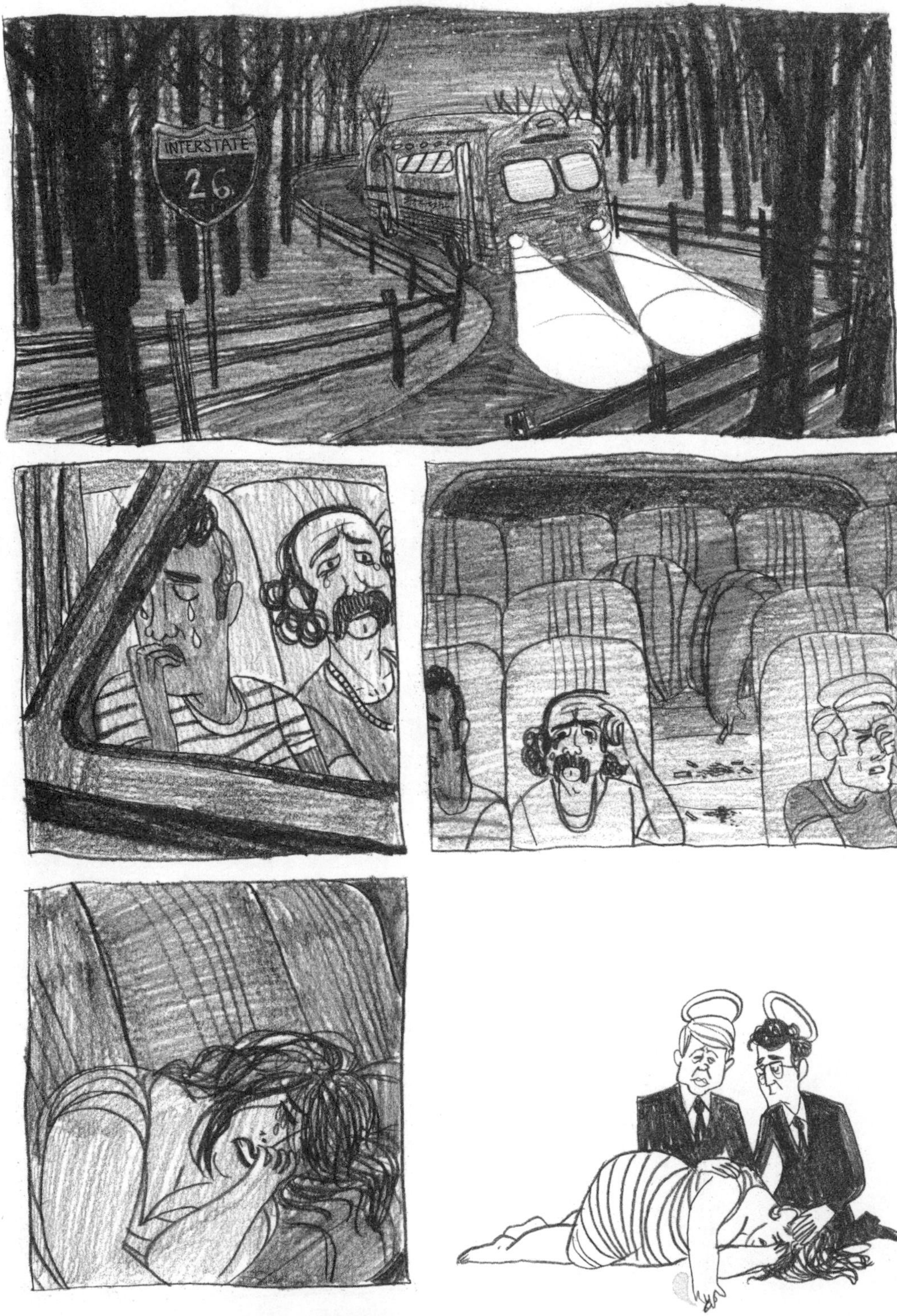
INTERSTATE
26

10-Jim

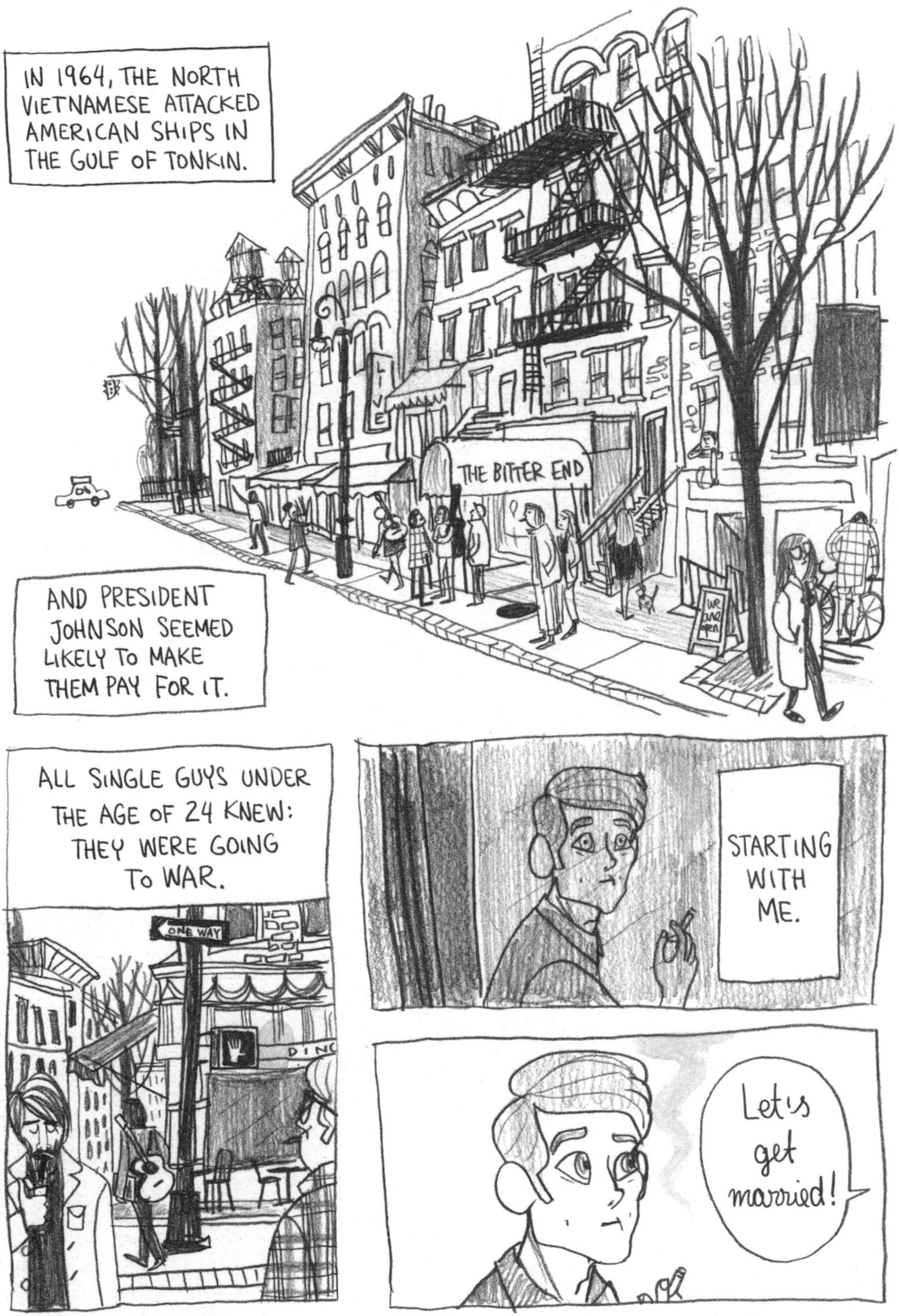
IN 1964, THE NORTH VIETNAMESE ATTACKED AMERICAN SHIPS IN THE GULF OF TONKIN.
THE BITTER END
AND PRESIDENT JOHNSON SEEMED LIKELY TO MAKE THEM PAY FOR IT.
ALL SINGLE GUYS UNDER THE AGE OF 24 KNEW: THEY WERE GOING TO WAR.
ONE WAY
STARTING WITH ME.
Let's get married!

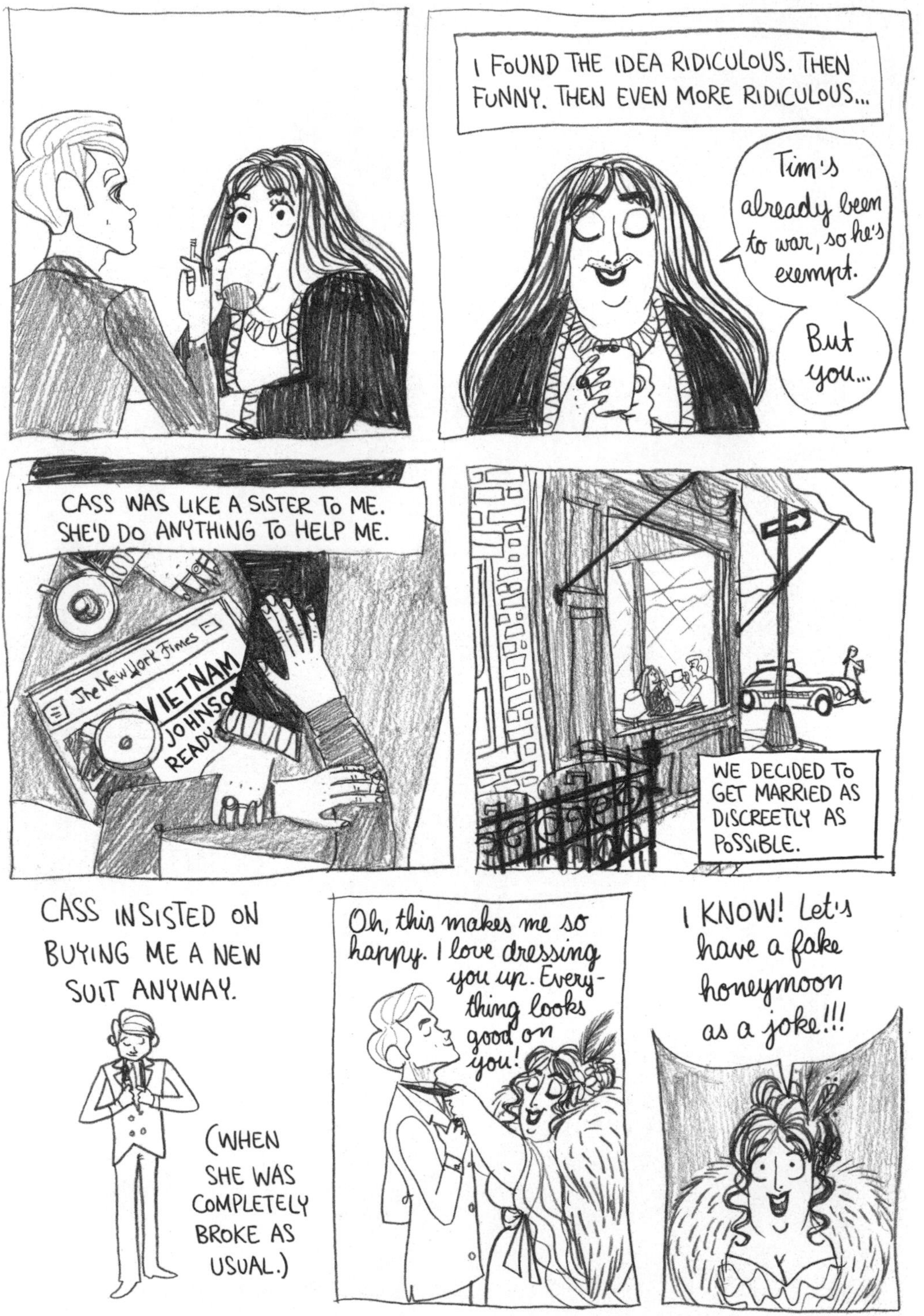
I FOUND THE IDEA RIDICULOUS. THEN FUNNY. THEN EVEN MORE RIDICULOUS...
Tim's already been to war, so he's exempt.
But you...
CASS WAS LIKE A SISTER TO ME. SHE'D DO ANYTHING TO HELP ME.
The New York Times
VIETNAM
WE DECIDED TO GET MARRIED AS DISCREETLY AS POSSIBLE.
CASS INSISTED ON BUYING ME A NEW SUIT ANYWAY.
(WHEN SHE WAS COMPLETELY BROKE AS USUAL.)
Oh, this makes me so happy. I love dressing you up. Everything looks good on you!
I KNOW! Let's have a fake honeymoon as a joke!!!

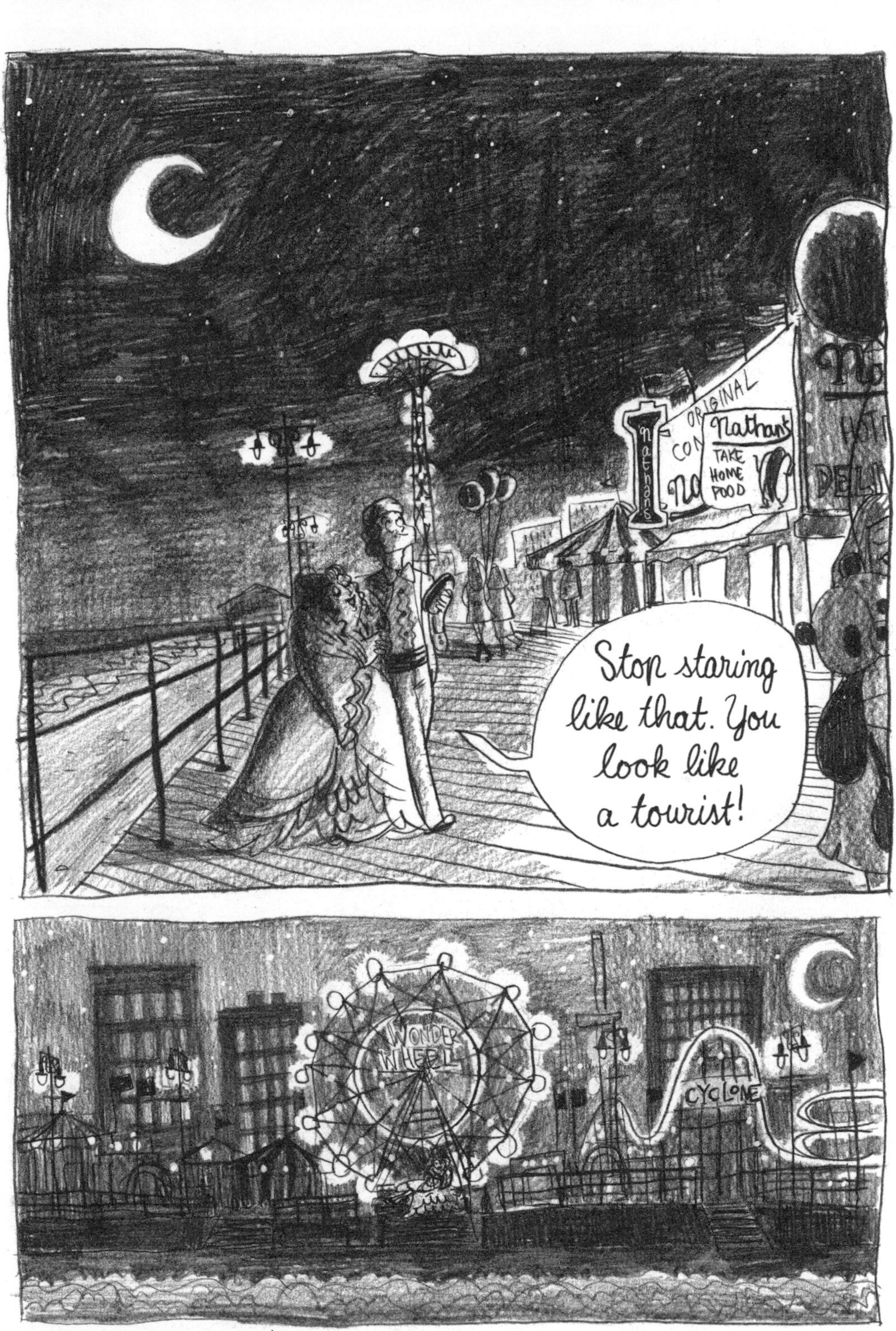
ORIGINAL
Nathan's
Stop staring like that. You look like a tourist!
WONDER WHEEL
CYCLONE

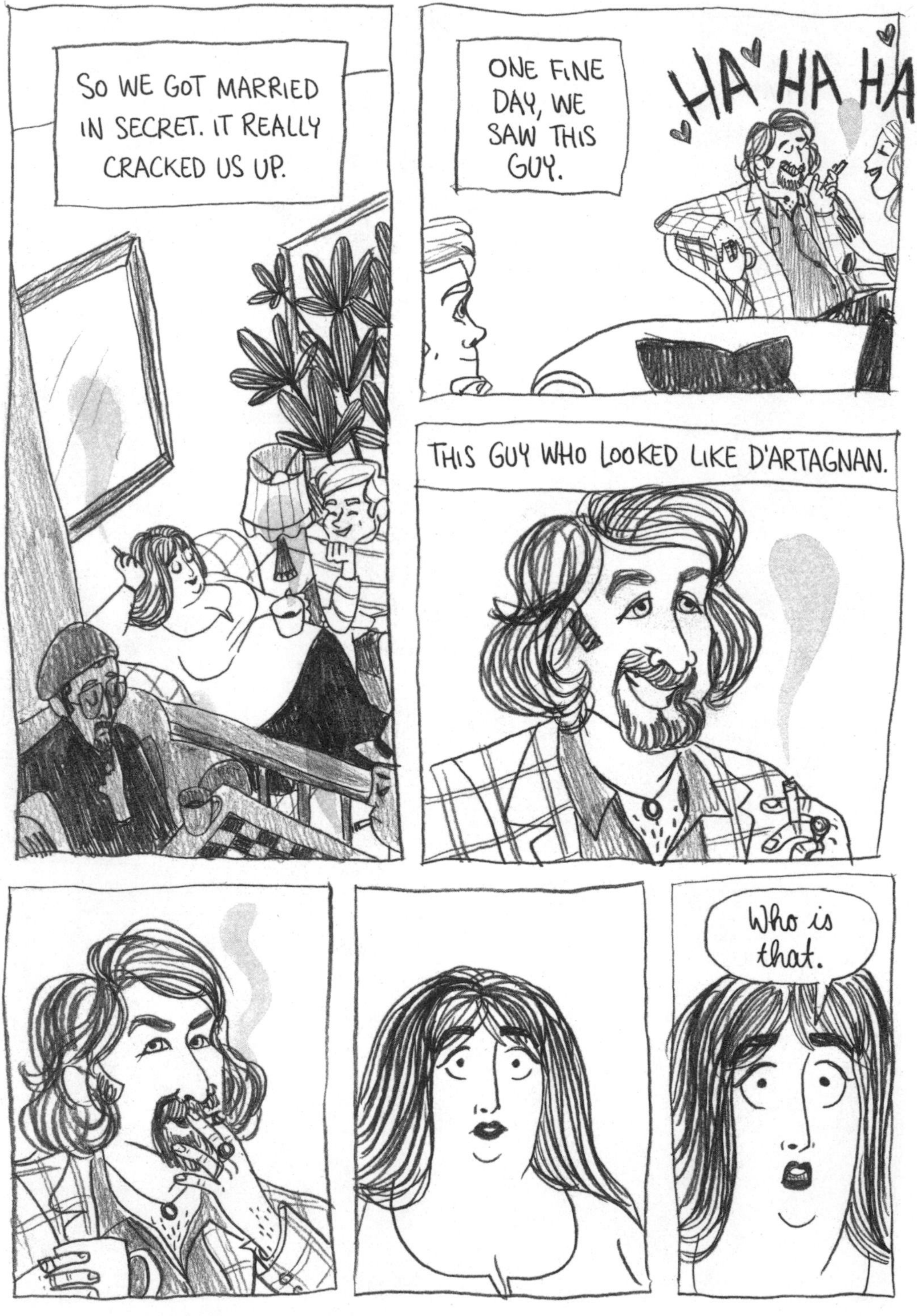

SO WE GOT MARRIED IN SECRET. IT REALLY CRACKED US UP.
ONE FINE DAY, WE SAW THIS GUY.
HA HA HA
THIS GUY WHO LOOKED LIKE D'ARTAGNAN.
Who is that.

Him? He's a singer. I've seen him lots of times. He's, umm...

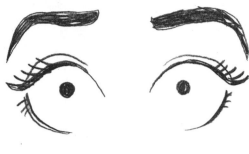

Denny I-don't-remember-what...

Great voice. Really. One of the best voices I've heard...

I'm amazed you haven't bumped into him. He's not too bad at open-microphone nights.

In fact, I wonder if the Journeymen...

Okay, you're not listening to me at all anymore.

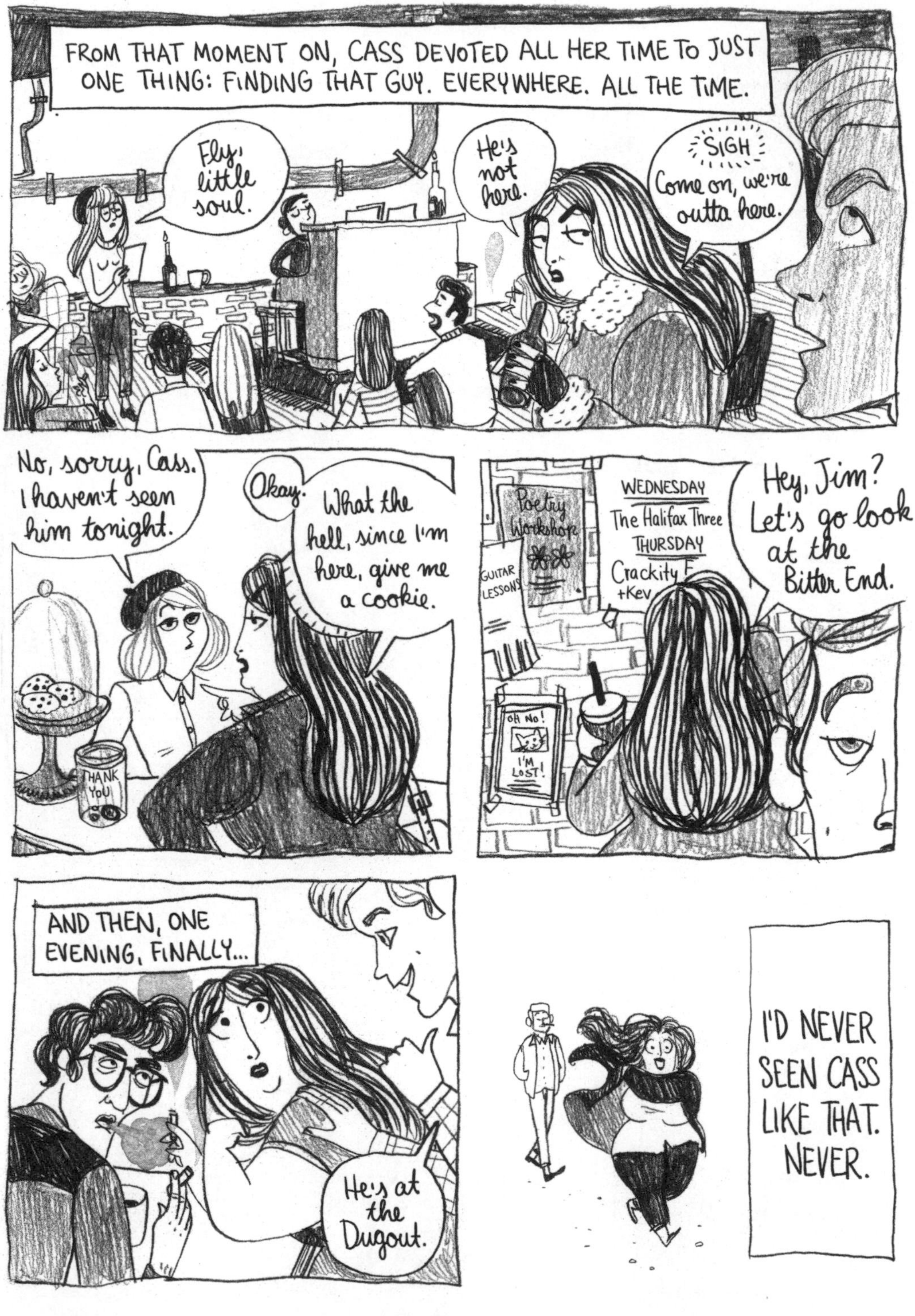
FROM THAT MOMENT ON, CASS DEVOTED ALL HER TIME TO JUST ONE THING: FINDING THAT GUY. EVERYWHERE. ALL THE TIME.
Fly, little soul.
He's not here.
SIGH
Come on, we're outta here.
No, sorry, Cass. I haven't seen him tonight.
Okay.
What the hell, since I'm here, give me a cookie.
THANK YOU
Poetry Workshop
GUITAR LESSONS
WEDNESDAY
The Halifax Three
THURSDAY
Crackity F
+Kev
OH NO!
I'M LOST!
Hey, Jim? Let's go look at the Bitter End.
AND THEN, ONE EVENING, FINALLY...
He's at the Dugout.
I'D NEVER SEEN CASS LIKE THAT. NEVER.

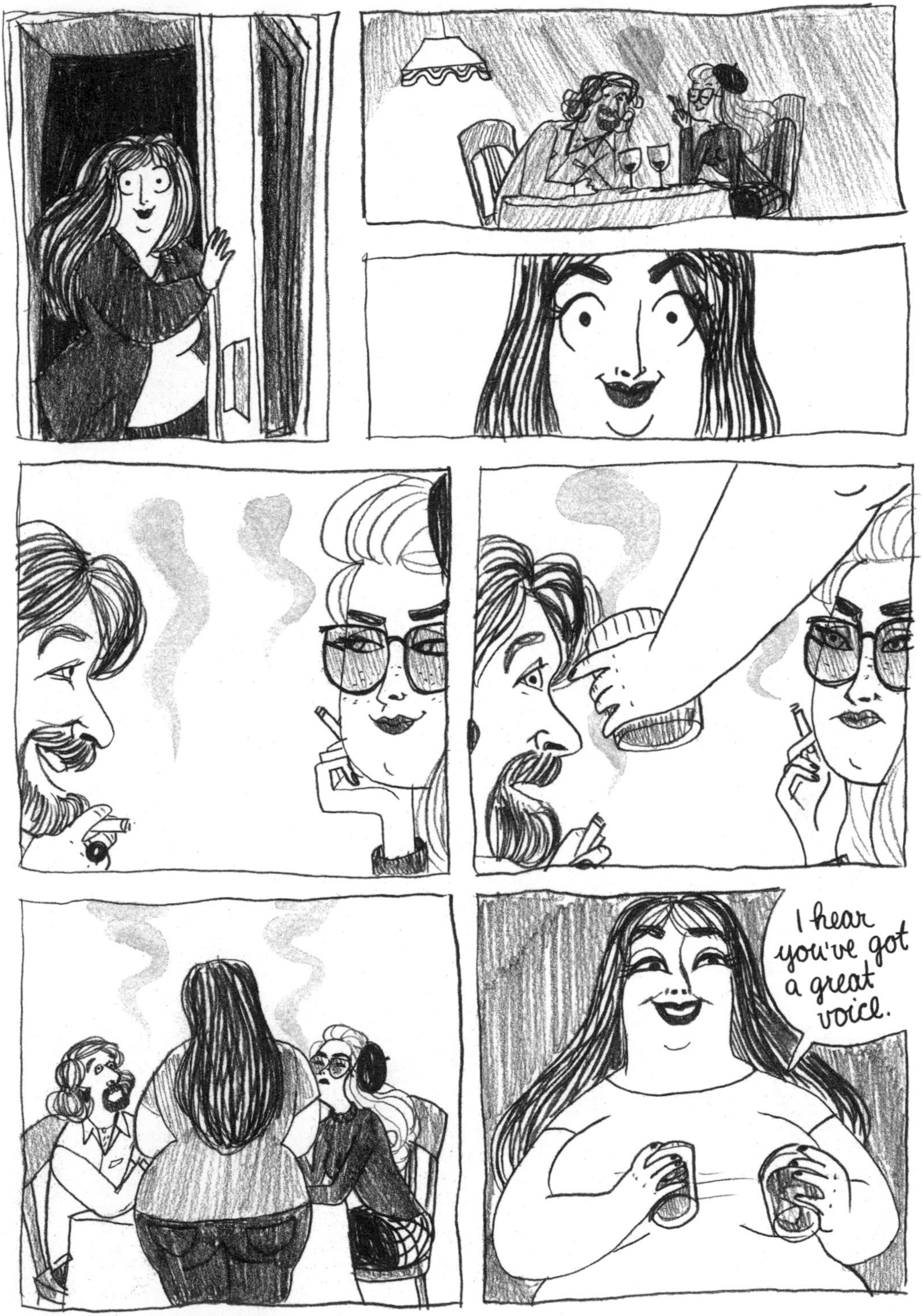
I hear you've got a great voice.

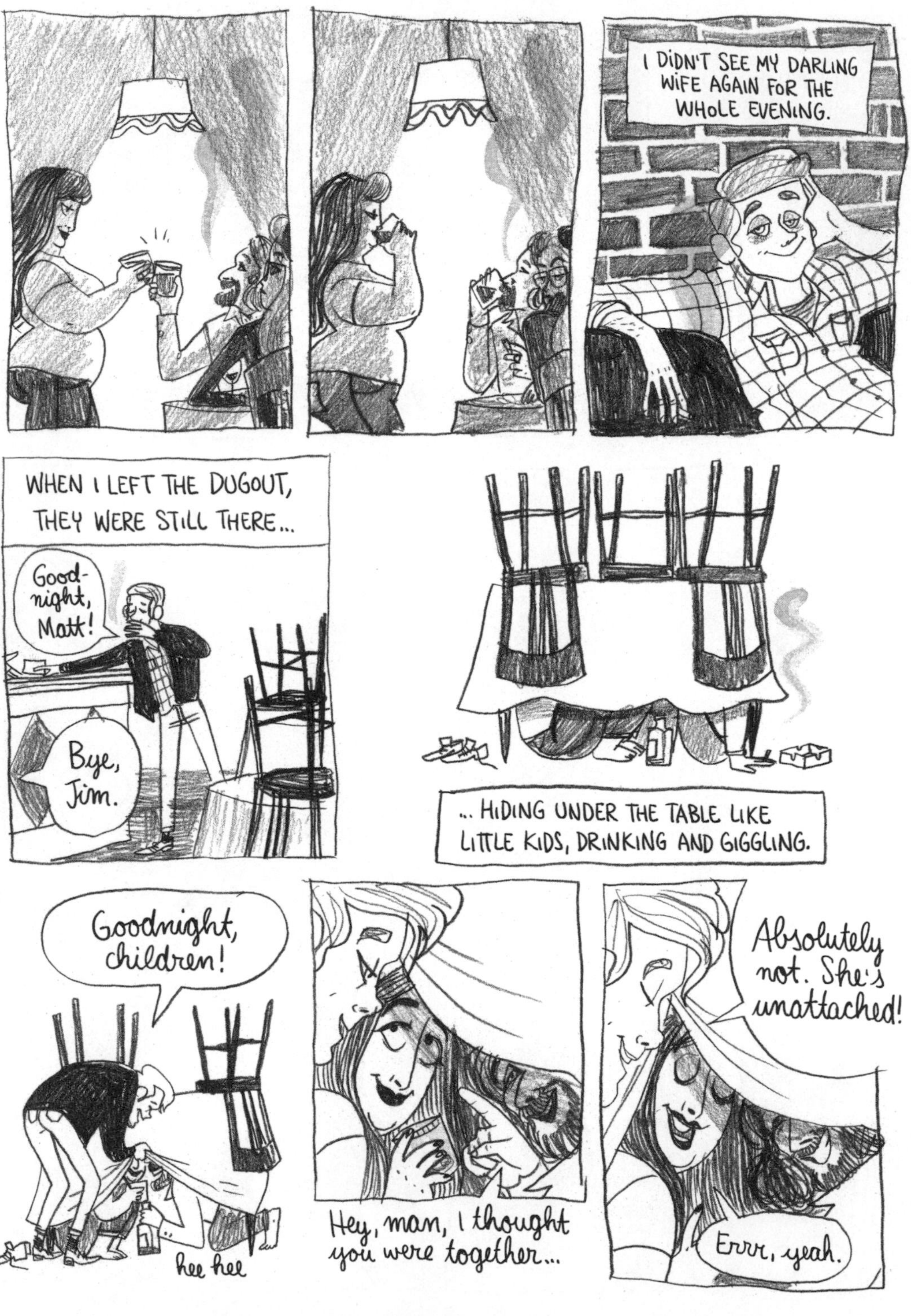
I DIDN'T SEE MY DARLING WIFE AGAIN FOR THE WHOLE EVENING.
WHEN I LEFT THE DUGOUT, THEY WERE STILL THERE...
Good-night, Matt!
Bye, Jim.
... HIDING UNDER THE TABLE LIKE LITTLE KIDS, DRINKING AND GIGGLING.
Goodnight, children!
hee hee
Hey, man, I thought you were together...
Absolutely not. She's unattached!
Errr, yeah.

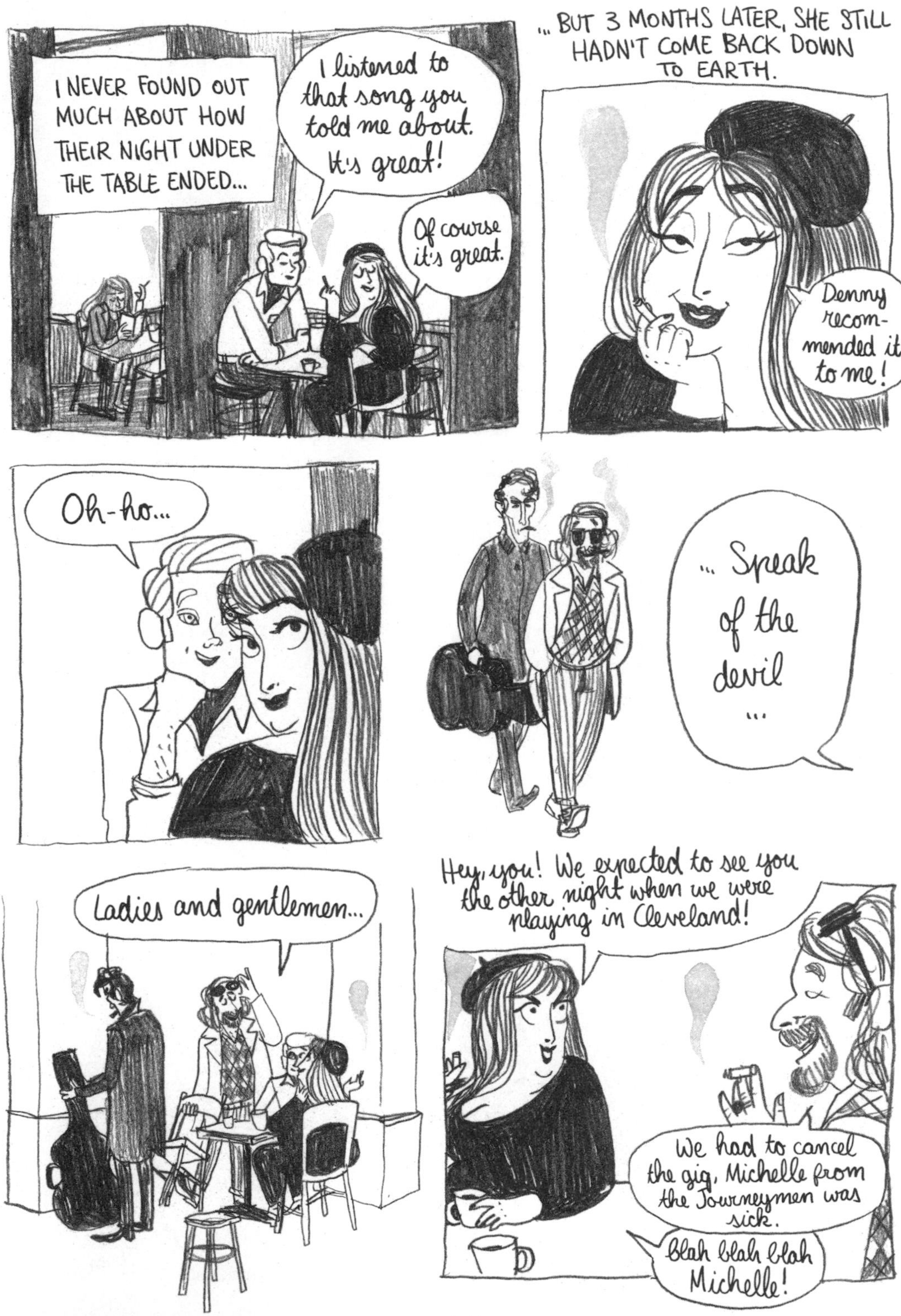
I NEVER FOUND OUT MUCH ABOUT HOW THEIR NIGHT UNDER THE TABLE ENDED...
I listened to that song you told me about. It's great!
Of course it's great.
... BUT 3 MONTHS LATER, SHE STILL HADN'T COME BACK DOWN TO EARTH.
Denny recom-mended it to me!
Oh-ho...
... Speak of the devil ...
Ladies and gentlemen...
Hey, you! We expected to see you the other night when we were playing in Cleveland!
We had to cancel the gig, Michelle from the Journeymen was sick.
Blah blah blah Michelle!

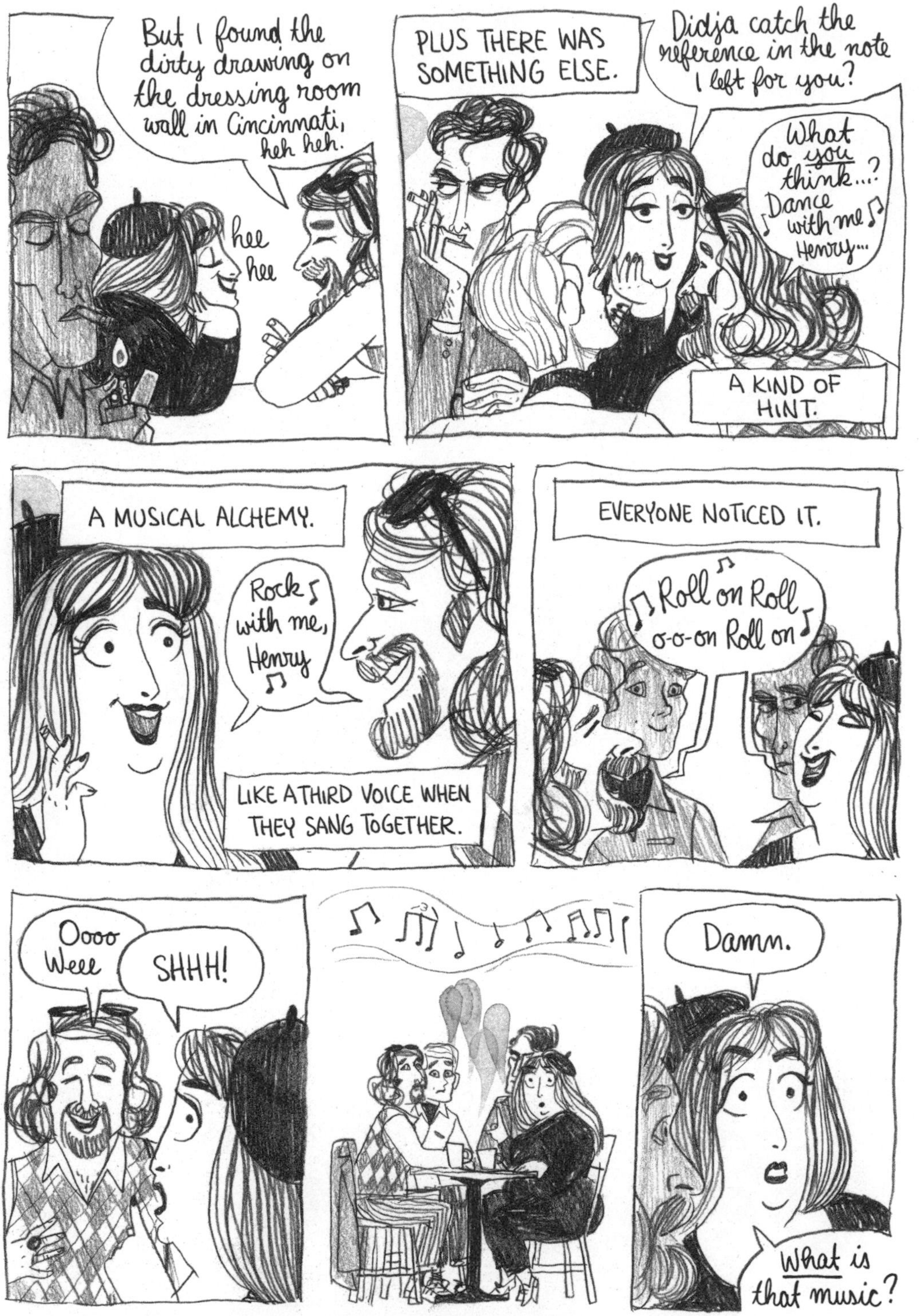
But I found the dirty drawing on the dressing room wall in Cincinnati, heh heh.
hee hee
PLUS THERE WAS SOMETHING ELSE.
Didja catch the reference in the note I left for you?
What do you think...? Dance with me Henry...
A KIND OF HINT.
A MUSICAL ALCHEMY.
Rock with me, Henry
LIKE A THIRD VOICE WHEN THEY SANG TOGETHER.
EVERYONE NOTICED IT.
Roll on Roll o-o-on Roll on
Oooo Weee
SHHH!
Damn.
What is that music?

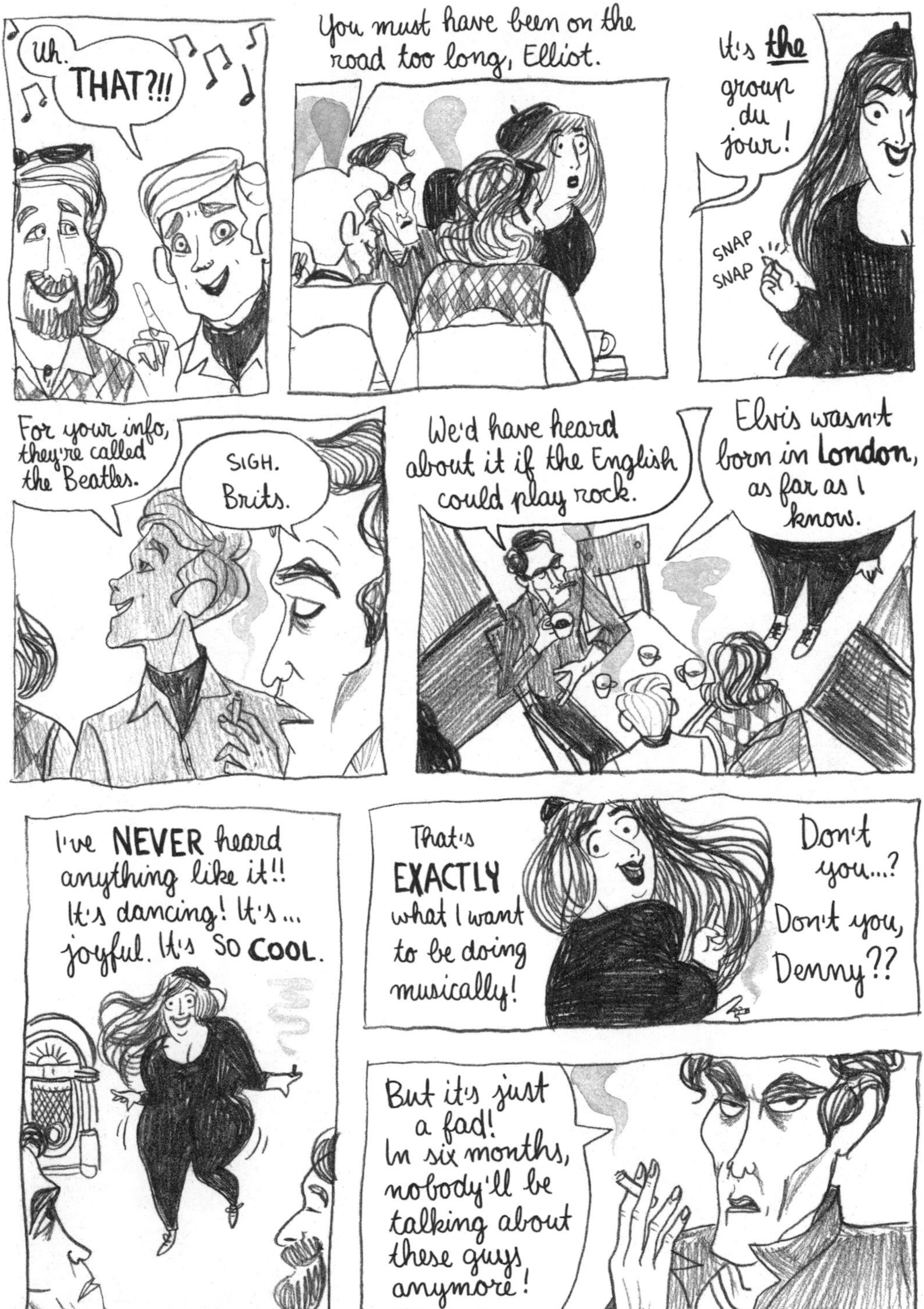
Uh.
THAT?!!
You must have been on the road too long, Elliot.
It's the group du jour!
SNAP
SNAP
For your info, they're called the Beatles.
SIGH. Brits.
We'd have heard about it if the English could play rock.
Elvis wasn't born in London, as far as I know.
I've NEVER heard anything like it!! It's dancing! It's... joyful. It's SO COOL.
That's EXACTLY what I want to be doing musically!
Don't you...? Don't you, Denny??
But it's just a fad! In six months, nobody'll be talking about these guys anymore!

Tim. Brace yourself... but...

Folk music... it's over.

That's it.

Come on! Let's start a new group!

A name like... "the somethings"! With... with an *electric* guitar!

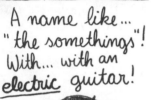

and... DRUMS!!

With you too, Denny!!

So c'mon, already!! Say yes, guys!

THE MUGWUMPS. IT WAS DENNY WHO CHOSE OUR NAME.

11- Art

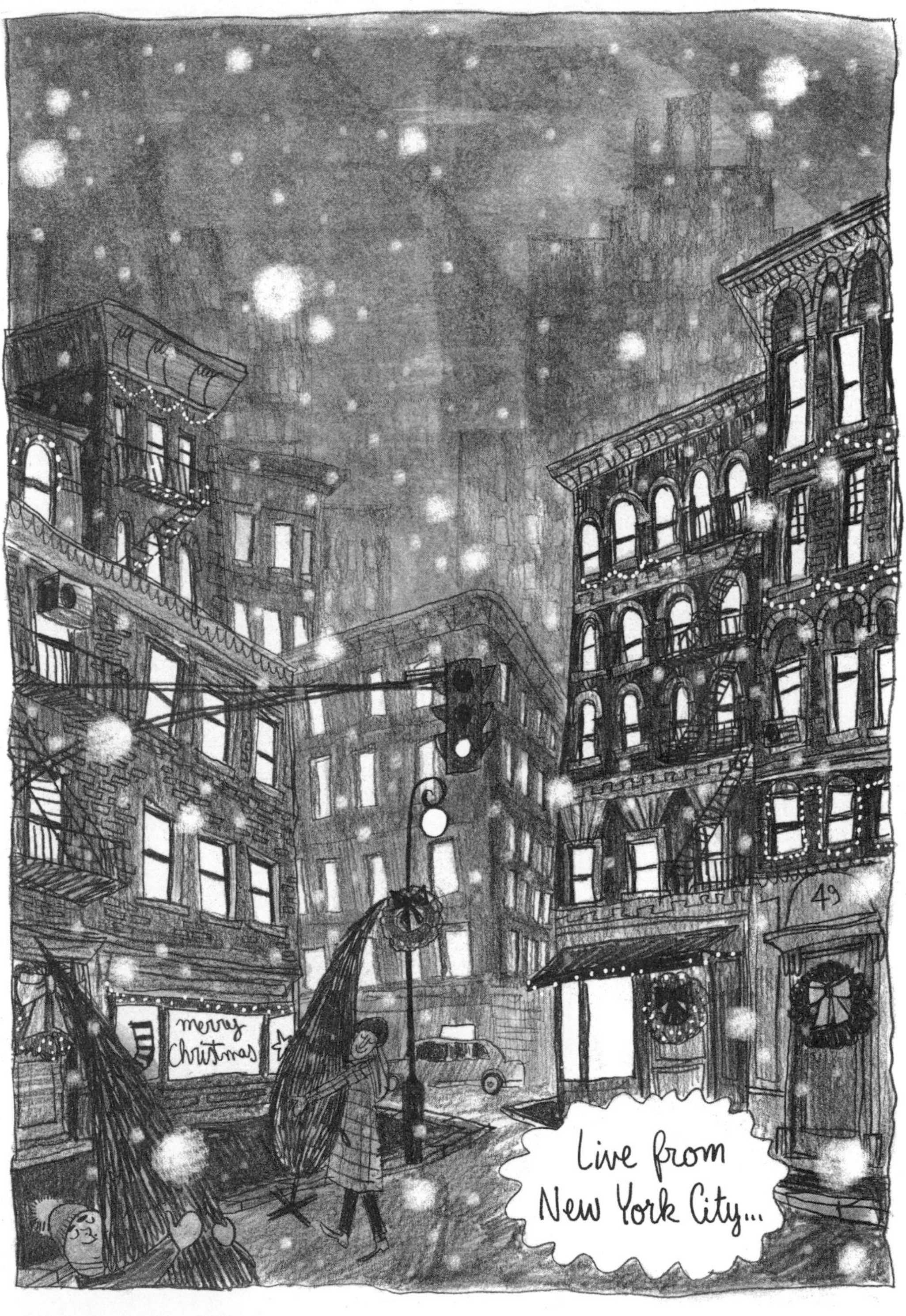
merry Christmas
49
Live from New York City...

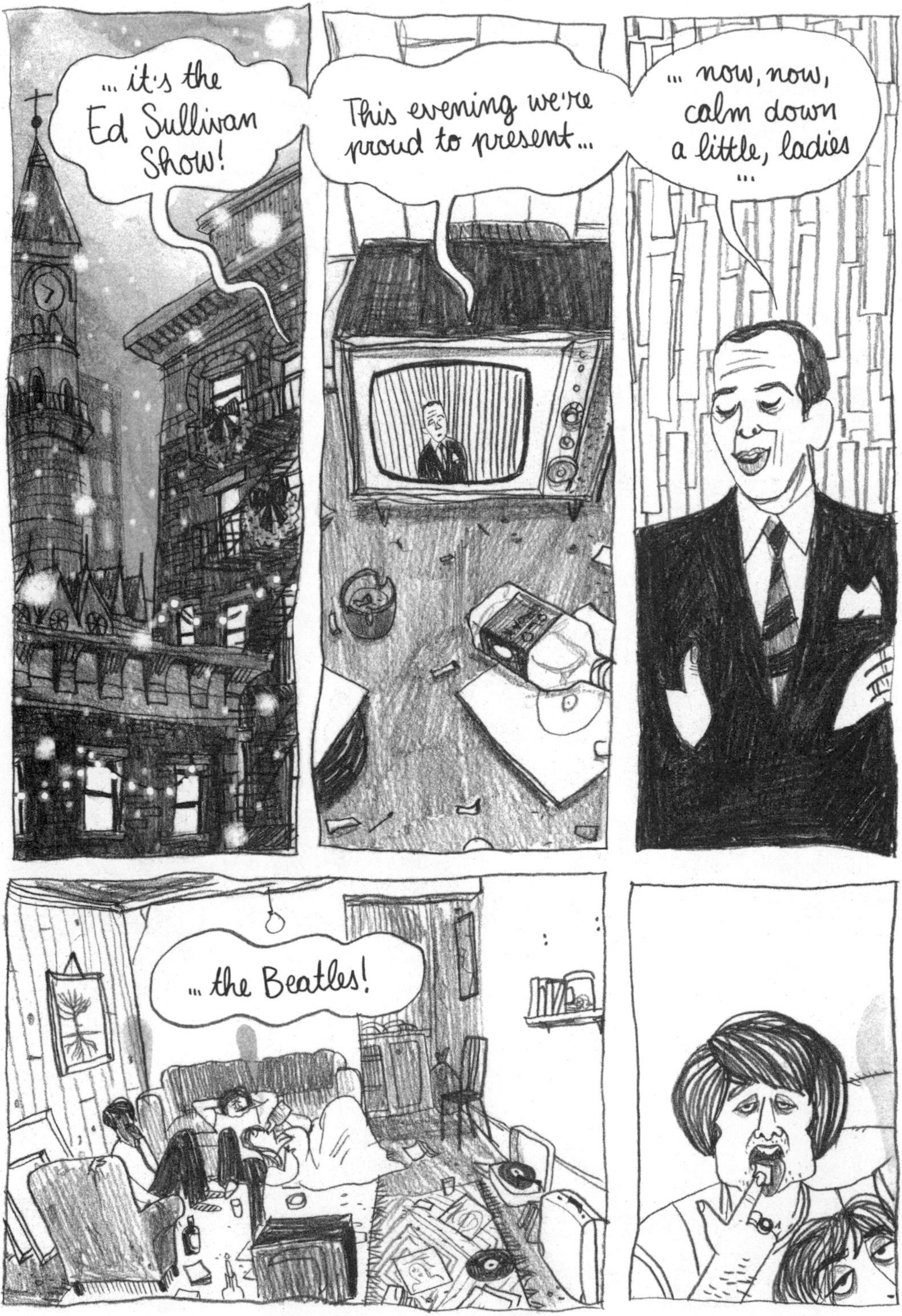

... it's the Ed Sullivan Show!
This evening we're proud to present...
... now, now, calm down a little, ladies ...
... the Beatles!

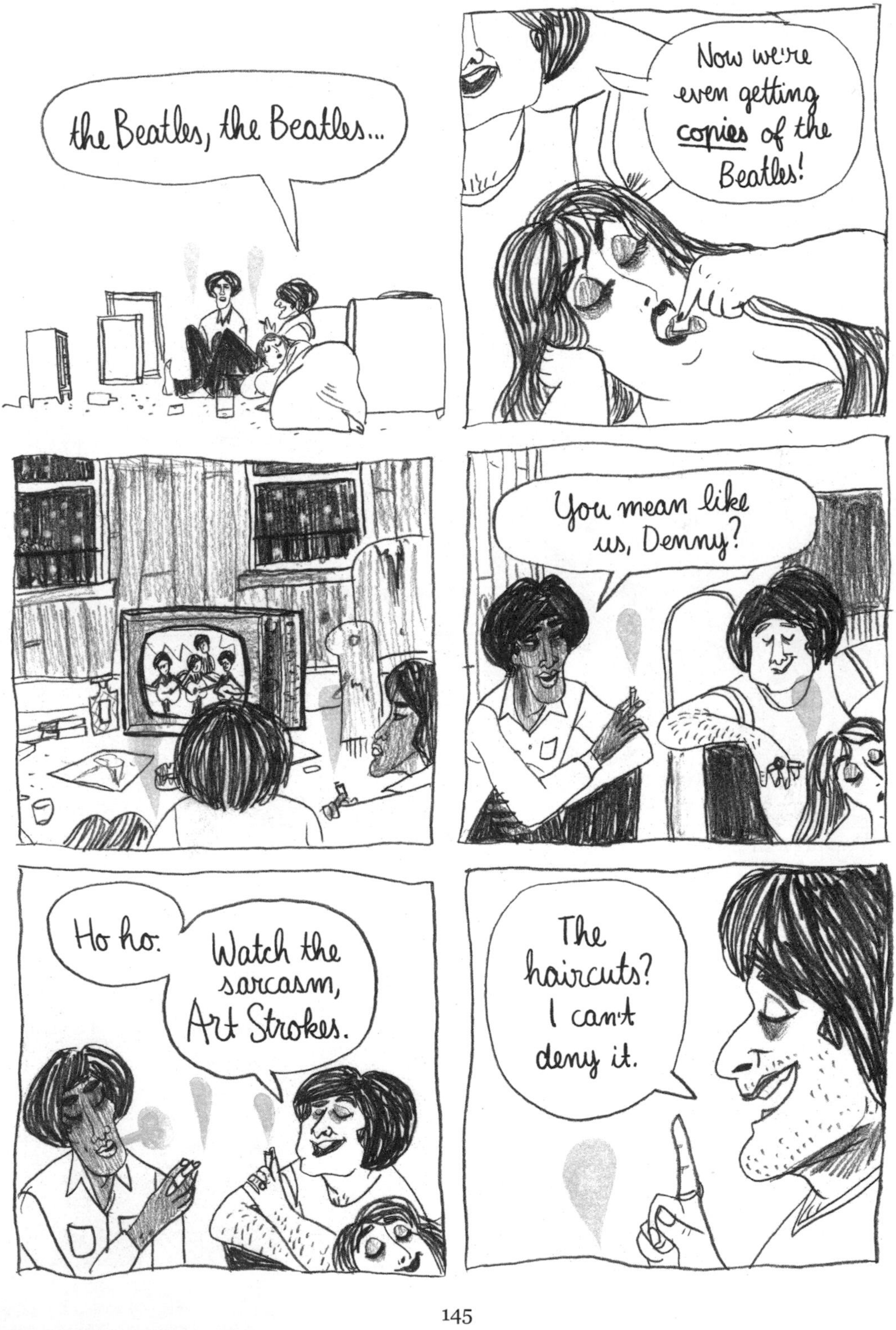
the Beatles, the Beatles...
Now we're even getting copies of the Beatles!
You mean like us, Denny?
Ho ho.
Watch the sarcasm, Art Strokes.
The haircuts? I can't deny it.

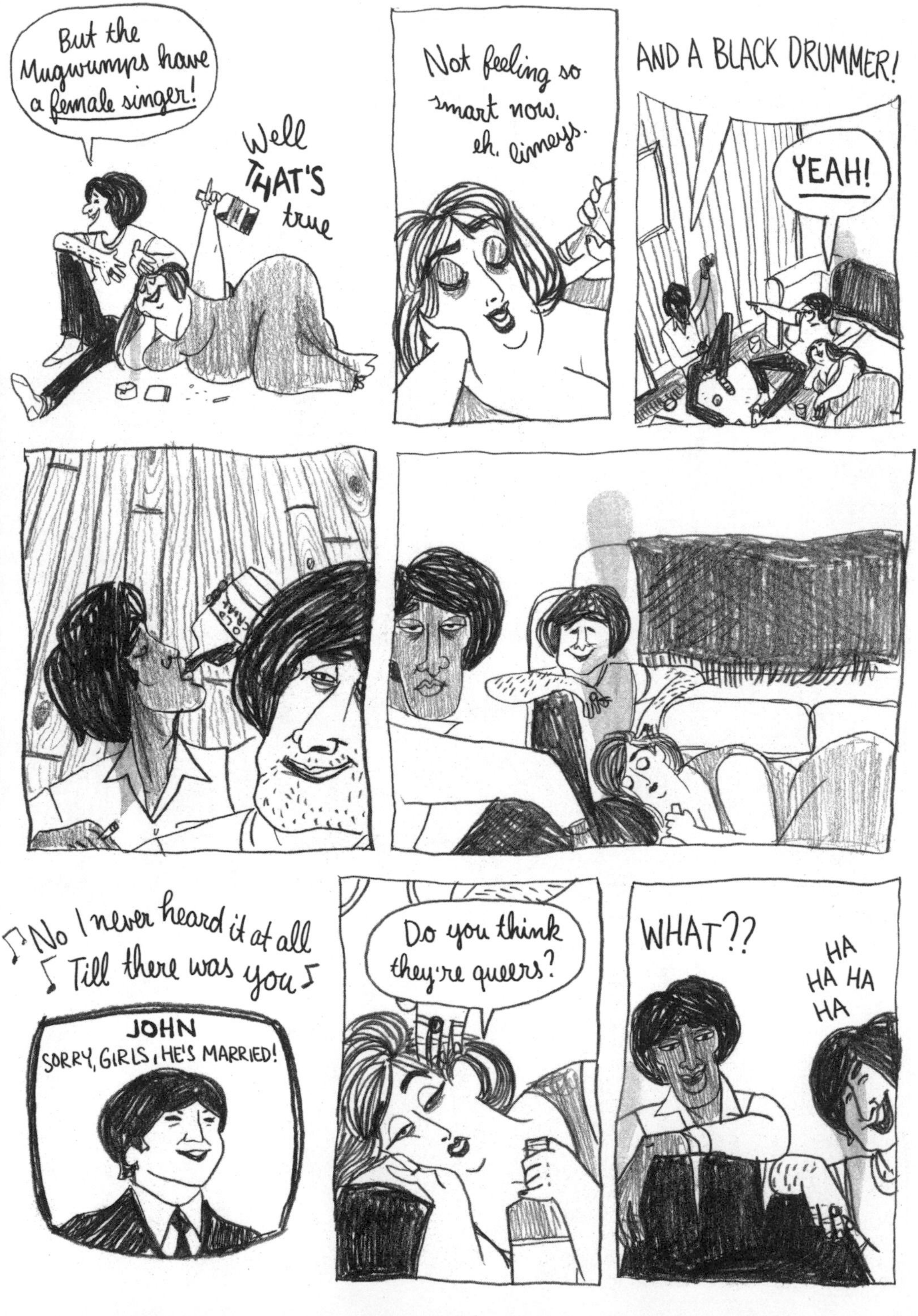
But the Mugwumps have a female singer!
Well THAT'S true
Not feeling so smart now, eh, limeys.
AND A BLACK DRUMMER!
YEAH!
No I never heard it at all
Till there was you
JOHN
SORRY, GIRLS, HE'S MARRIED!
Do you think they're queers?
WHAT??
HA HA HA HA

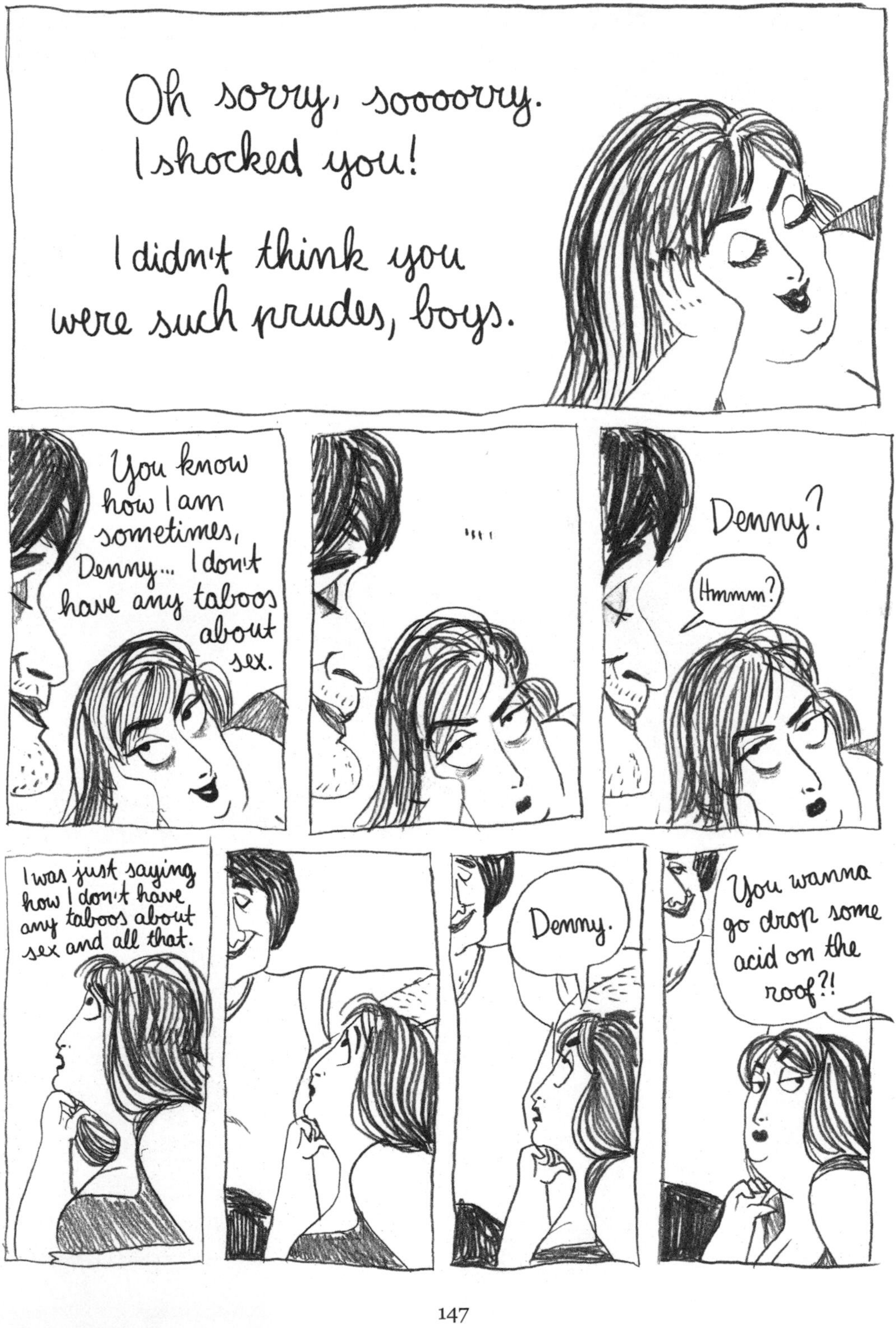
Oh sorry, soooorry. I shocked you!
I didn't think you were such prudes, boys.
You know how I am sometimes, Denny... I don't have any taboos about sex.
...
Denny?
Hmmm?
I was just saying how I don't have any taboos about sex and all that.
Denny.
You wanna go drop some acid on the roof?!

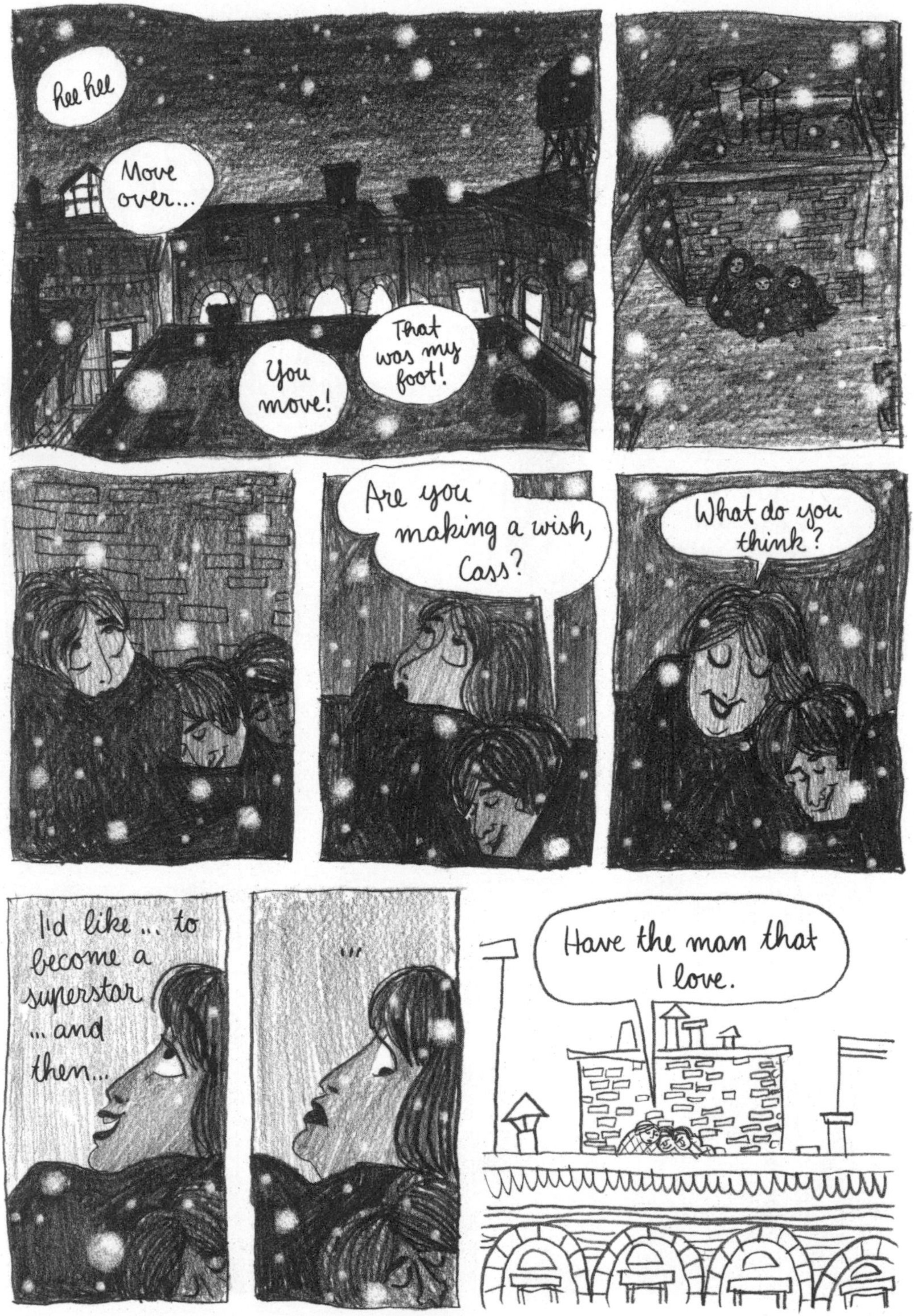
Hee hee
Move over...
You move!
That was my foot!
Are you making a wish, Cass?
What do you think?
I'd like ... to become a superstar ... and then...
...
Have the man that I love.

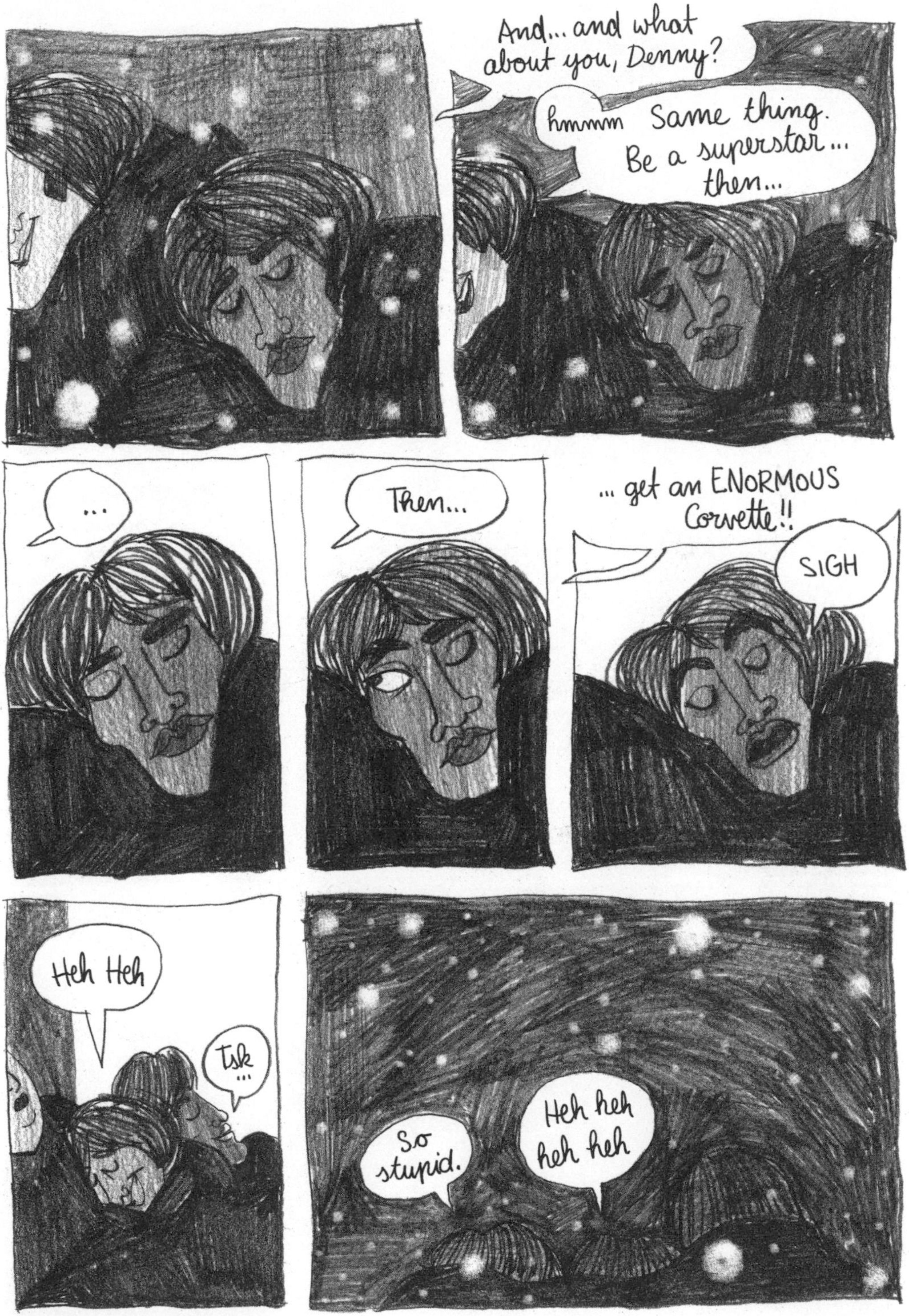
And... and what about you, Denny?
hmmm Same thing. Be a superstar... then...
...
Then...
... get an ENORMOUS Corvette!!
SIGH
Heh Heh
Tsk ...
So stupid.
Heh heh heh heh

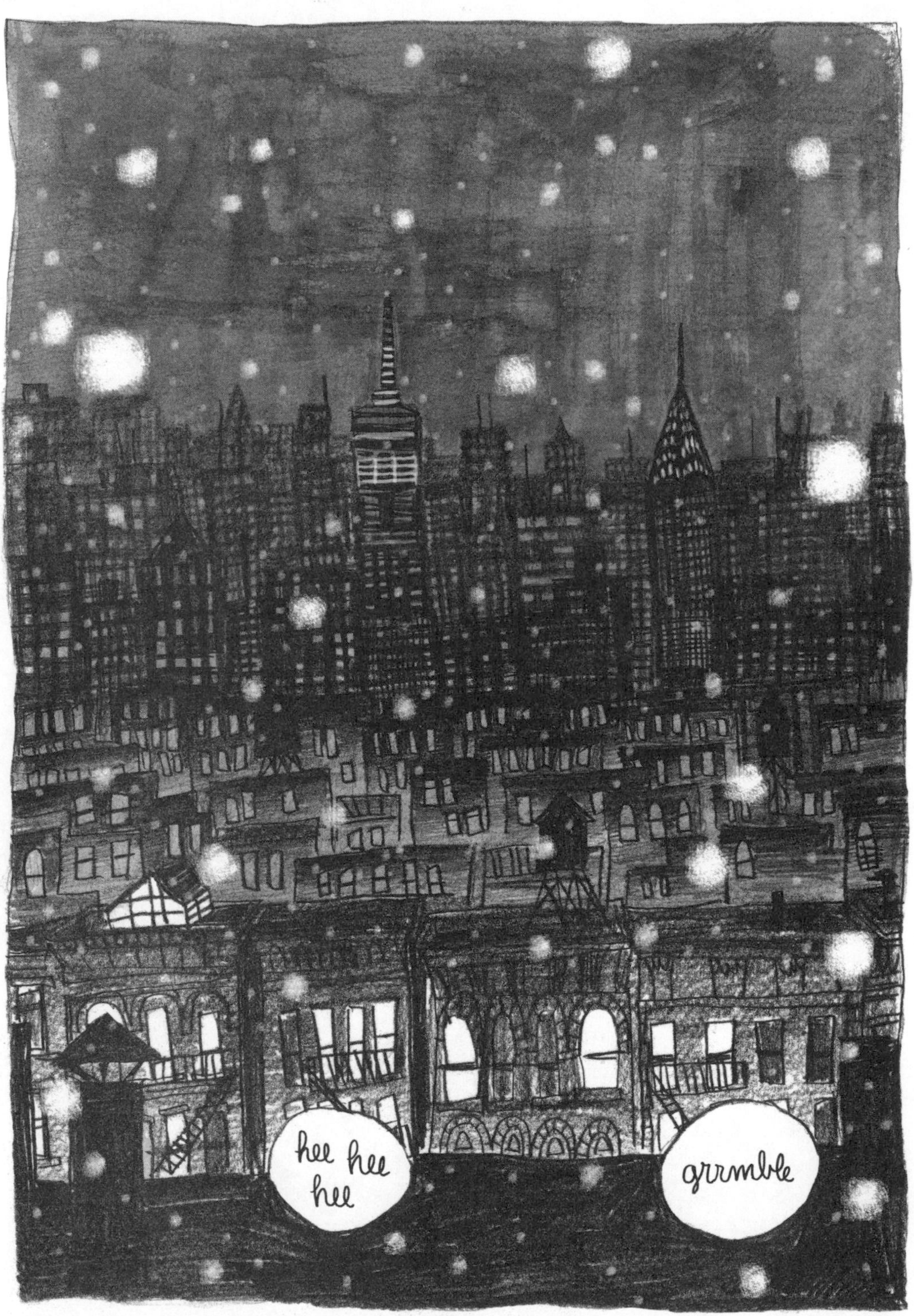
hee hee
hee
grrmble

12- Phil

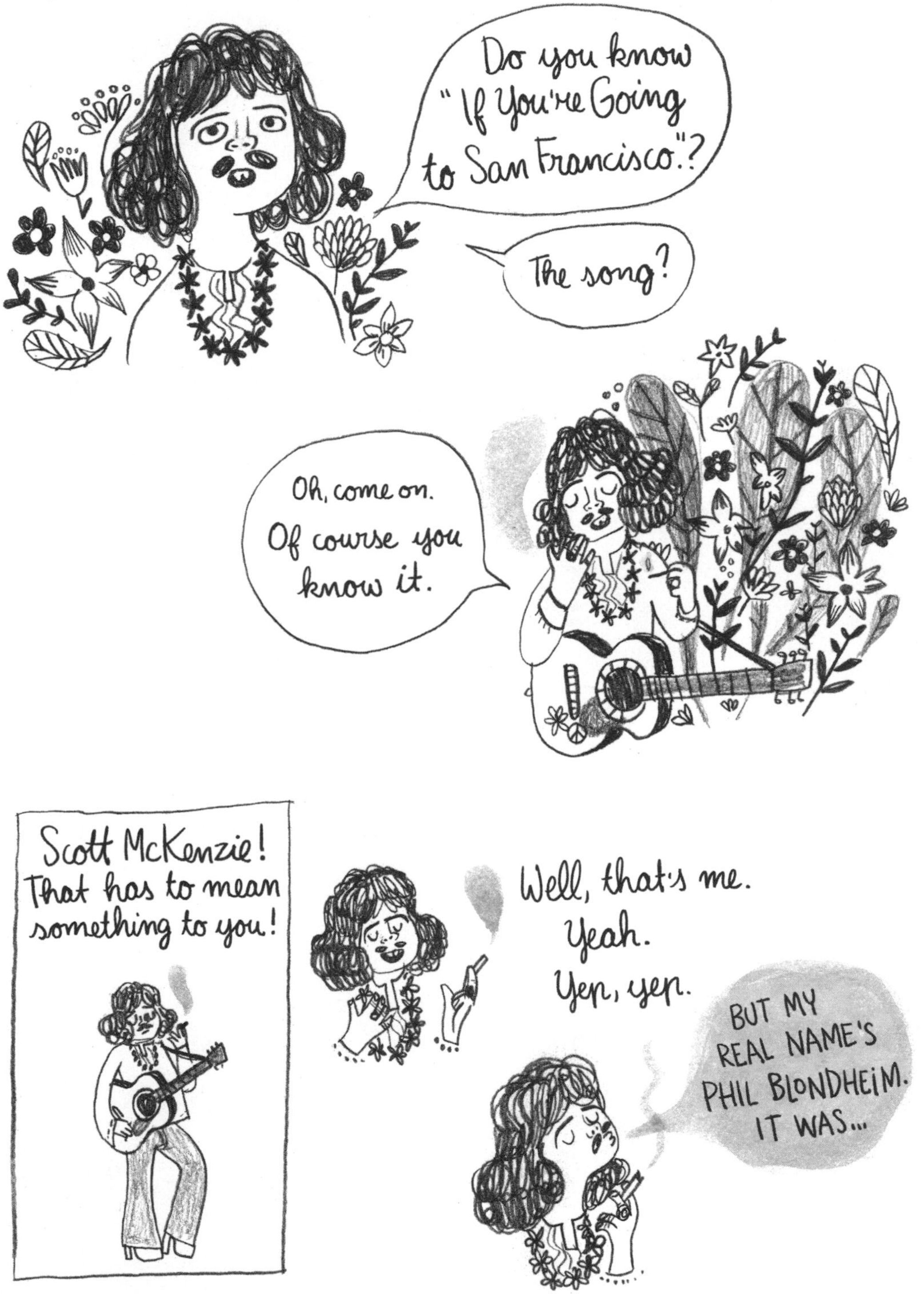
Do you know "If You're Going to San Francisco"?
The song?
Oh, come on. Of course you know it.
Scott McKenzie! That has to mean something to you!
Well, that's me. Yeah. Yep, yep.
BUT MY REAL NAME'S PHIL BLONDHEIM. IT WAS...

...A LOOOONG TIME AGO...

(me in 1964)

(YEAH, YEAH, THE HAIR. IT WAS ALMOST MANDATORY AT THE TIME.)

←

I WAS PART OF A GROUP CALLED THE

Journeymen

ORIGINALLY, THERE WERE:

JOHN PHILLIPS

A BIT OF A CONTROLLING, BORDERLINE PETTY TYRANT, BUT YOU HAVE TO ADMIT HE KNEW HOW TO WRITE SONGS, THE BASTARD.

ONE DAY, JOHN MET A 17-YEAR-OLD MODEL:

MICHELLE

AHHHH. MICHELLE.

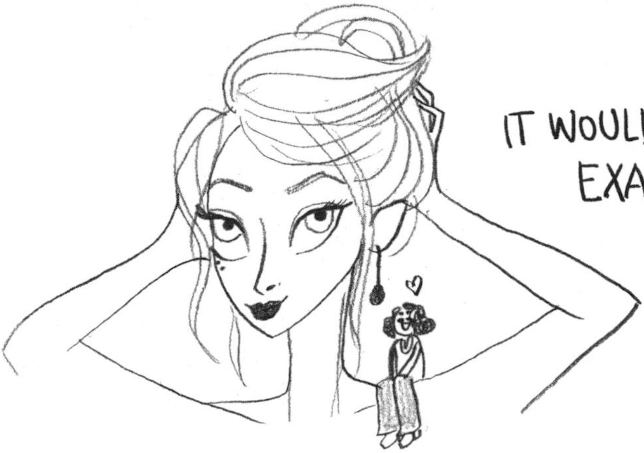

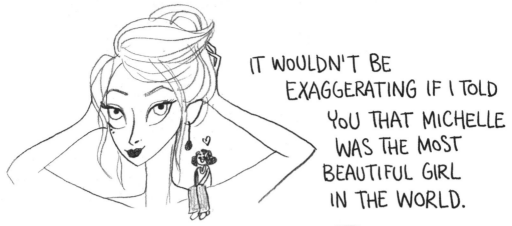

IT WOULDN'T BE EXAGGERATING IF I TOLD YOU THAT MICHELLE WAS THE MOST BEAUTIFUL GIRL IN THE WORLD.

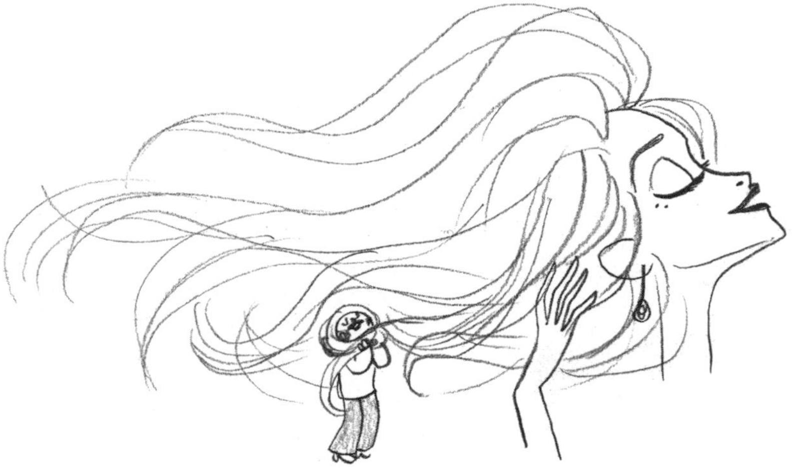

MICHELLE...

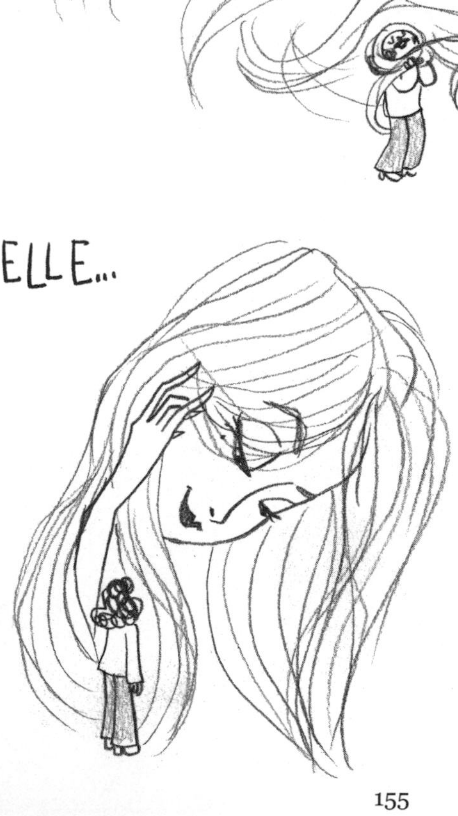

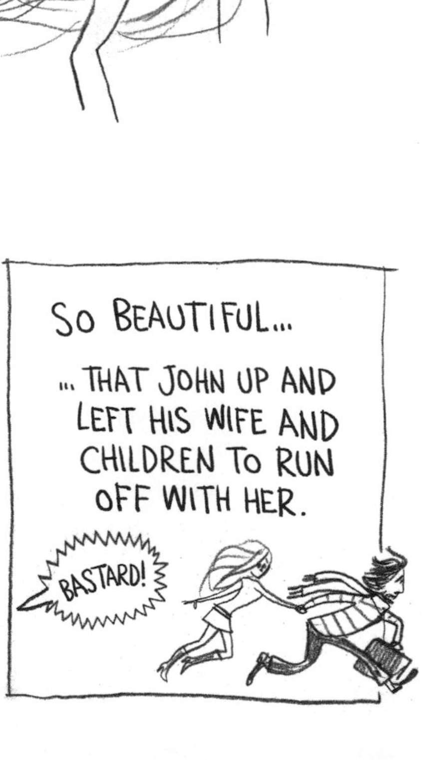
SO BEAUTIFUL...
... THAT JOHN UP AND LEFT HIS WIFE AND CHILDREN TO RUN OFF WITH HER.
BASTARD!

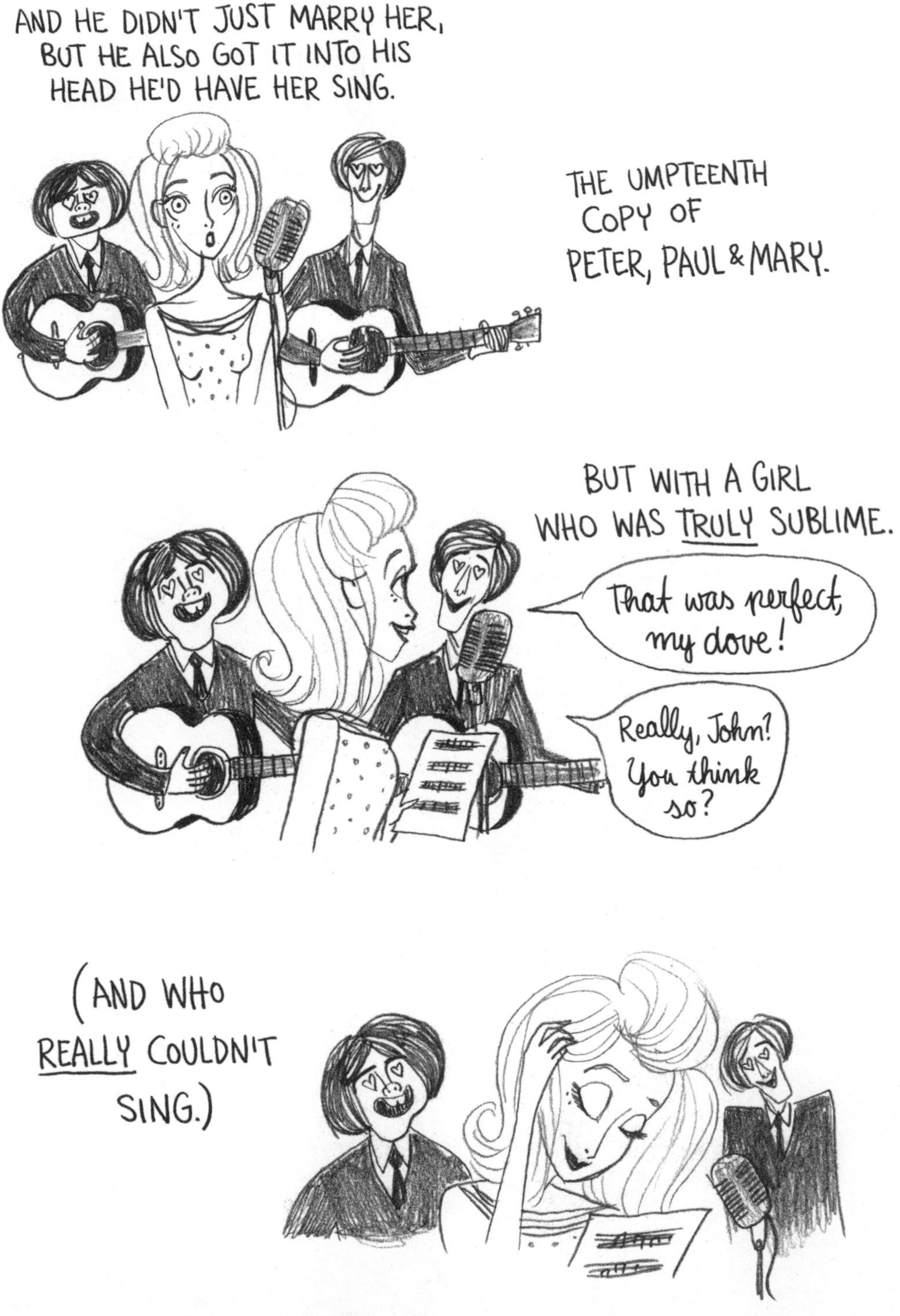
AND HE DIDN'T JUST MARRY HER, BUT HE ALSO GOT IT INTO HIS HEAD HE'D HAVE HER SING.
THE UMPTEENTH COPY OF PETER, PAUL & MARY.
BUT WITH A GIRL WHO WAS TRULY SUBLIME.
That was perfect, my dove!
Really, John? You think so?
(AND WHO REALLY COULDN'T SING.)

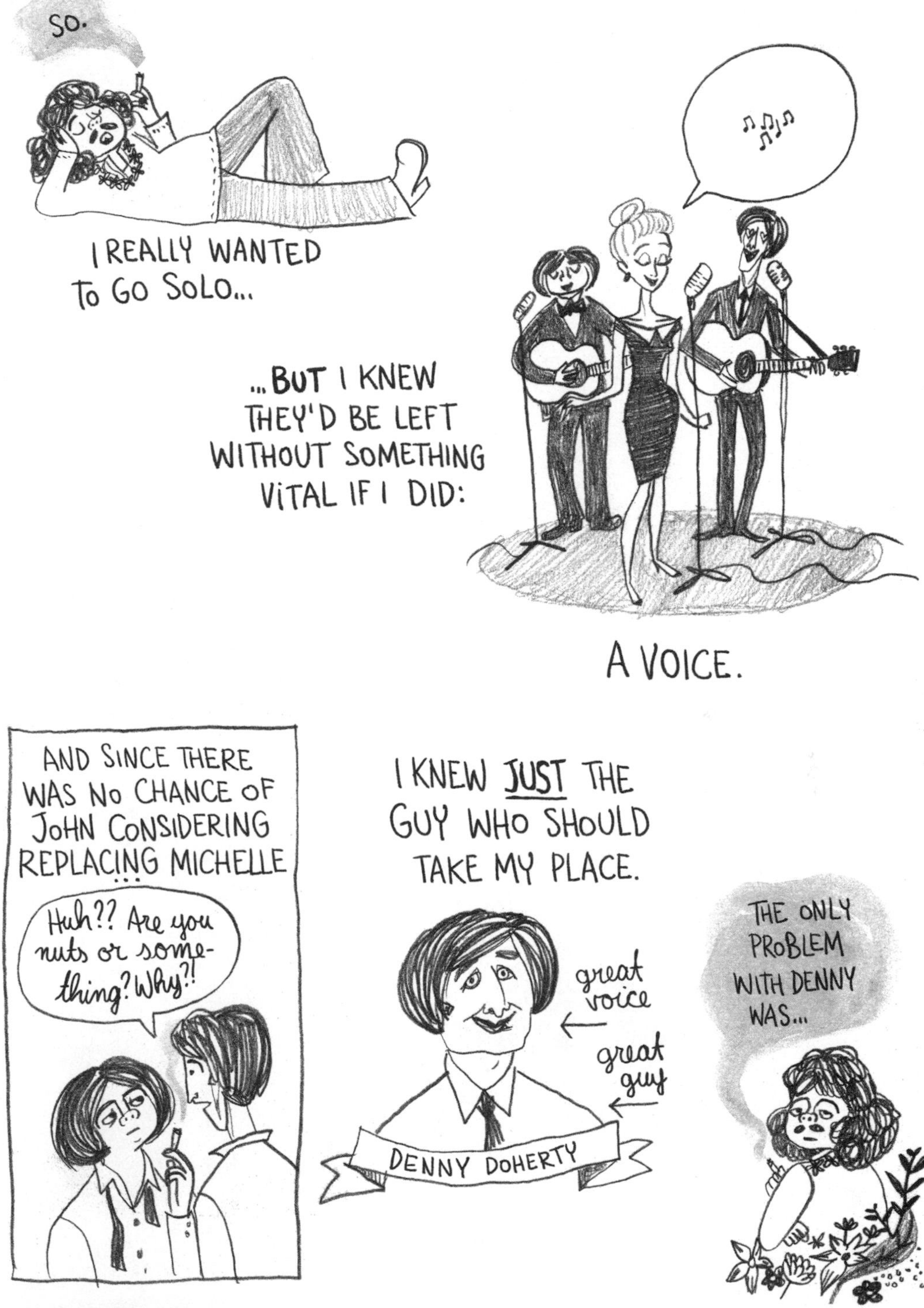
SO.
I REALLY WANTED TO GO SOLO...
...BUT I KNEW THEY'D BE LEFT WITHOUT SOMETHING VITAL IF I DID:
A VOICE.
AND SINCE THERE WAS NO CHANCE OF JOHN CONSIDERING REPLACING MICHELLE ...
Huh?? Are you nuts or something? Why?!
I KNEW JUST THE GUY WHO SHOULD TAKE MY PLACE.
great voice
great guy
DENNY DOHERTY
THE ONLY PROBLEM WITH DENNY WAS...

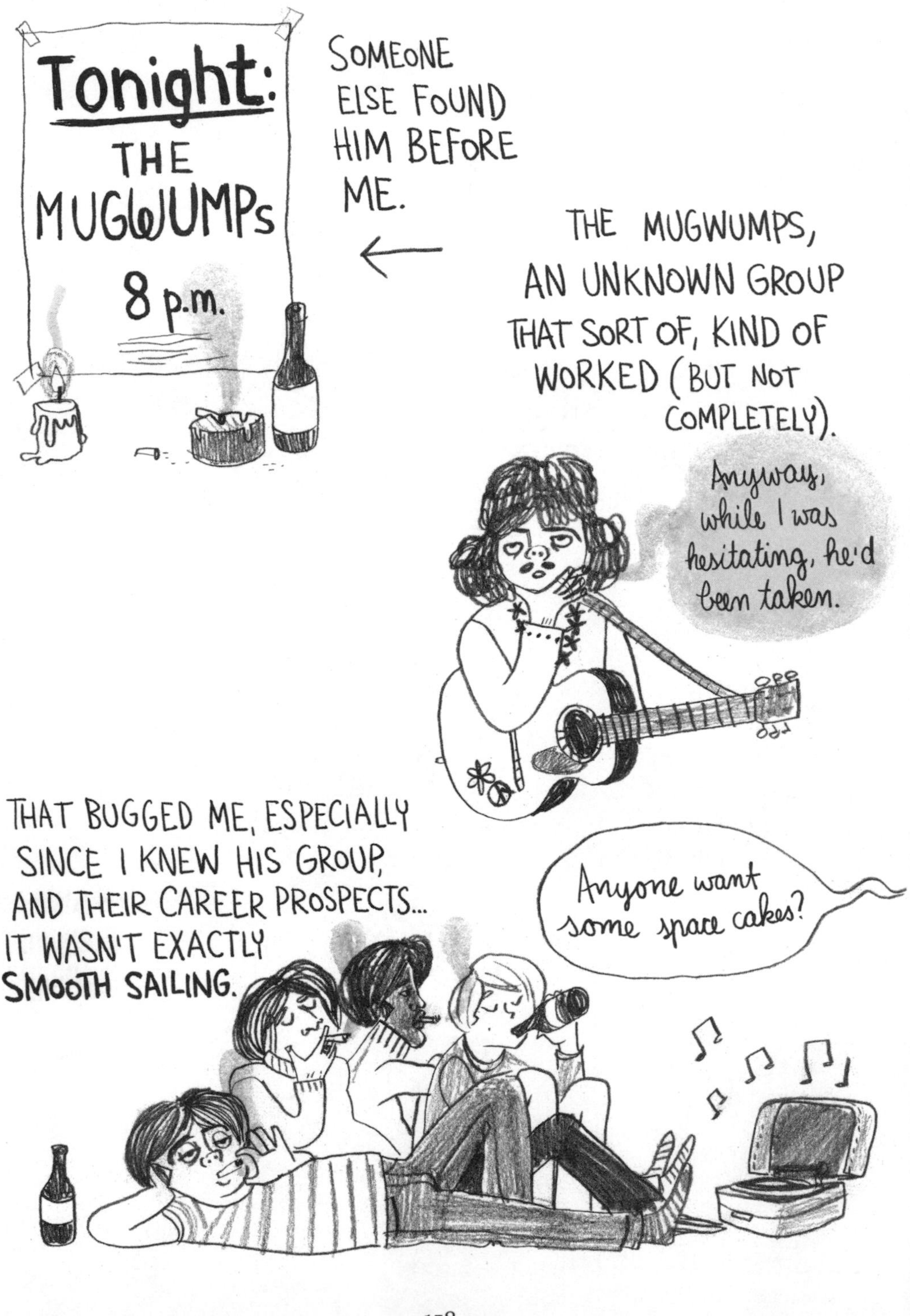
Tonight:
THE MUGWUMPs
8 p.m.
SOMEONE ELSE FOUND HIM BEFORE ME.
THE MUGWUMPS, AN UNKNOWN GROUP THAT SORT OF, KIND OF WORKED (BUT NOT COMPLETELY).
Anyway, while I was hesitating, he'd been taken.
THAT BUGGED ME, ESPECIALLY SINCE I KNEW HIS GROUP, AND THEIR CAREER PROSPECTS... IT WASN'T EXACTLY SMOOTH SAILING.
Anyone want some space cakes?

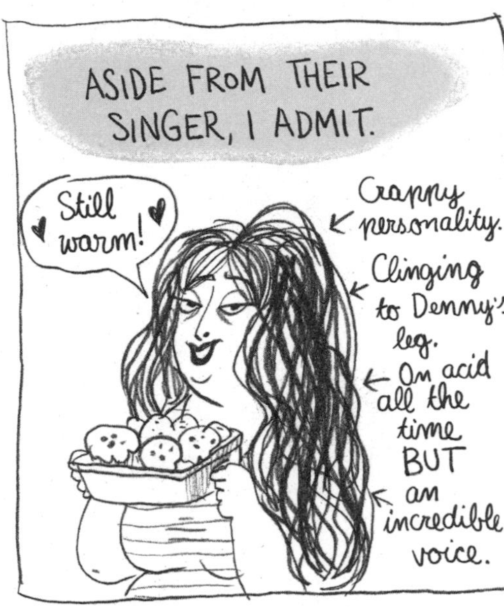
ASIDE FROM THEIR SINGER, I ADMIT.
Still warm!
Crappy personality.
Clinging to Denny's leg.
On acid all the time BUT an incredible voice.

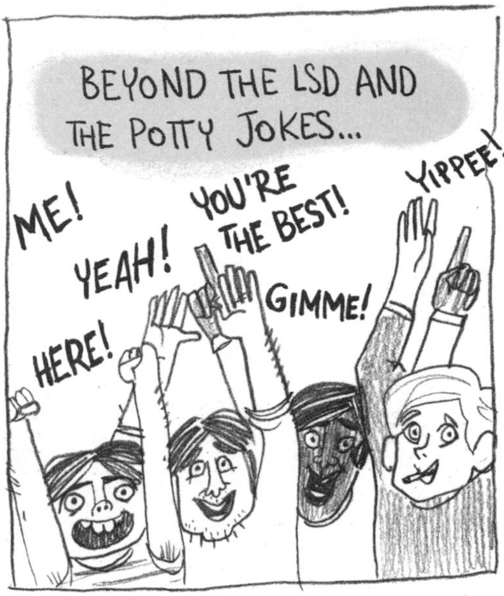
BEYOND THE LSD AND THE POTTY JOKES...
ME!
YEAH!
YOU'RE THE BEST!
YIPPEE!
GIMME!
HERE!

... THE MUGWUMPS WEREN'T OVERFLOWING WITH BIG PLANS FOR THE FUTURE.

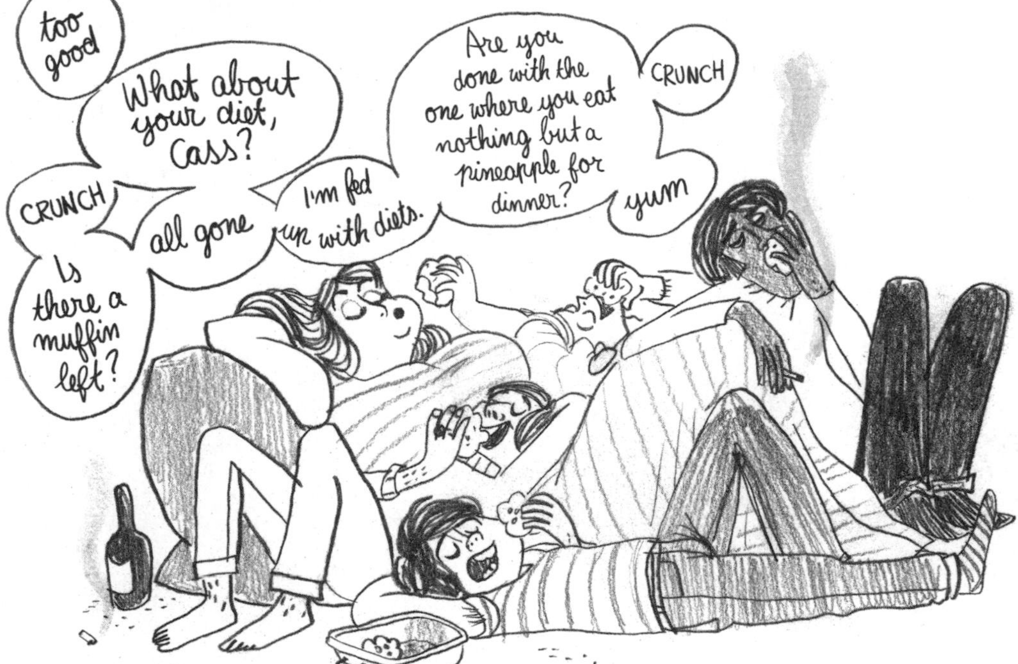
too good
What about your diet, Cass?
CRUNCH
Is there a muffin left?
all gone
I'm fed up with diets.
Are you done with the one where you eat nothing but a pineapple for dinner?
CRUNCH
yum

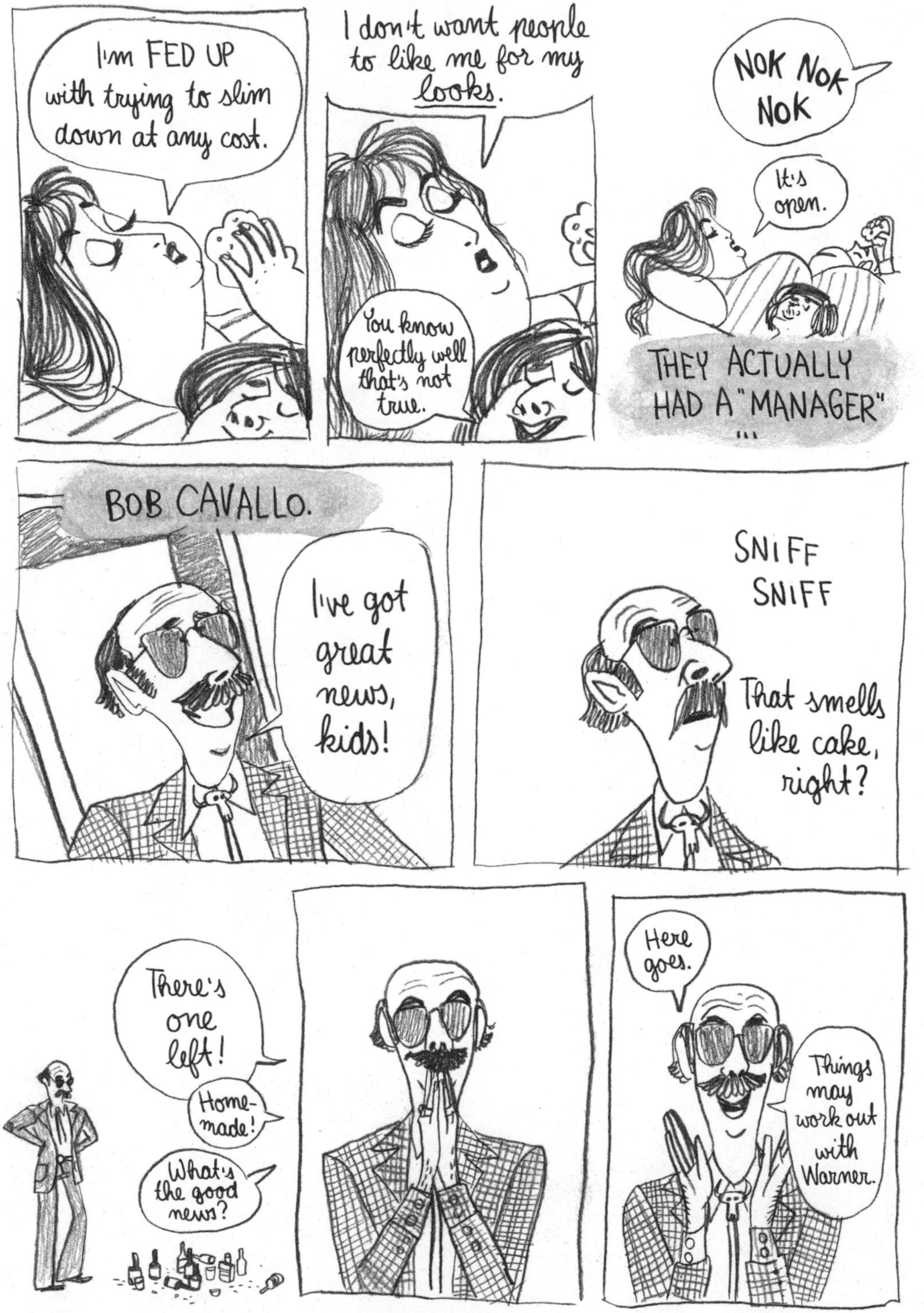
I'm FED UP with trying to slim down at any cost.
I don't want people to like me for my looks.
You know perfectly well that's not true.
NOK NOK NOK
It's open.
THEY ACTUALLY HAD A "MANAGER"...
BOB CAVALLO.
I've got great news, kids!
SNIFF SNIFF
That smells like cake, right?
There's one left!
Home-made!
What's the good news?
Here goes.
Things may work out with Warner.

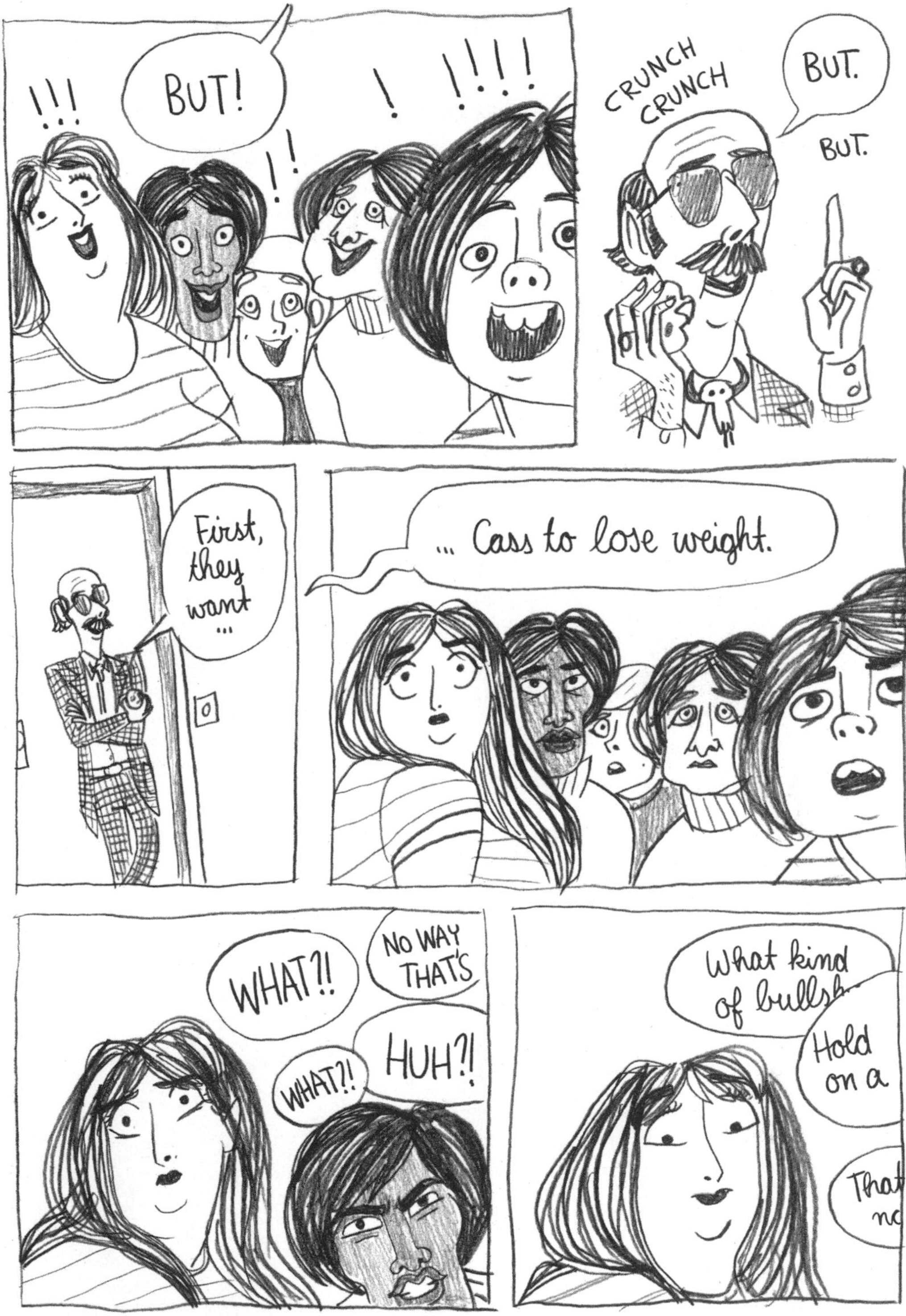
!!!
BUT!
!!
! !!!!
CRUNCH
CRUNCH
BUT.
BUT.
First, they want ...
... Cass to lose weight.
WHAT?!
NO WAY THAT'S
WHAT?!
HUH?!
What kind of bullsh...
Hold on a
That

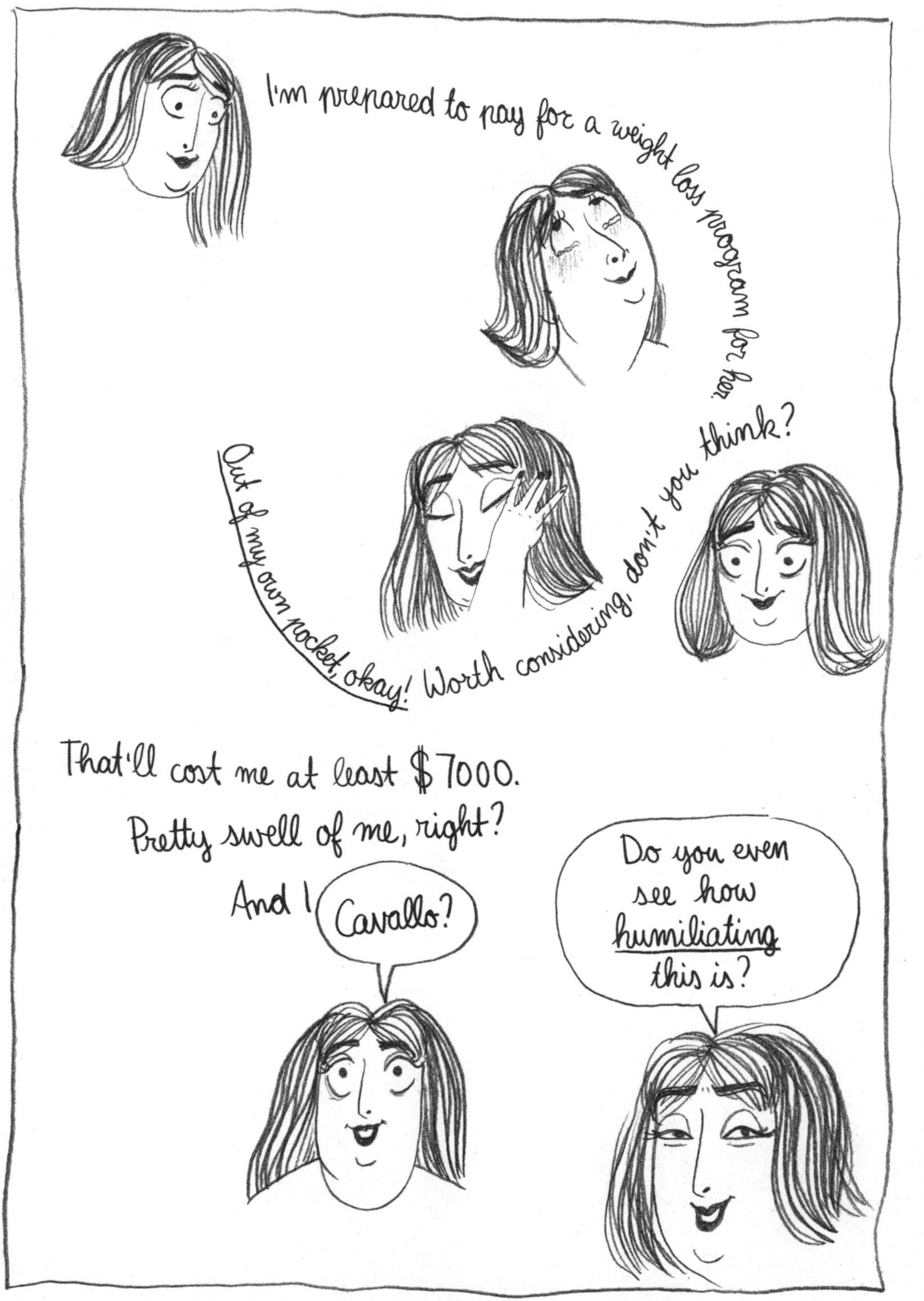

I'm prepared to pay for a weight loss program for her.
Out of my own pocket, okay! Worth considering, don't you think?
That'll cost me at least $7000.
Pretty swell of me, right?
And I
Cavallo?
Do you even see how humiliating this is?

Do you _realize_ that you're saying...

... in front of my group...

... that if we don't get famous...

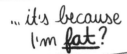

... it's because I'm _fat_?

That's garbage! They can go fuck themselves!

Cass is perfect the way she is!

Exact-ly!

And she's the best singer there is!

We don't give a shit! We don't need her to be _beautiful_!

IN SHORT, THE MUGWUMPS WERE HUGELY BUMMED OUT.

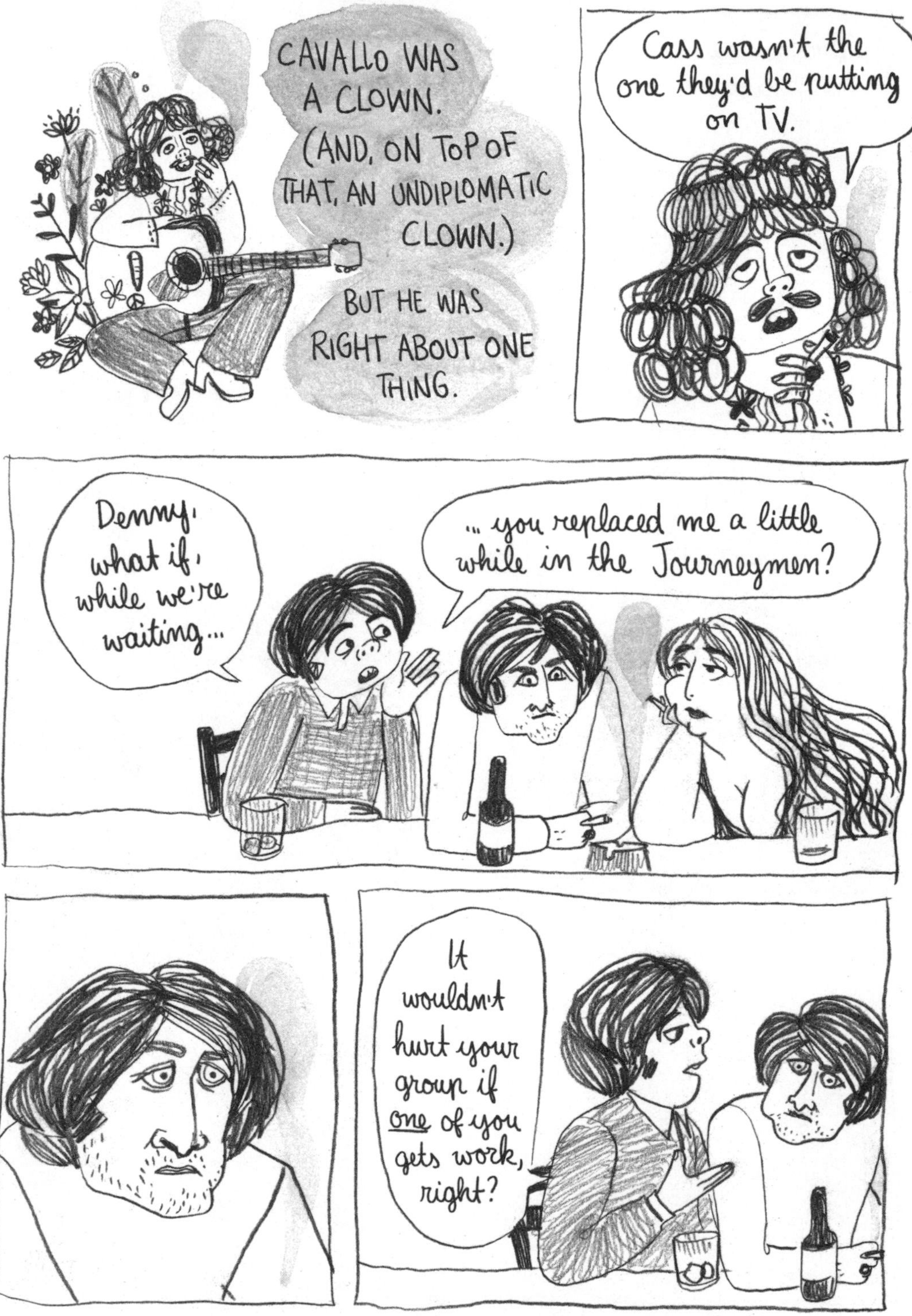
CAVALLO WAS A CLOWN. (AND, ON TOP OF THAT, AN UNDIPLOMATIC CLOWN.)
BUT HE WAS RIGHT ABOUT ONE THING.
Cass wasn't the one they'd be putting on TV.
Denny, what if, while we're waiting...
... you replaced me a little while in the Journeymen?
It wouldn't hurt your group if one of you gets work, right?

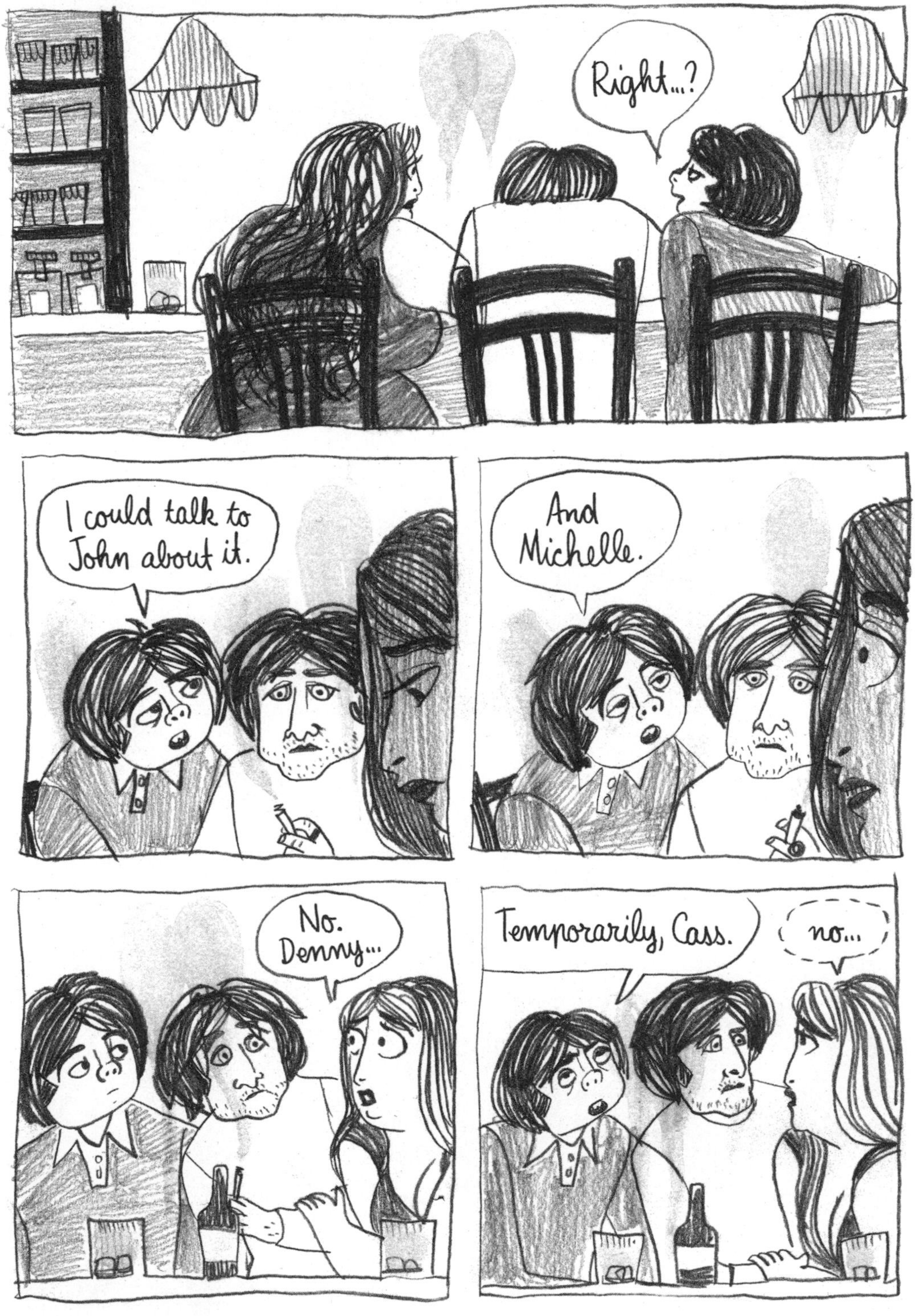
Right...?
I could talk to John about it.
And Michelle.
No. Denny...
Temporarily, Cass.
no...

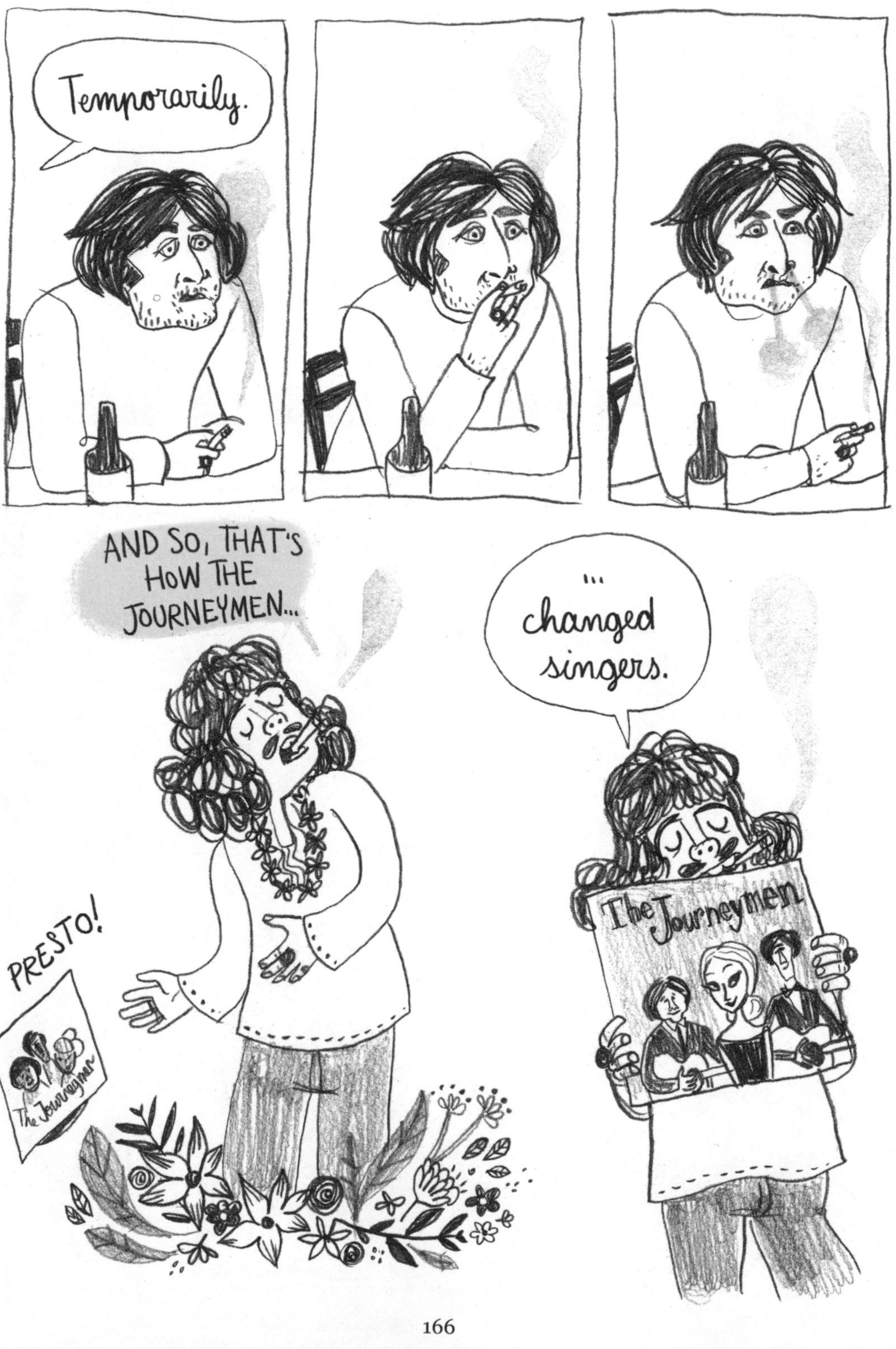
Temporarily.
AND SO, THAT'S HOW THE JOURNEYMEN...
... changed singers.
PRESTO!
The Journeymen

13-Denny

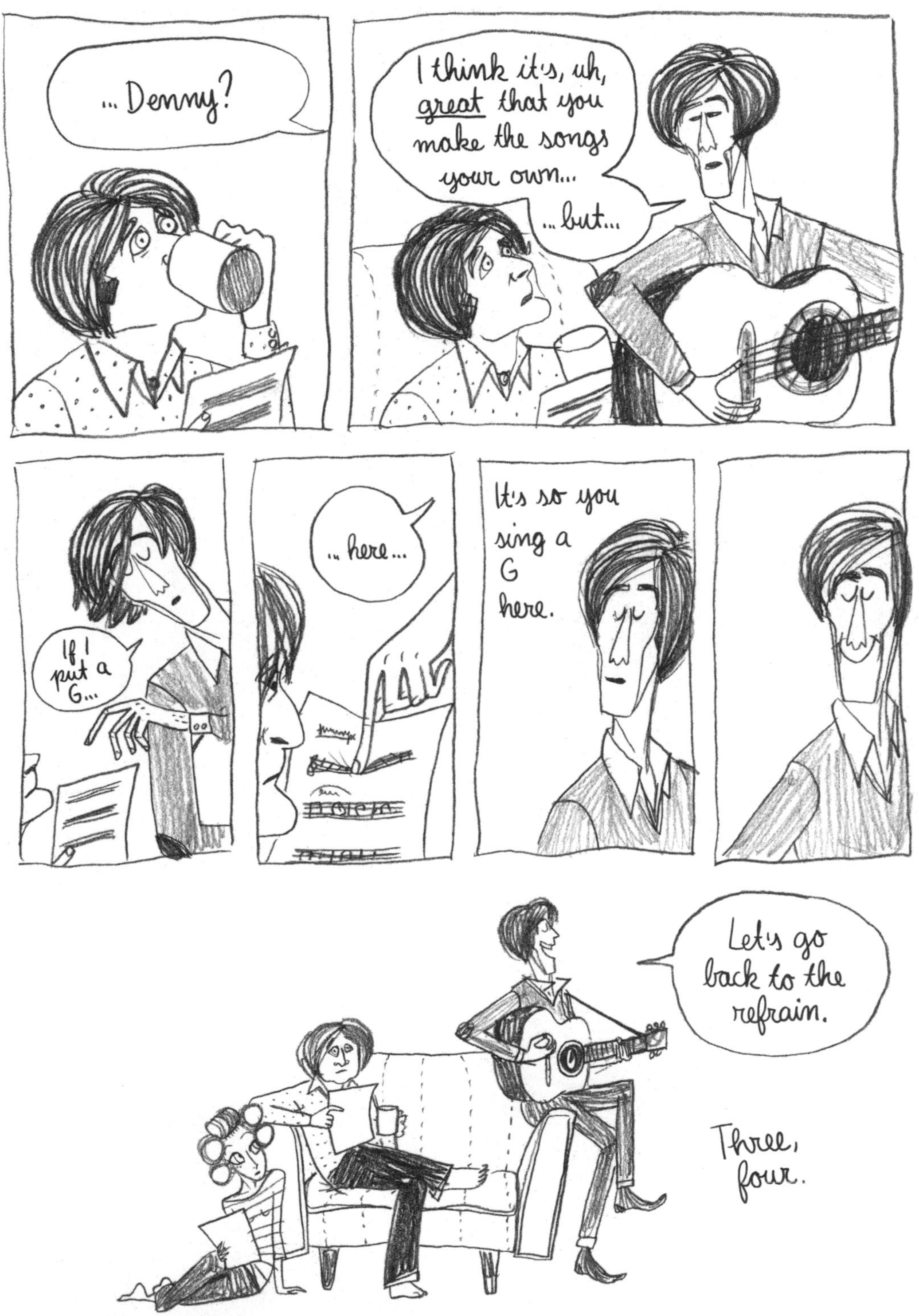
... Denny?
I think it's, uh, great that you make the songs your own...
... but...
If I put a G...
... here...
It's so you sing a G here.
Let's go back to the refrain.
Three, four.

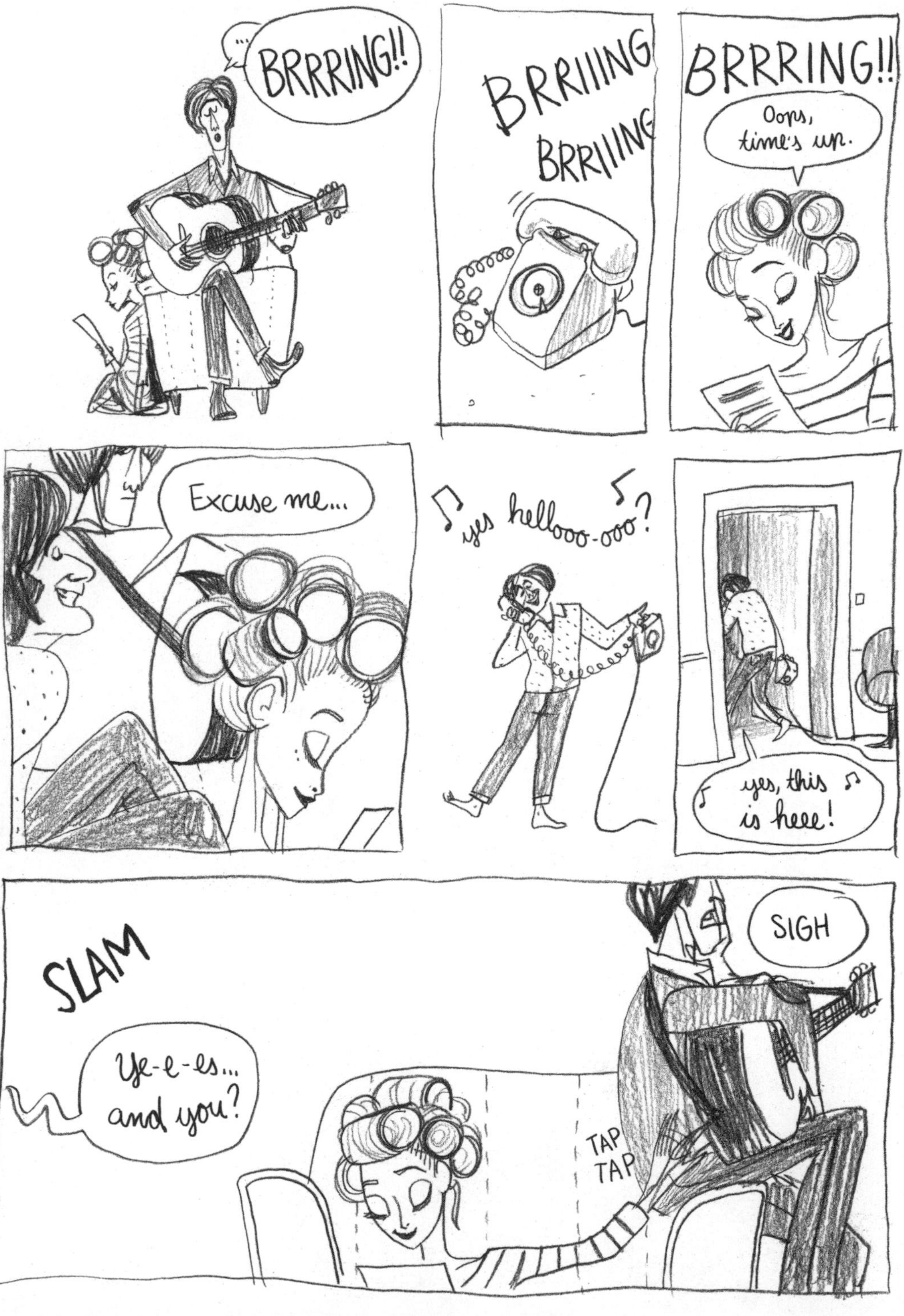
...
BRRRING!!
BRRIIING
BRRIIING
BRRRING!!
Oops, time's up.
Excuse me...
yes hellooo-ooo?
yes, this is heee!
SLAM
SIGH
Ye-e-es... and you?
TAP TAP

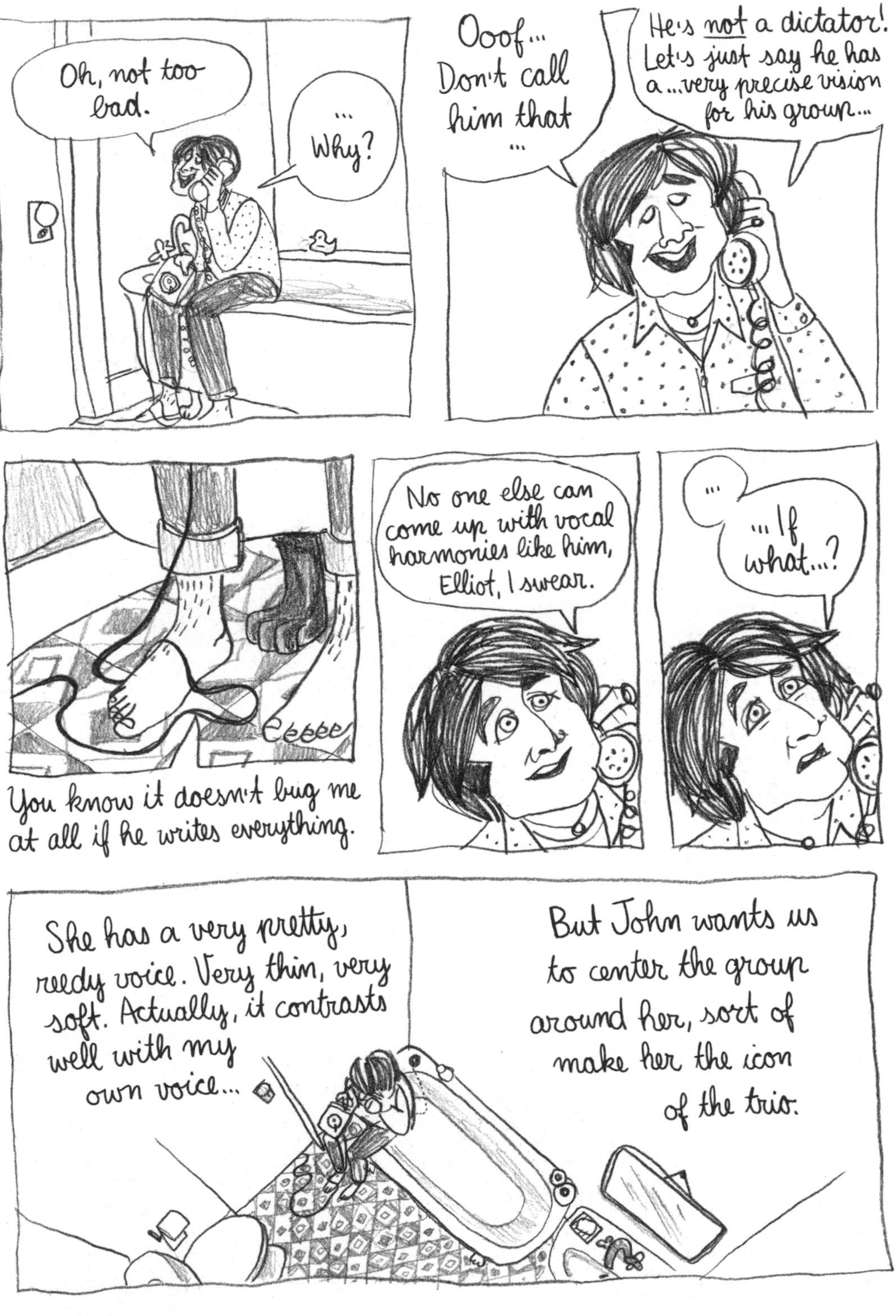

Oh, not too bad.
... Why?
Ooof... Don't call him that ...
He's not a dictator! Let's just say he has a... very precise vision for his group...
Eeeee
You know it doesn't bug me at all if he writes everything.
No one else can come up with vocal harmonies like him, Elliot, I swear.
...
... If what...?
She has a very pretty, reedy voice. Very thin, very soft. Actually, it contrasts well with my own voice...
But John wants us to center the group around her, sort of make her the icon of the trio.

Capitalize on her beauty.

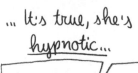

... It's true, she's hypnotic...

Yeah, yeah. I get it.

Okay, I'm fed up with hearing about your Michelle, Denny.

I want to meet her.

You'll be surprised, you know.

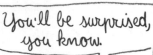

She's not as superficial as you seem to think.

She lost her mother when she was very young. She's lived through some hard times...

I can hear you making a face, you know.

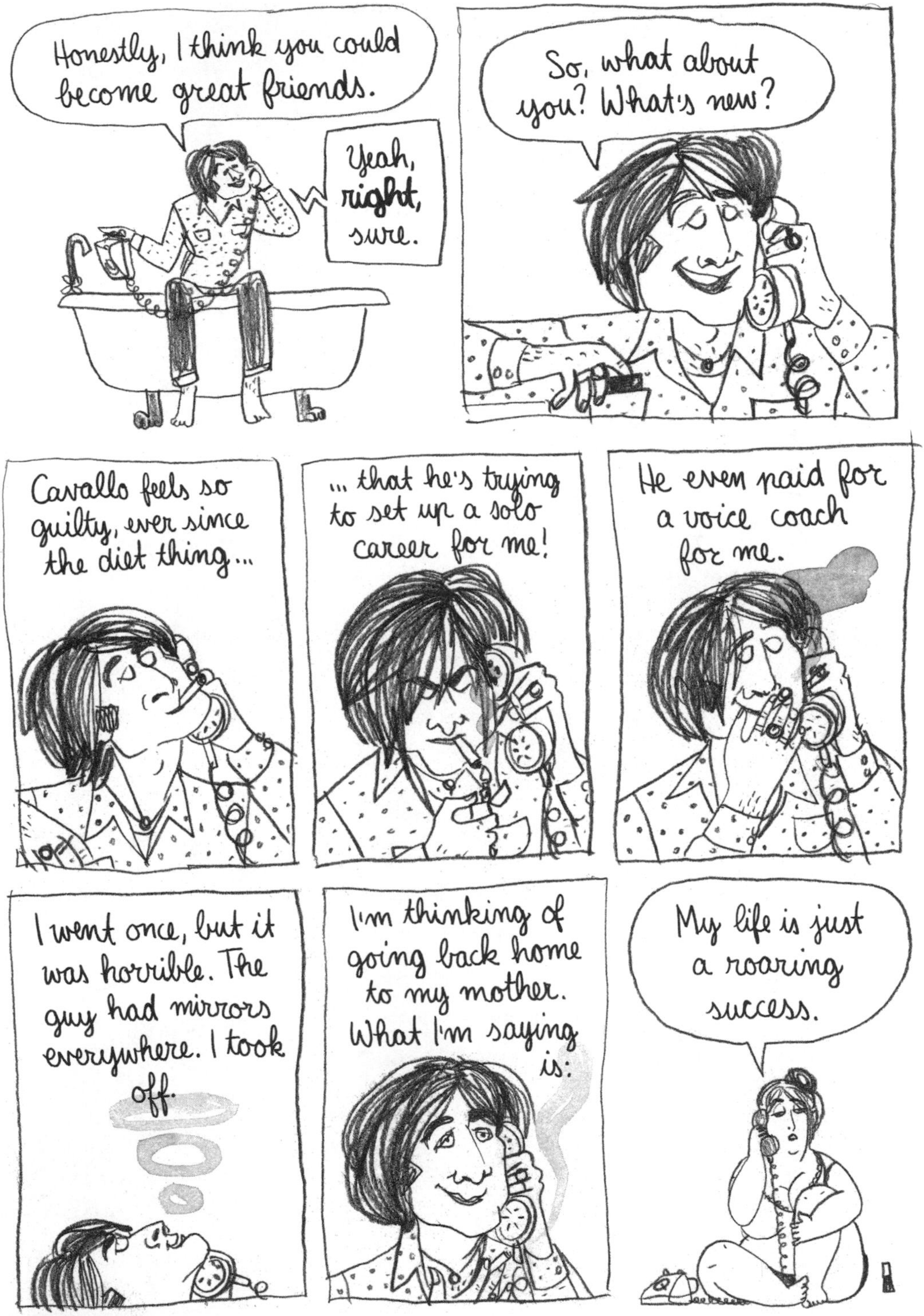
Honestly, I think you could become great friends.
Yeah, right, sure.
So, what about you? What's new?
Cavallo feels so guilty, ever since the diet thing...
... that he's trying to set up a solo career for me!
He even paid for a voice coach for me.
I went once, but it was horrible. The guy had mirrors everywhere. I took off.
I'm thinking of going back home to my mother. What I'm saying is:
My life is just a roaring success.

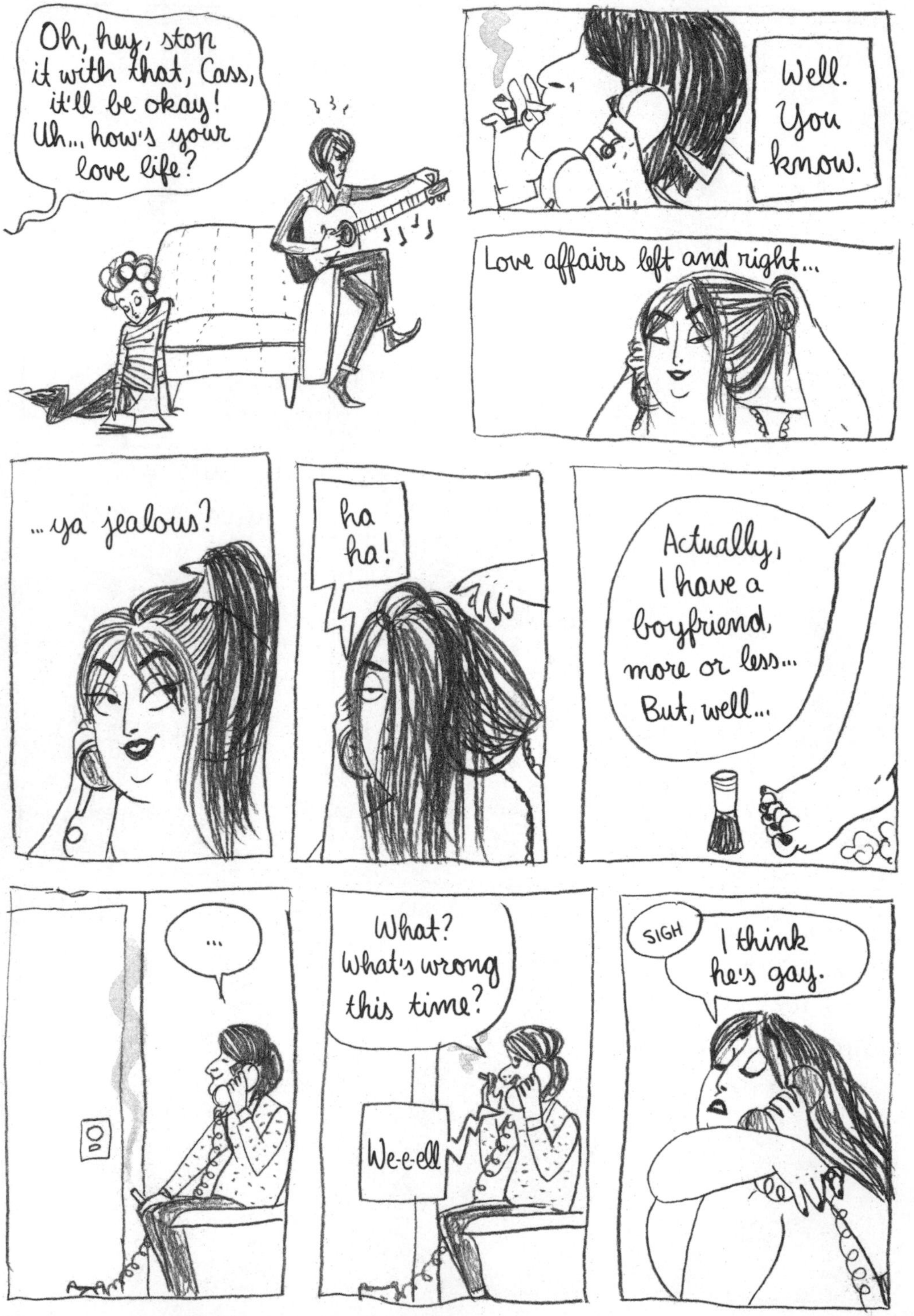
Oh, hey, stop it with that, Cass, it'll be okay! Uh..., how's your love life?
Well. You know.
Love affairs left and right...
... ya jealous?
ha ha!
Actually, I have a boyfriend, more or less... But, well...
...
What? What's wrong this time?
We-e-ell
SIGH
I think he's gay.

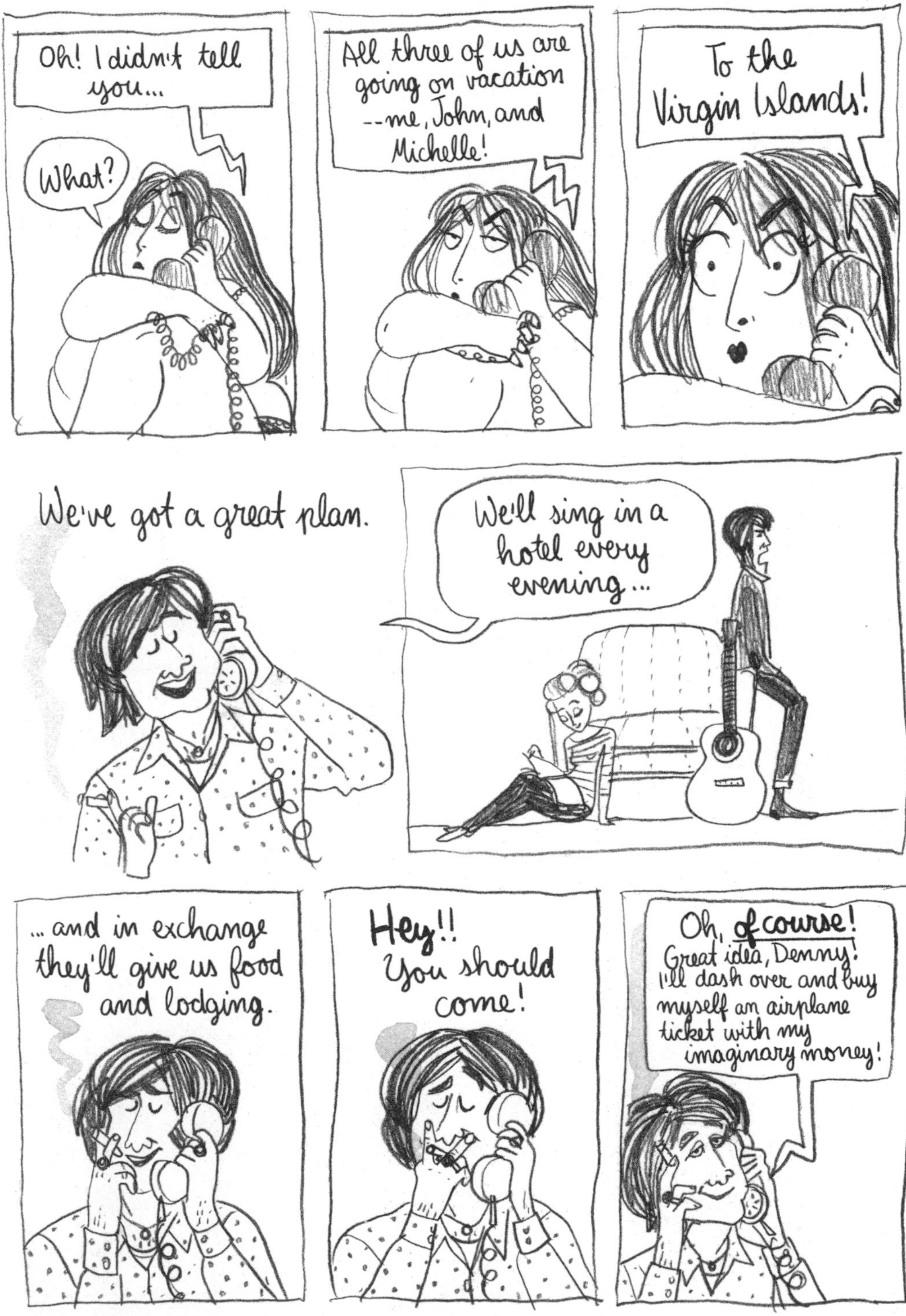

Oh! I didn't tell you...
What?
All three of us are going on vacation --me, John, and Michelle!
To the Virgin Islands!
We've got a great plan.
We'll sing in a hotel every evening...
... and in exchange they'll give us food and lodging.
Hey!! You should come!
Oh, of course! Great idea, Denny! I'll dash over and buy myself an airplane ticket with my imaginary money!

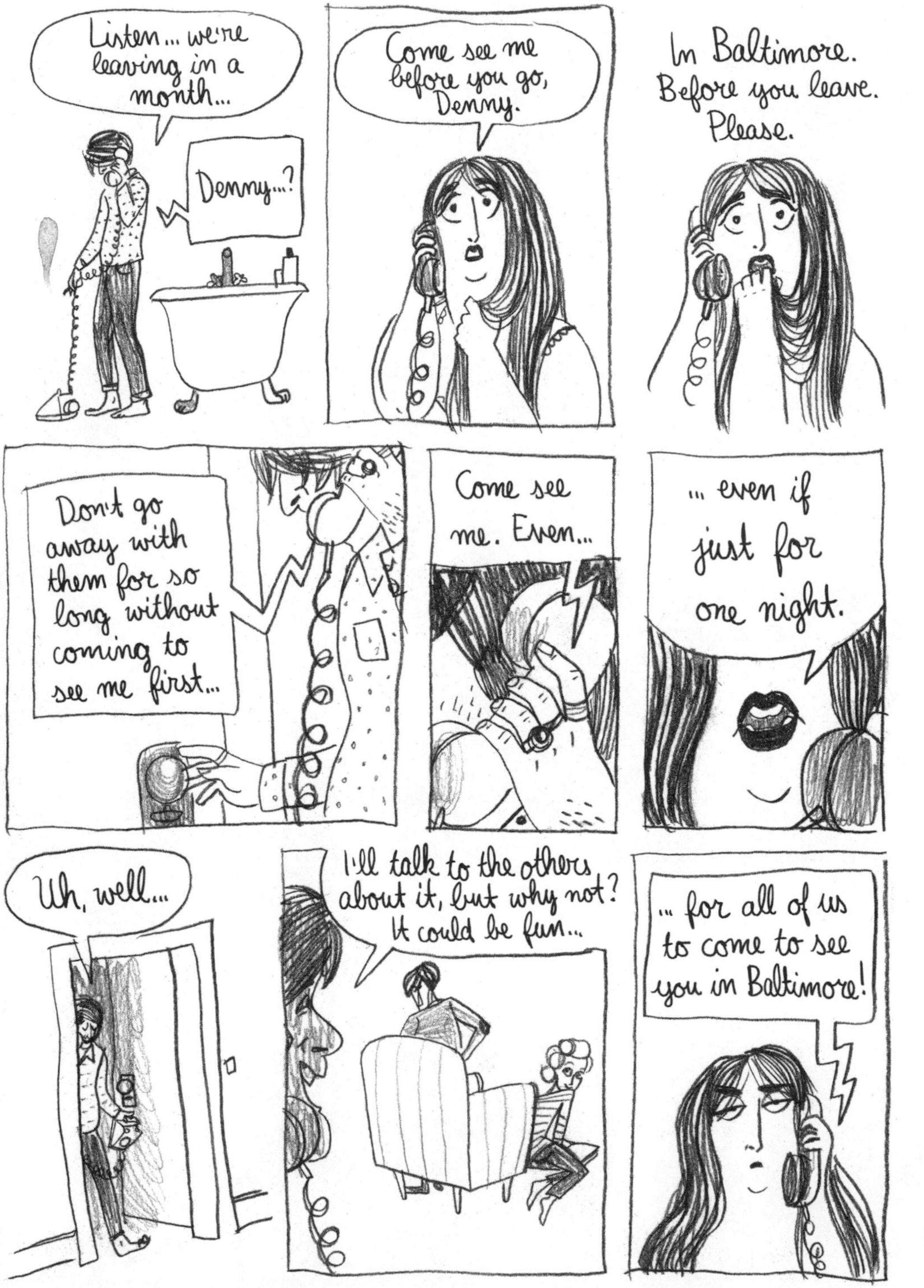
Listen... we're leaving in a month...
Denny...?
Come see me before you go, Denny.
In Baltimore. Before you leave. Please.
Don't go away with them for so long without coming to see me first...
Come see me. Even...
... even if just for one night.
Uh, well...
I'll talk to the others about it, but why not? It could be fun...
... for all of us to come to see you in Baltimore!

14-Bess

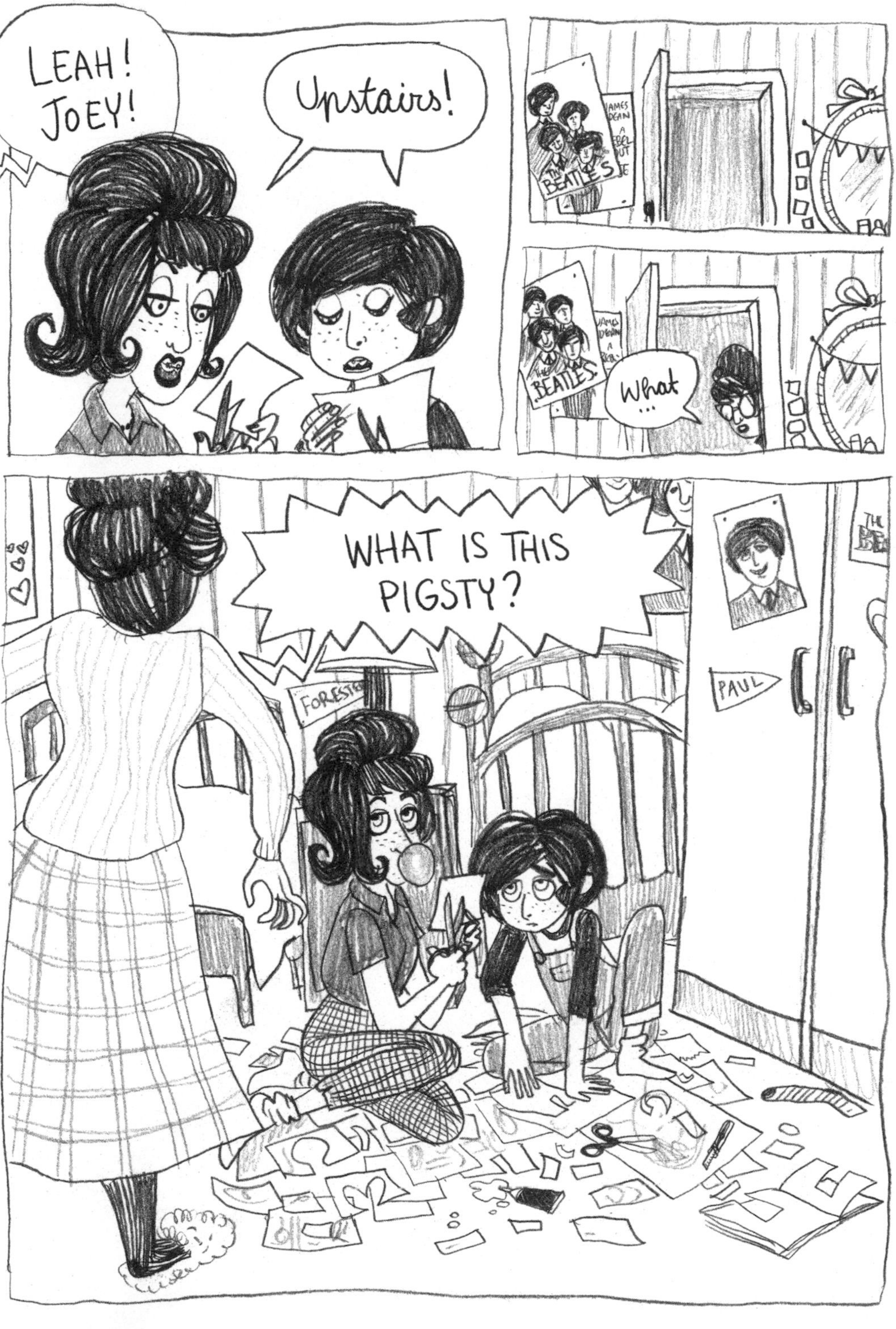
LEAH! JOEY!
Upstairs!
THE BEATLES
JAMES DEAN
THE BEATLES
What ...
WHAT IS THIS PIGSTY?
FOREST
PAUL

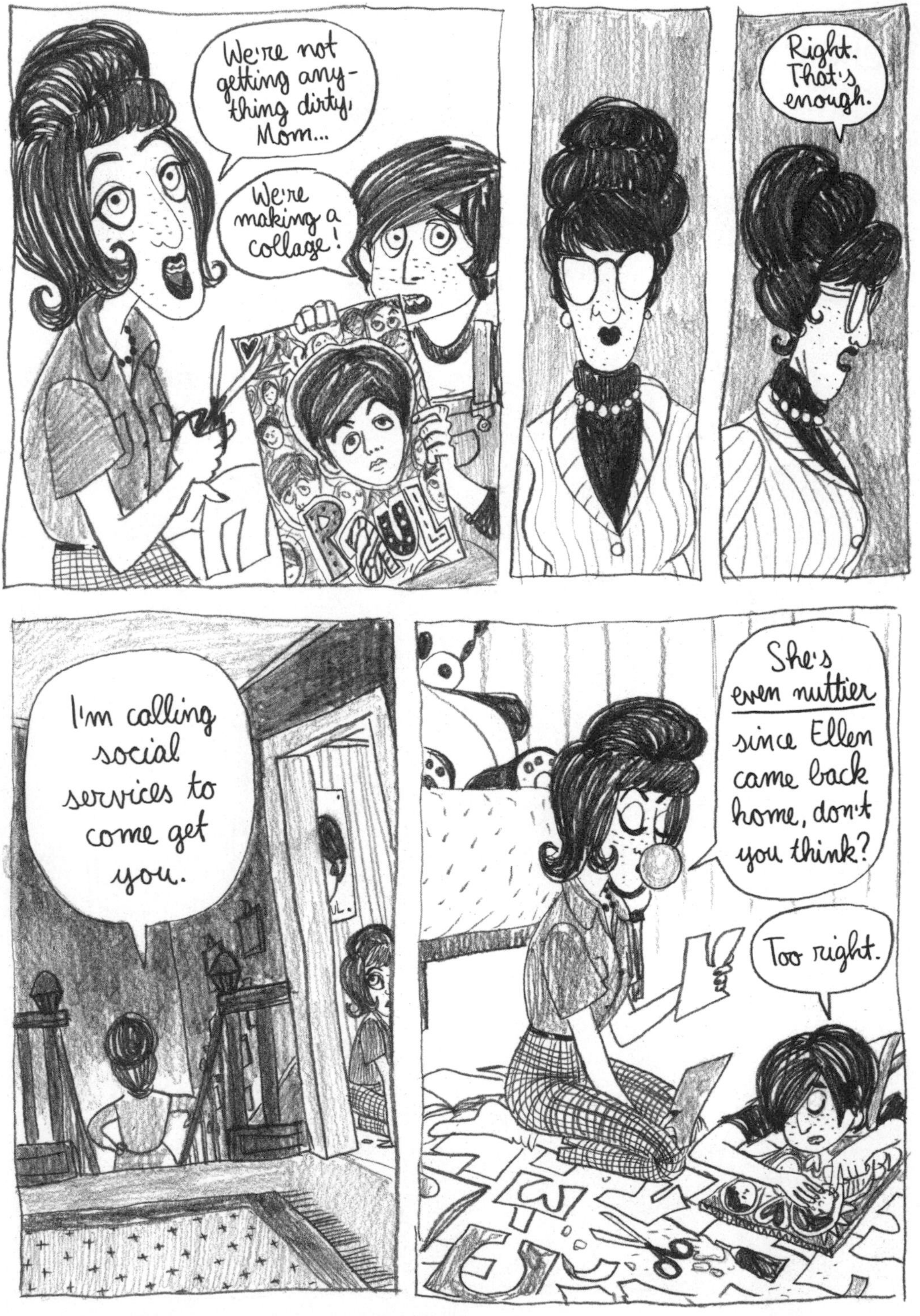

We're not getting anything dirty, Mom...
We're making a collage!
PAUL
Right. That's enough.
I'm calling social services to come get you.
She's even nuttier since Ellen came back home, don't you think?
Too right.

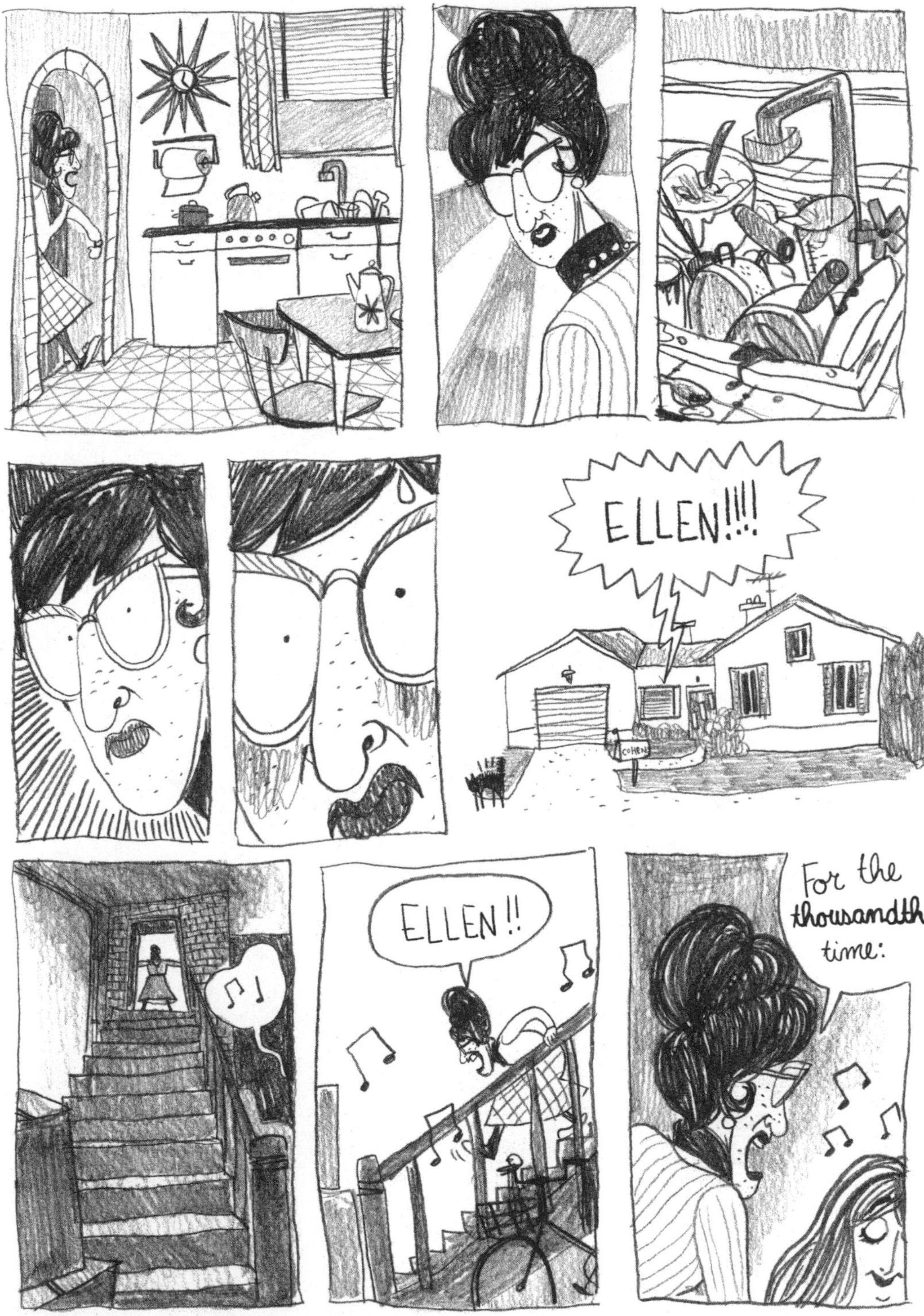
ELLEN!!!!
COHEN
ELLEN!!
For the thousandth time:

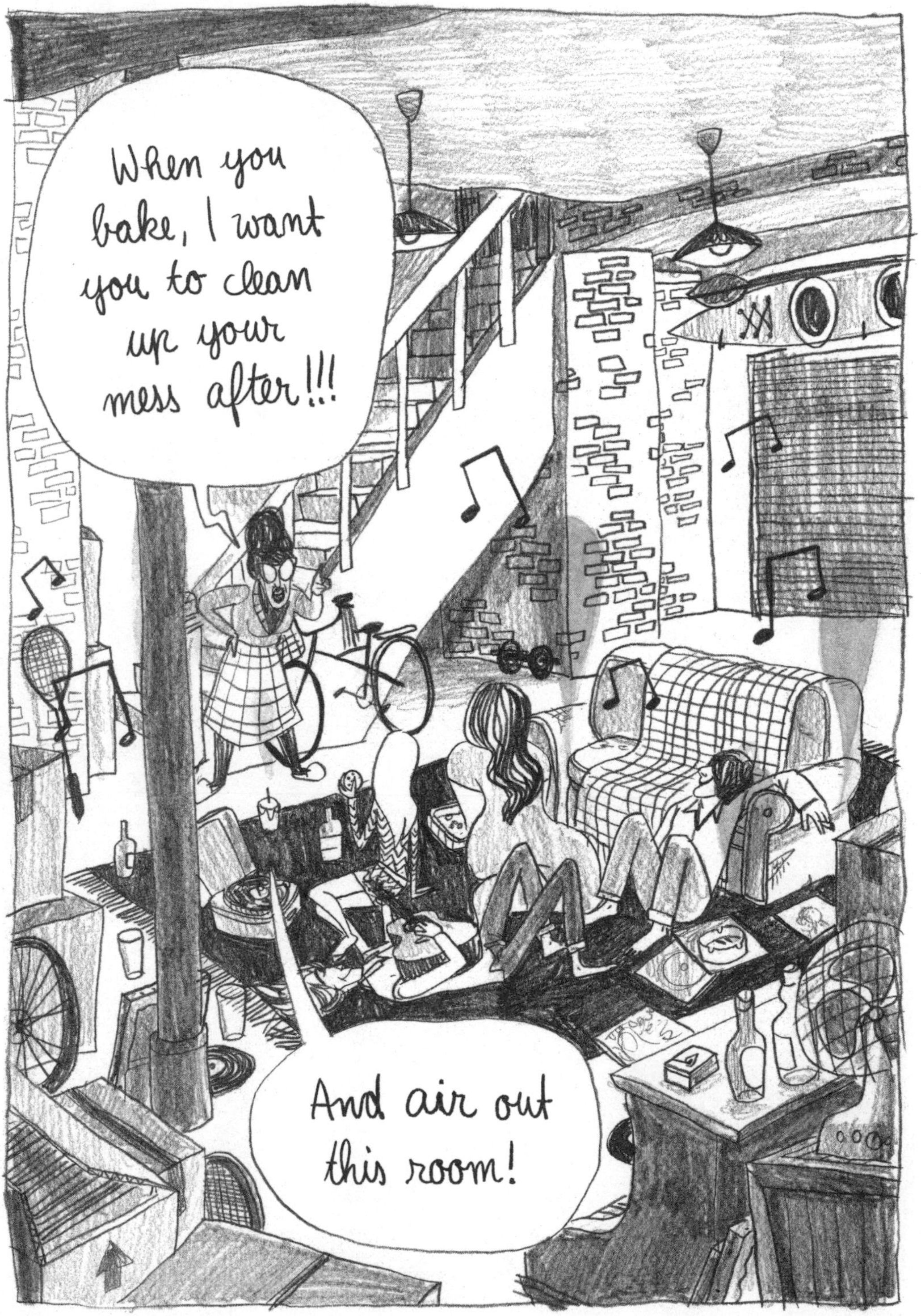
When you bake, I want you to clean up your mess after!!!
And air out this room!

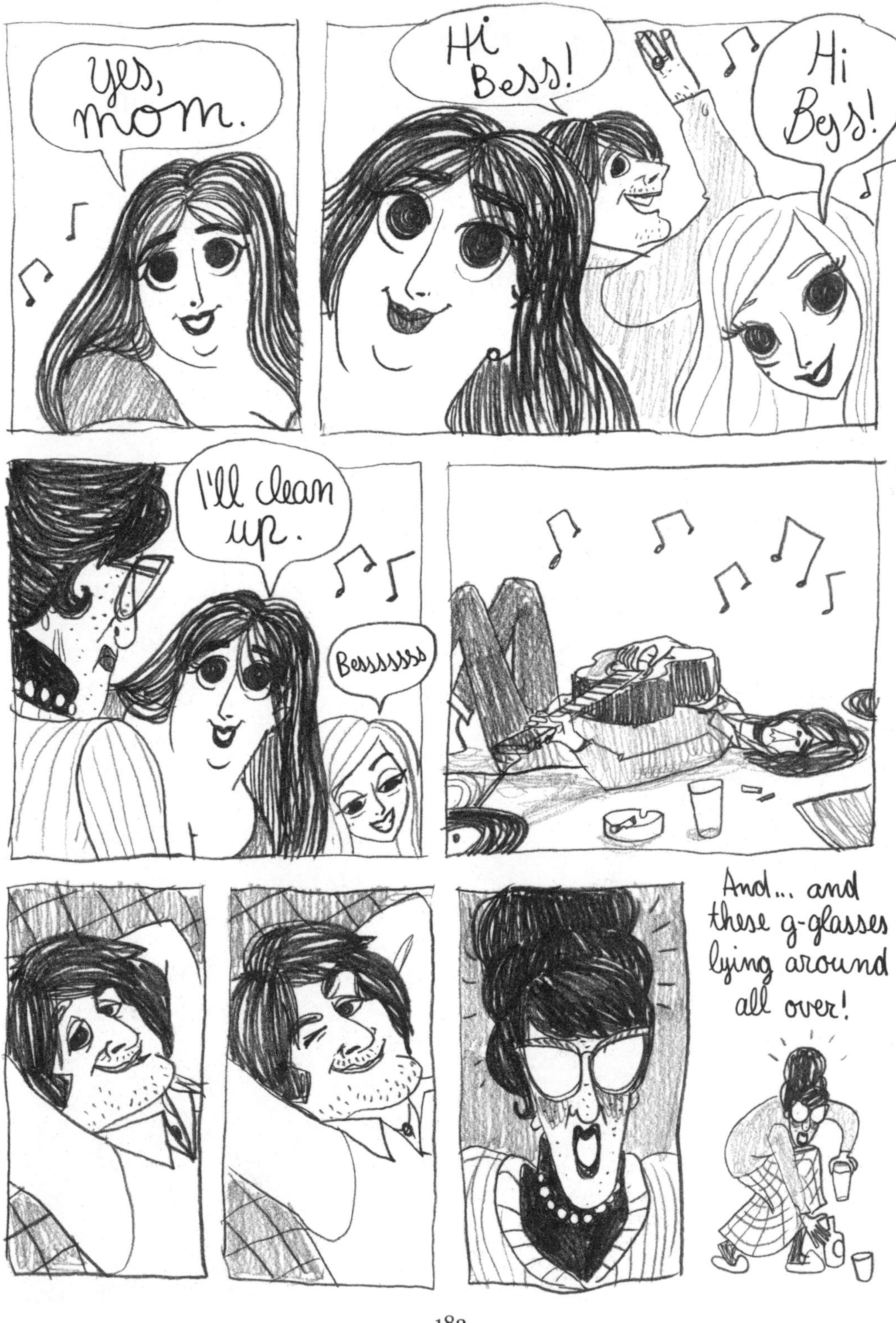
Yes, mom.
Hi Bess!
Hi Bess!
I'll clean up.
Bessssss
And... and these g-glasses lying around all over!

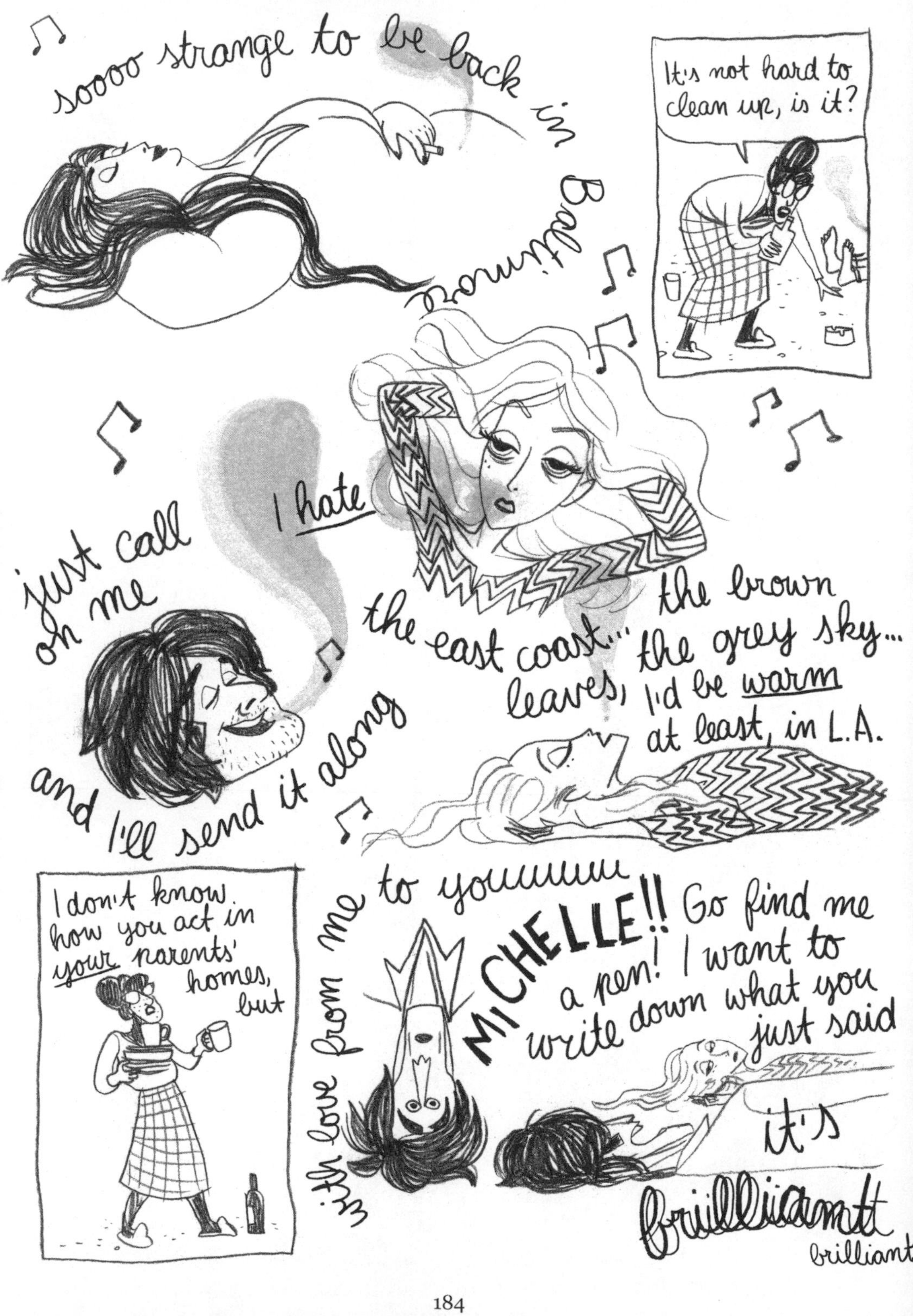

sooooo strange to be back in Baltimore
It's not hard to clean up, is it?
just call on me
I hate
the east coast... the brown leaves, the grey sky... I'd be warm at least, in L.A.
and I'll send it along
with love from me to youuuuuu
I don't know how you act in your parents' homes, but
MICHELLE!! Go find me a pen! I want to write down what you just said
it's
brilliant
brilliant

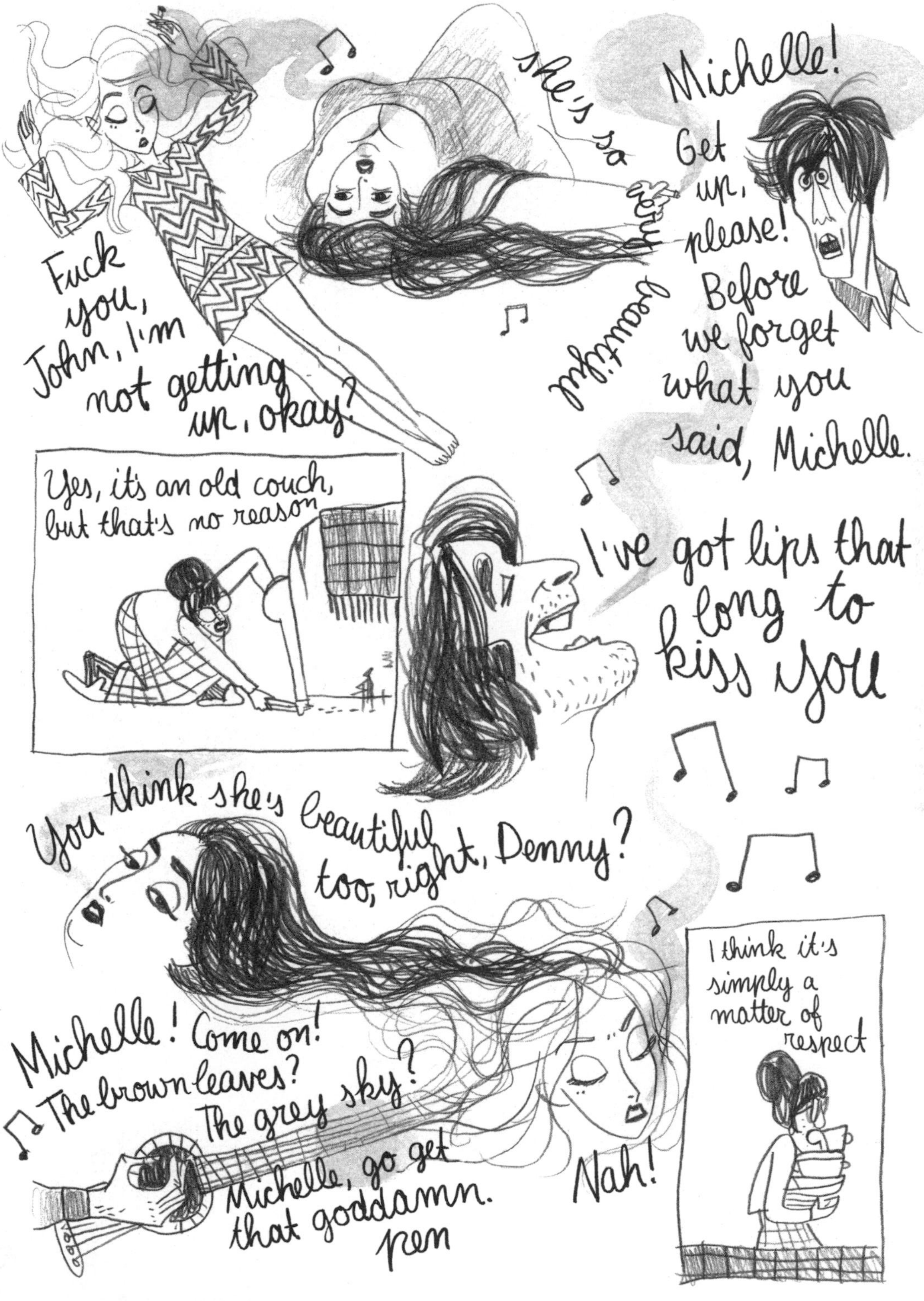
Fuck you, John, I'm not getting up, okay?
She's so very beautiful
Michelle!
Get up, please! Before we forget what you said, Michelle.
Yes, it's an old couch, but that's no reason
I've got lips that long to kiss you
You think she's beautiful too, right, Denny?
Michelle! Come on! The brown leaves? The grey sky?
Michelle, go get that goddamn. pen
Nah!
I think it's simply a matter of respect

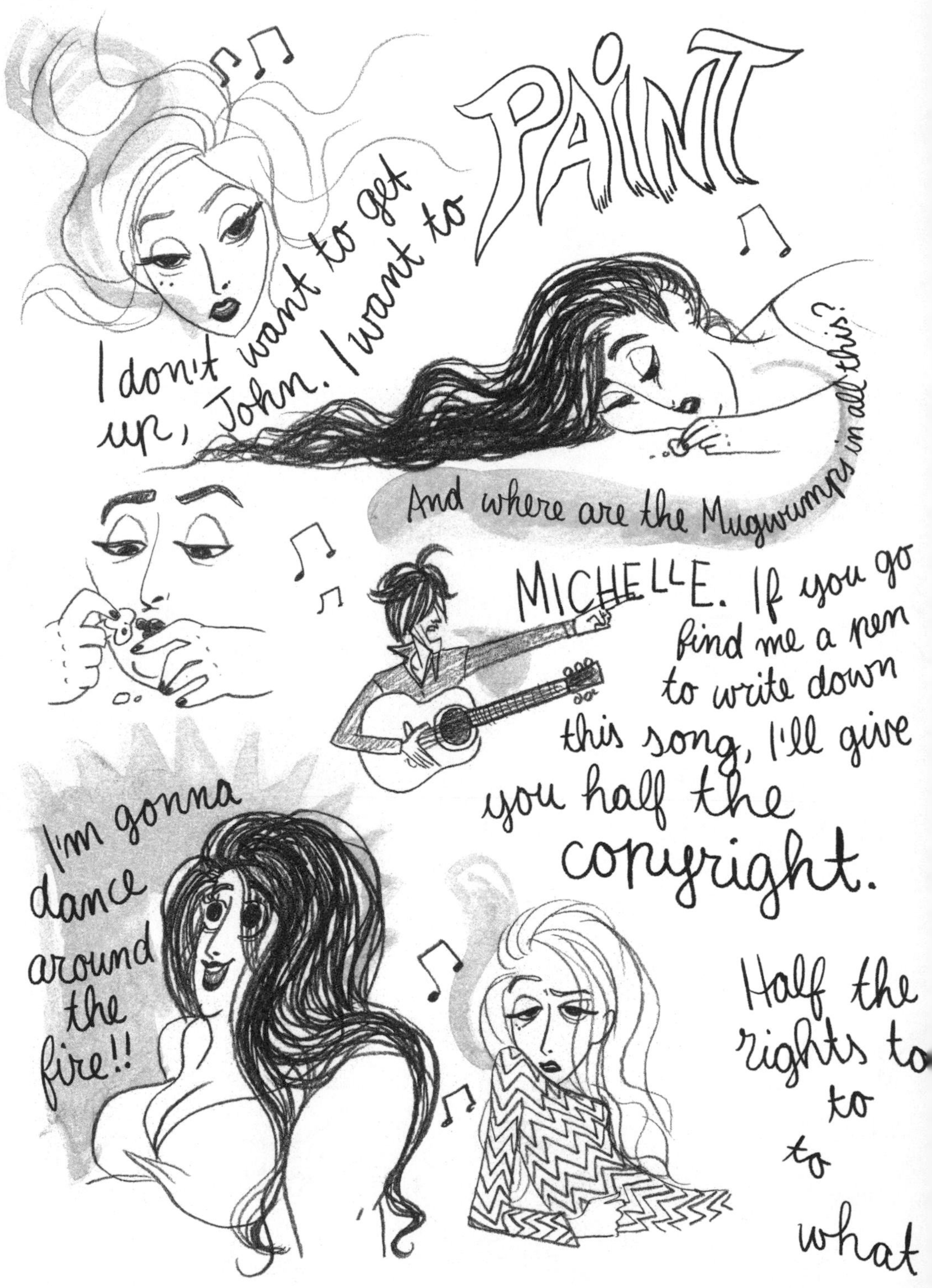

PAINT
I don't want to get up, John. I want to
And where are the Mugwumps in all this?
MICHELLE. If you go find me a pen to write down this song, I'll give you half the copyright.
I'm gonna dance around the fire!!
Half the rights to to to what

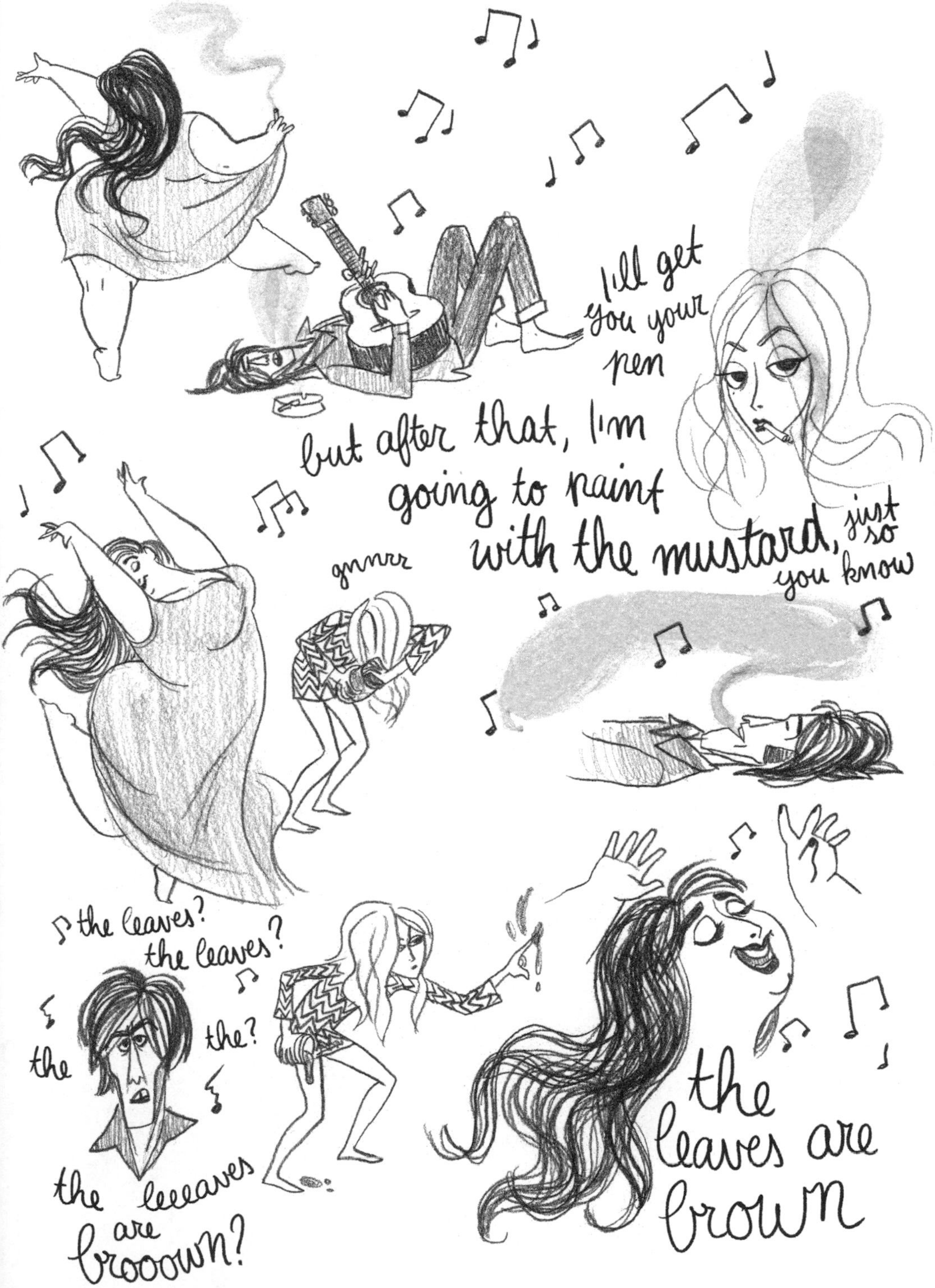

I'll get you your pen
but after that, I'm going to paint with the mustard, just so you know
gnnrr
the leaves? the leaves?
the
the?
the leeeaves are brooown?
the leaves are brown

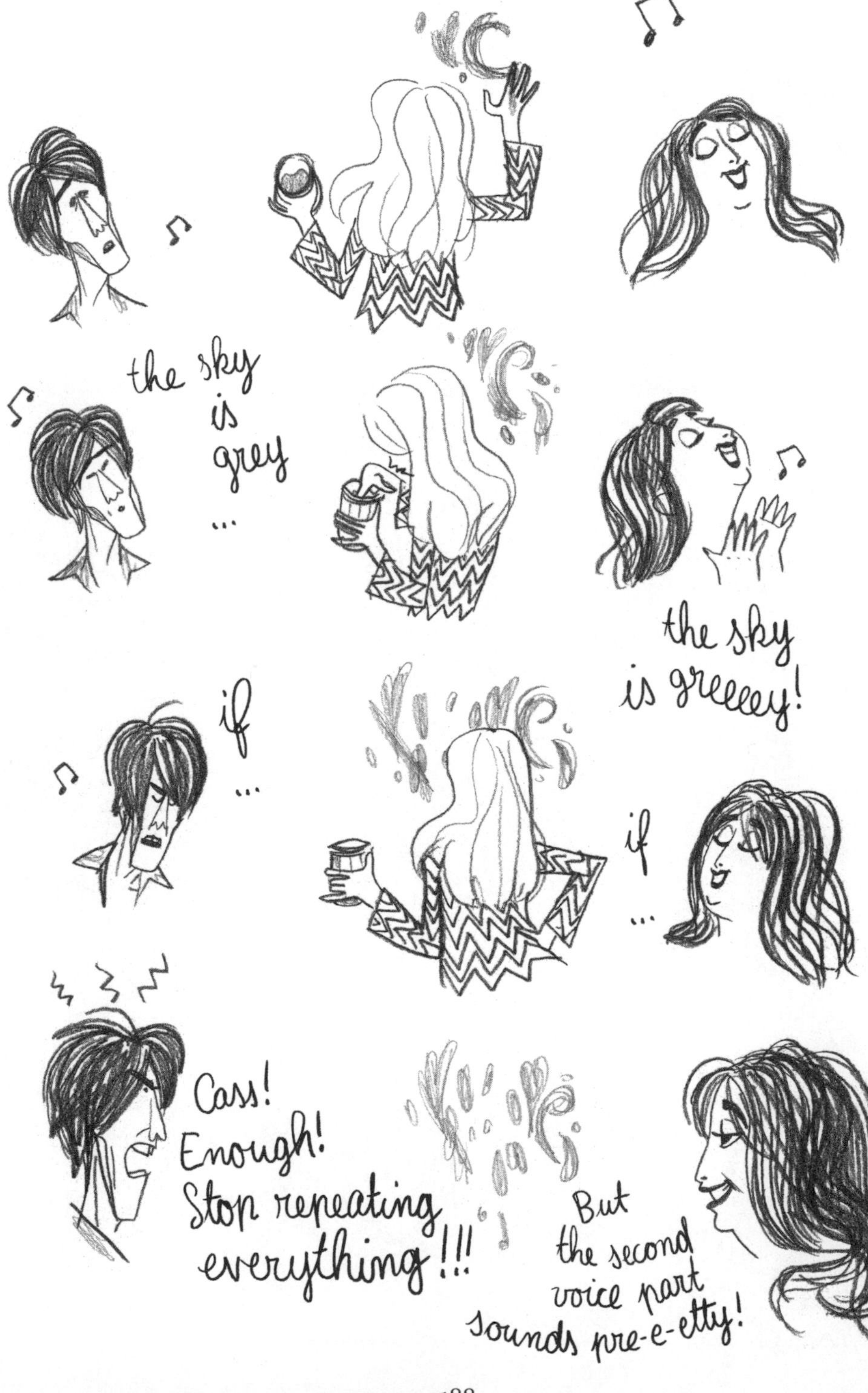

the sky is grey ...
the sky is greeeey!
if ...
if ...
Cass! Enough! Stop repeating everything!!!
But the second voice part sounds pre-e-etty!

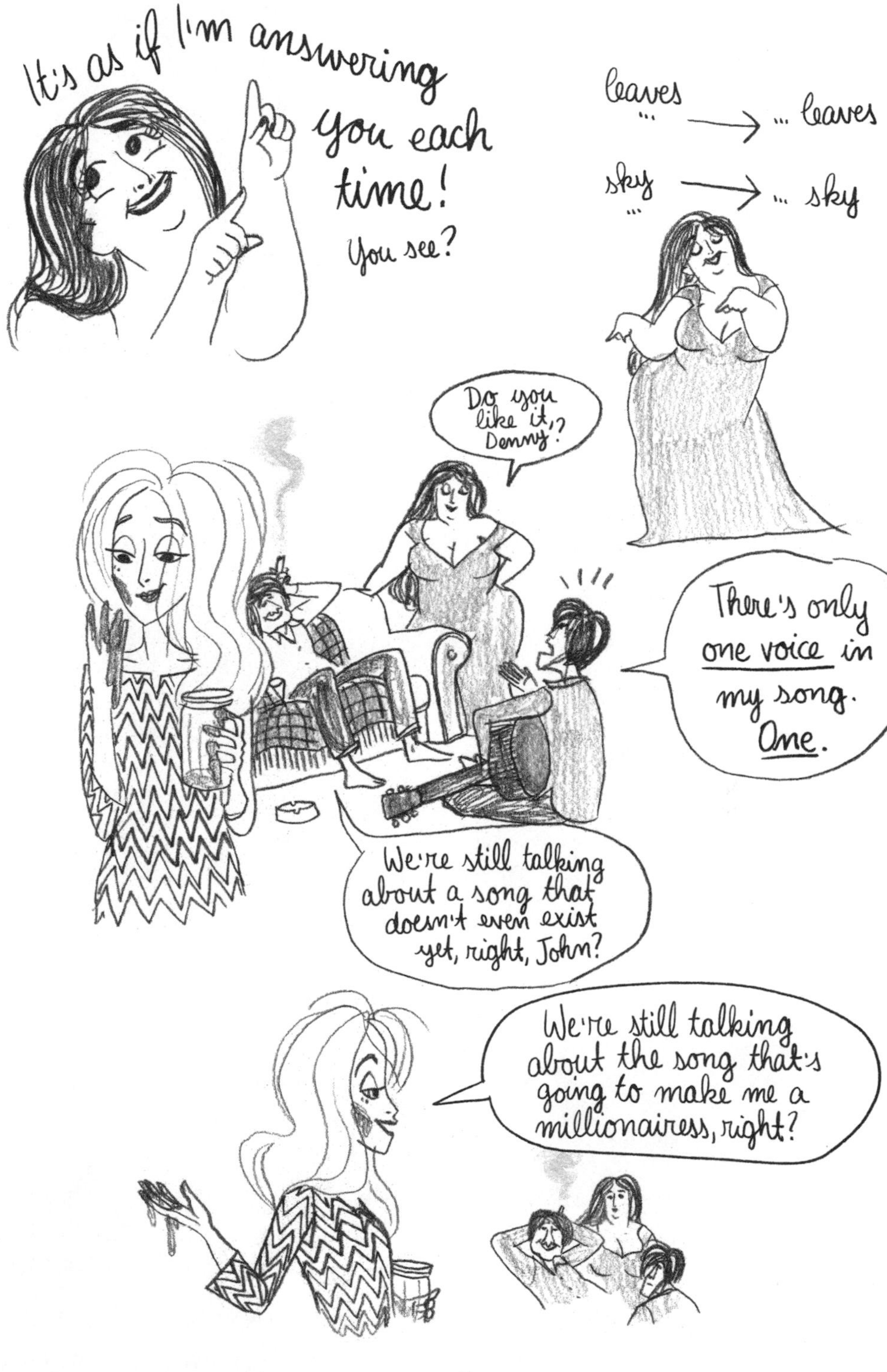
It's as if I'm answering you each time!
You see?
leaves ... → ... leaves
sky ... → ... sky
Do you like it, Denny?
There's only one voice in my song. One.
We're still talking about a song that doesn't even exist yet, right, John?
We're still talking about the song that's going to make me a millionairess, right?

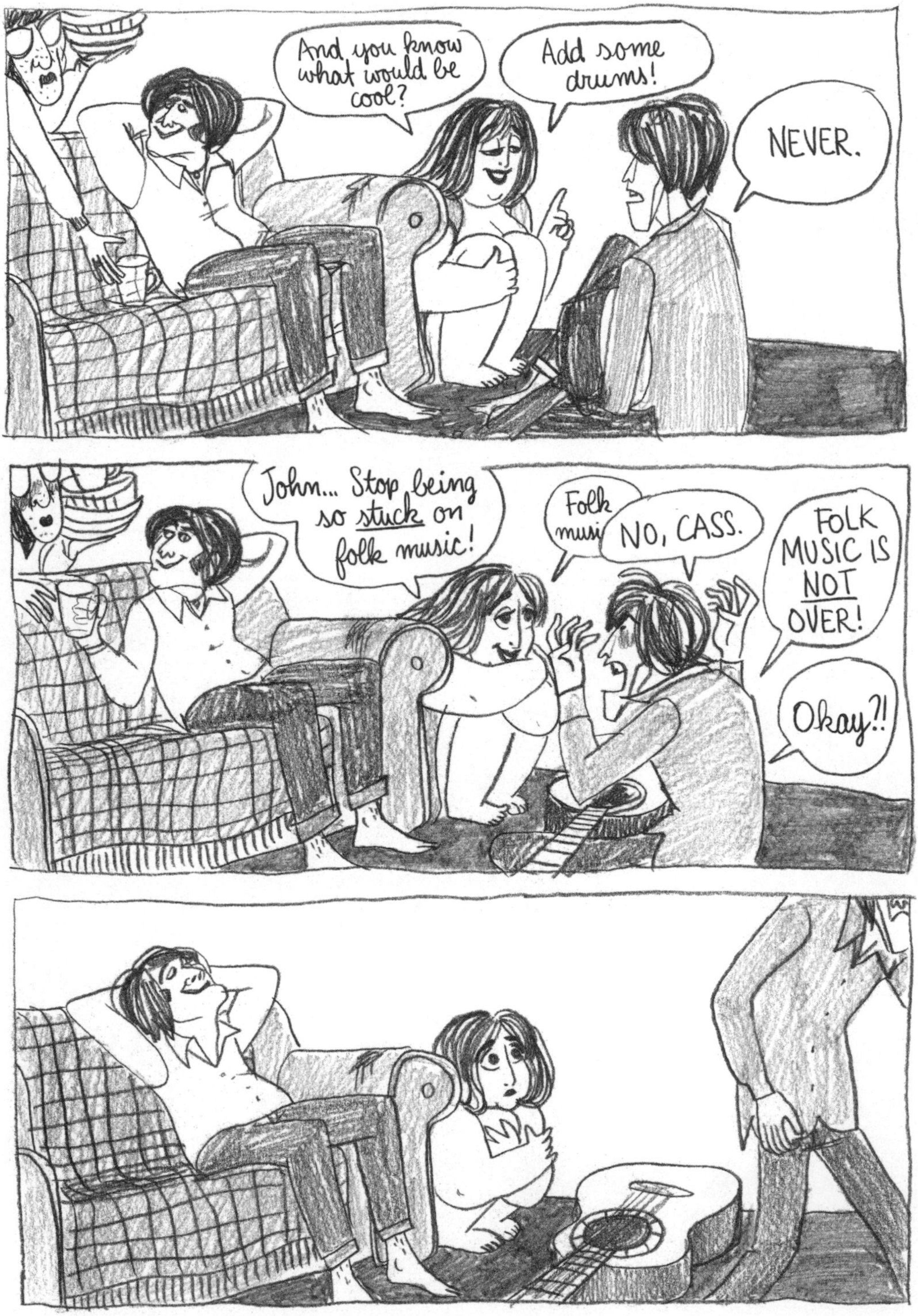
And you know what would be cool?
Add some drums!
NEVER.
John... Stop being so stuck on folk music!
Folk musi
NO, CASS.
FOLK MUSIC IS NOT OVER!
Okay?!

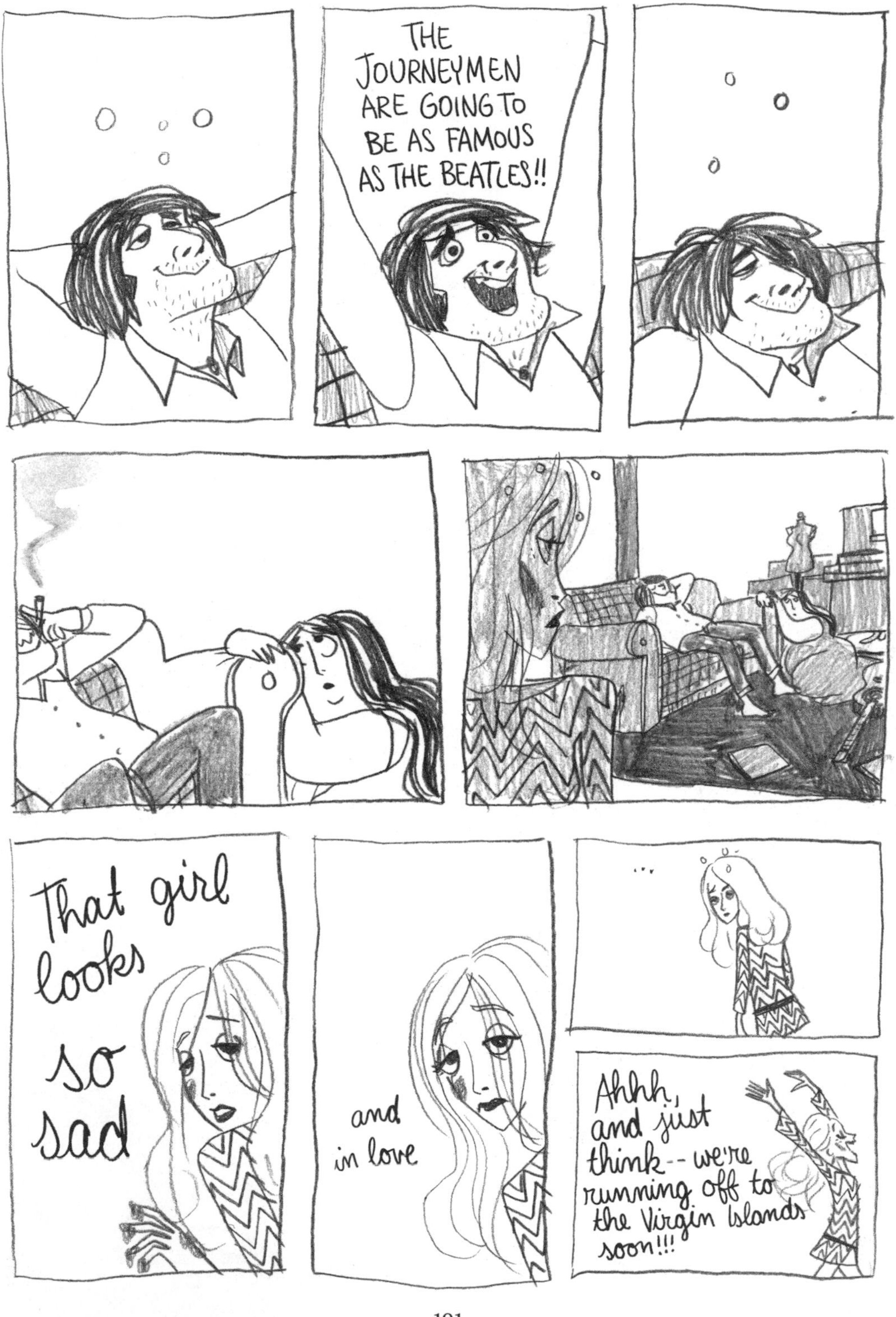
THE JOURNEYMEN ARE GOING TO BE AS FAMOUS AS THE BEATLES!!
That girl looks so sad
and in love
...
Ahhh, and just think-- we're running off to the Virgin Islands soon!!!

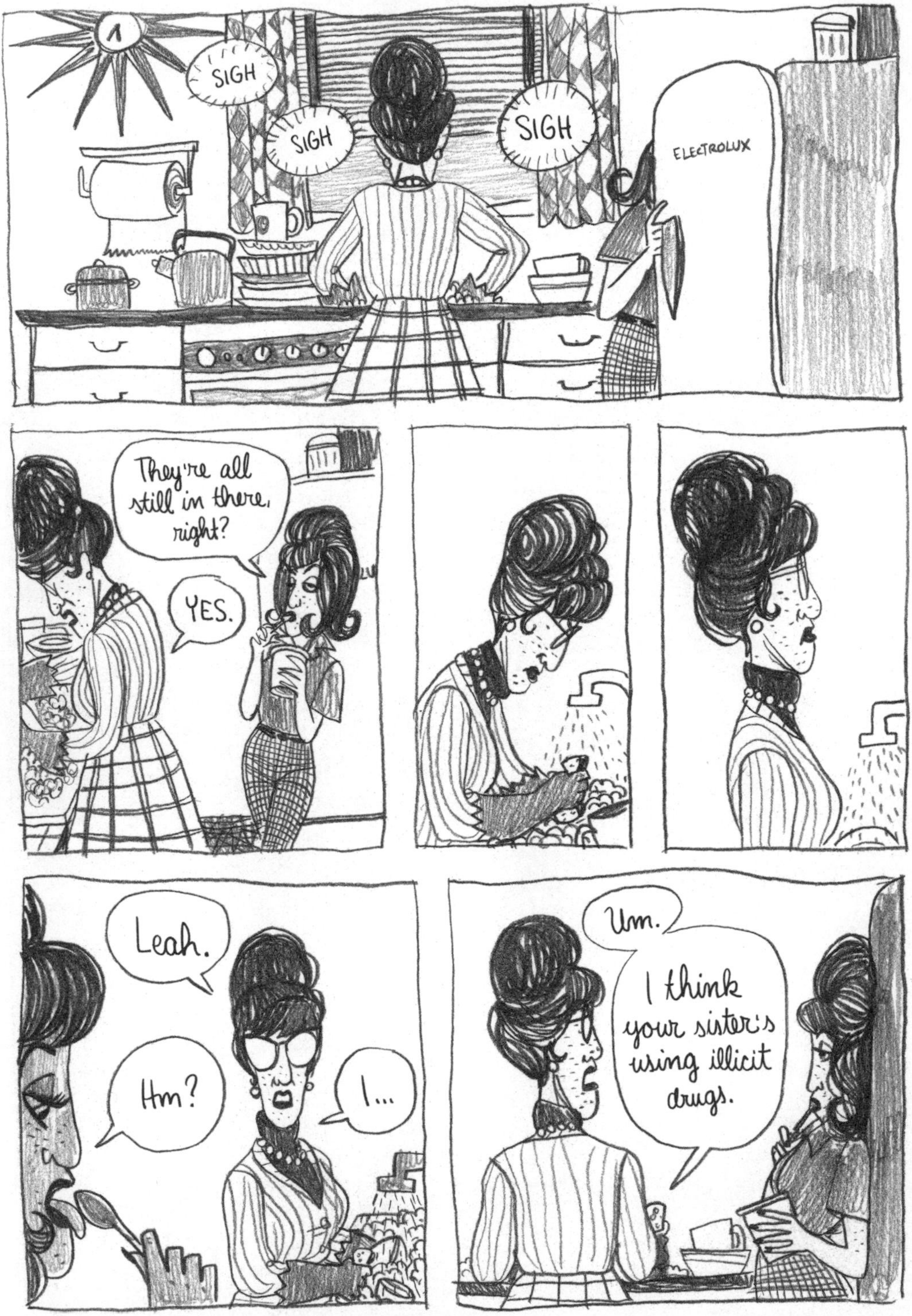
SIGH
SIGH
SIGH
ELECTROLUX
They're all still in there, right?
YES.
Leah.
Hm?
I...
Um.
I think your sister's using illicit drugs.

15-Michelle

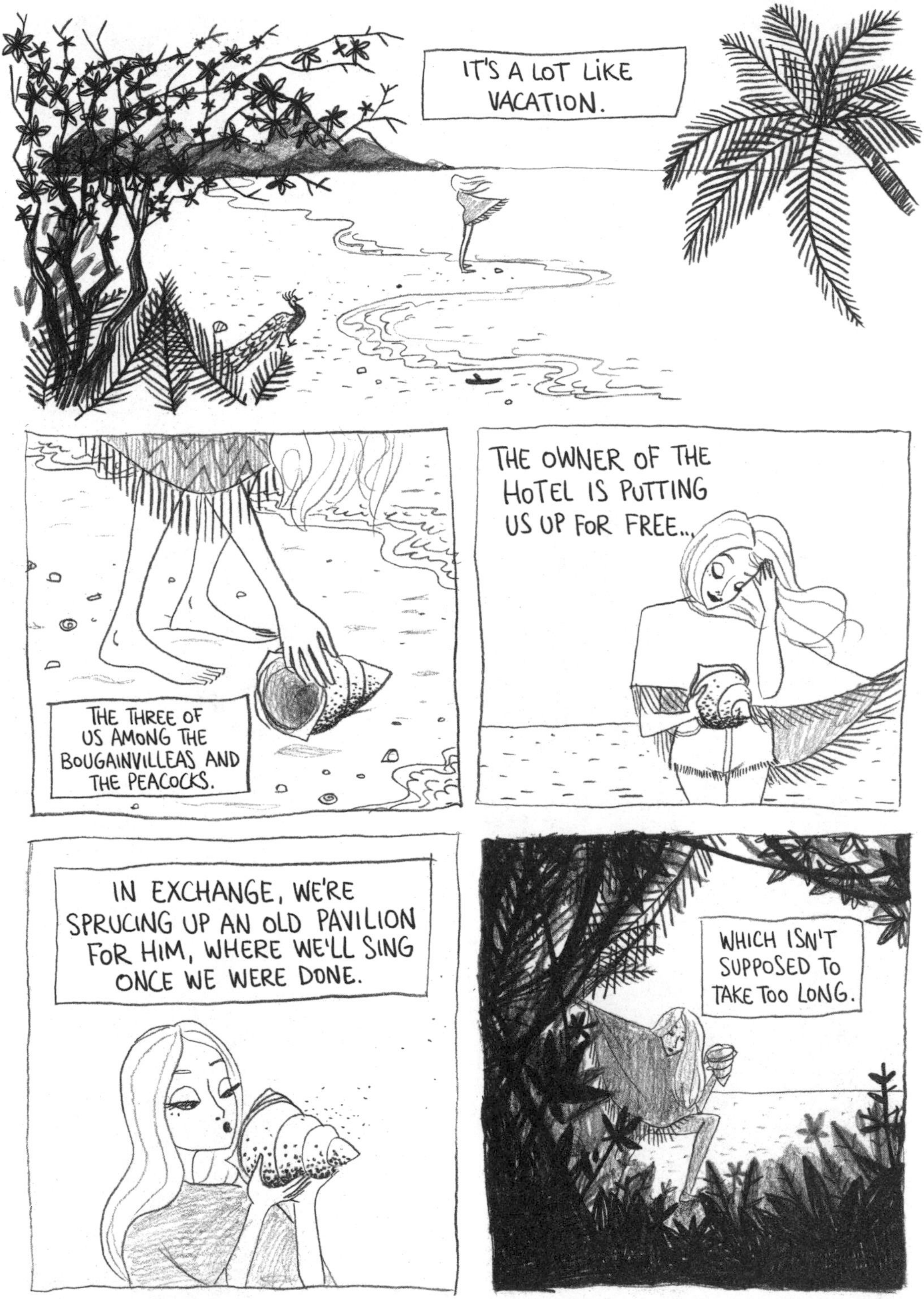
IT'S A LOT LIKE VACATION.
THE THREE OF US AMONG THE BOUGAINVILLEAS AND THE PEACOCKS.
THE OWNER OF THE HOTEL IS PUTTING US UP FOR FREE...
IN EXCHANGE, WE'RE SPRUCING UP AN OLD PAVILION FOR HIM, WHERE WE'LL SING ONCE WE WERE DONE.
WHICH ISN'T SUPPOSED TO TAKE TOO LONG.

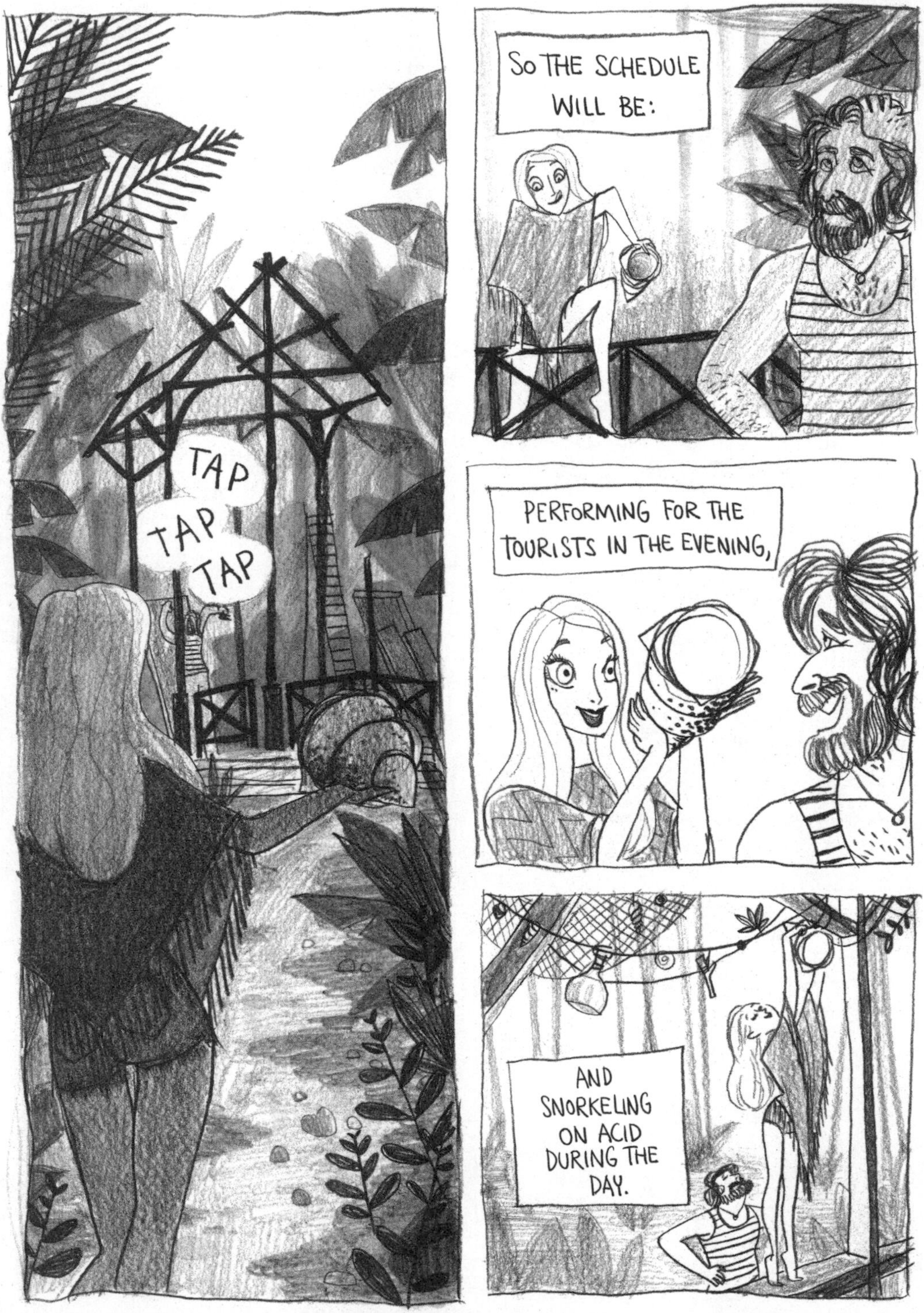
TAP
TAP
TAP
SO THE SCHEDULE WILL BE:
PERFORMING FOR THE TOURISTS IN THE EVENING,
AND SNORKELING ON ACID DURING THE DAY.

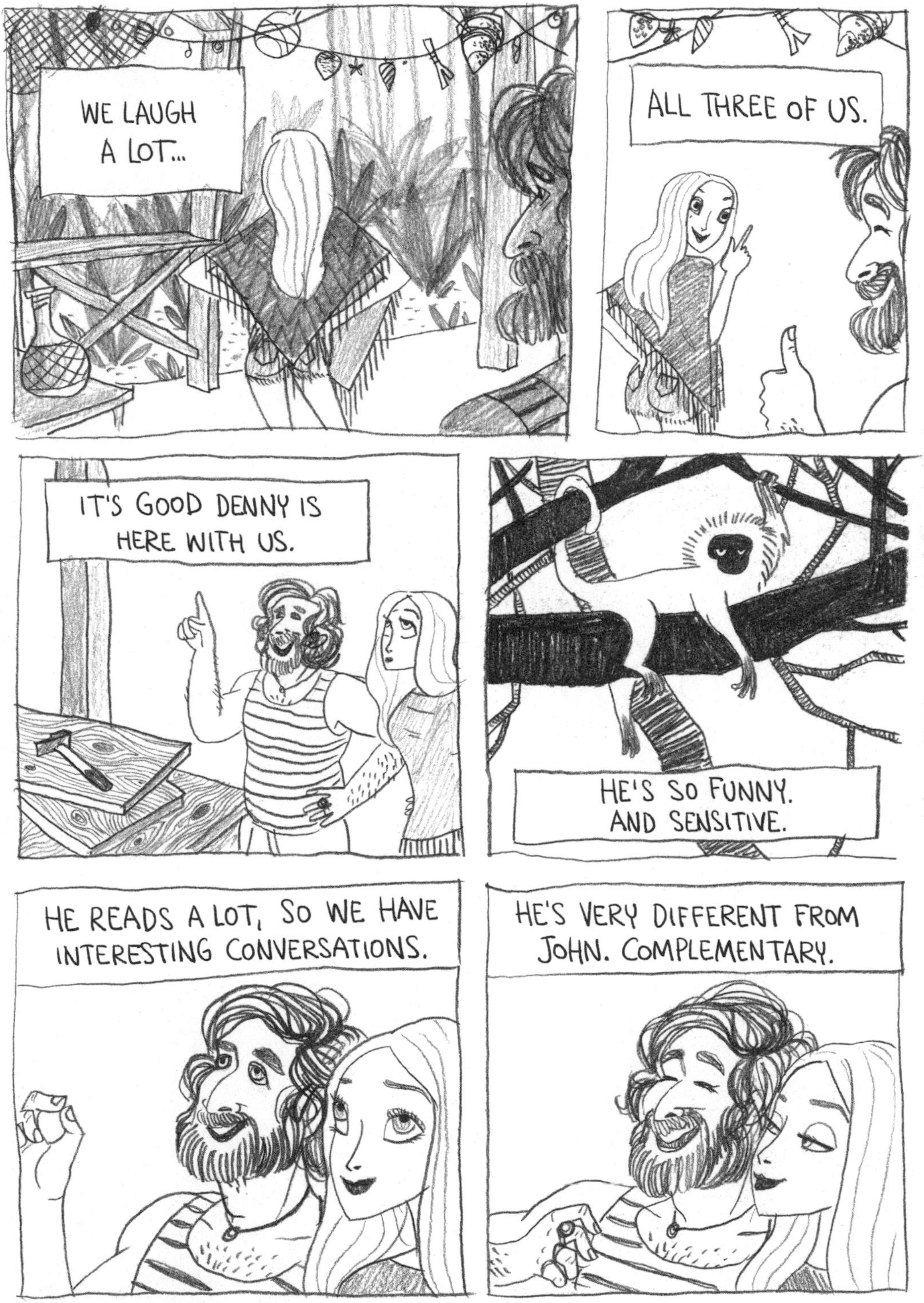
WE LAUGH A LOT...
ALL THREE OF US.
IT'S GOOD DENNY IS HERE WITH US.
HE'S SO FUNNY. AND SENSITIVE.
HE READS A LOT, SO WE HAVE INTERESTING CONVERSATIONS.
HE'S VERY DIFFERENT FROM JOHN. COMPLEMENTARY.

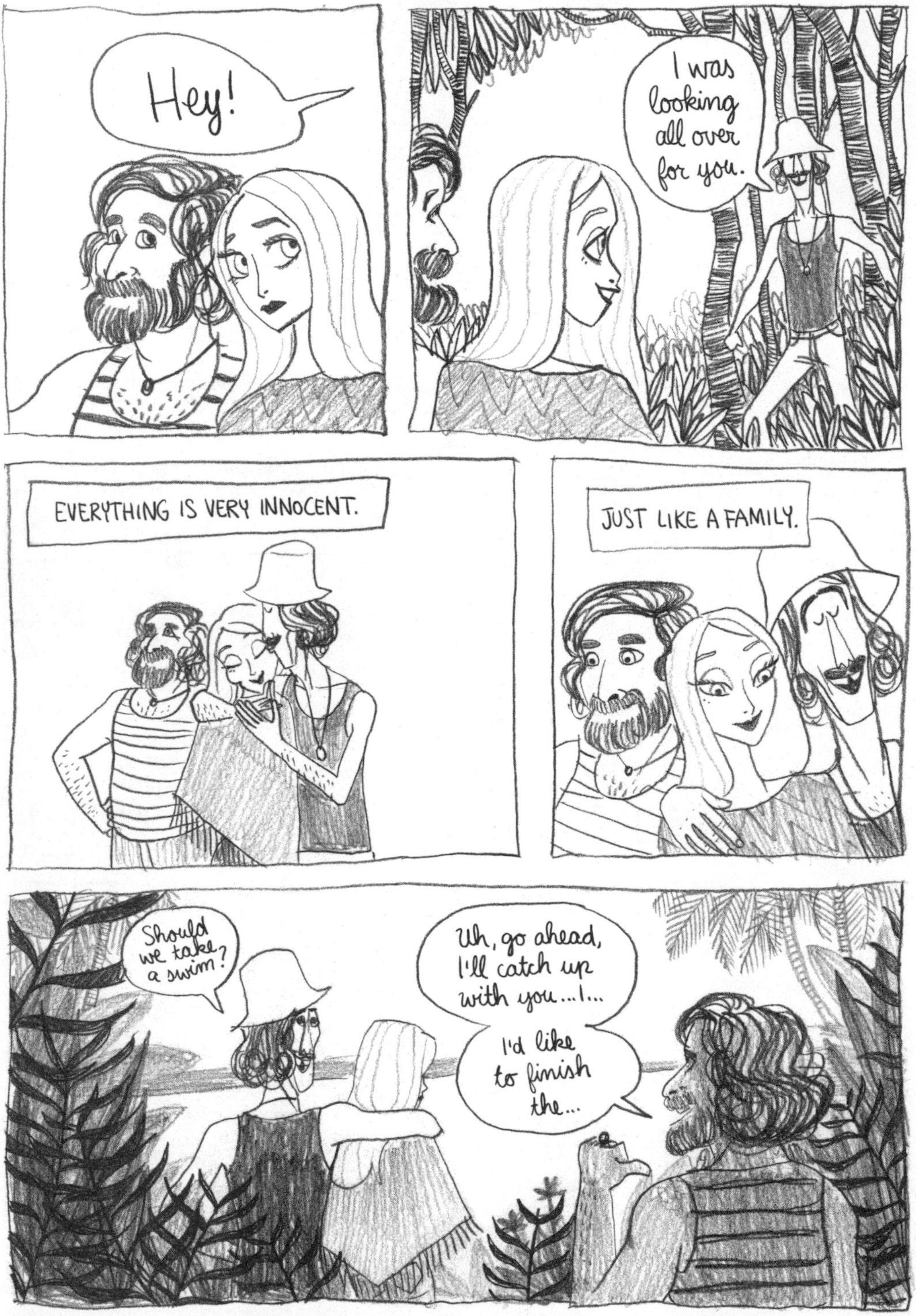
Hey!
I was looking all over for you.
EVERYTHING IS VERY INNOCENT.
JUST LIKE A FAMILY.
Should we take a swim?
Uh, go ahead, I'll catch up with you... I...
I'd like to finish the...

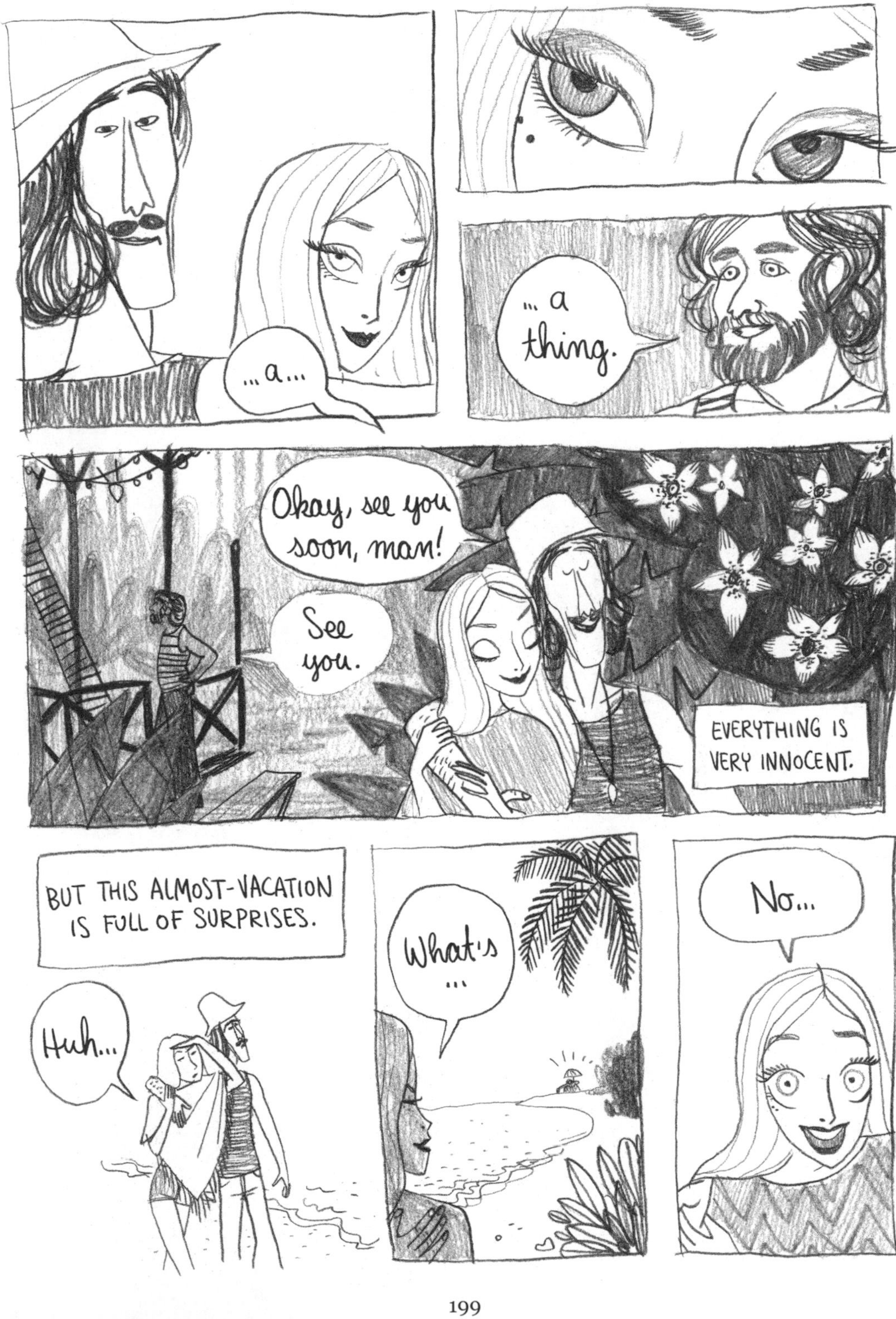
...a...
... a thing.
Okay, see you soon, man!
See you.
EVERYTHING IS VERY INNOCENT.
BUT THIS ALMOST-VACATION IS FULL OF SURPRISES.
Huh...
What's ...
No...

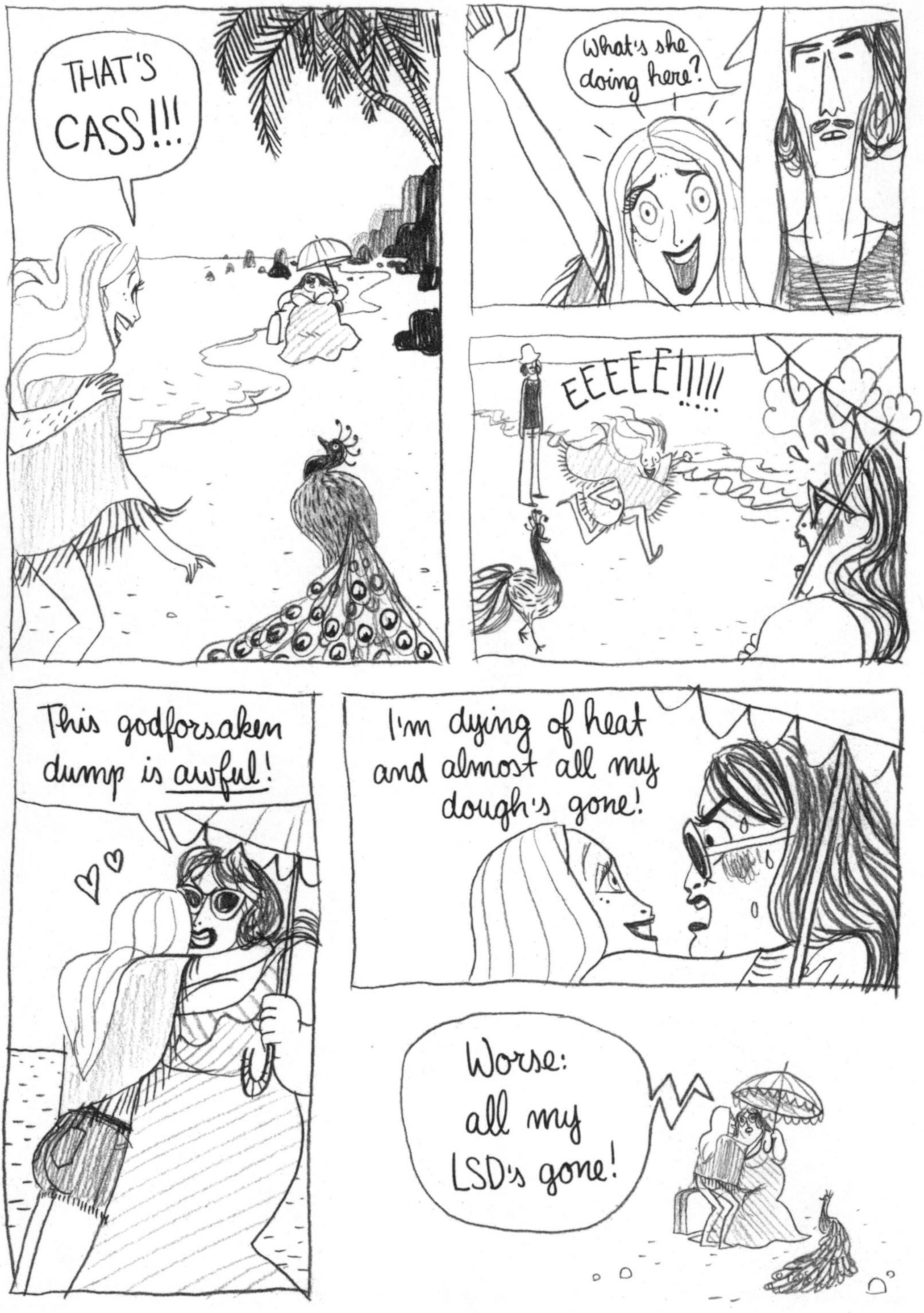
THAT'S CASS!!!...
What's she doing here?
EEEEE!!!!!....
This godforsaken dump is awful!
I'm dying of heat and almost all my dough's gone!
Worse: all my LSD's gone!

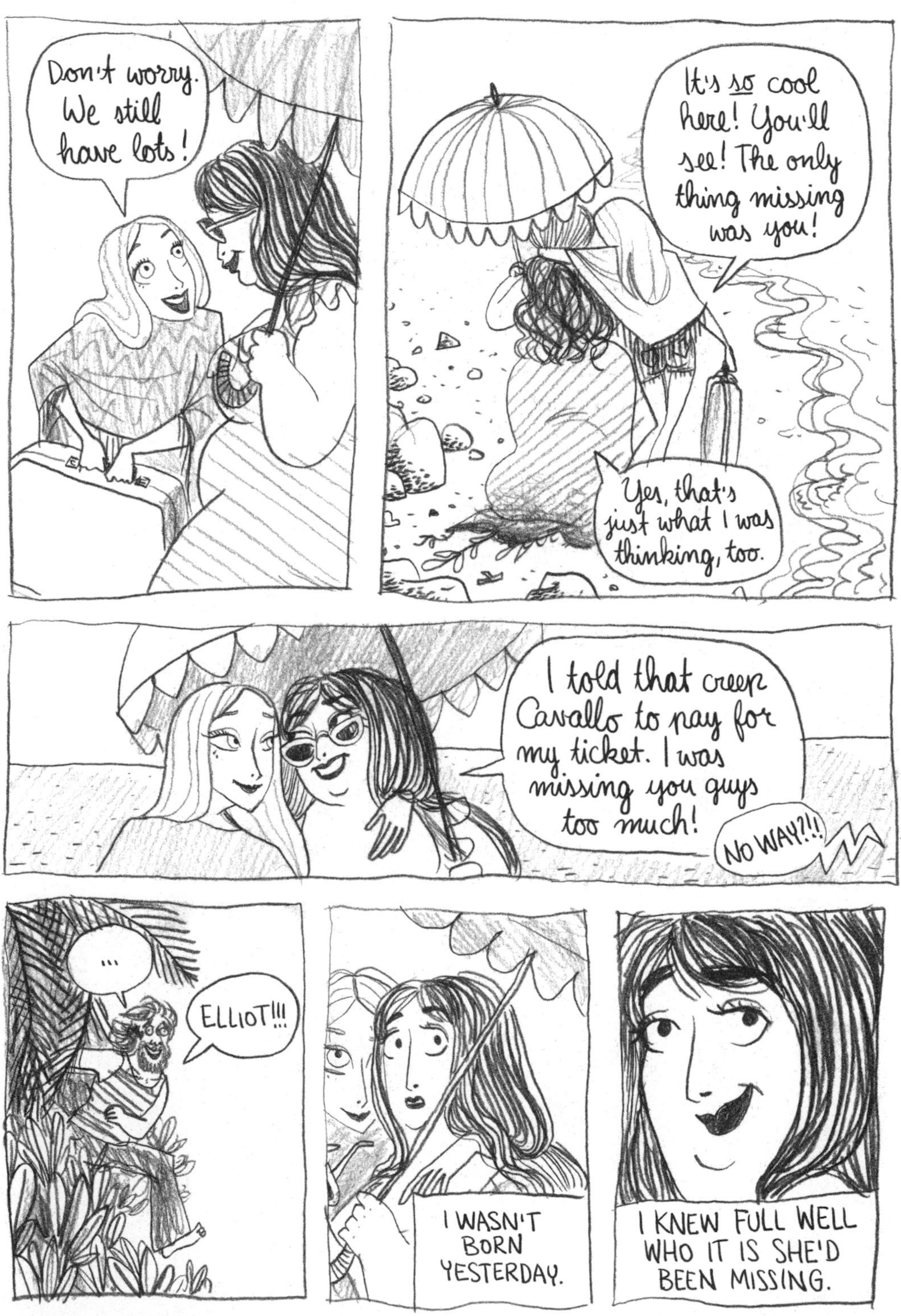
Don't worry. We still have lots!
It's so cool here! You'll see! The only thing missing was you!
Yes, that's just what I was thinking, too.
I told that creep Cavallo to pay for my ticket. I was missing you guys too much!
NO WAY?!!
...
ELLIOT!!!
I WASN'T BORN YESTERDAY.
I KNEW FULL WELL WHO IT IS SHE'D BEEN MISSING.

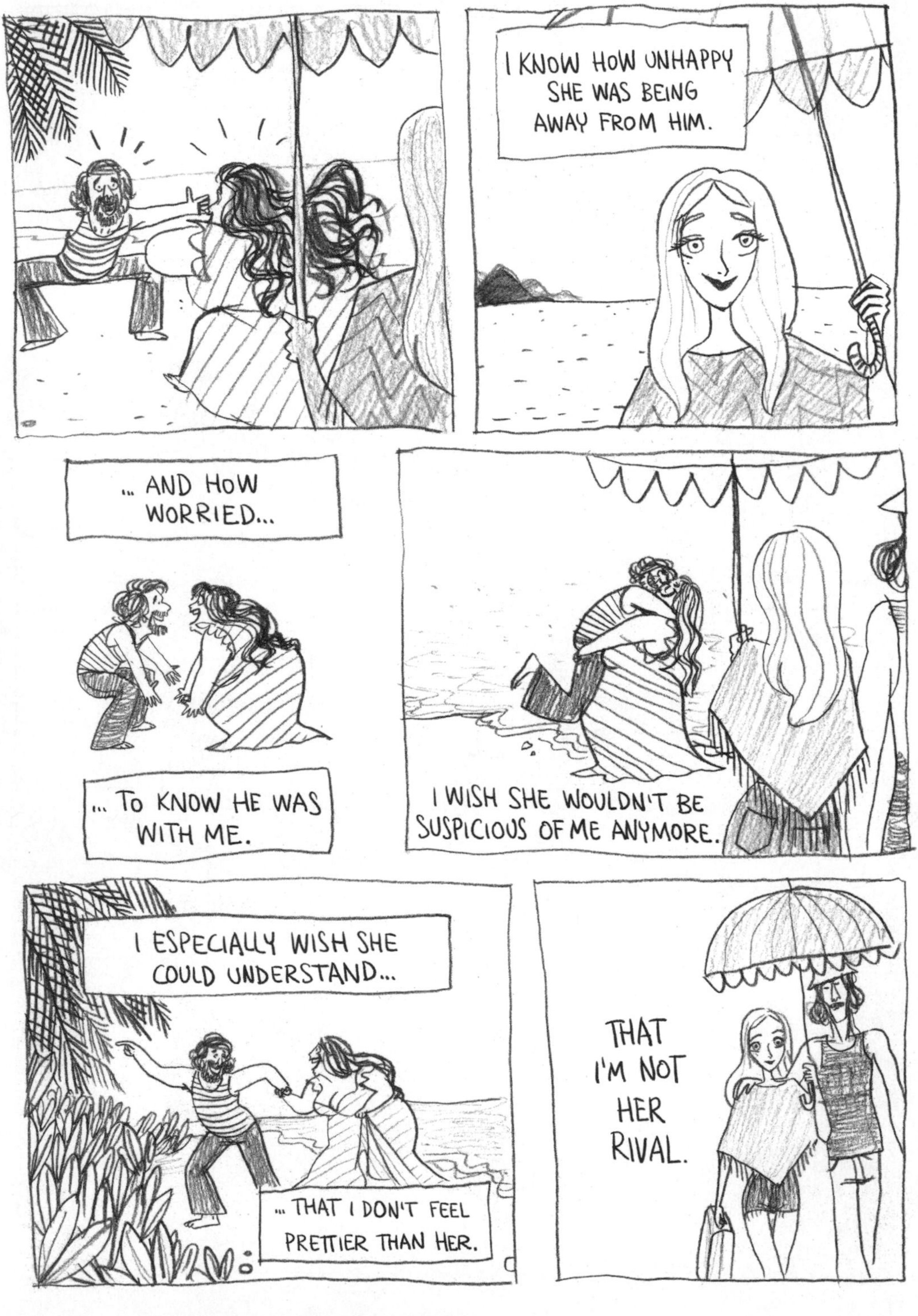
I KNOW HOW UNHAPPY SHE WAS BEING AWAY FROM HIM.
... AND HOW WORRIED...
... TO KNOW HE WAS WITH ME.
I WISH SHE WOULDN'T BE SUSPICIOUS OF ME ANYMORE.
I ESPECIALLY WISH SHE COULD UNDERSTAND...
... THAT I DON'T FEEL PRETTIER THAN HER.
THAT I'M NOT HER RIVAL.

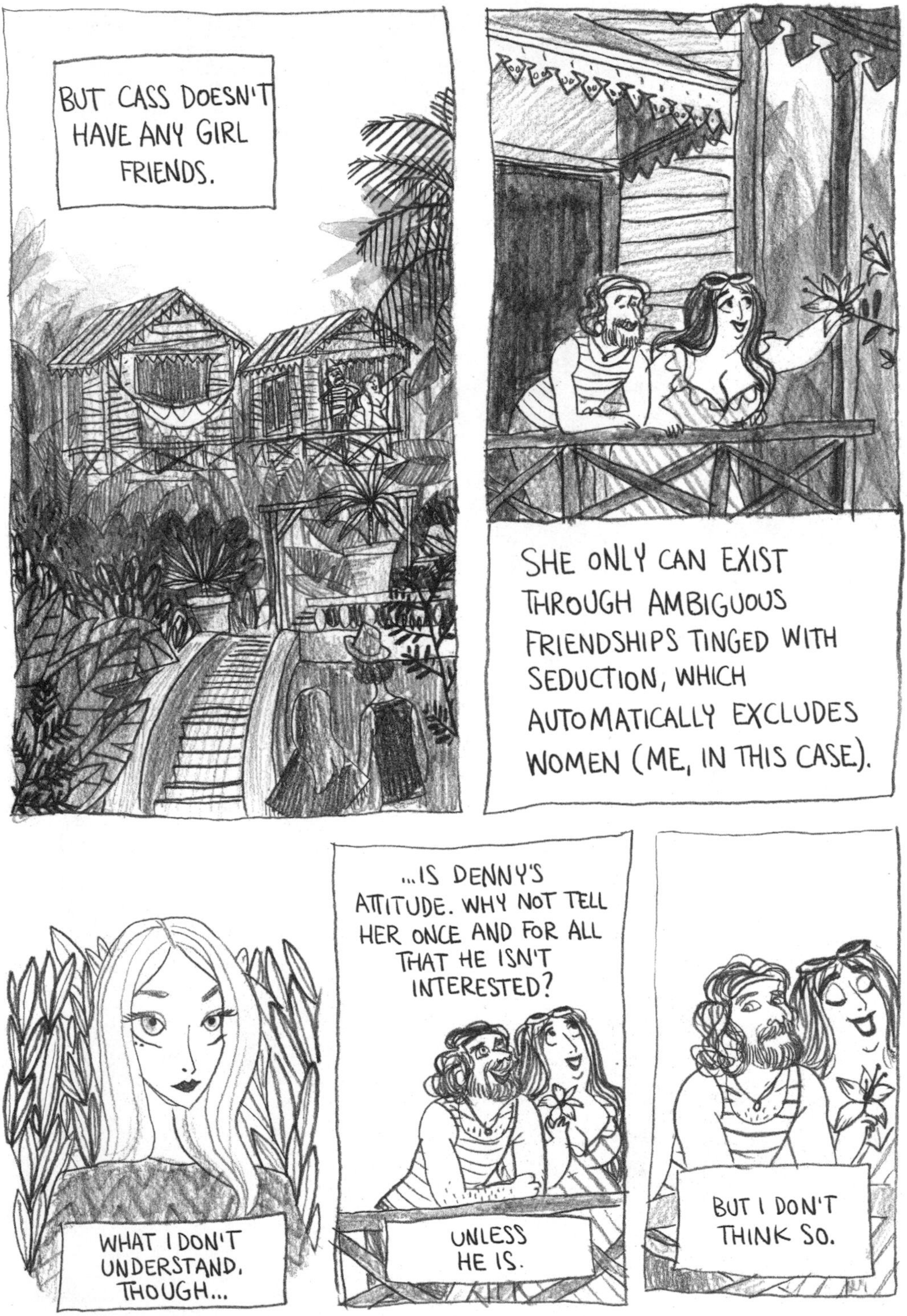
BUT CASS DOESN'T HAVE ANY GIRL FRIENDS.
SHE ONLY CAN EXIST THROUGH AMBIGUOUS FRIENDSHIPS TINGED WITH SEDUCTION, WHICH AUTOMATICALLY EXCLUDES WOMEN (ME, IN THIS CASE).
WHAT I DON'T UNDERSTAND, THOUGH...
...IS DENNY'S ATTITUDE. WHY NOT TELL HER ONCE AND FOR ALL THAT HE ISN'T INTERESTED?
UNLESS HE IS.
BUT I DON'T THINK SO.

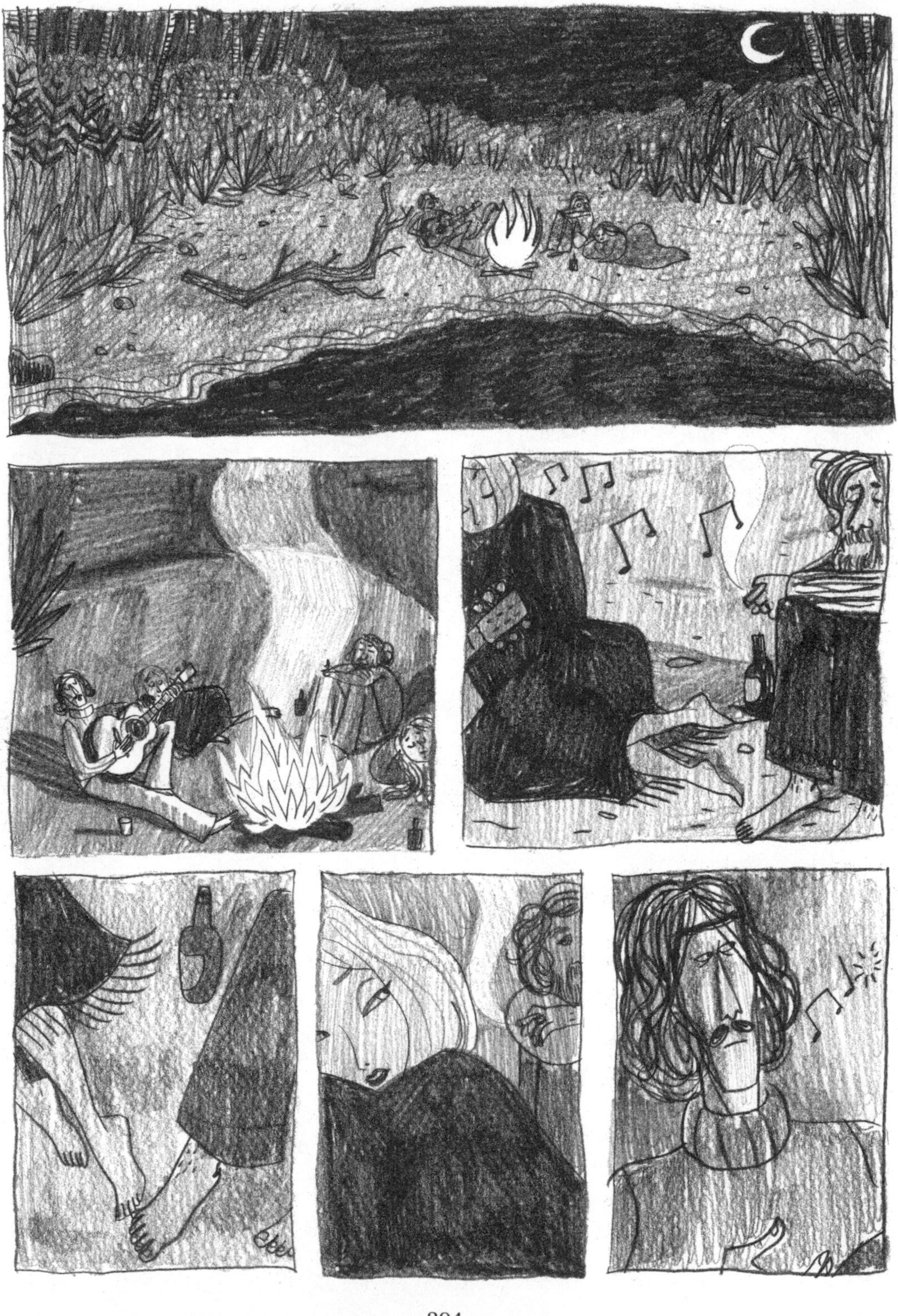

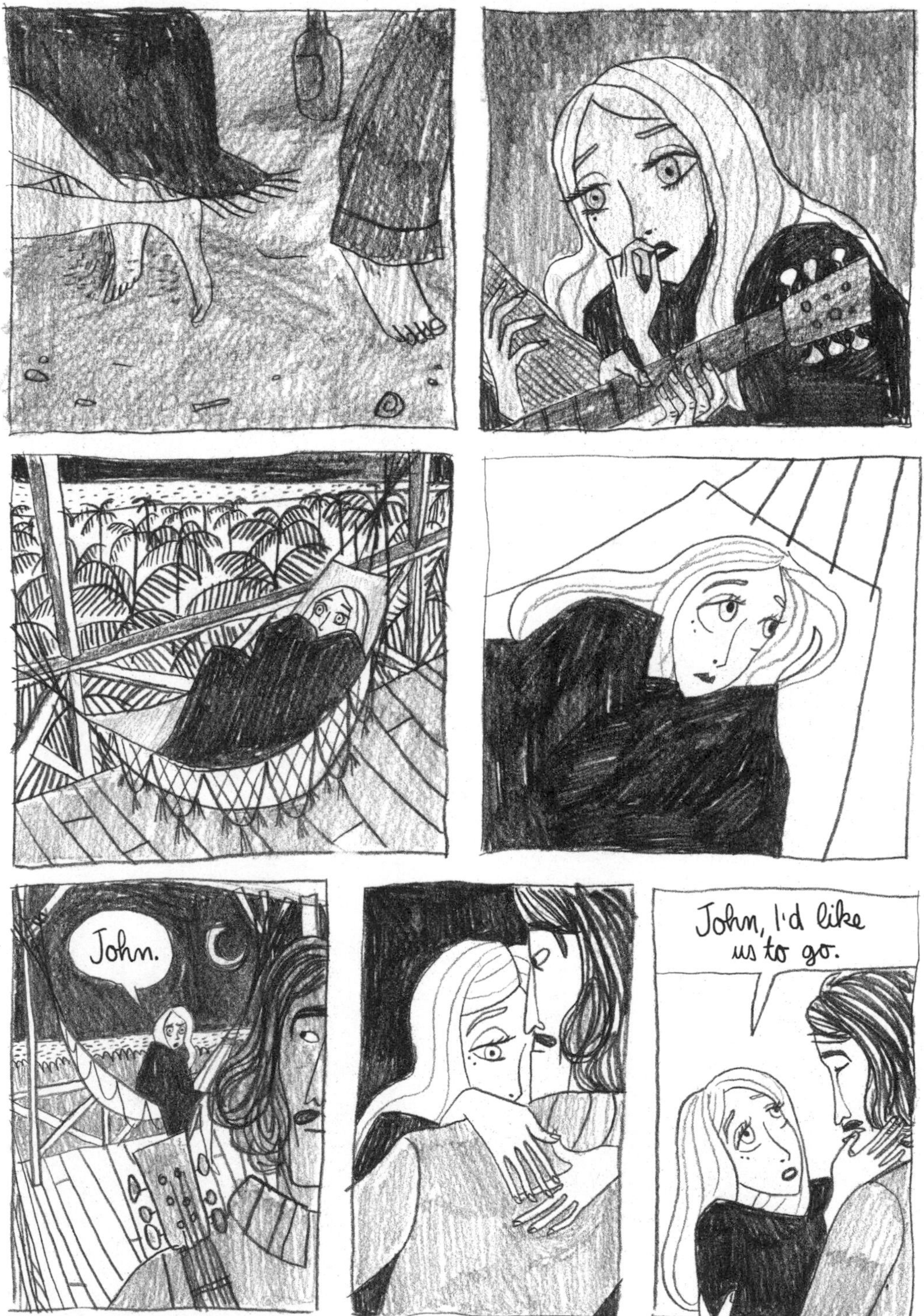
John.
John, I'd like us to go.

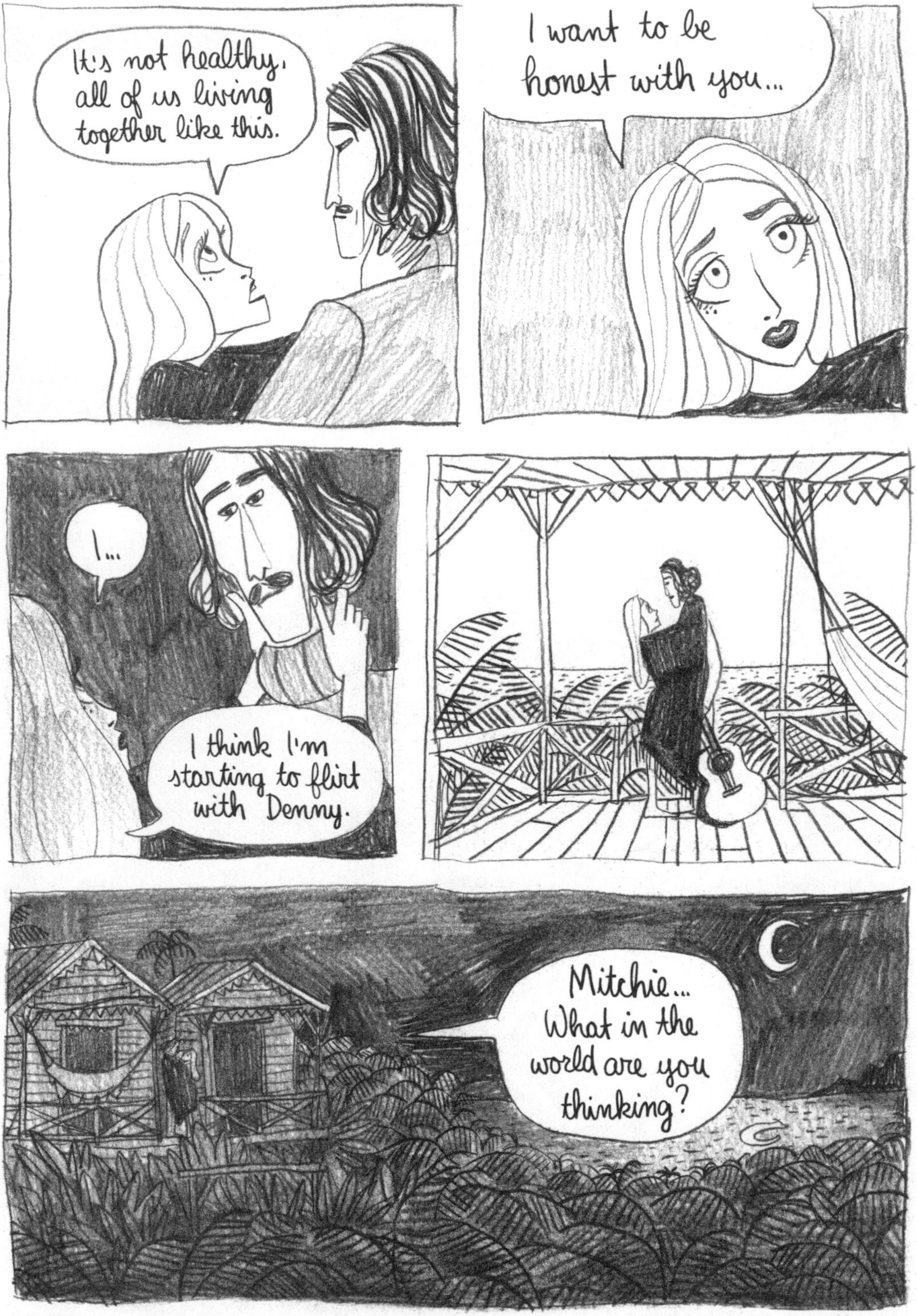
It's not healthy, all of us living together like this.
I want to be honest with you...
I...
I think I'm starting to flirt with Denny.
Mitchie... What in the world are you thinking?

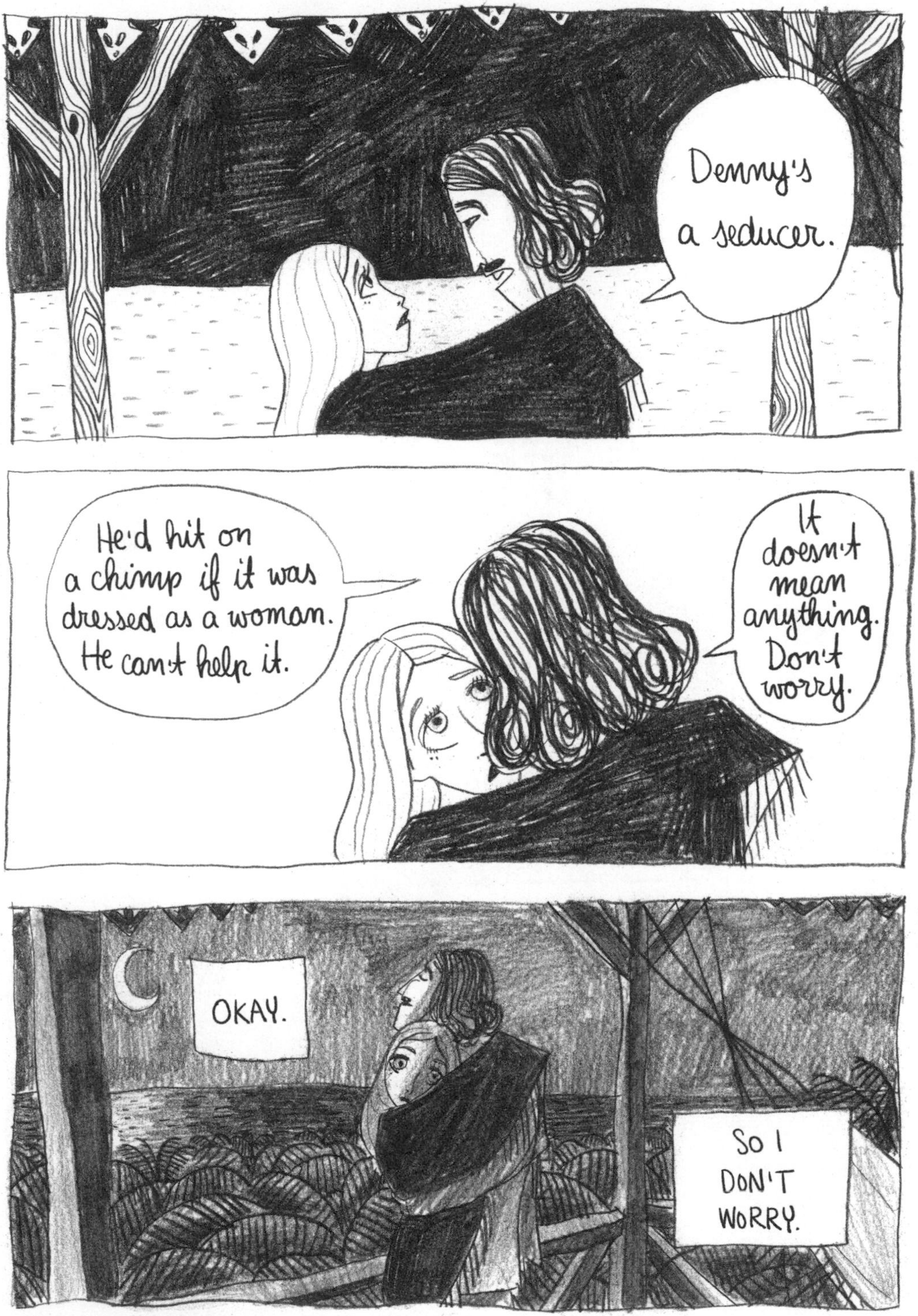
Denny's a seducer.
He'd hit on a chimp if it was dressed as a woman. He can't help it.
It doesn't mean anything. Don't worry.
OKAY.
SO I DON'T WORRY.

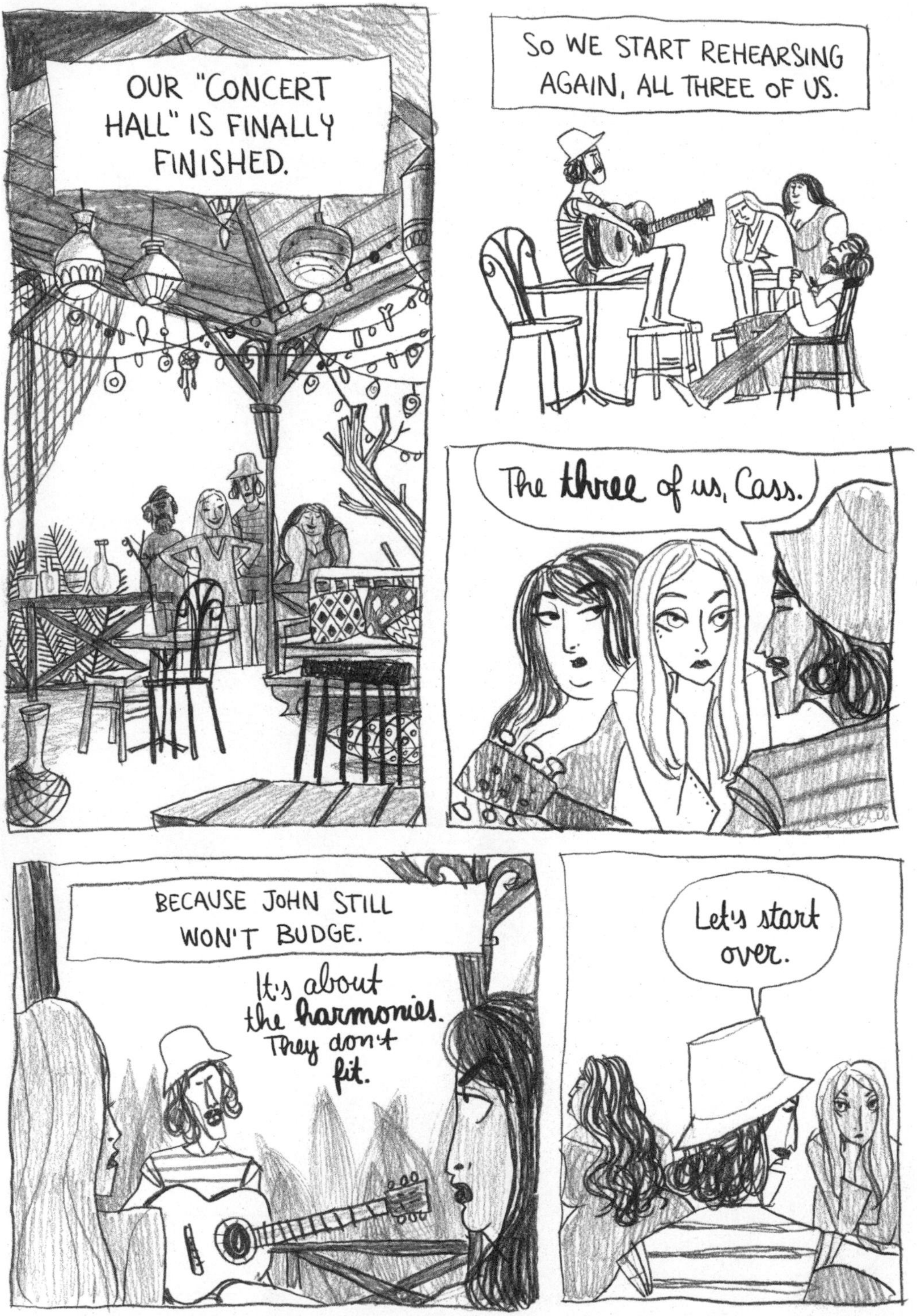
OUR "CONCERT HALL" IS FINALLY FINISHED.
SO WE START REHEARSING AGAIN, ALL THREE OF US.
The three of us, Cass.
BECAUSE JOHN STILL WON'T BUDGE.
It's about the harmonies. They don't fit.
Let's start over.

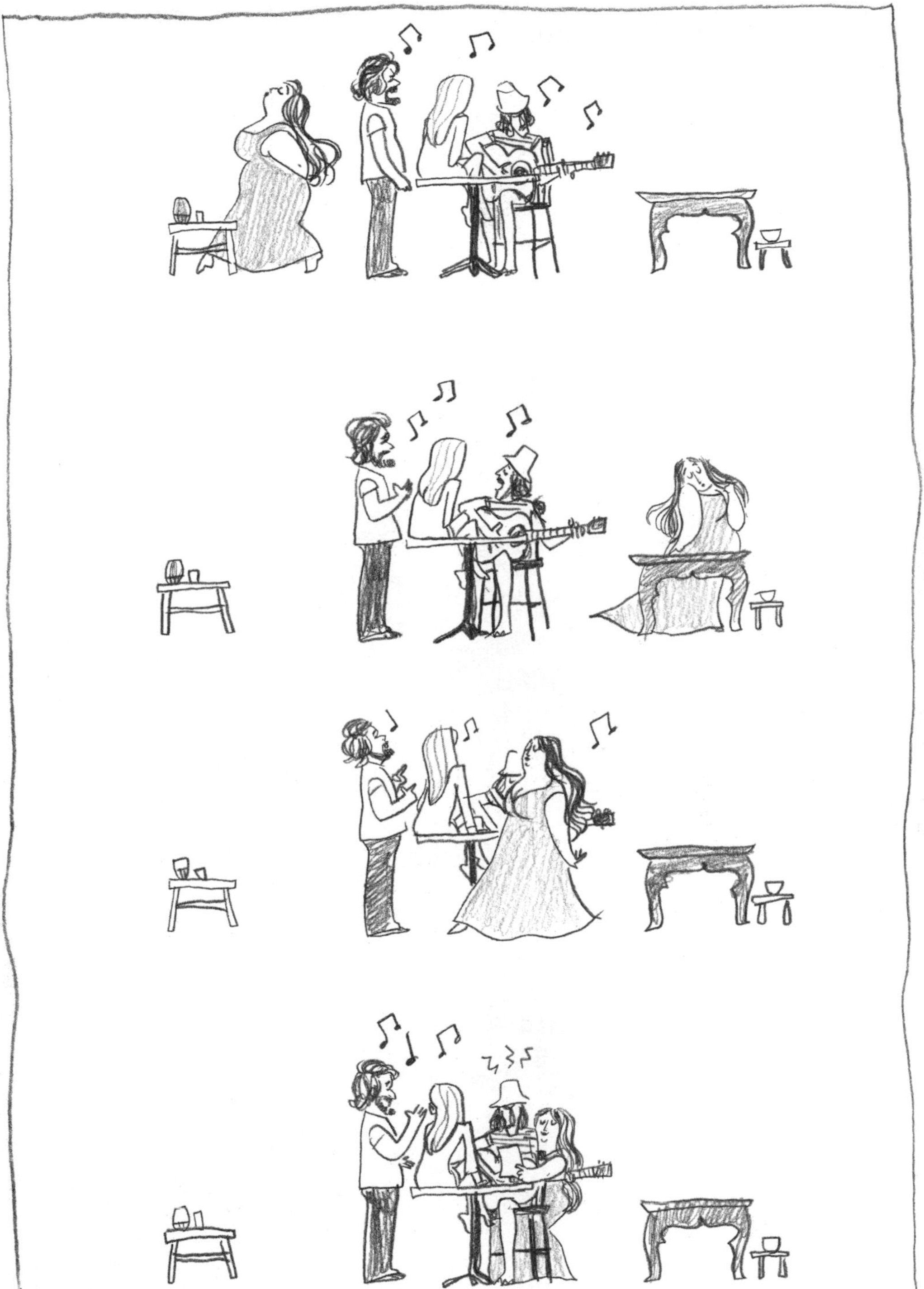

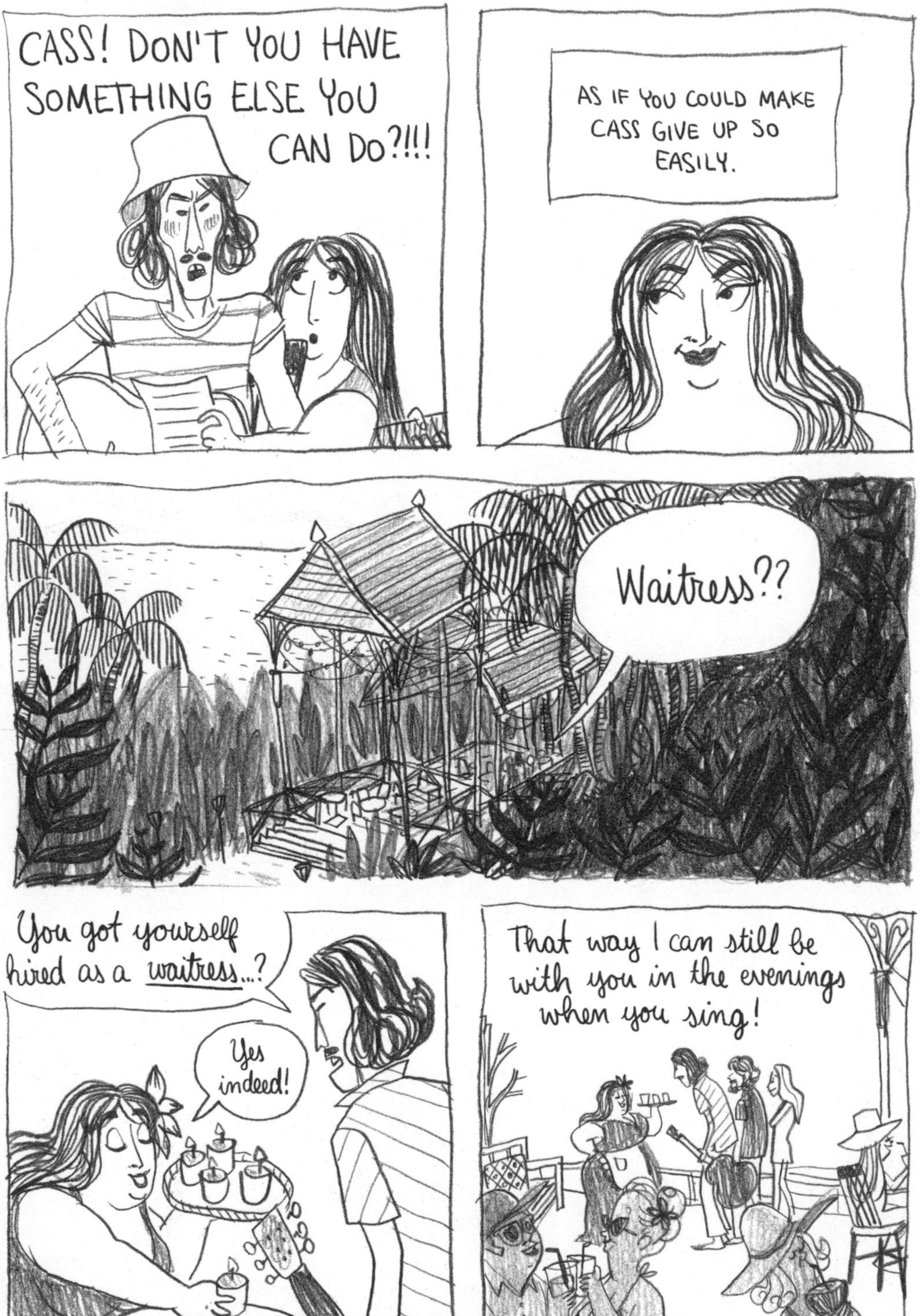
CASS! DON'T YOU HAVE SOMETHING ELSE YOU CAN DO?!!!
AS IF YOU COULD MAKE CASS GIVE UP SO EASILY.
Waitress??
You got yourself hired as a waitress...?
Yes indeed!
That way I can still be with you in the evenings when you sing!

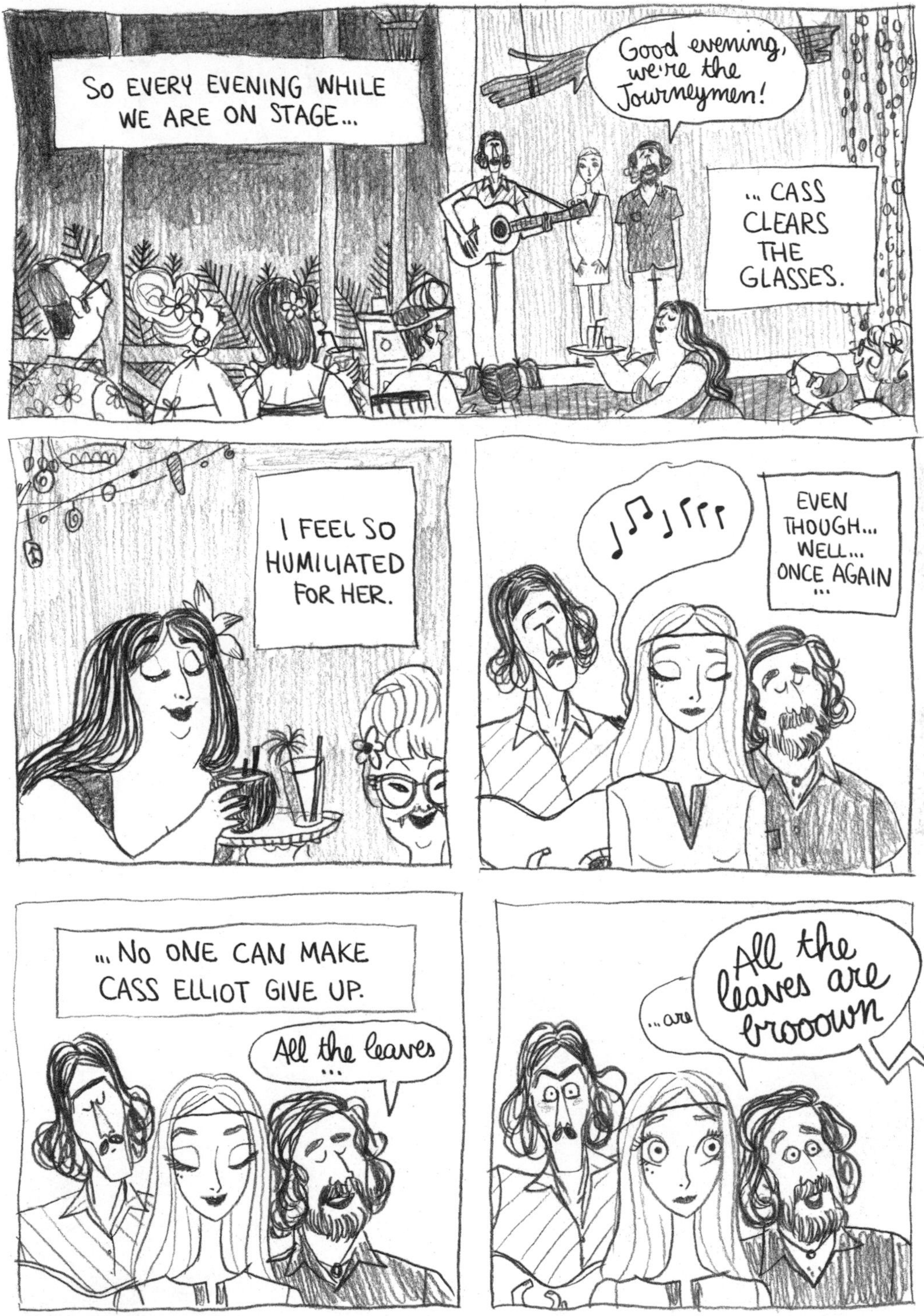

So EVERY EVENING WHILE WE ARE ON STAGE...
Good evening, we're the Journeymen!
... CASS CLEARS THE GLASSES.
I FEEL SO HUMILIATED FOR HER.
EVEN THOUGH... WELL... ONCE AGAIN ...
... No ONE CAN MAKE CASS ELLIOT GIVE UP.
All the leaves ...
... are
All the leaves are brooown

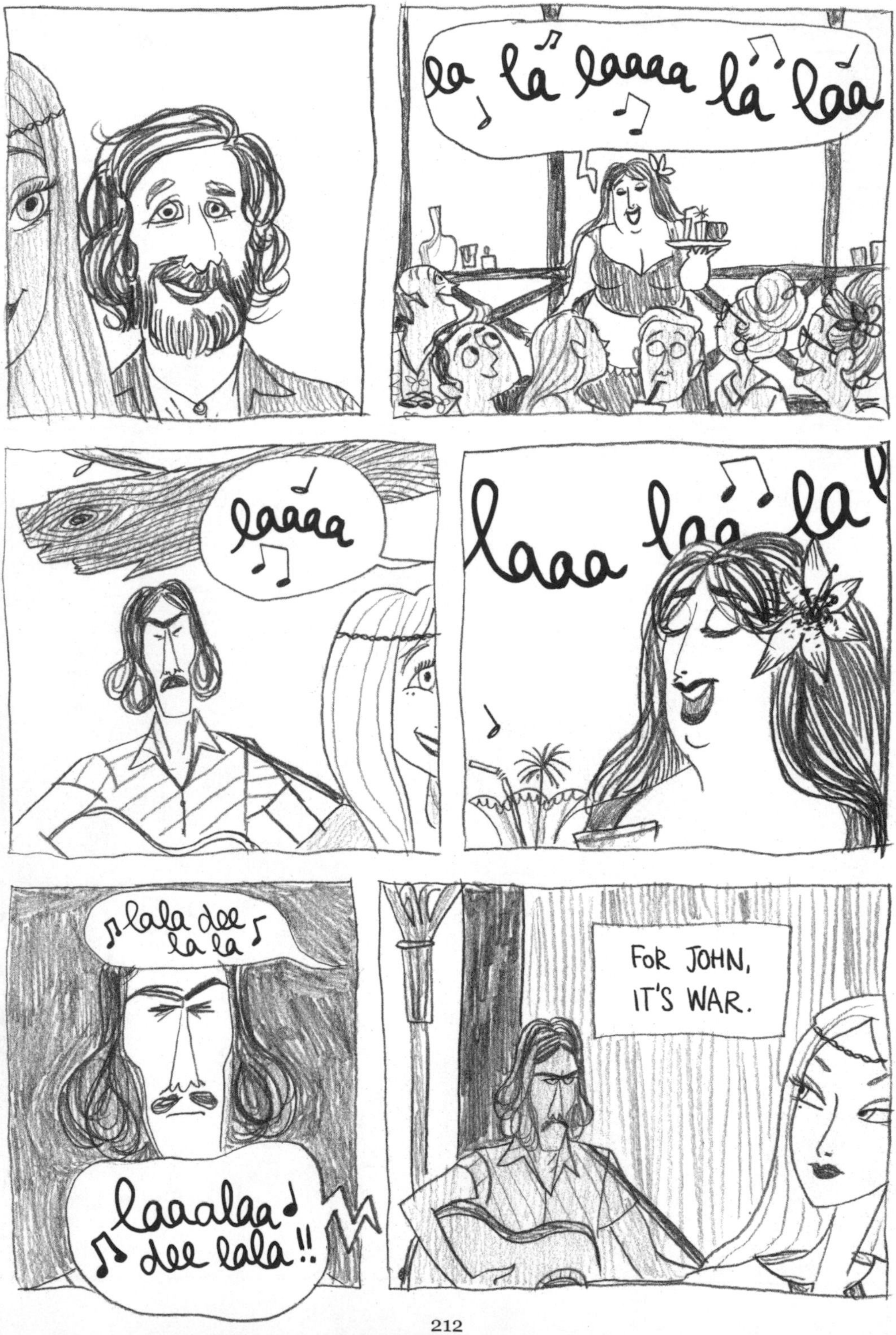

la la laaaa la laa
laaaa
laaa laa la
lala dee la la
laaalaa dee lala!!
FOR JOHN, IT'S WAR.

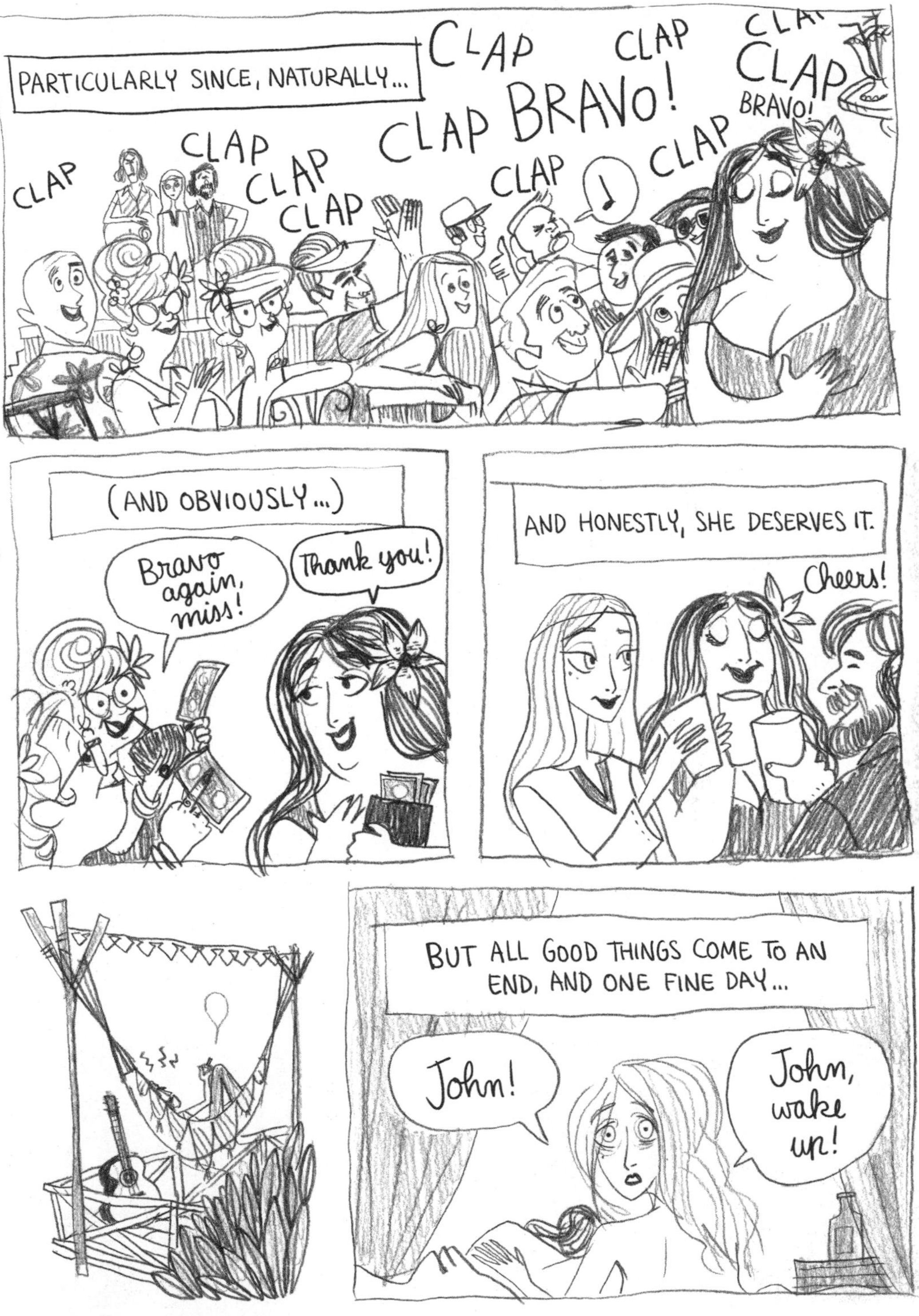
PARTICULARLY SINCE, NATURALLY...
CLAP
CLAP
CLAP
CLAP
CLAP BRAVO!
CLAP
CLAP
CLAP
CLAP
CLAP
BRAVO!
CLAP
(AND OBVIOUSLY...)
Bravo again, miss!
Thank you!
AND HONESTLY, SHE DESERVES IT.
Cheers!
BUT ALL GOOD THINGS COME TO AN END, AND ONE FINE DAY...
John!
John, wake up!

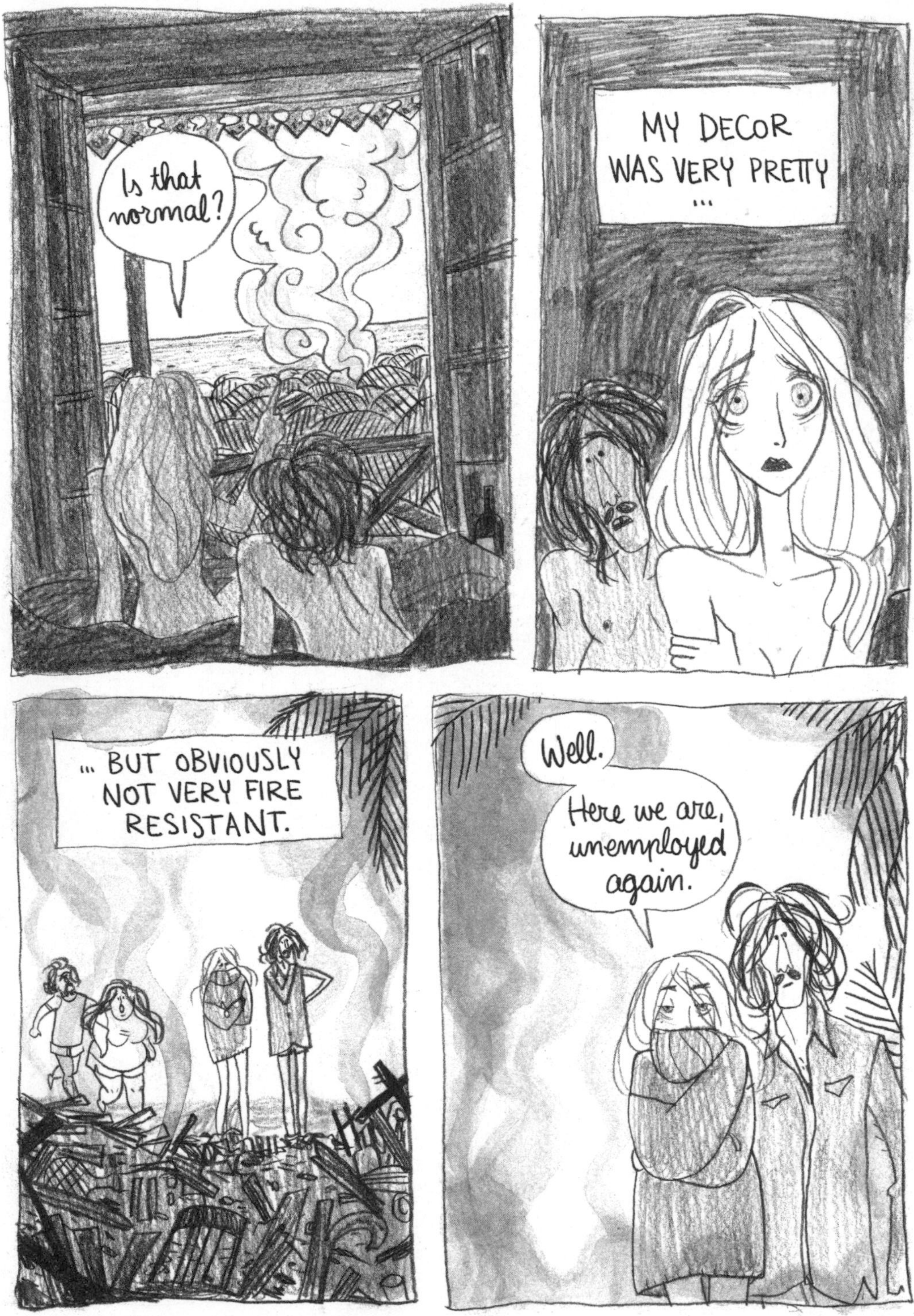
Is that normal?
MY DECOR WAS VERY PRETTY ...
... BUT OBVIOUSLY NOT VERY FIRE RESISTANT.
Well.
Here we are, unemployed again.

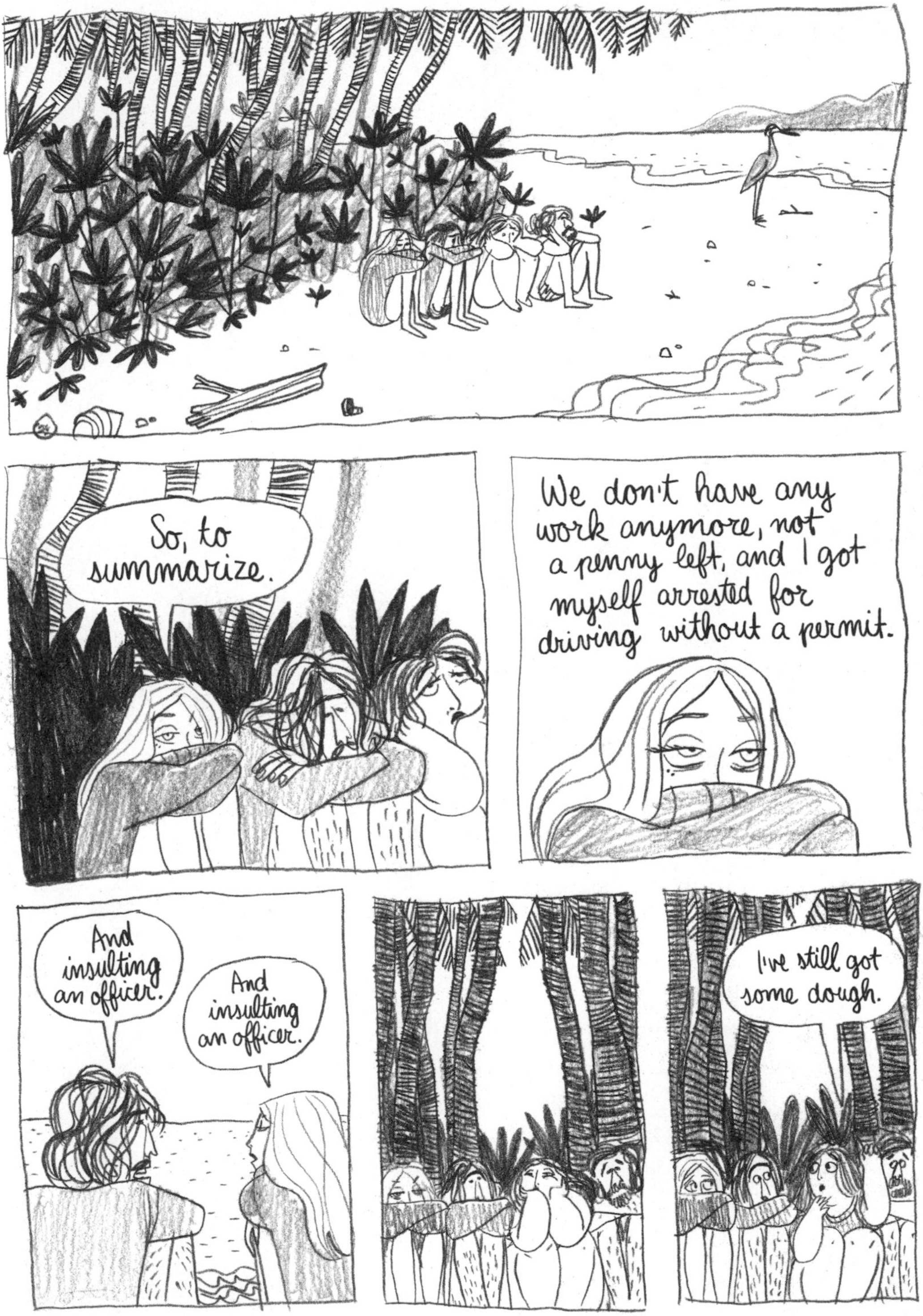
So, to summarize.
We don't have any work anymore, not a penny left, and I got myself arrested for driving without a permit.
And insulting an officer.
And insulting an officer.
I've still got some dough.

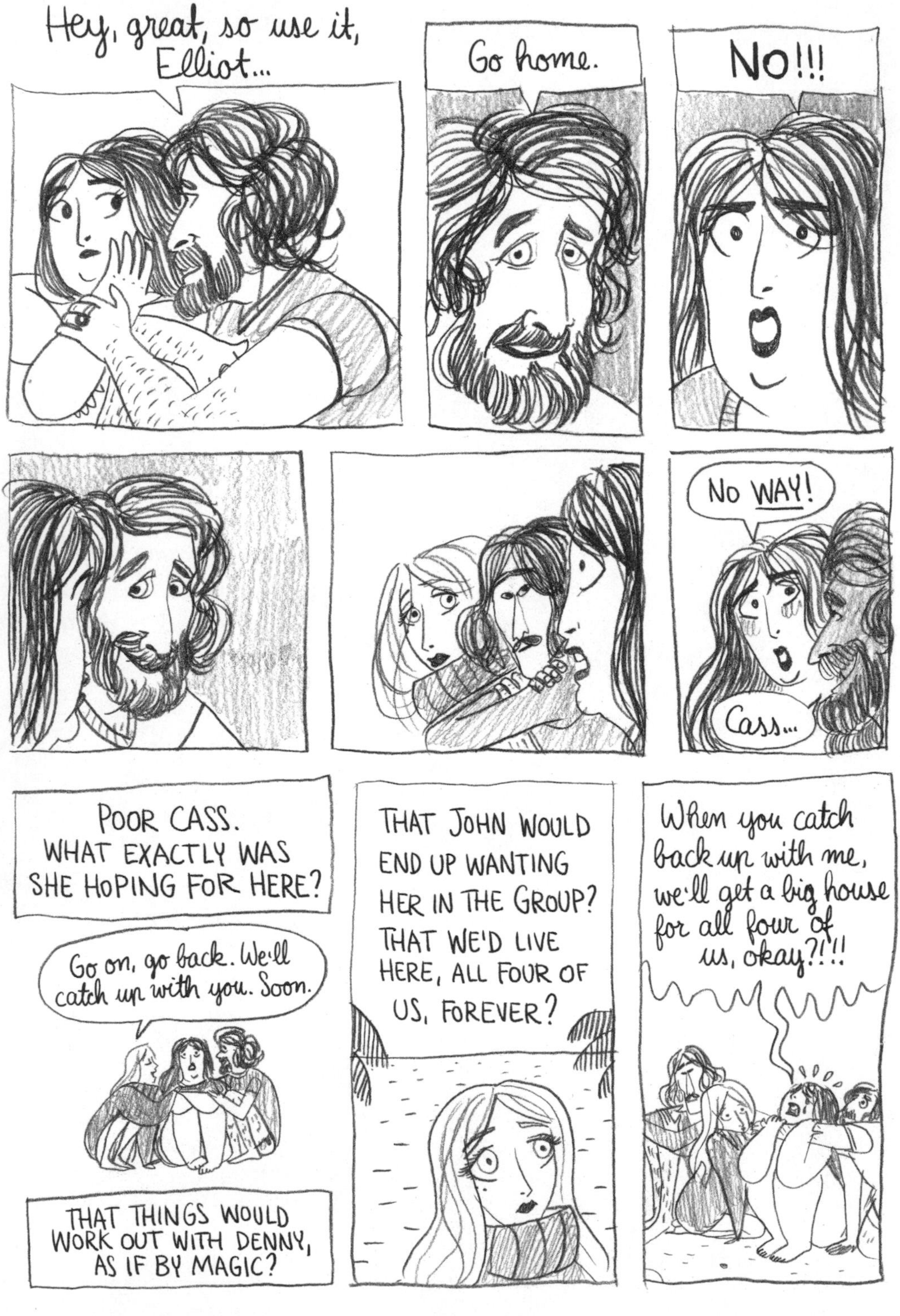
Hey, great, so use it, Elliot...
Go home.
NO!!!
No WAY!
Cass...
POOR CASS. WHAT EXACTLY WAS SHE HOPING FOR HERE?
Go on, go back. We'll catch up with you. Soon.
THAT THINGS WOULD WORK OUT WITH DENNY, AS IF BY MAGIC?
THAT JOHN WOULD END UP WANTING HER IN THE GROUP? THAT WE'D LIVE HERE, ALL FOUR OF US, FOREVER?
When you catch back up with me, we'll get a big house for all four of us, okay?!!!

16-John

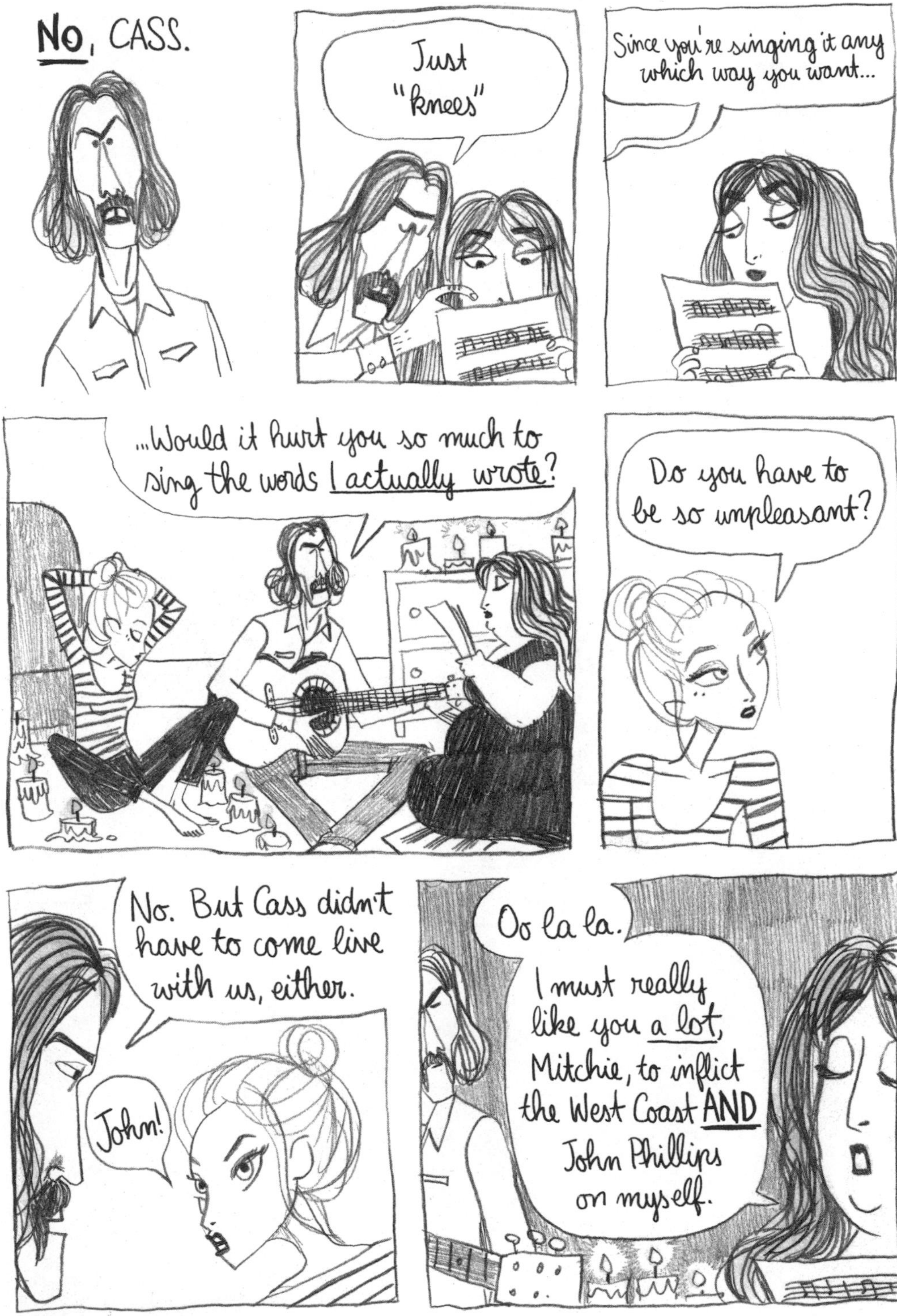

NO, CASS.
Just "knees"
Since you're singing it any which way you want...
...Would it hurt you so much to sing the words I actually wrote?
Do you have to be so unpleasant?
No. But Cass didn't have to come live with us, either.
John!
Oo la la.
I must really like you a lot, Mitchie, to inflict the West Coast AND John Phillips on myself.

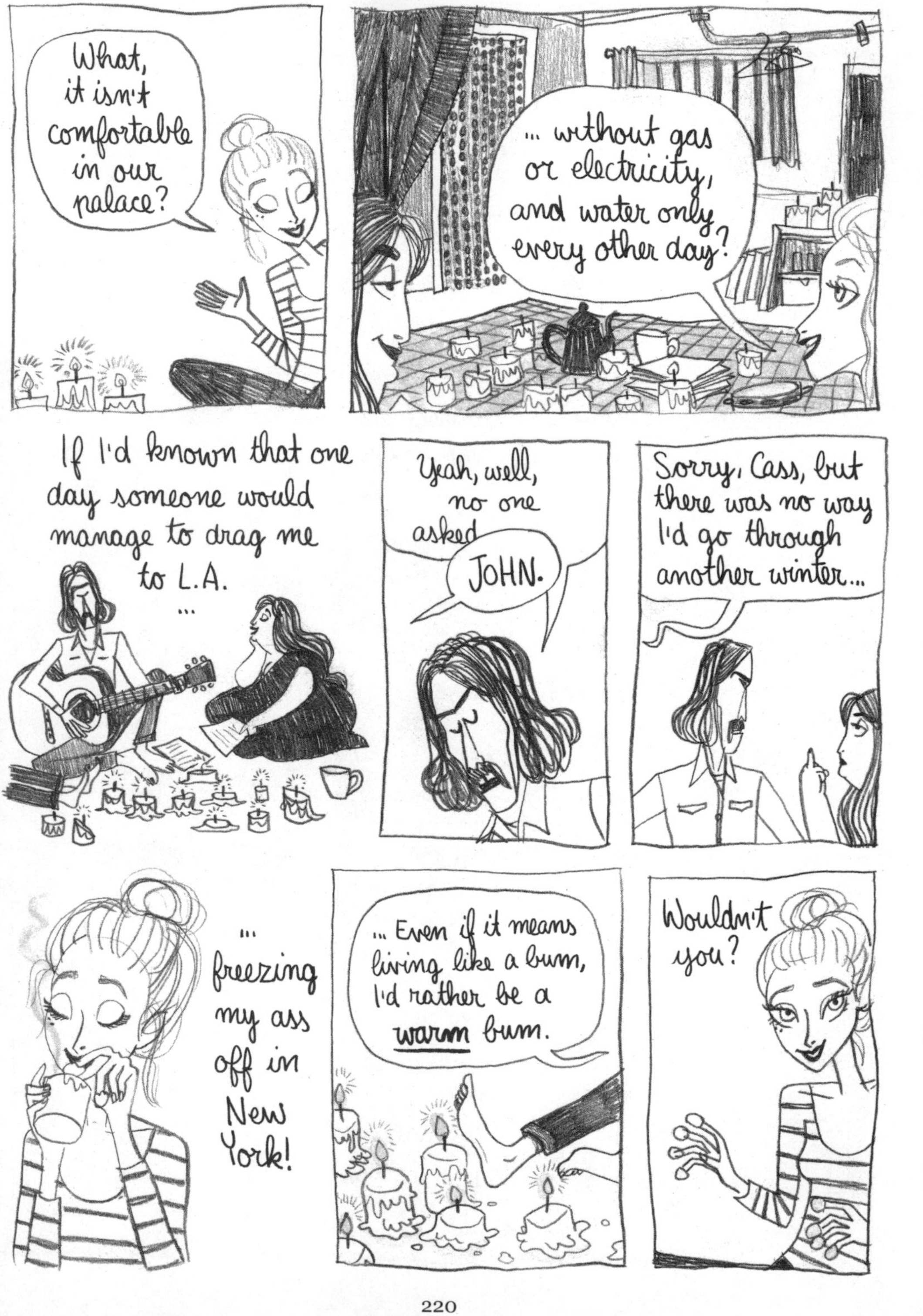

What, it isn't comfortable in our palace?
... without gas or electricity, and water only every other day?
If I'd known that one day someone would manage to drag me to L.A. ...
Yeah, well, no one asked
JOHN.
Sorry, Cass, but there was no way I'd go through another winter...
... freezing my ass off in New York!
... Even if it means living like a bum, I'd rather be a warm bum.
Wouldn't you?

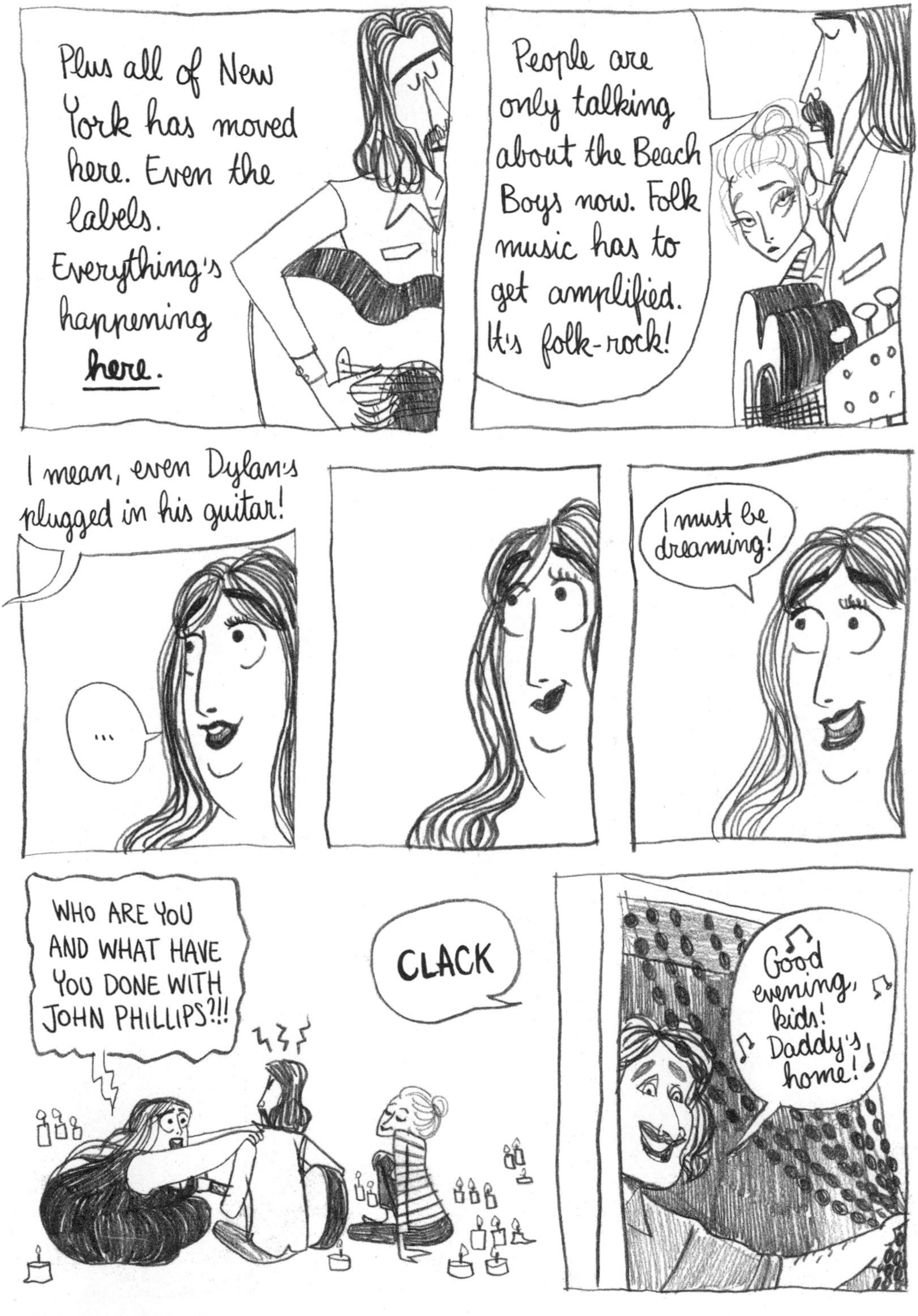
Plus all of New York has moved here. Even the labels. Everything's happening **here**.
People are only talking about the Beach Boys now. Folk music has to get amplified. It's folk-rock!
I mean, even Dylan's plugged in his guitar!
...
I must be dreaming!
WHO ARE YOU AND WHAT HAVE YOU DONE WITH JOHN PHILLIPS?!!
CLACK
Good evening, kids! Daddy's home!

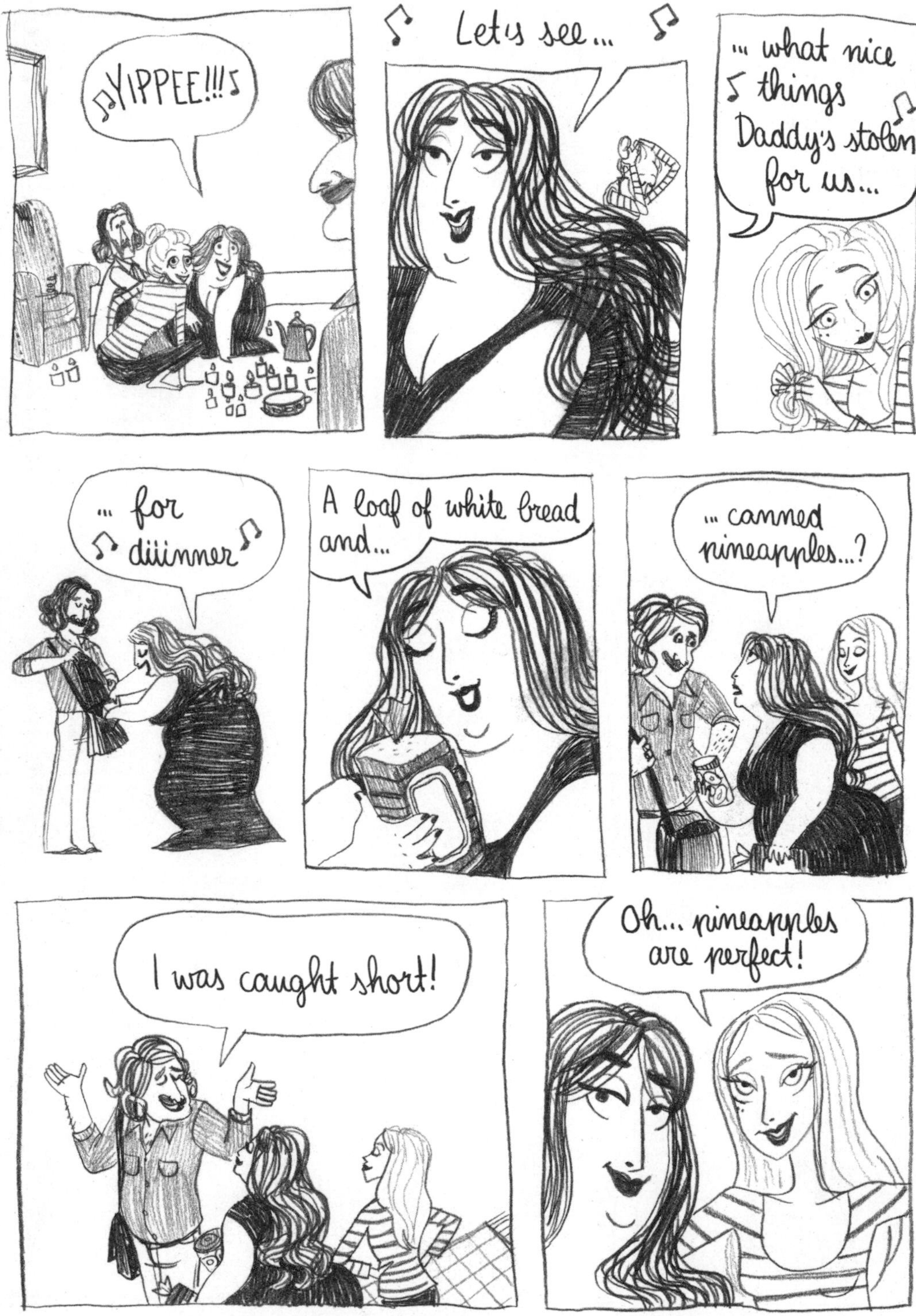
YIPPEE!!!
Let's see...
... what nice things Daddy's stolen for us...
... for diiinner
A loaf of white bread and...
... canned pineapples...?
I was caught short!
Oh... pineapples are perfect!

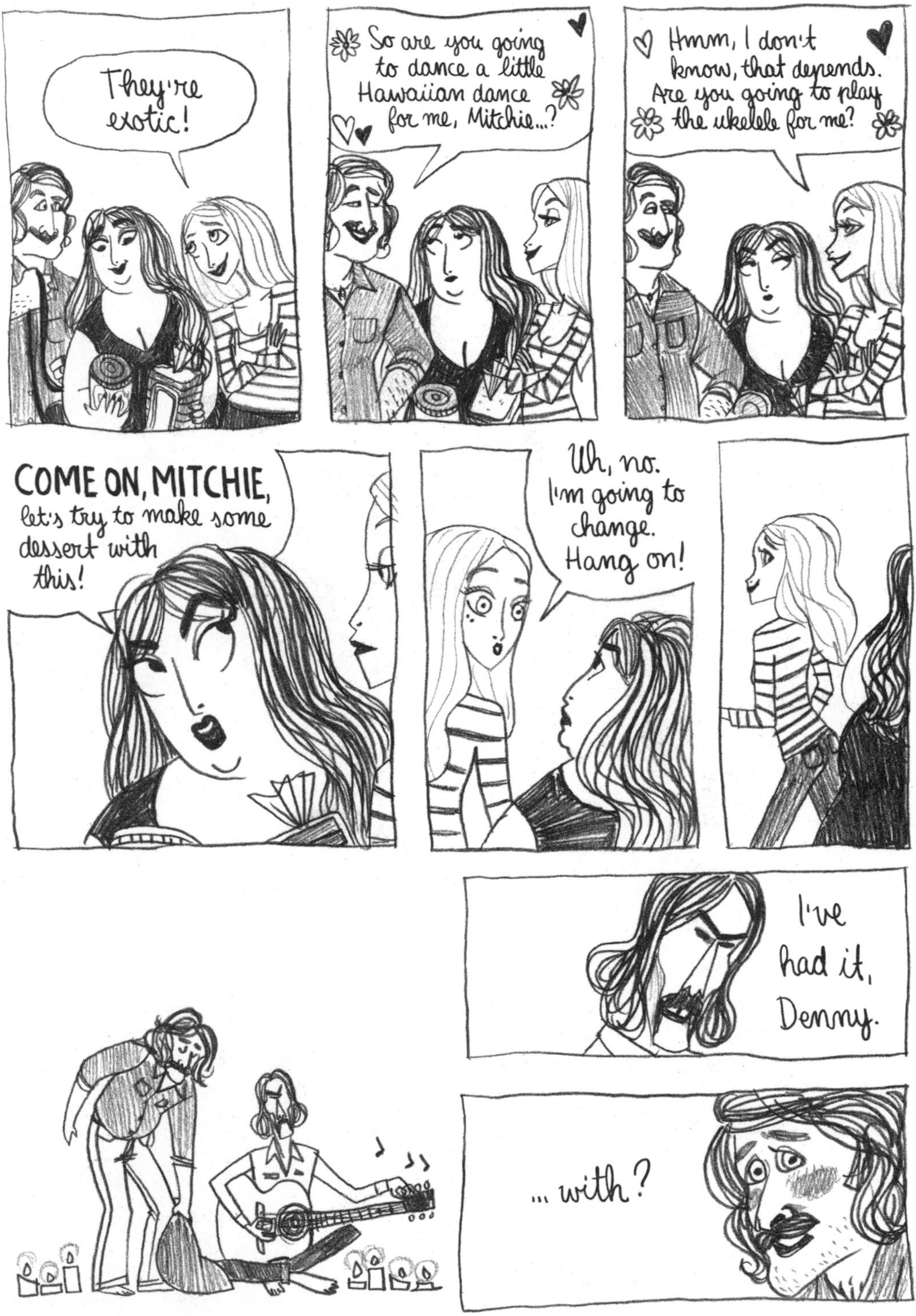
They're exotic!
So are you going to dance a little Hawaiian dance for me, Mitchie...?
Hmm, I don't know, that depends. Are you going to play the ukelele for me?
COME ON, MITCHIE, let's try to make some dessert with this!
Uh, no. I'm going to change. Hang on!
I've had it, Denny.
... with?

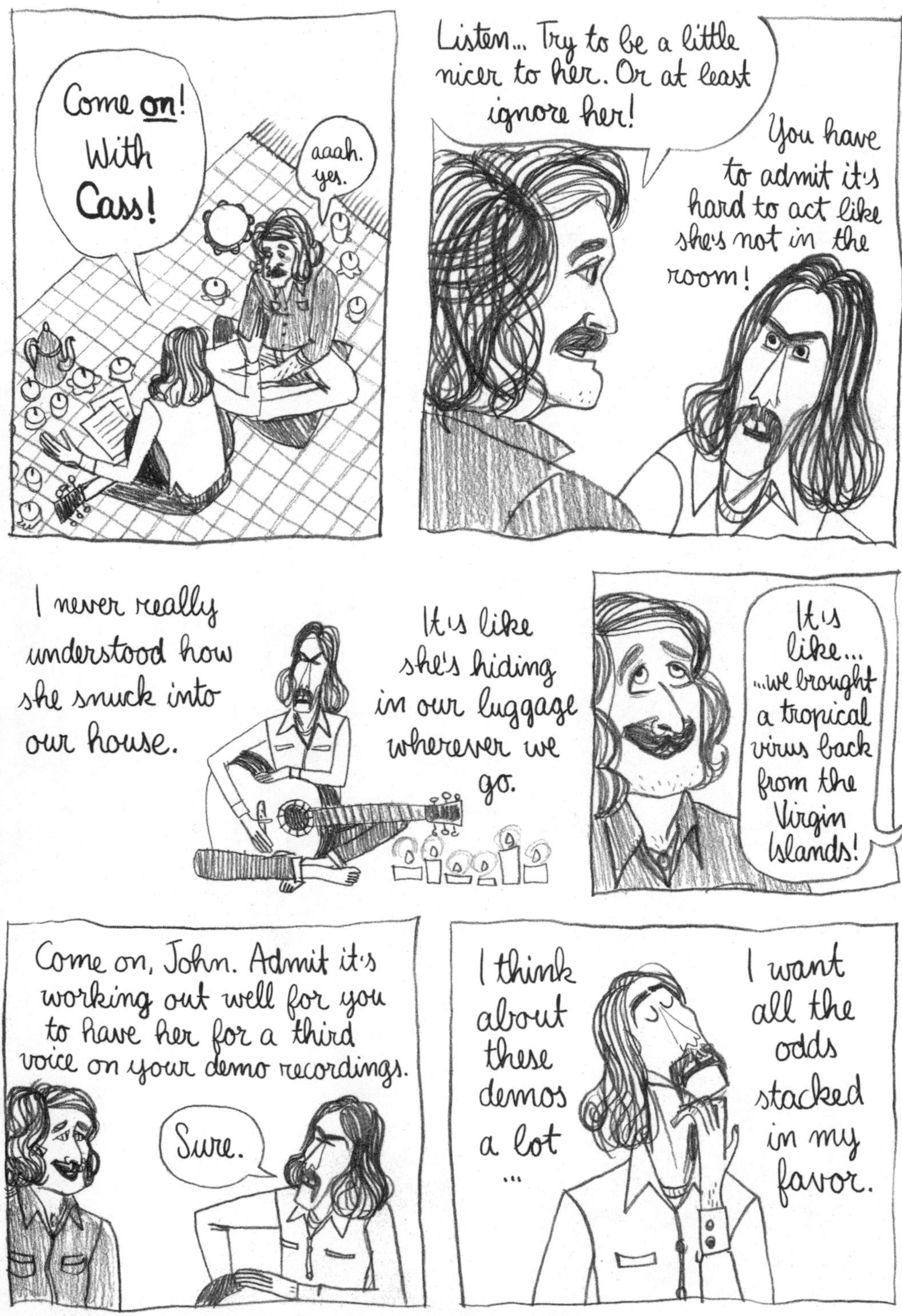
Come on! With Cass!
aaah. yes.
Listen... Try to be a little nicer to her. Or at least ignore her!
You have to admit it's hard to act like she's not in the room!
I never really understood how she snuck into our house.
It's like she's hiding in our luggage wherever we go.
It's like... ...we brought a tropical virus back from the Virgin Islands!
Come on, John. Admit it's working out well for you to have her for a third voice on your demo recordings.
Sure.
I think about these demos a lot ...
I want all the odds stacked in my favor.

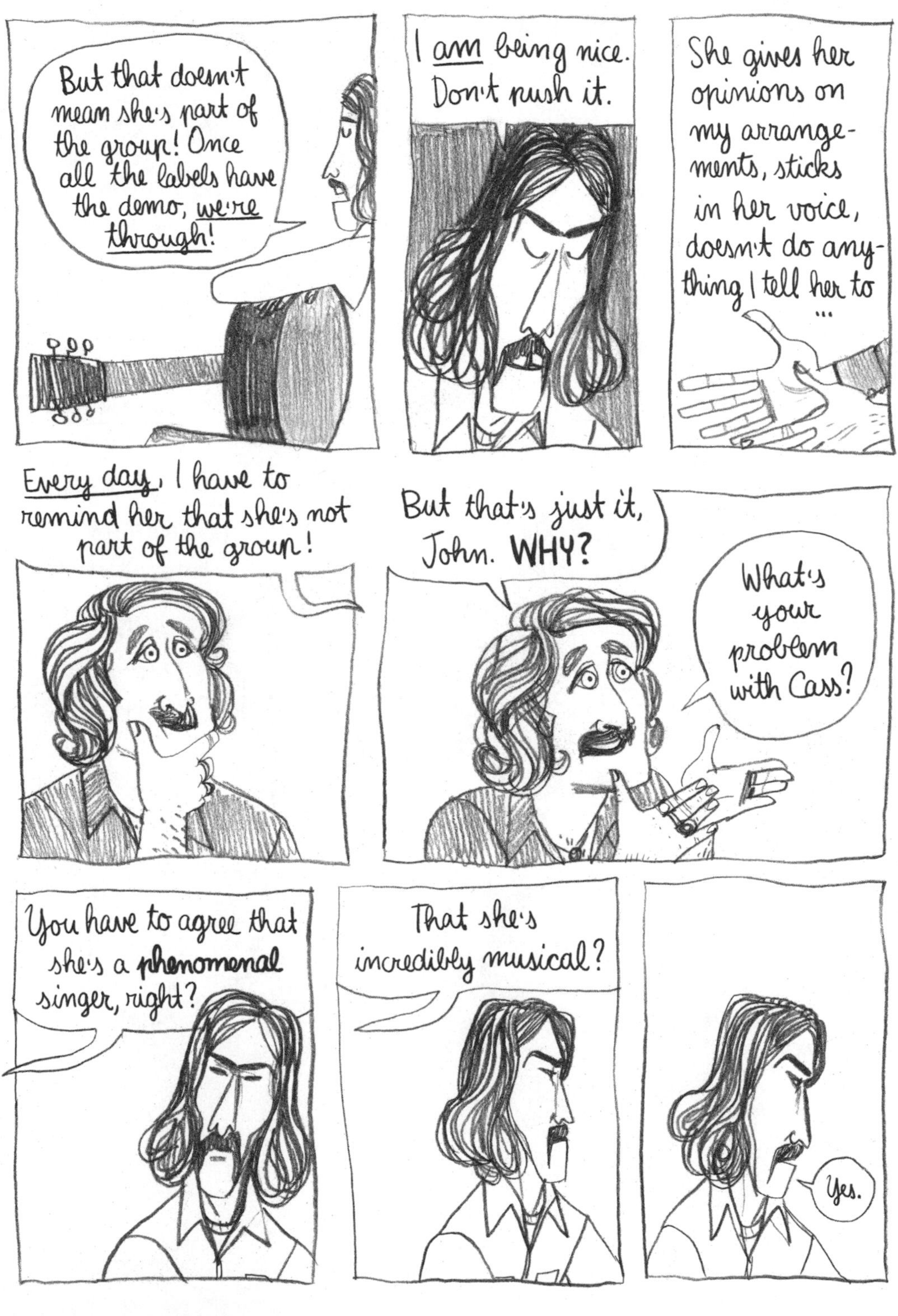
But that doesn't mean she's part of the group! Once all the labels have the demo, we're through!
I am being nice. Don't push it.
She gives her opinions on my arrangements, sticks in her voice, doesn't do anything I tell her to ...
Every day, I have to remind her that she's not part of the group!
But that's just it, John. WHY?
What's your problem with Cass?
You have to agree that she's a phenomenal singer, right?
That she's incredibly musical?
Yes.

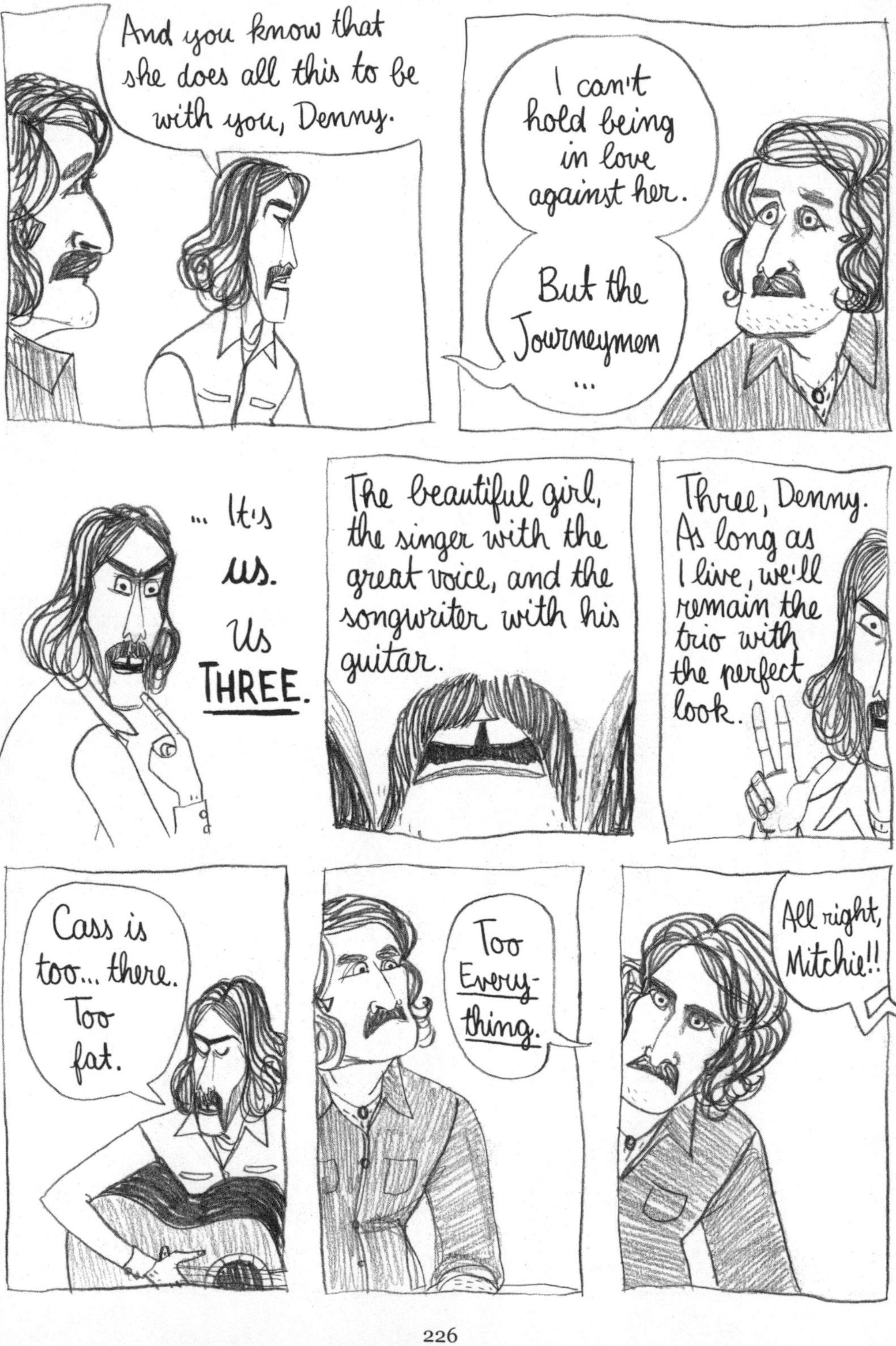

And you know that she does all this to be with you, Denny.
I can't hold being in love against her.
But the Journeymen ...
... It's us. Us THREE.
The beautiful girl, the singer with the great voice, and the songwriter with his guitar.
Three, Denny. As long as I live, we'll remain the trio with the perfect look.
Cass is too... there. Too fat.
Too Every-thing.
All right, Mitchie!!

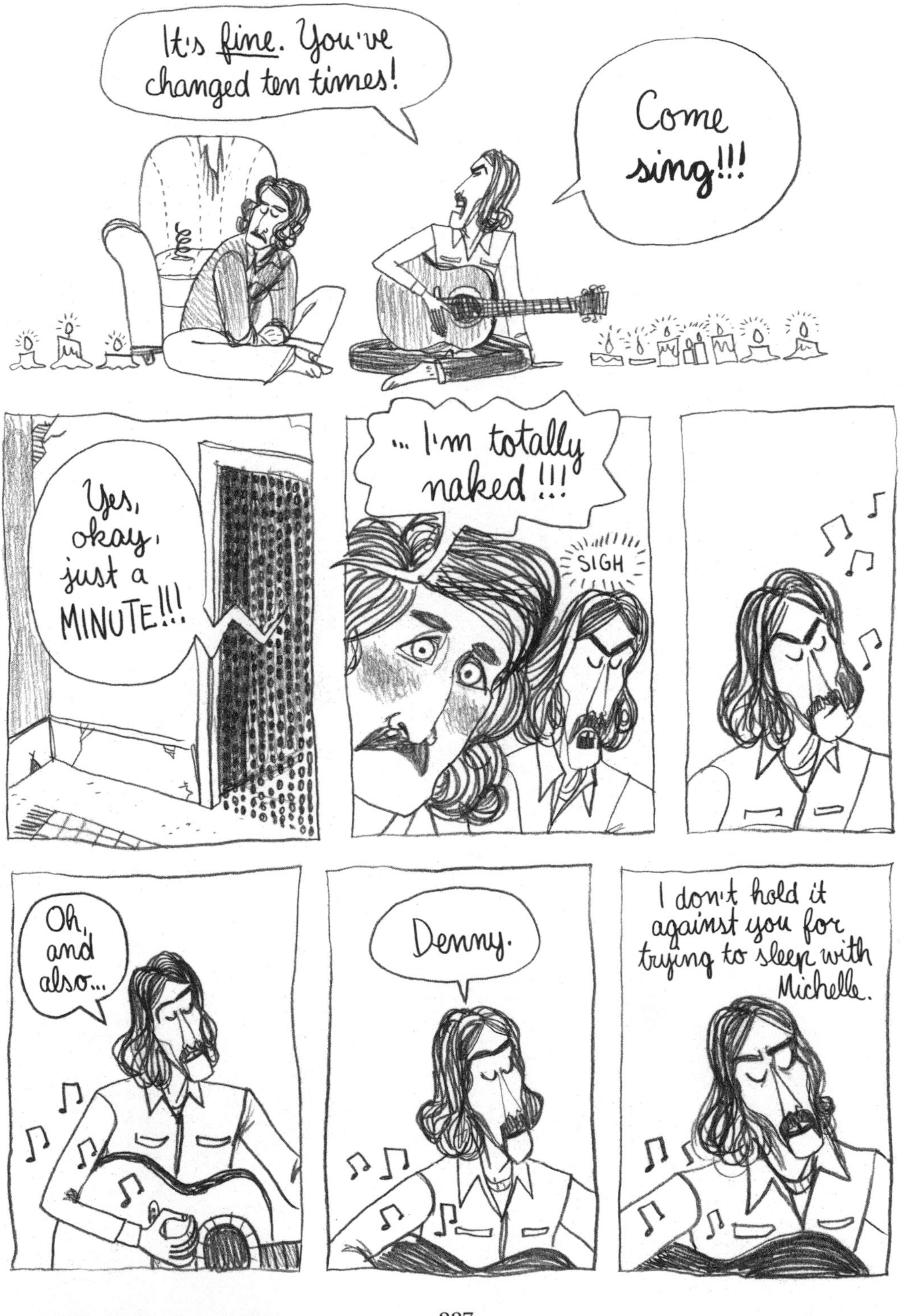
It's fine. You've changed ten times!
Come sing!!!
Yes, okay, just a MINUTE!!!
... I'm totally naked!!!
SIGH
Oh, and also...
Denny.
I don't hold it against you for trying to sleep with Michelle.

I understand it. She's the most beautiful woman in the world.

But Mitchie's an innocent. She's a child. She doesn't realize it.

She's completely unaware of her beauty. And the effect she has on guys.

OKAY, ARE WE GOING TO SING NOW OR DO MACRAMÉ?!!

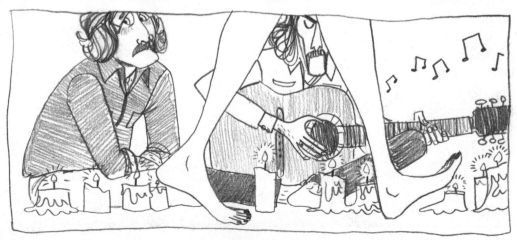

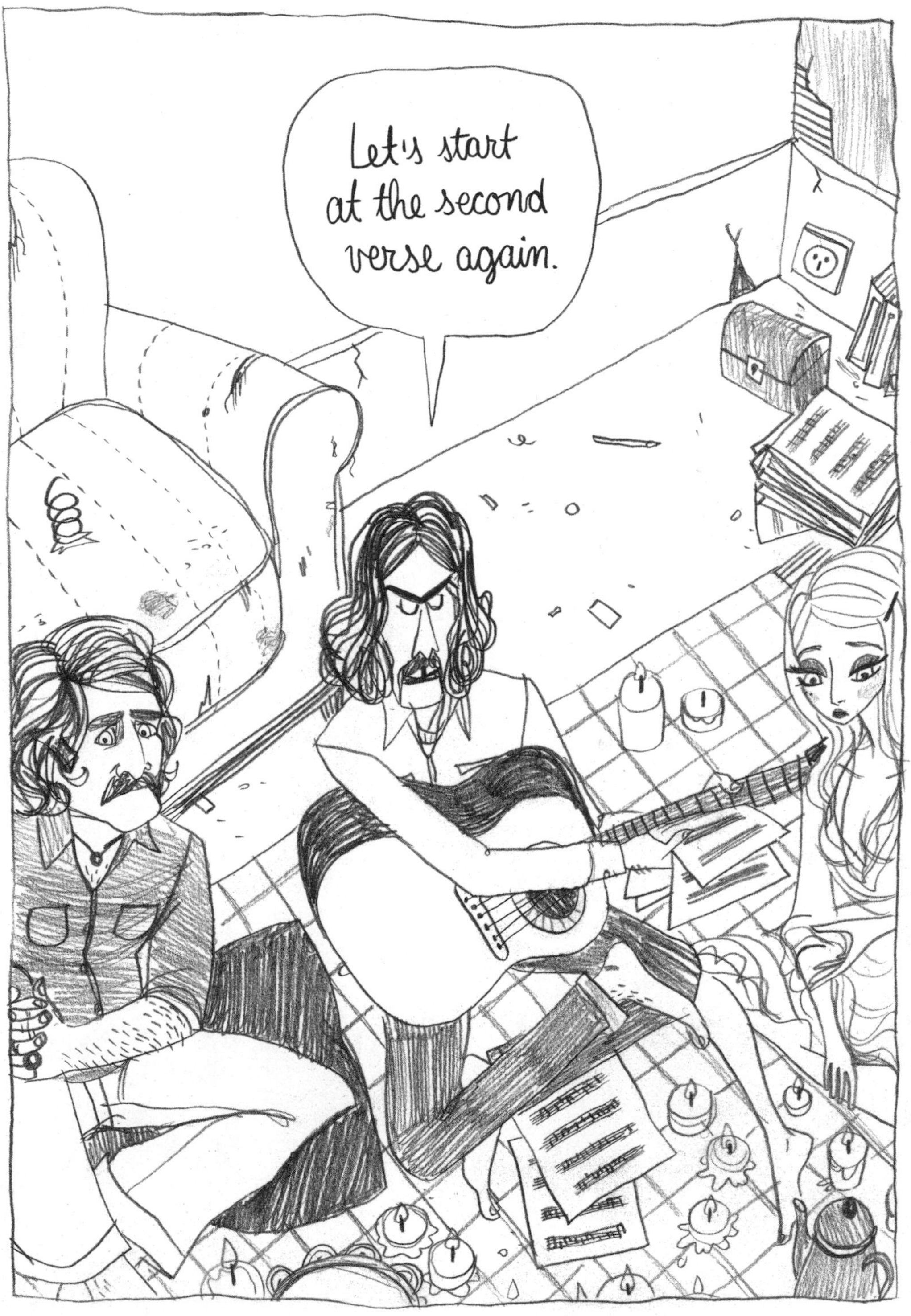
Let's start at the second verse again.

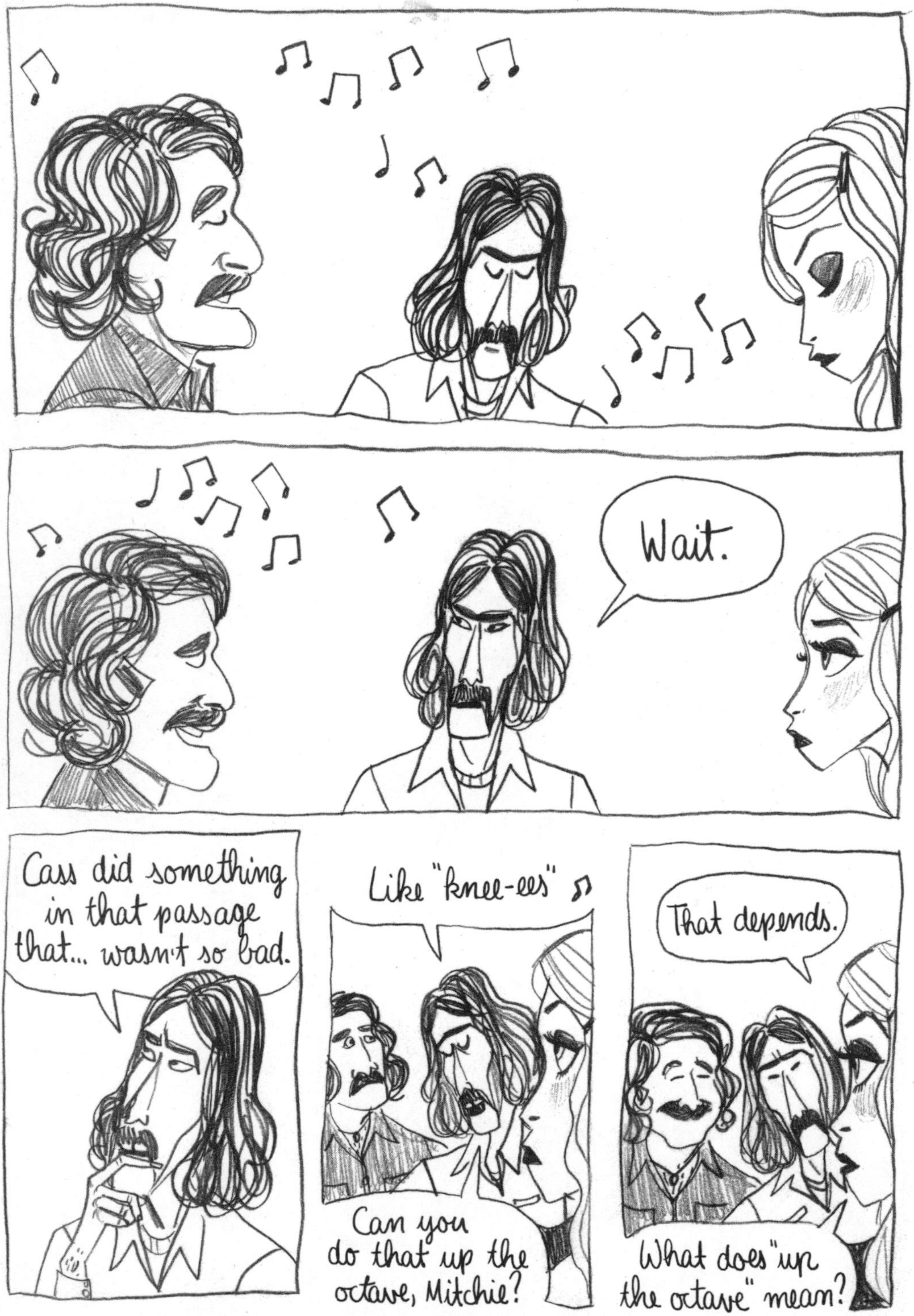
Wait.
Cass did something in that passage that... wasn't so bad.
Like "knee-ees"
Can you do that up the octave, Mitchie?
That depends.
What does "up the octave" mean?

17-Lou

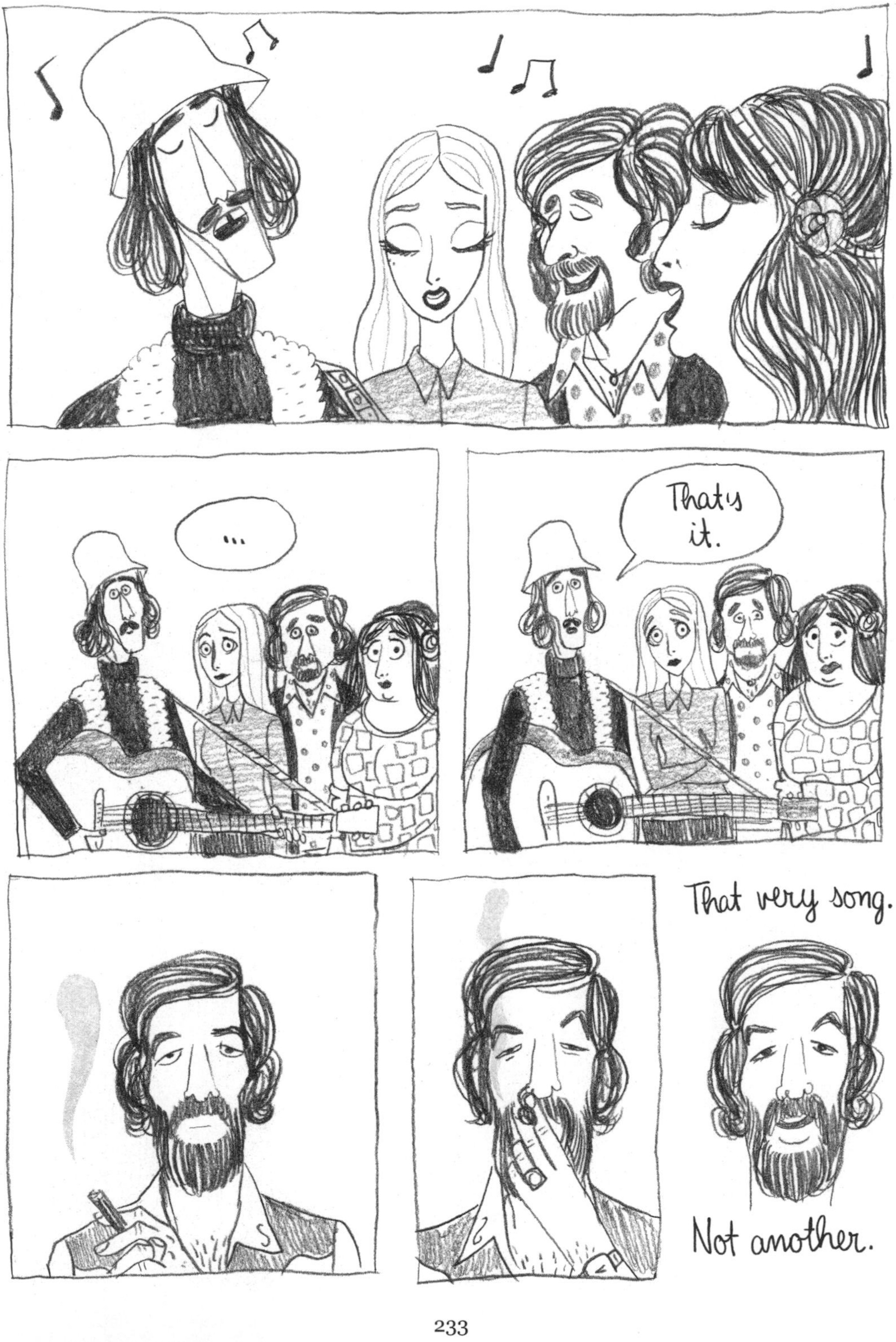
...
That's it.
That very song.
Not another.

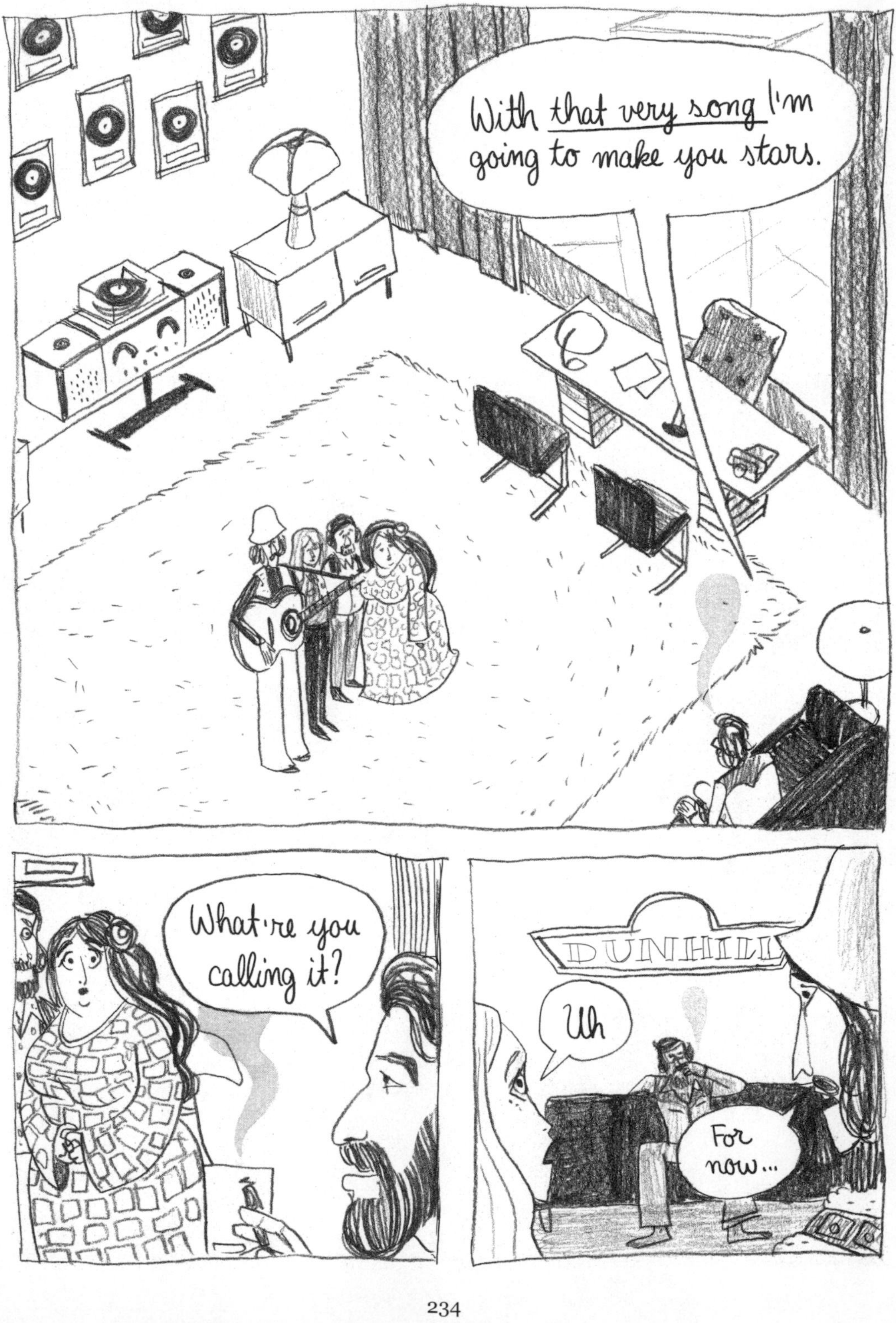
With that very song I'm going to make you stars.
What're you calling it?
DUNHILL
Uh
For now...

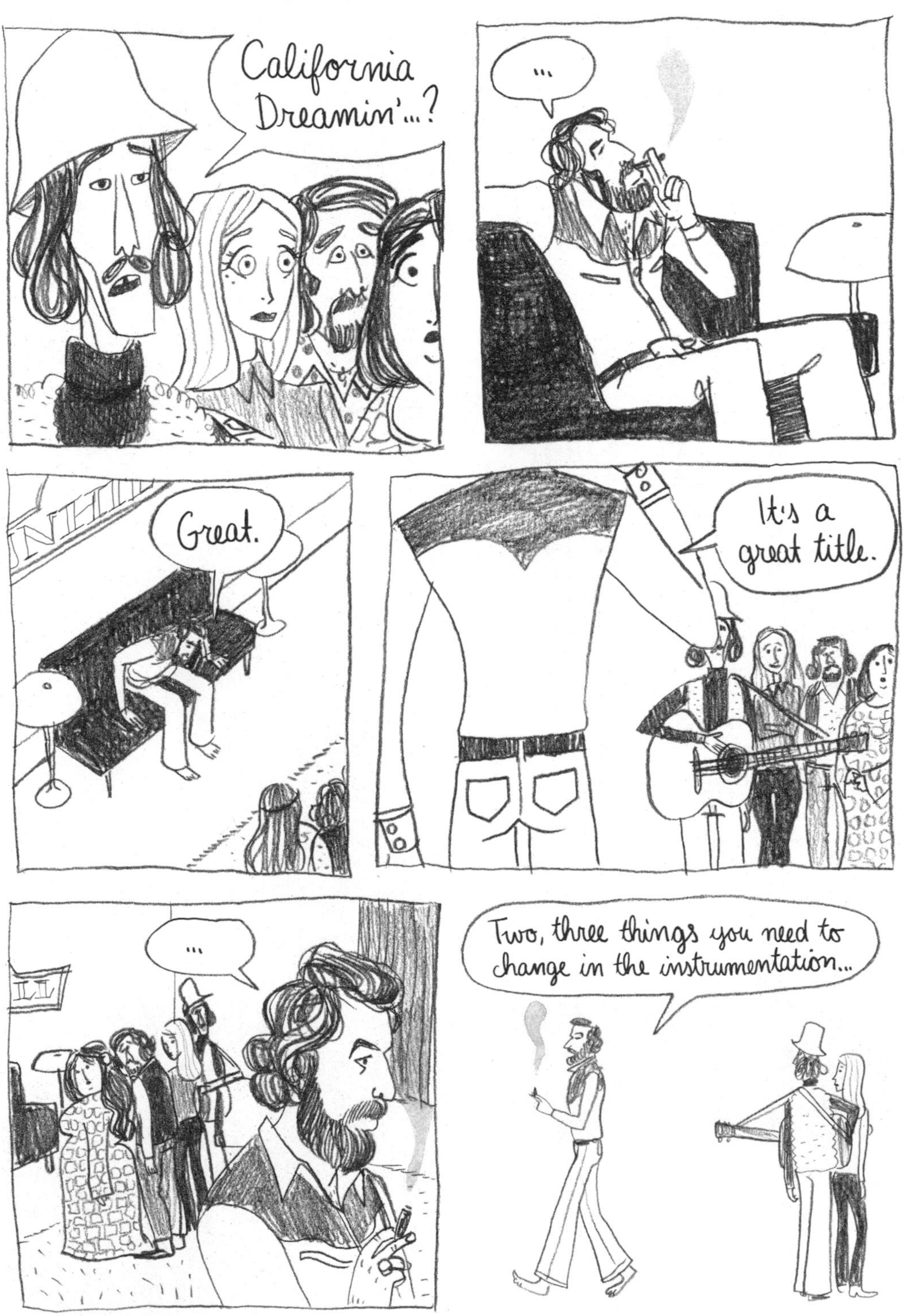
California Dreamin'...?
...
Great.
It's a great title.
...
Two, three things you need to change in the instrumentation...

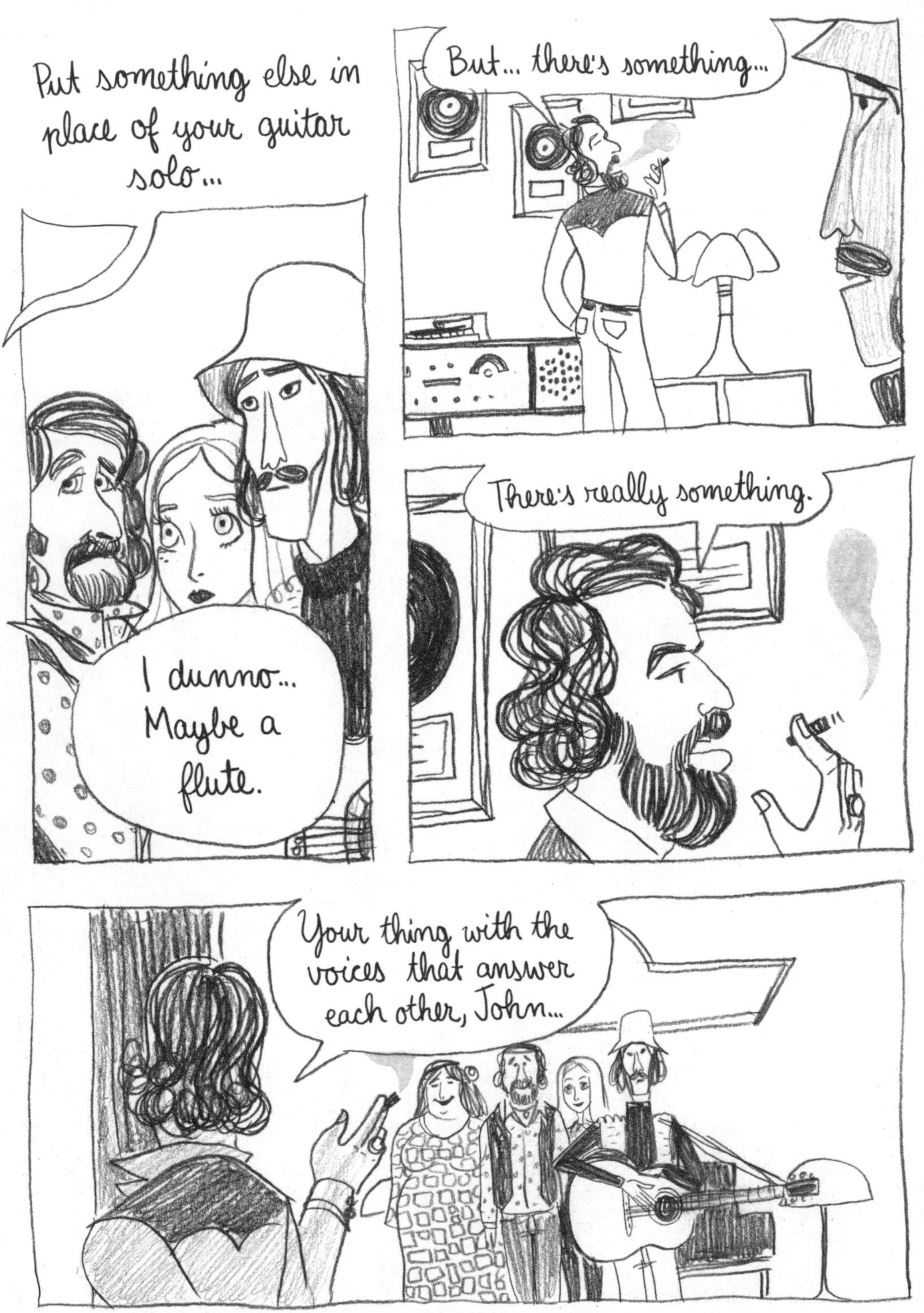
Put something else in place of your guitar solo...
I dunno... Maybe a flute.
But... there's something...
There's really something.
Your thing with the voices that answer each other, John...

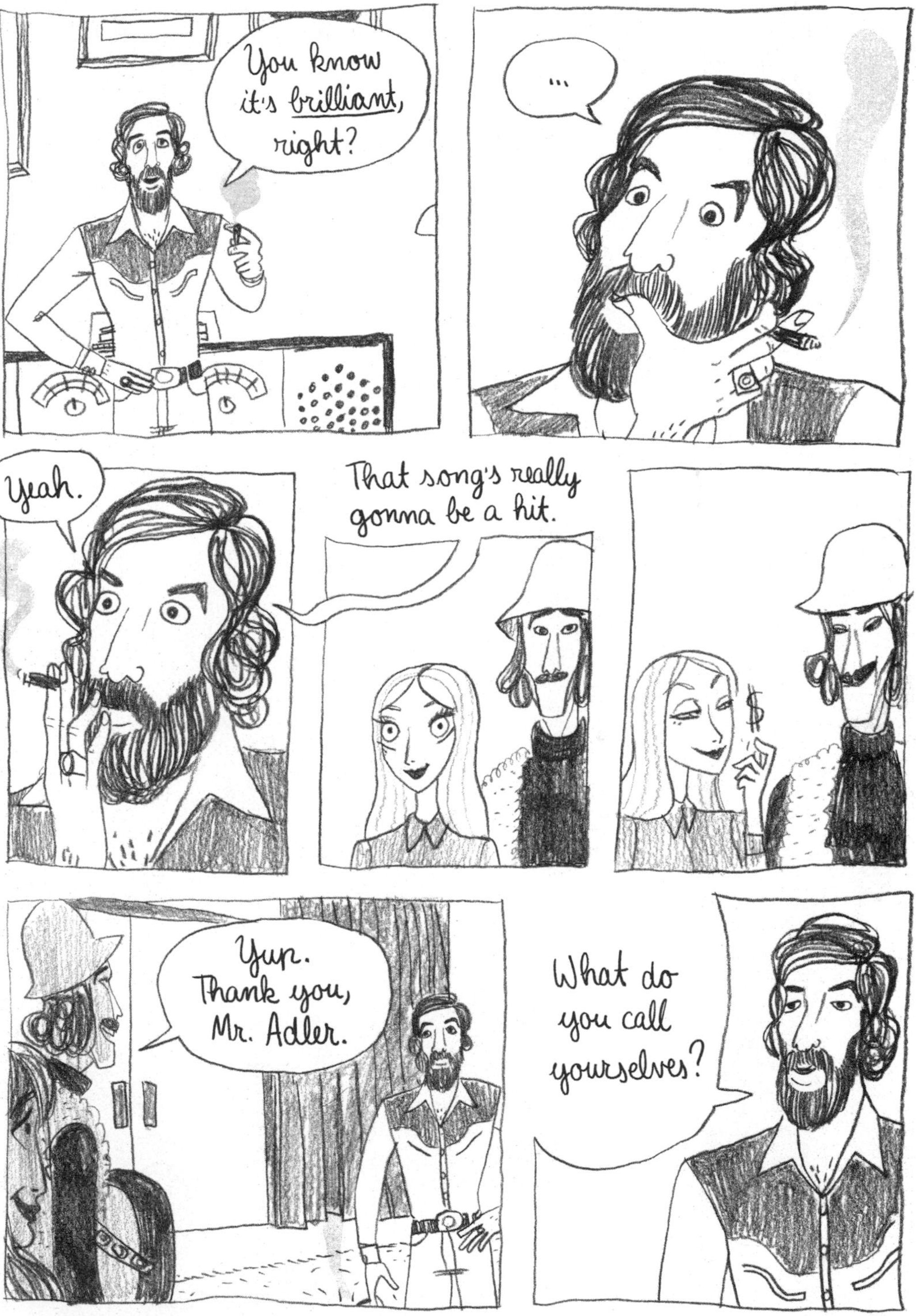
You know it's brilliant, right?
...
Yeah.
That song's really gonna be a hit.
$
Yup. Thank you, Mr. Adler.
What do you call yourselves?

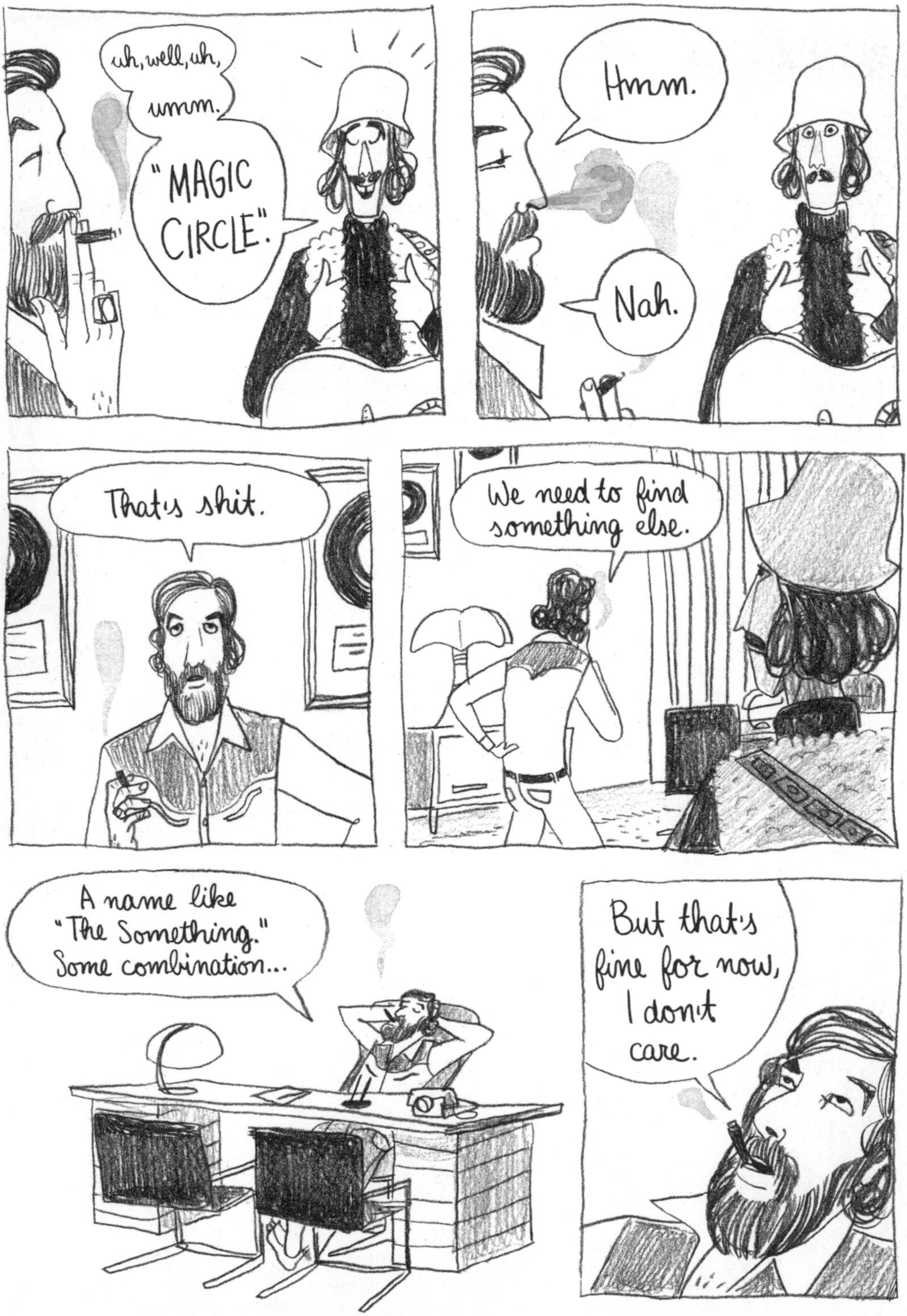
uh, well, uh,
umm.
"MAGIC CIRCLE".
Hmm.
Nah.
That's shit.
We need to find something else.
A name like "The Something." Some combination...
But that's fine for now, I don't care.

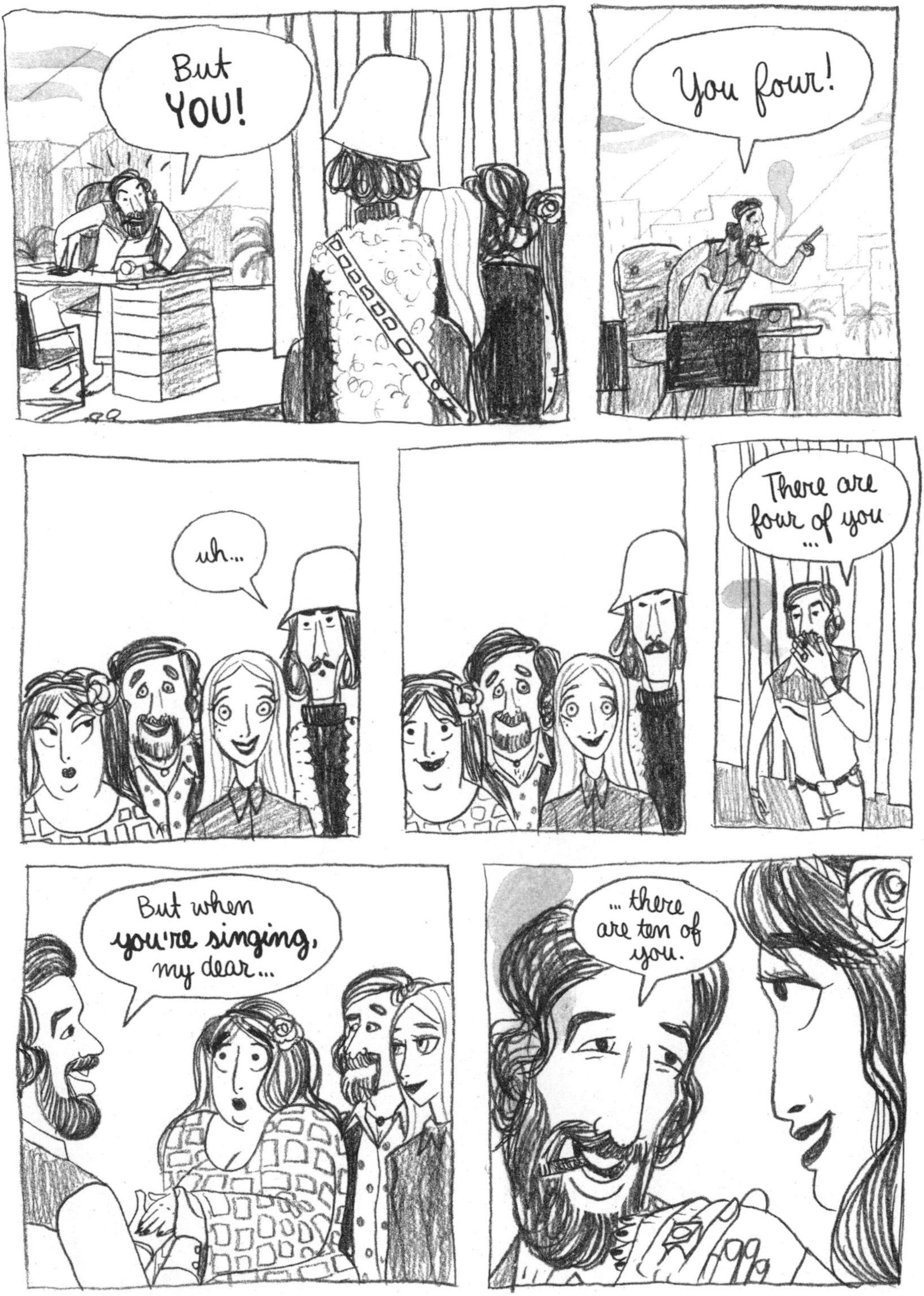
But YOU!
You four!
uh...
There are four of you ...
But when you're singing, my dear...
... there are ten of you.

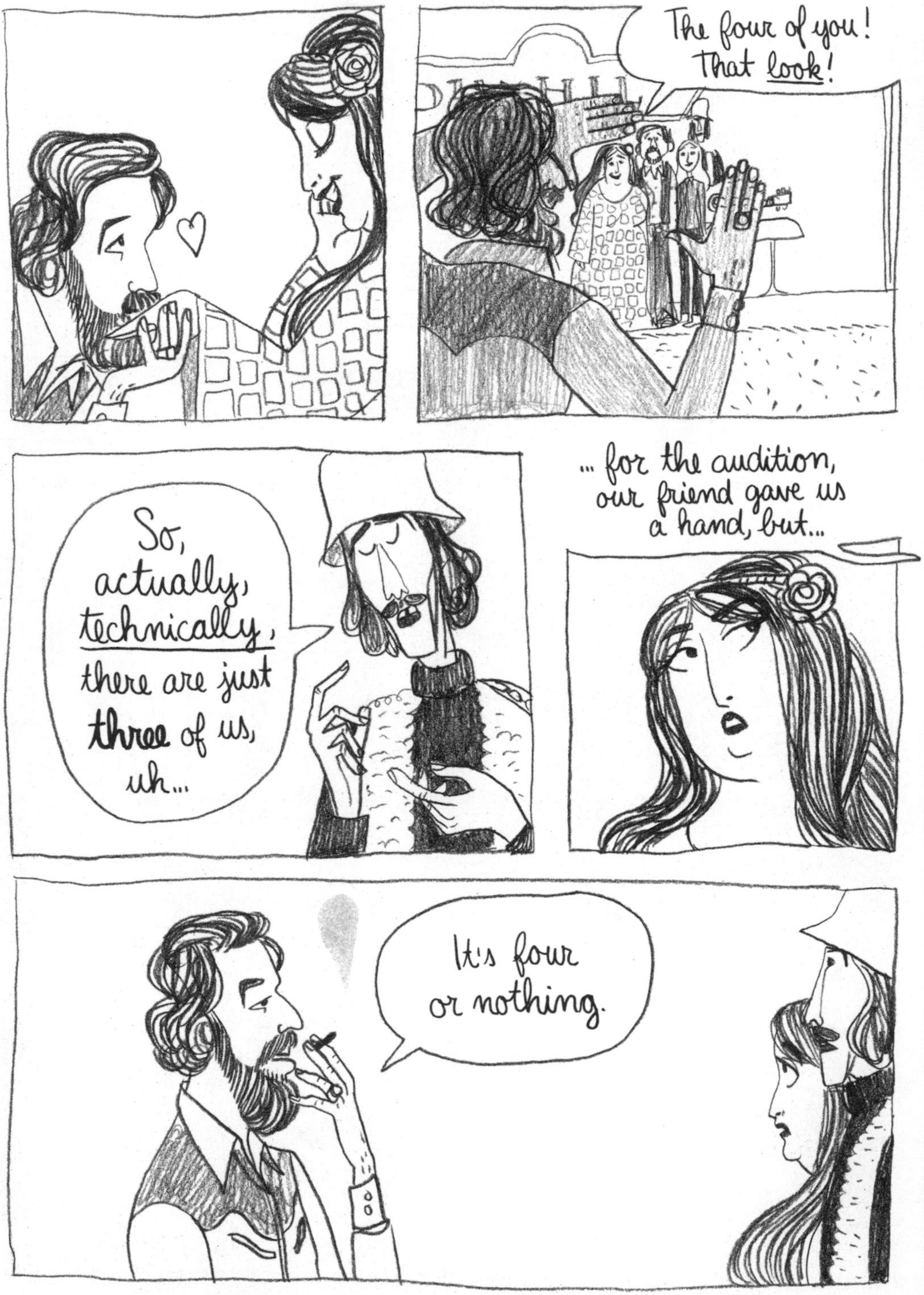
The four of you! That look!
So, actually, technically, there are just three of us, uh...
... for the audition, our friend gave us a hand, but...
It's four or nothing.

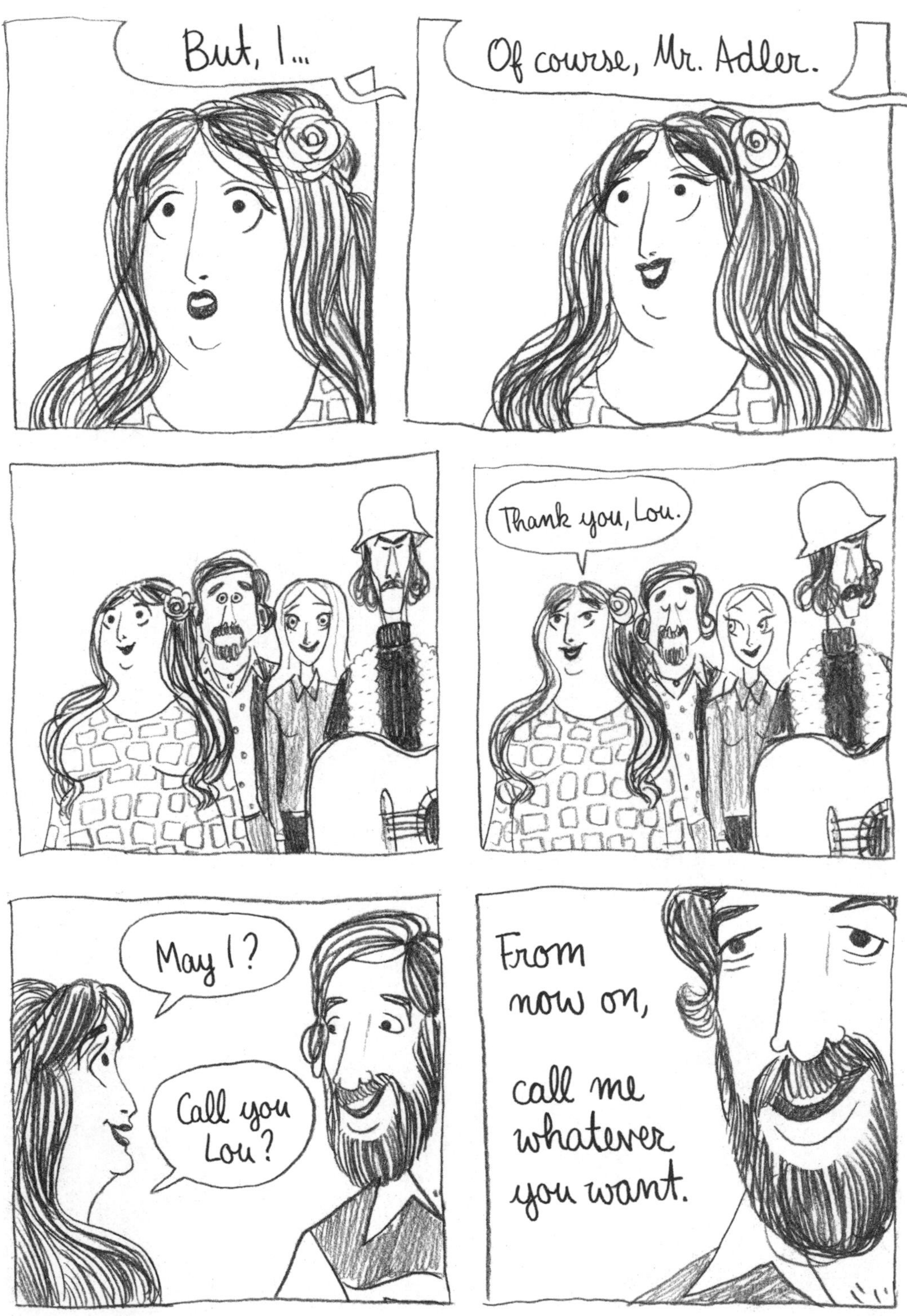
But, I...
Of course, Mr. Adler.
Thank you, Lou.
May I?
Call you Lou?
From now on, call me whatever you want.

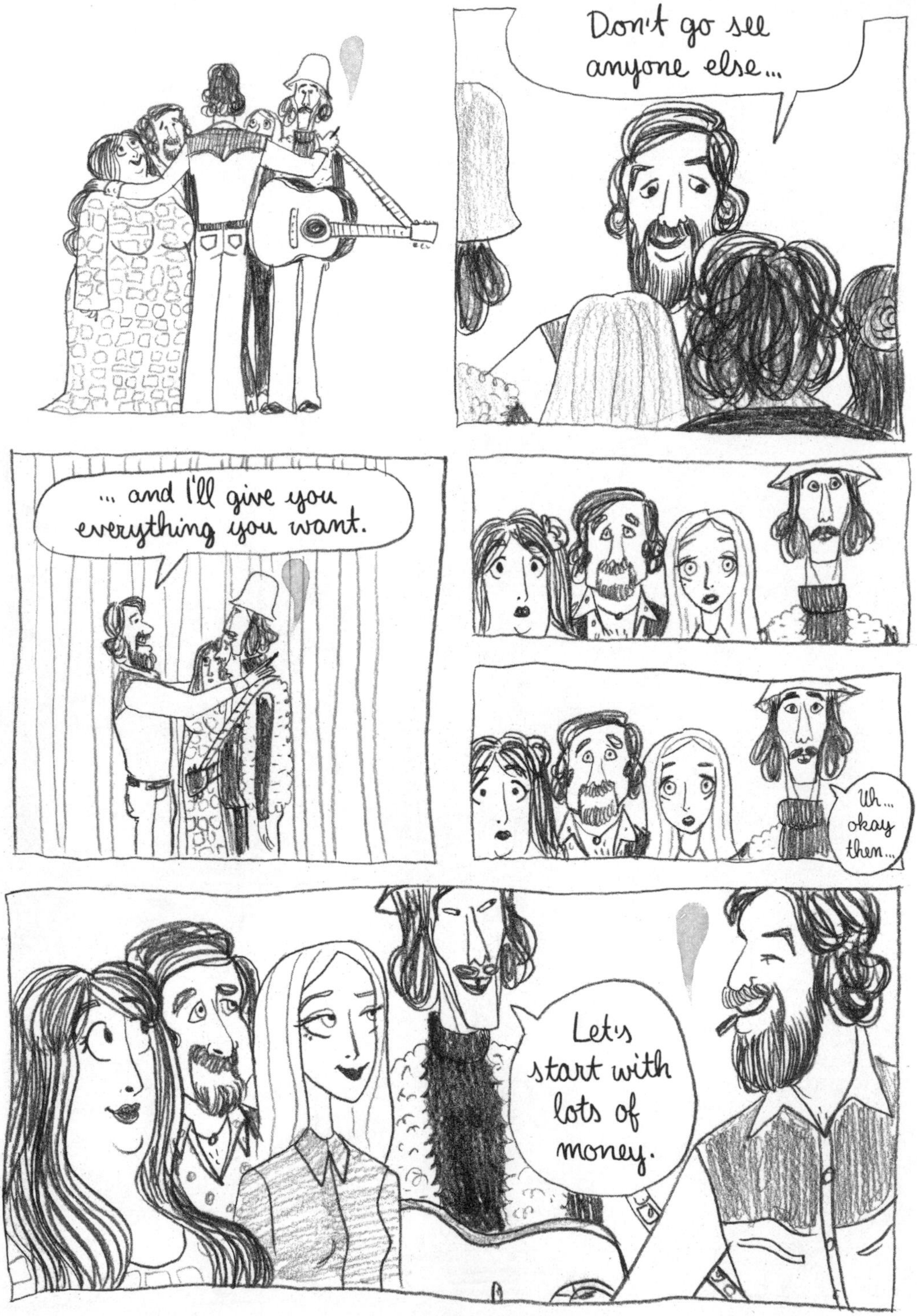
Don't go see anyone else...
... and I'll give you everything you want.
Uh... okay then...
Let's start with lots of money.

18

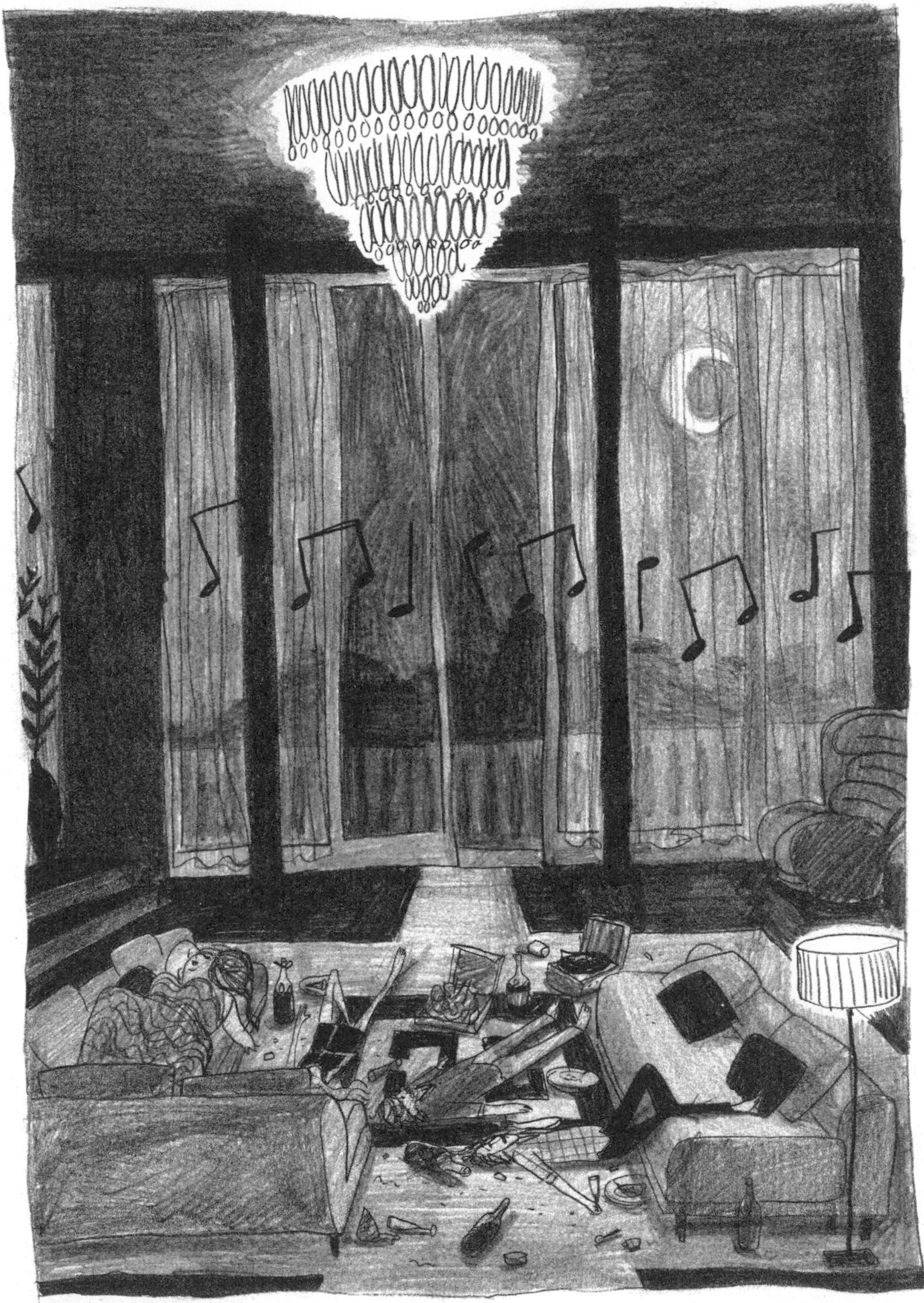

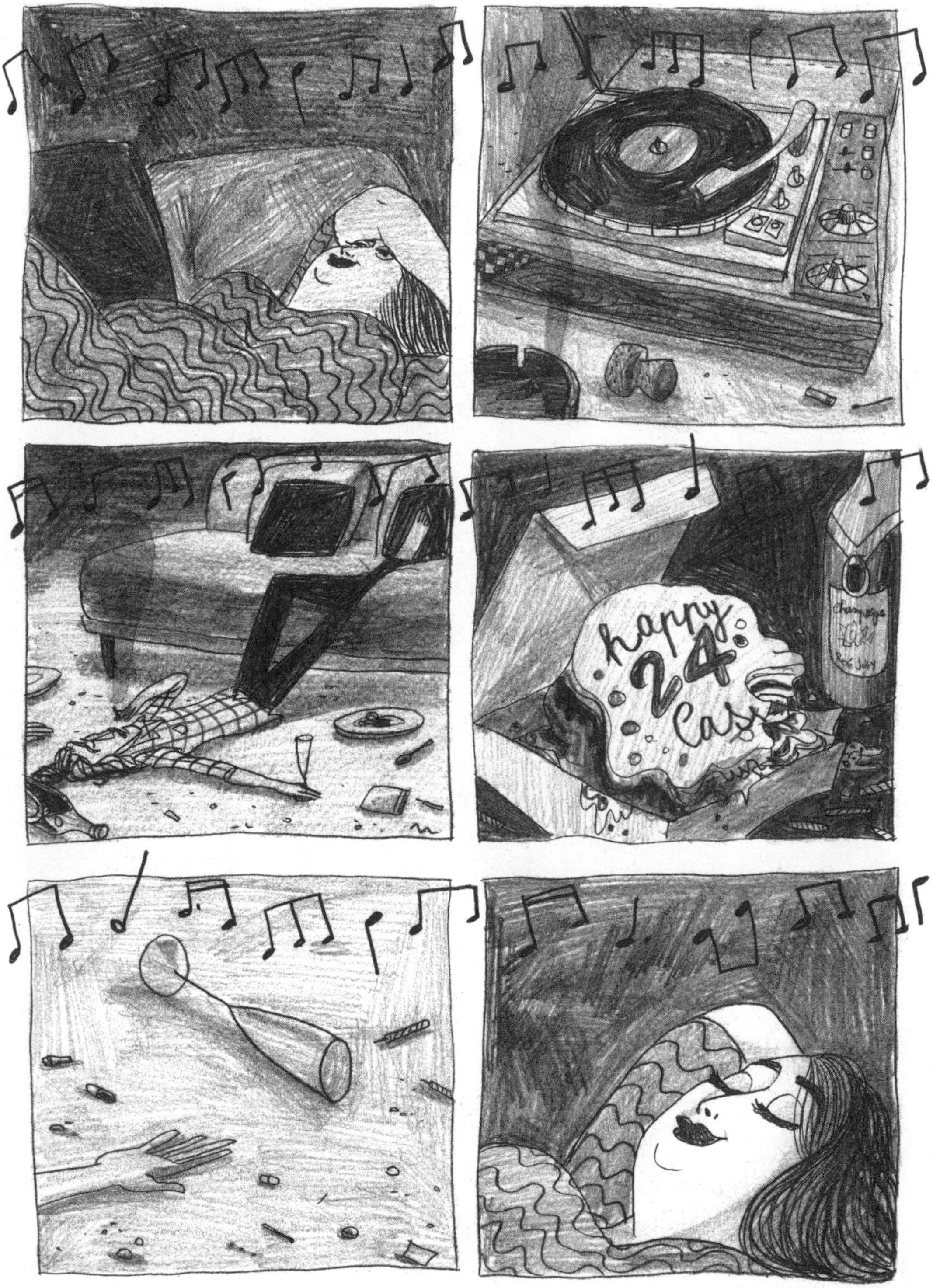
happy
24
Cas

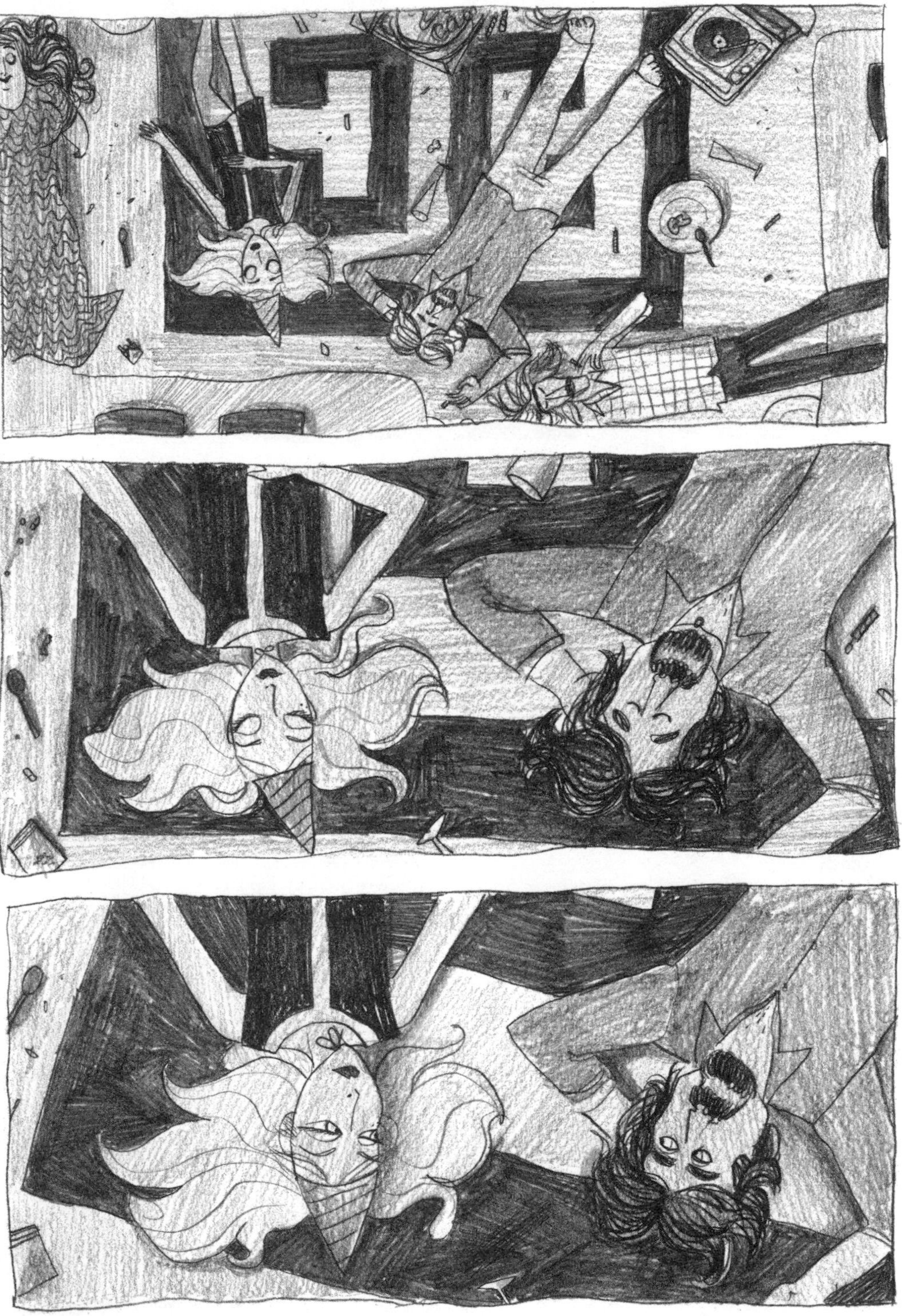

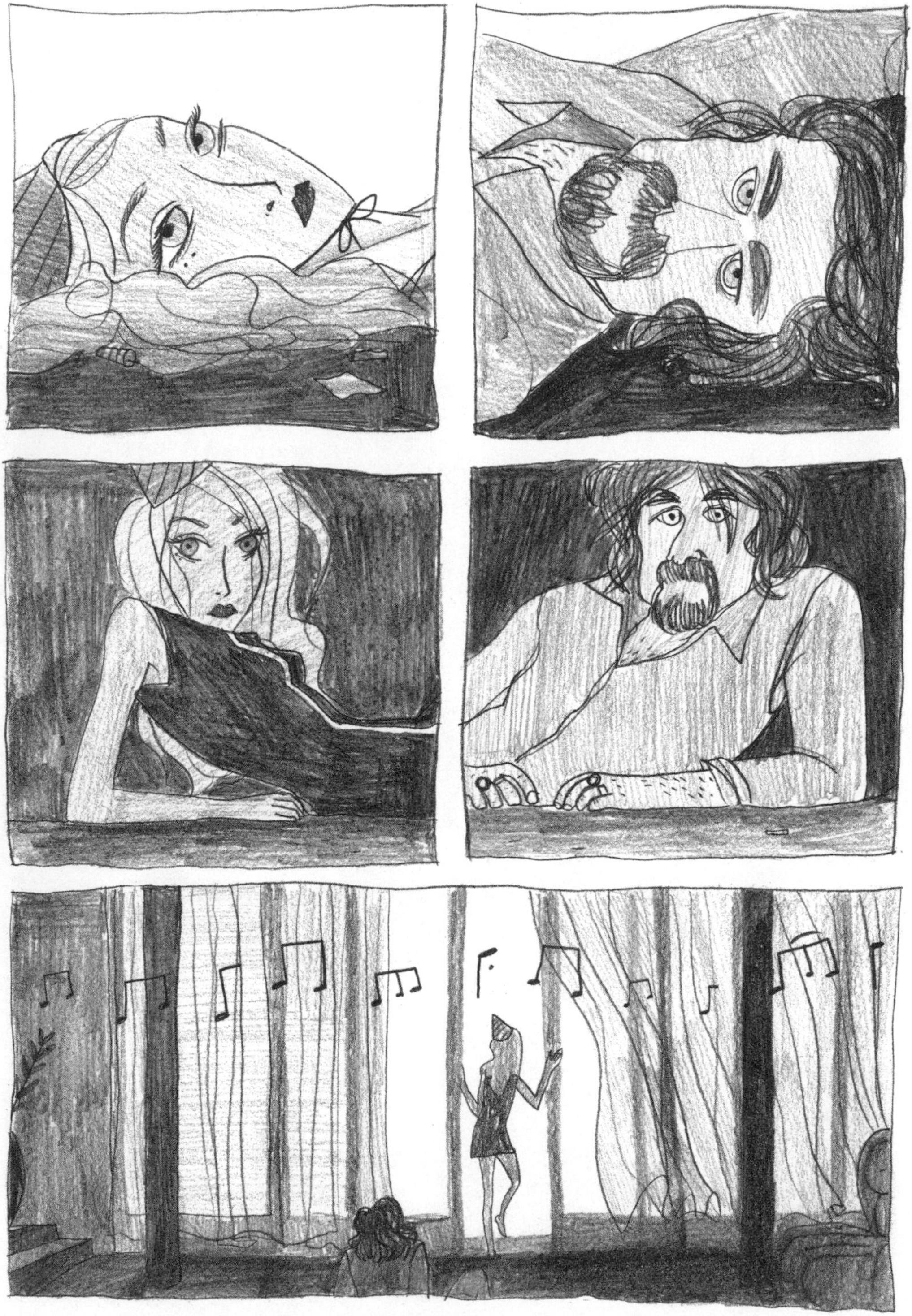

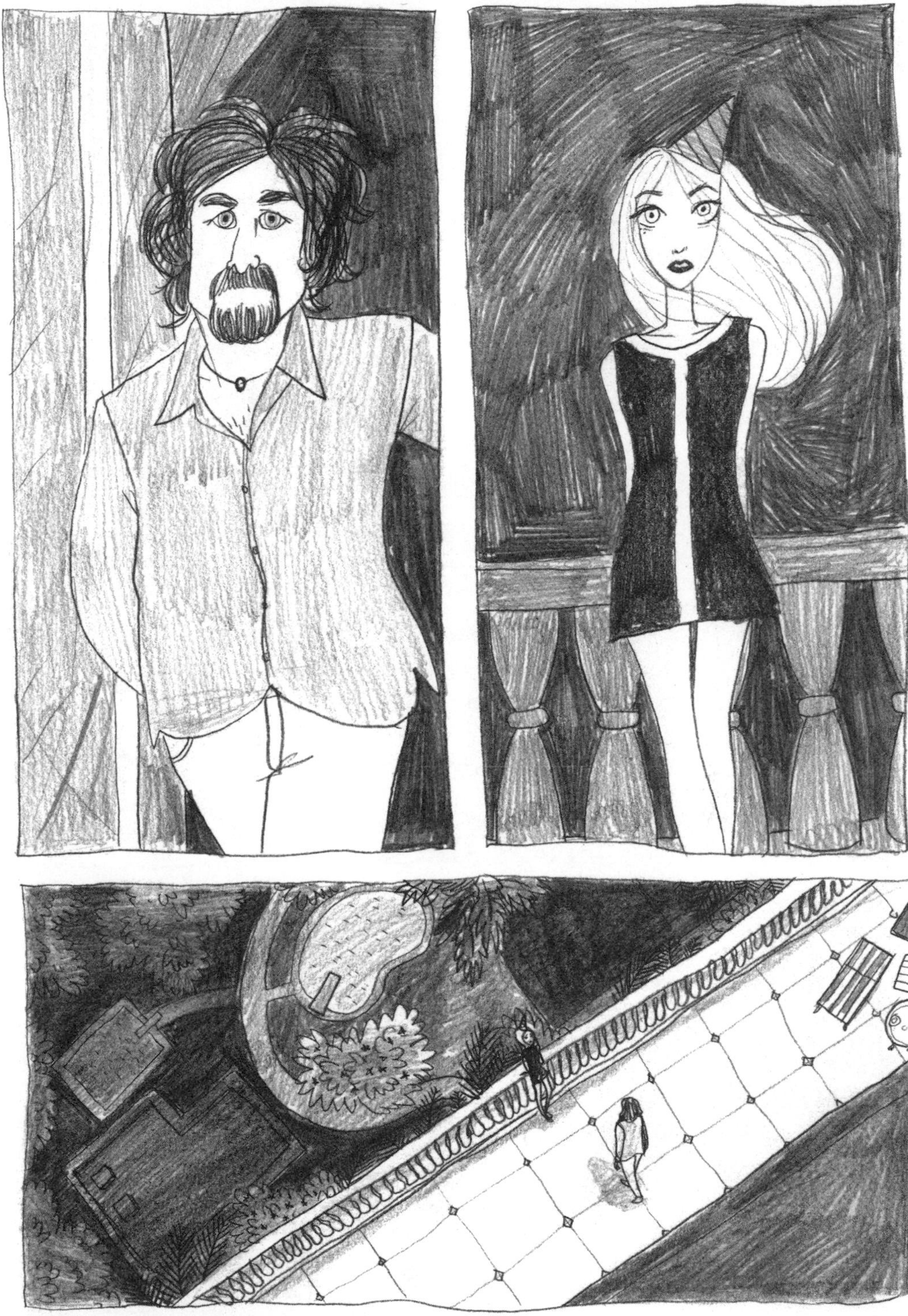

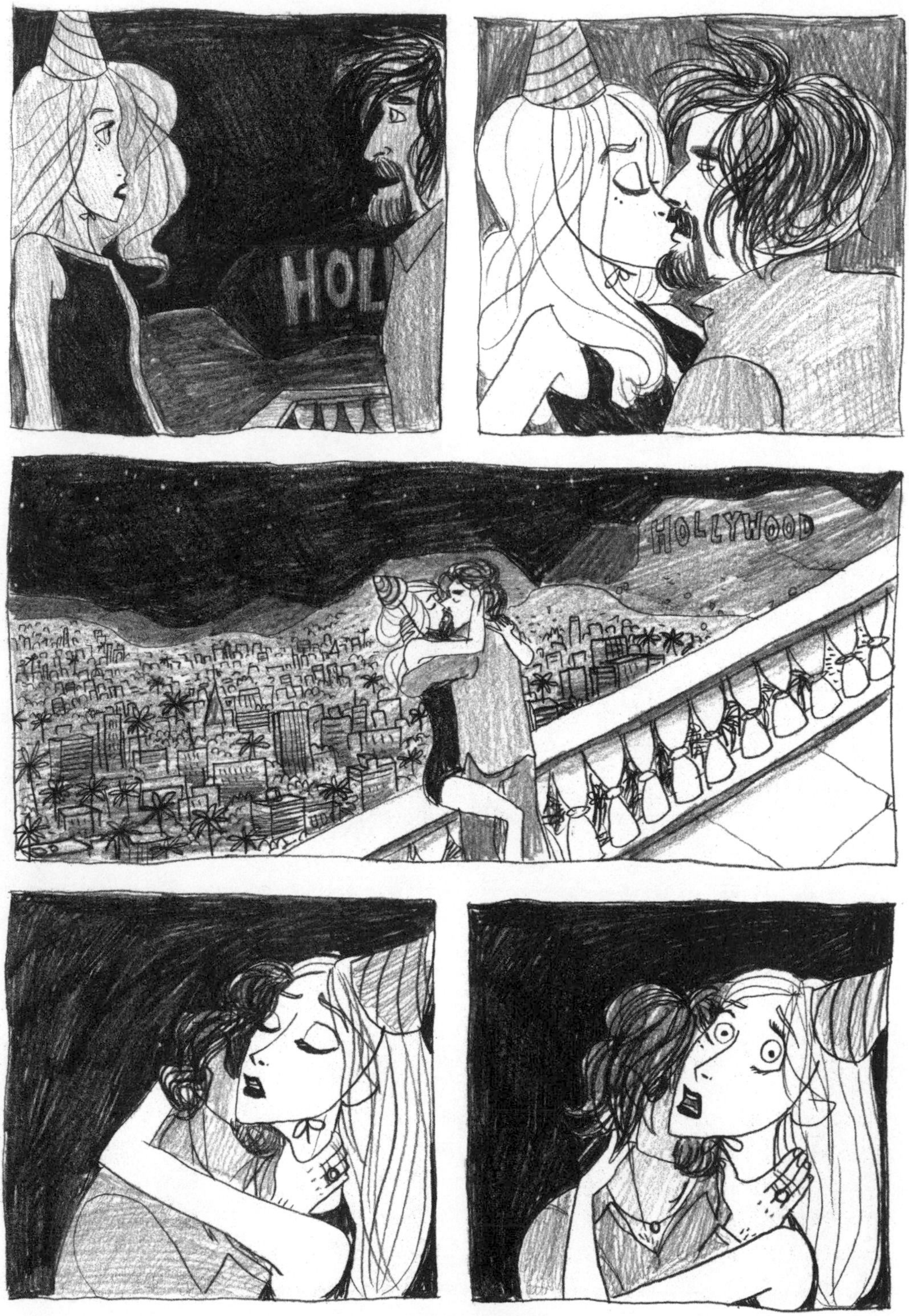
HOL
HOLLYWOOD

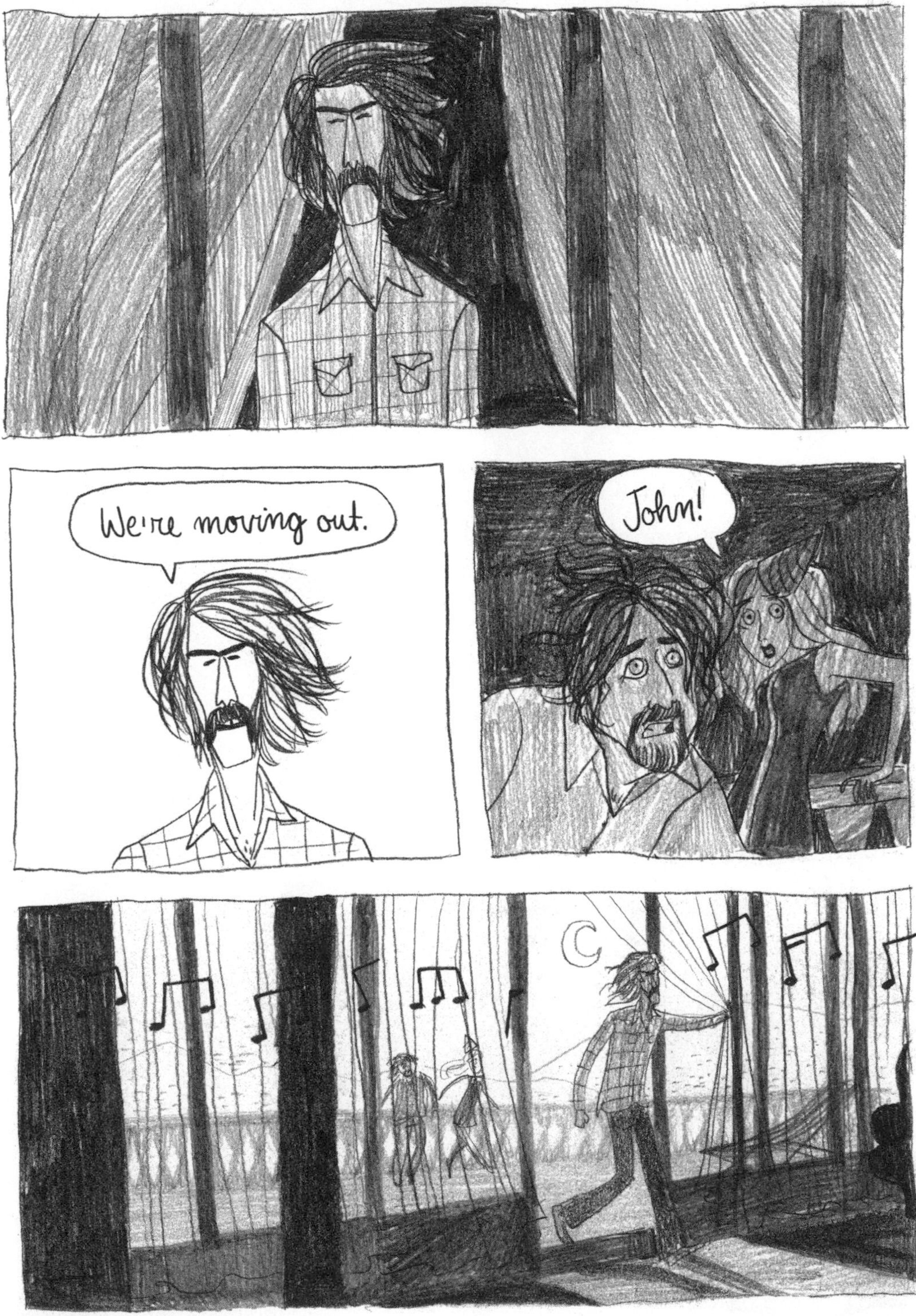
We're moving out.
John!

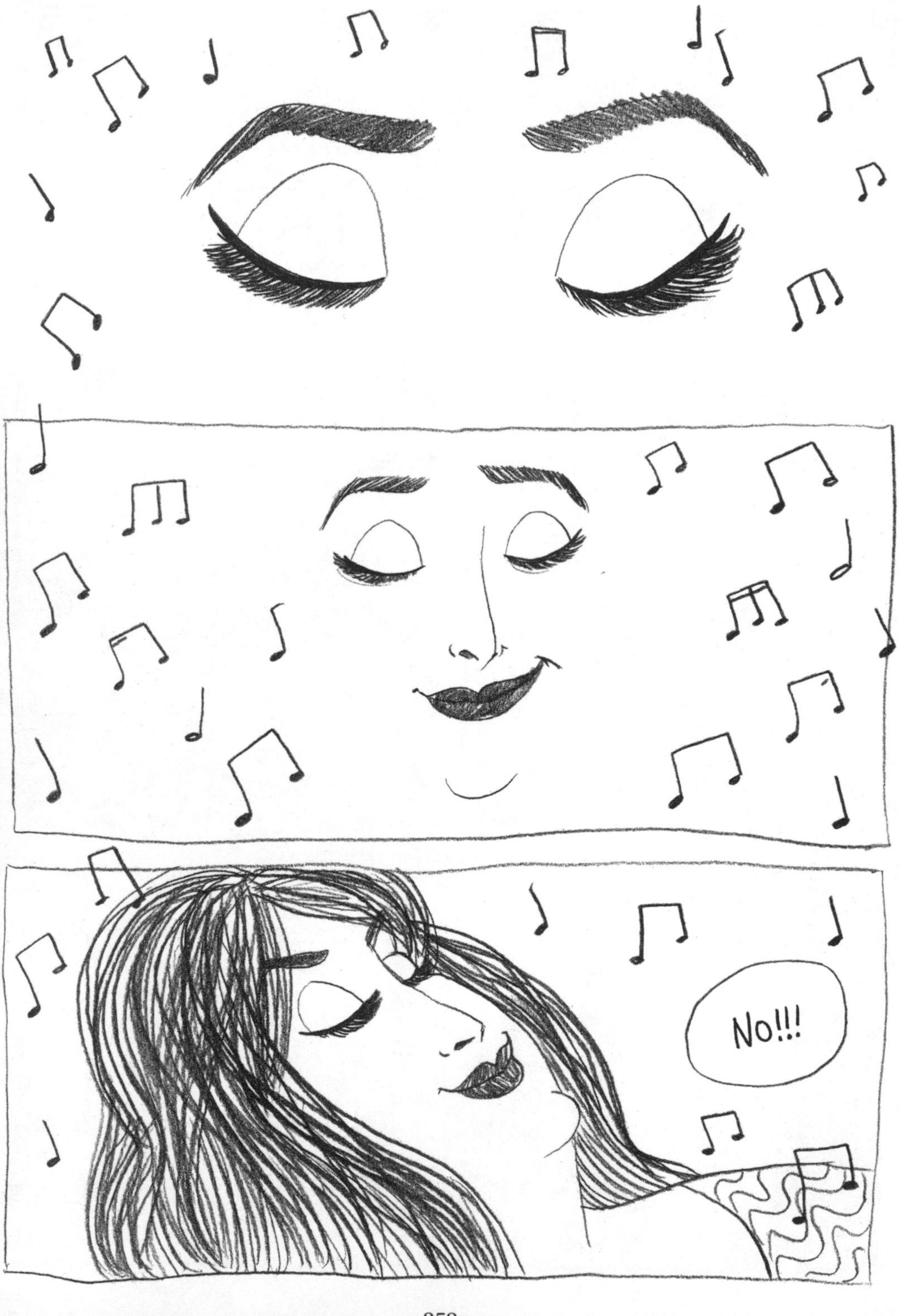
No!!!

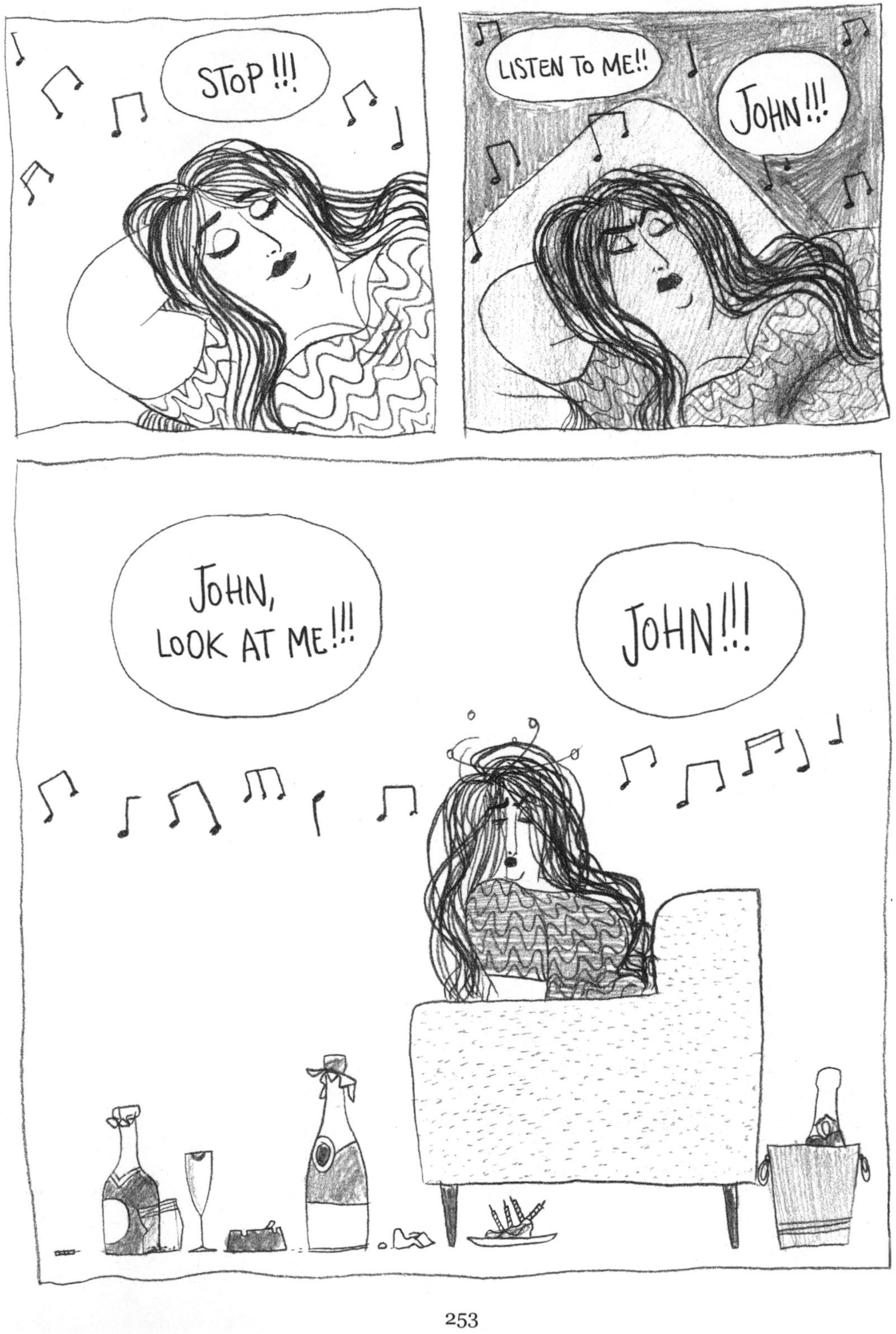
STOP!!!
LISTEN TO ME!!
JOHN!!!
JOHN,
LOOK AT ME!!!
JOHN!!!

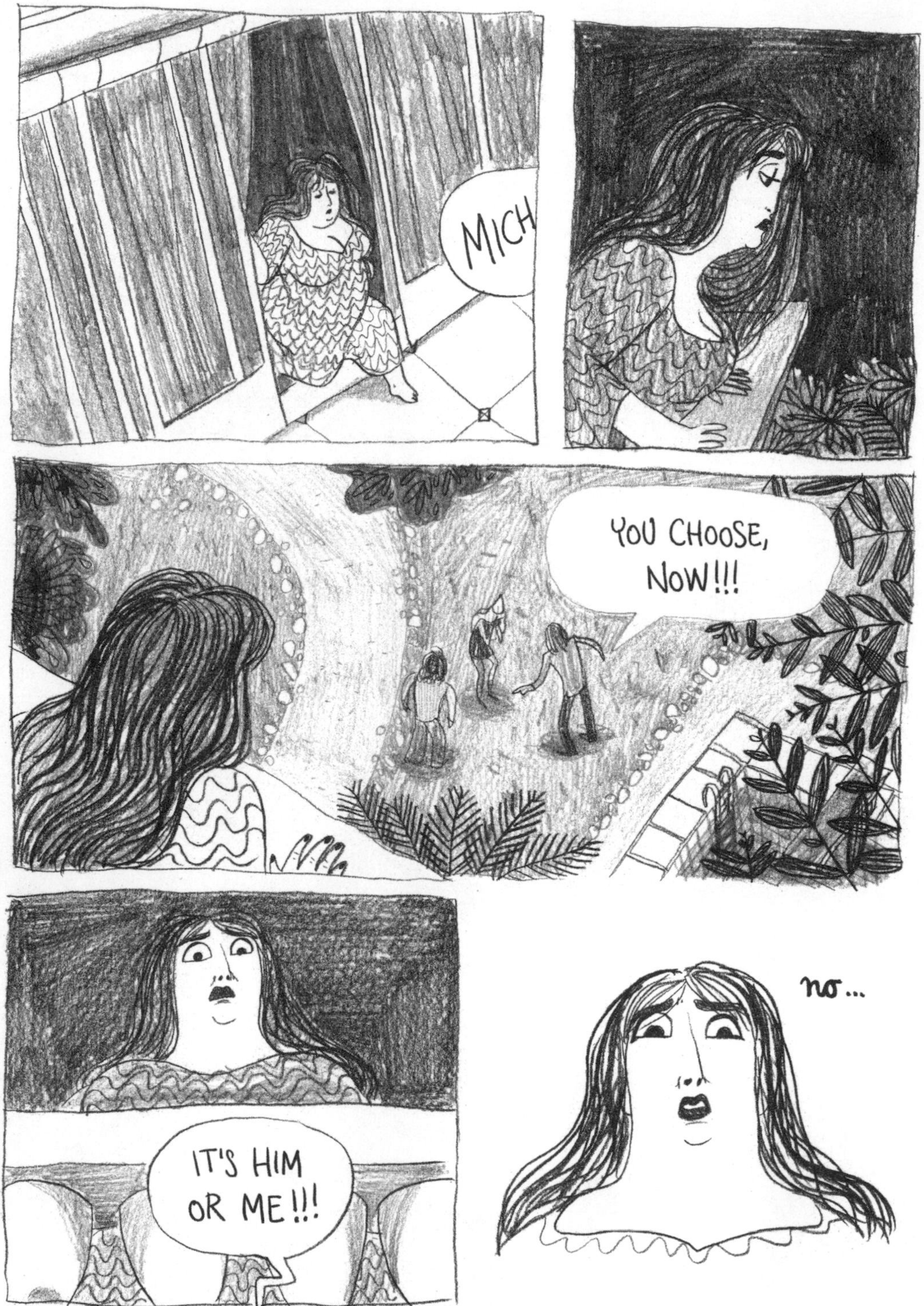
MICH
YOU CHOOSE, NOW!!!
IT'S HIM OR ME!!!
no...

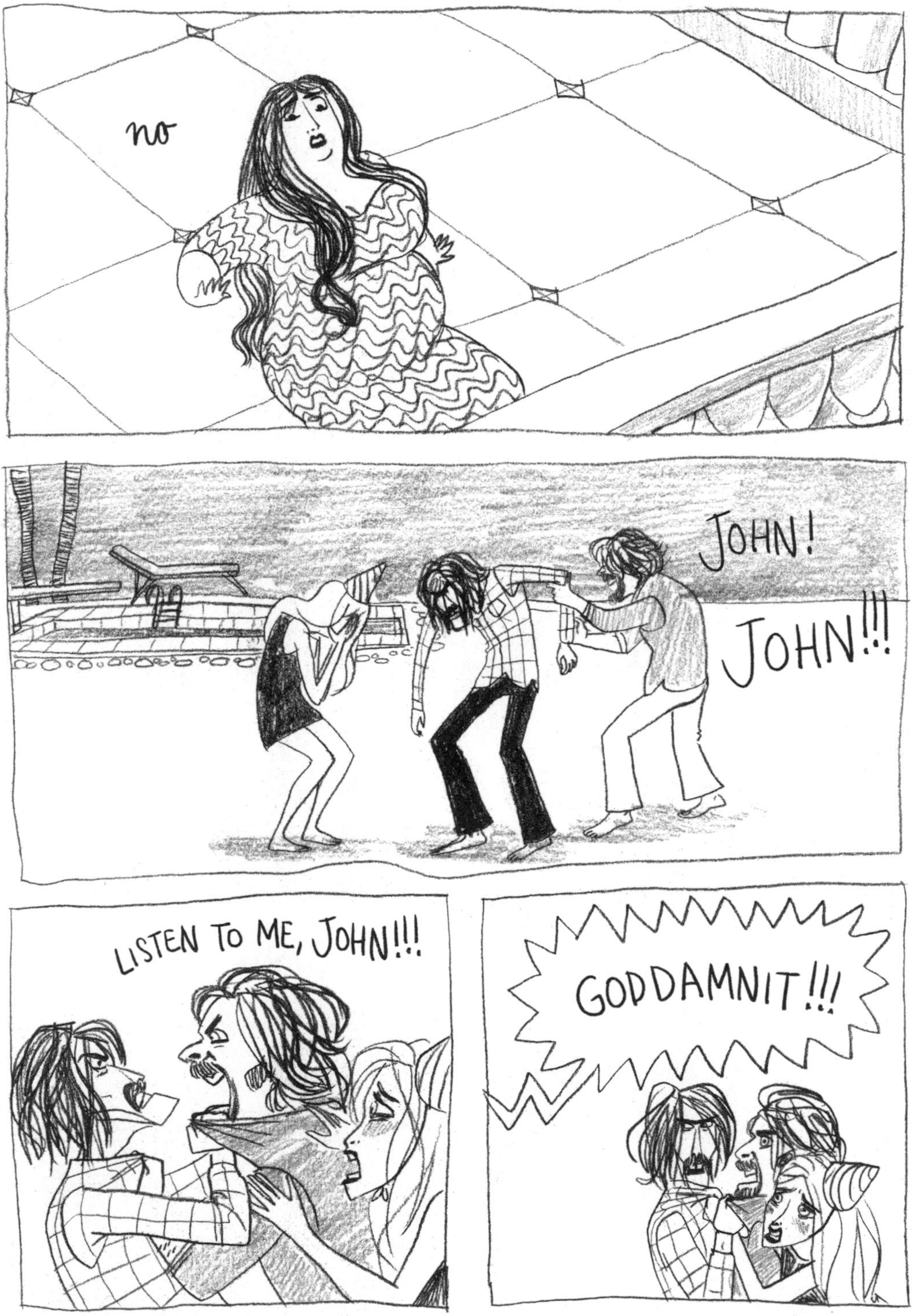
no
JOHN!
JOHN!!!
LISTEN TO ME, JOHN!!!
GODDAMNIT!!!

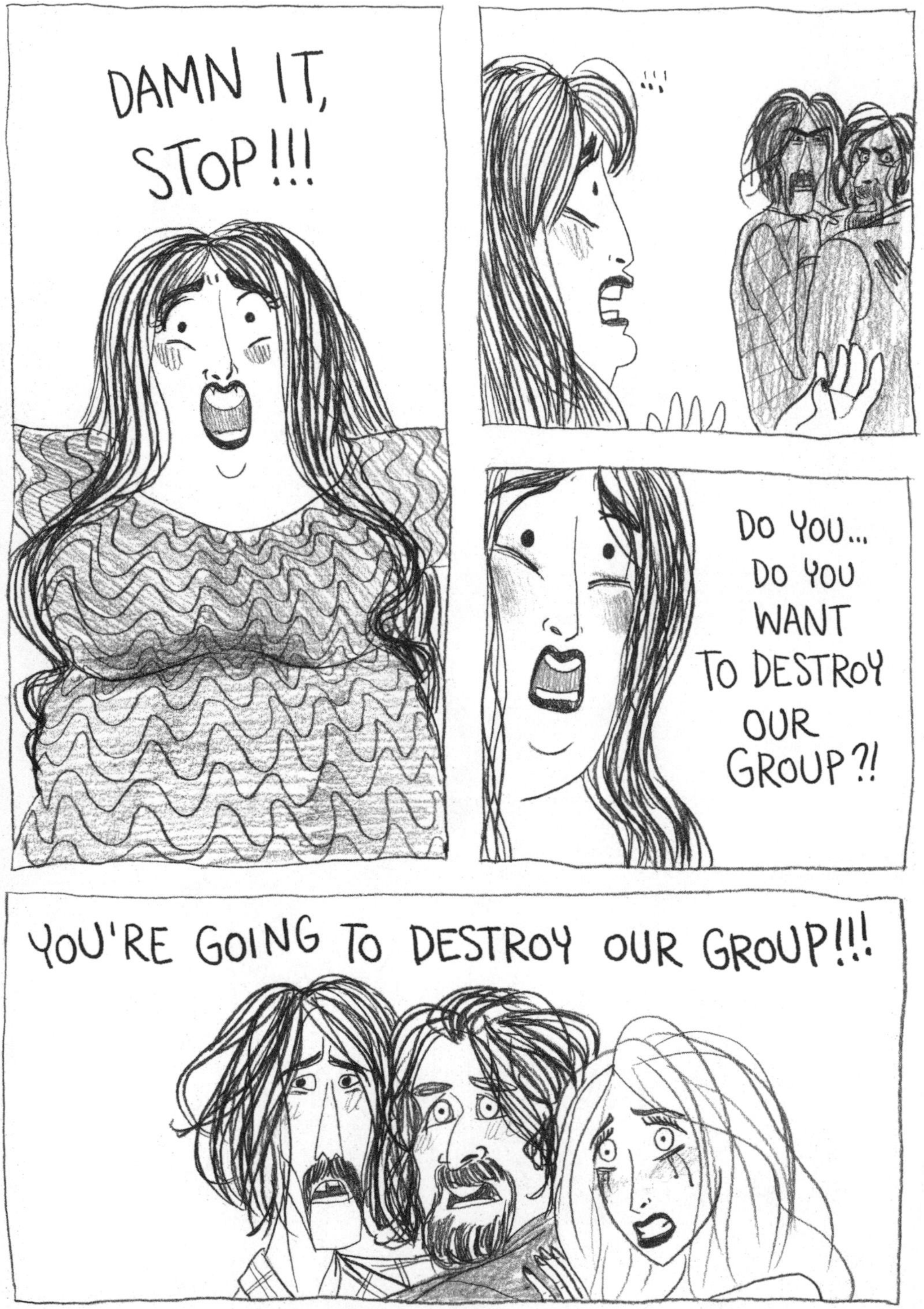
DAMN IT, STOP!!!
DO YOU... DO YOU WANT TO DESTROY OUR GROUP?!
YOU'RE GOING TO DESTROY OUR GROUP!!!

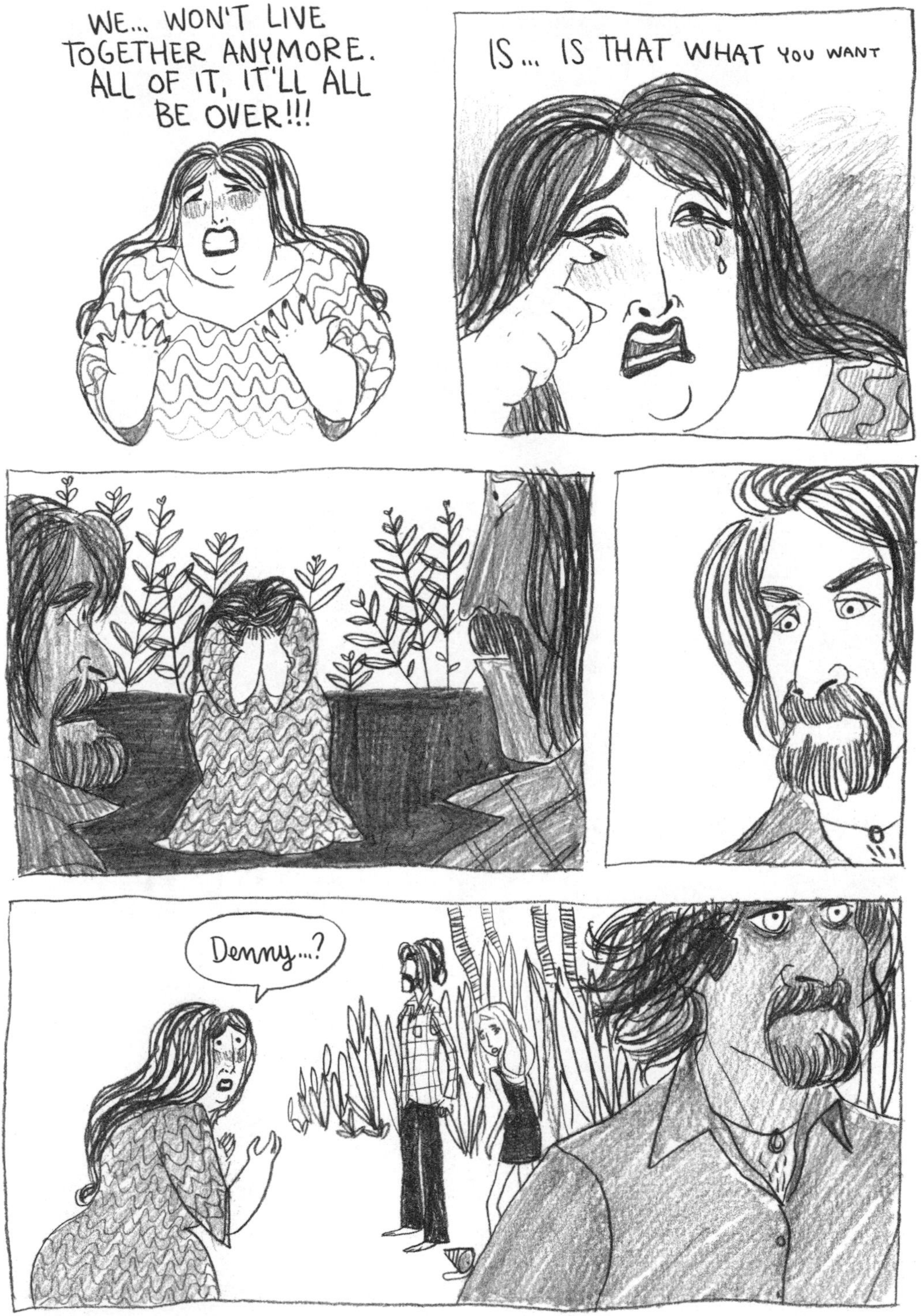
WE... WON'T LIVE TOGETHER ANYMORE. ALL OF IT, IT'LL ALL BE OVER!!!
IS... IS THAT WHAT YOU WANT
Denny...?

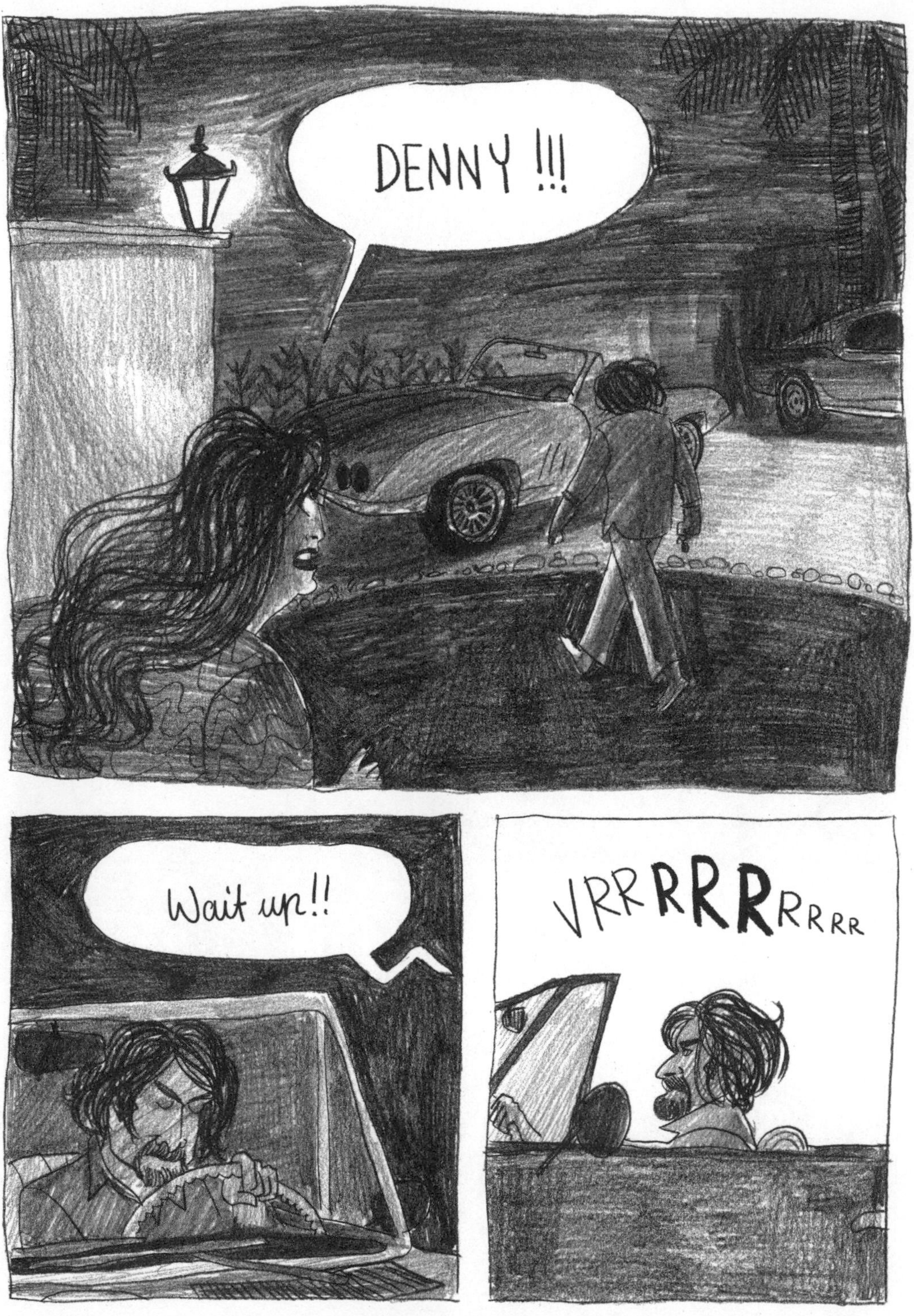
DENNY !!!
Wait up!!
VRRRRRRRRR

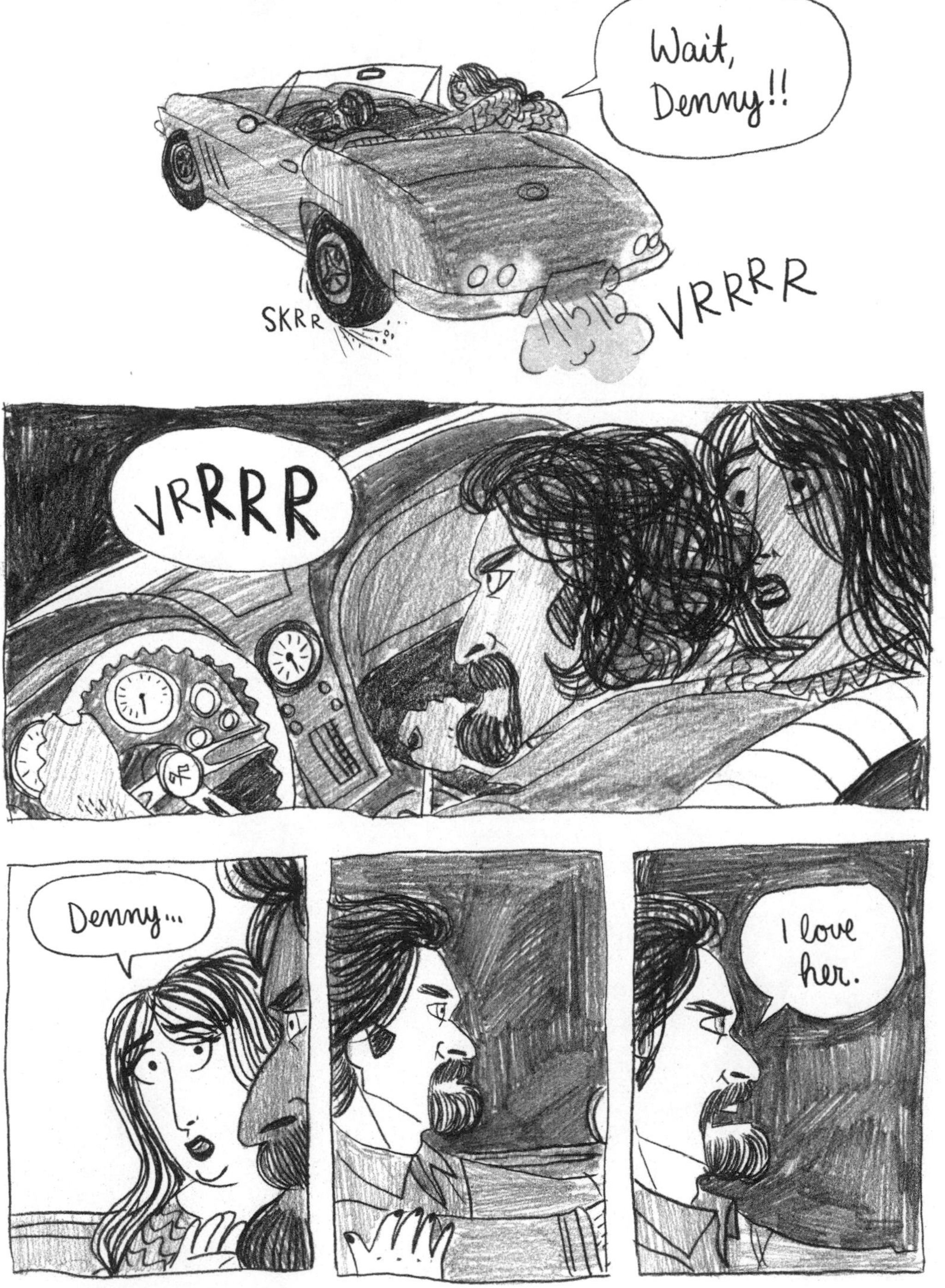
Wait, Denny!!
SKRR
VRRRR
VRRRR
Denny...
I love her.

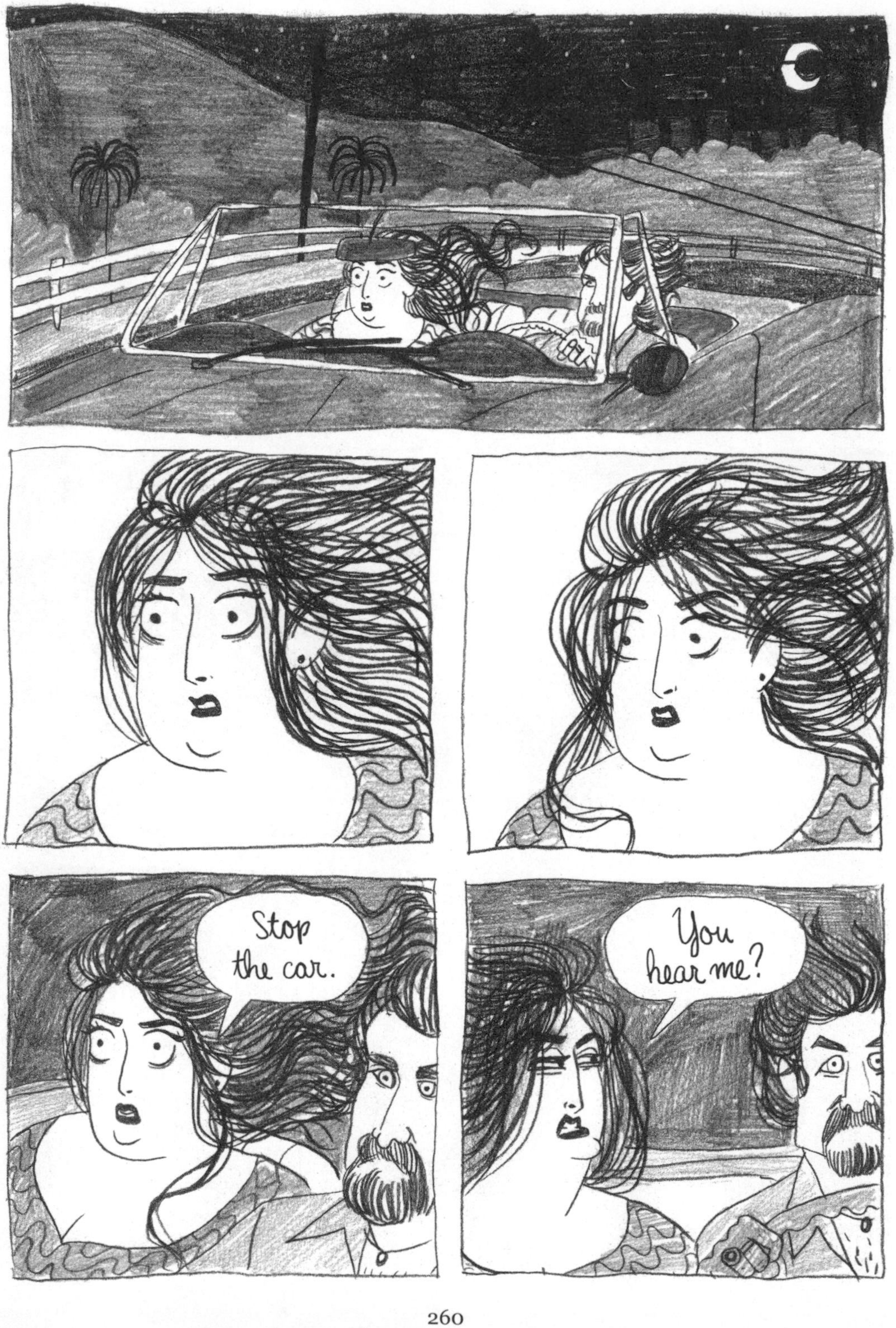
Stop the car.
You hear me?

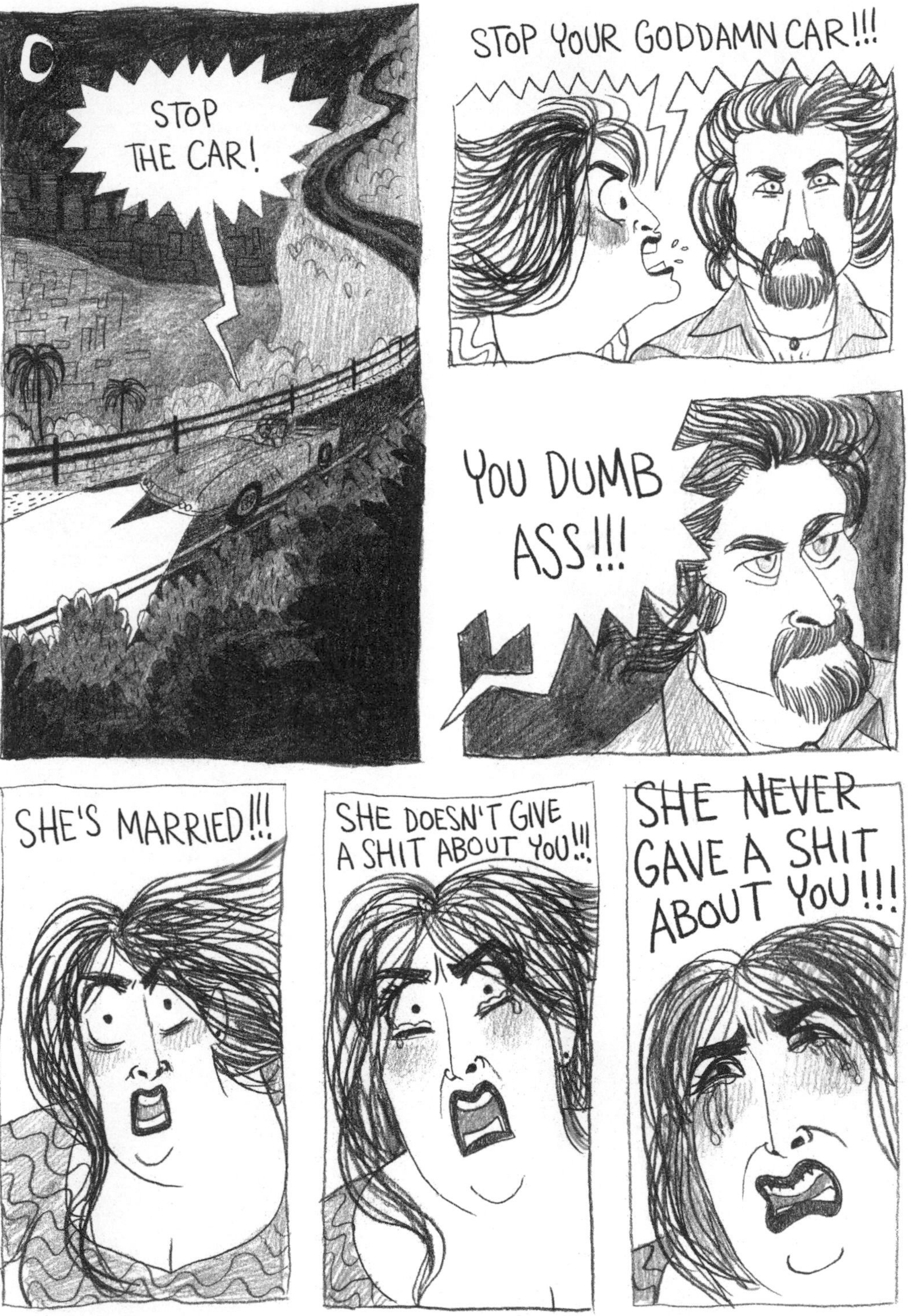
STOP THE CAR!
STOP YOUR GODDAMN CAR!!!
YOU DUMB ASS!!!
SHE'S MARRIED!!!
SHE DOESN'T GIVE A SHIT ABOUT YOU!!!
SHE NEVER GAVE A SHIT ABOUT YOU!!!

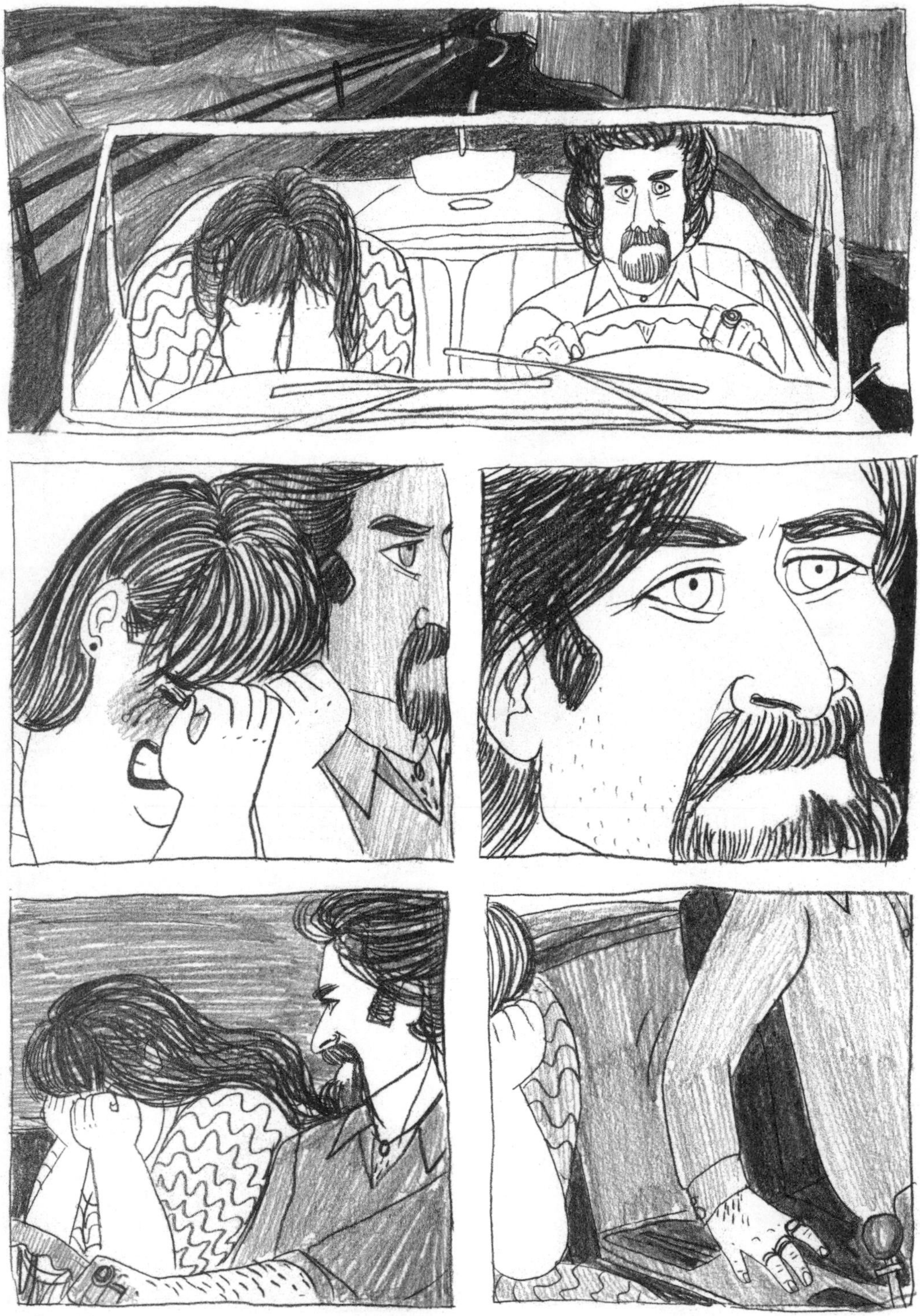

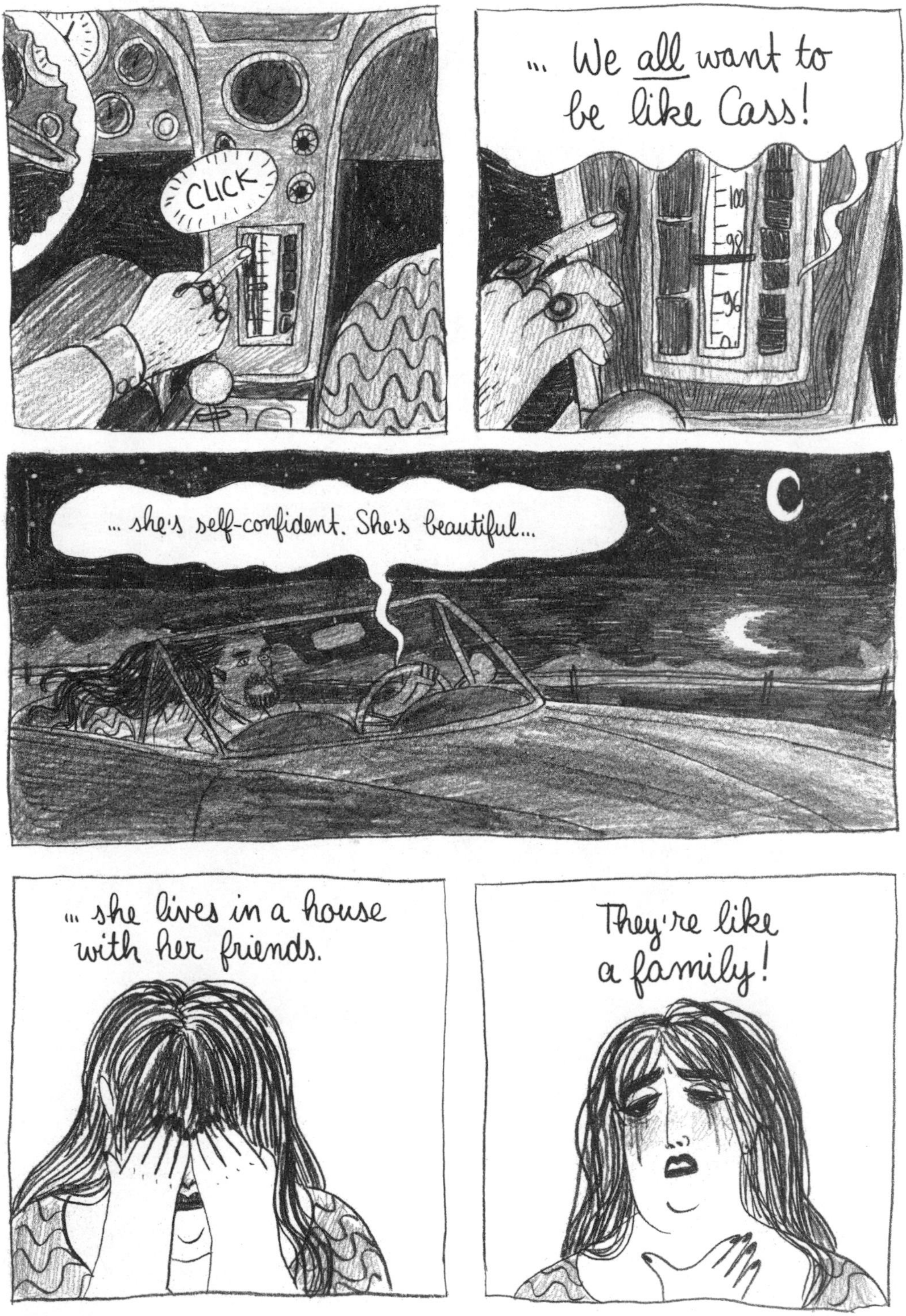
CLICK
... We all want to be like Cass!
... she's self-confident. She's beautiful...
... she lives in a house with her friends.
They're like a family!

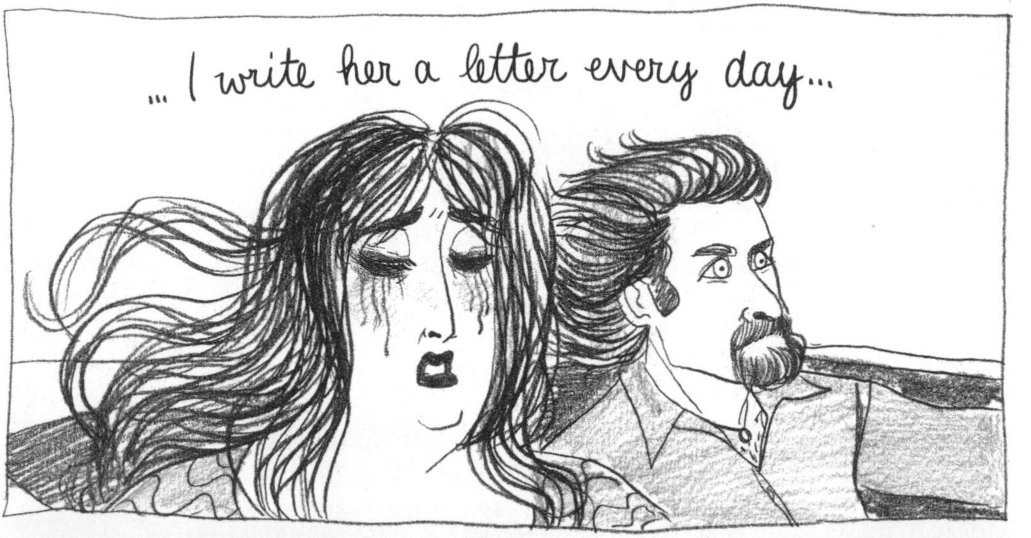
... I write her a letter every day...

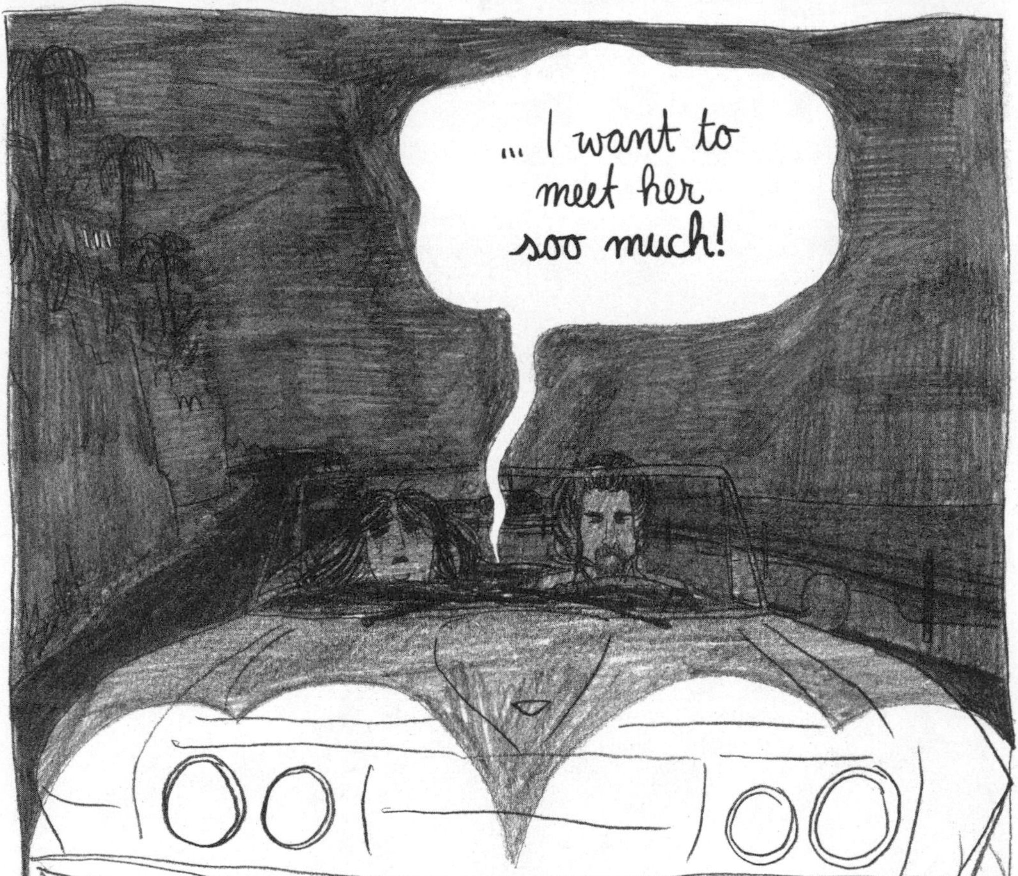
... I want to meet her soo much!

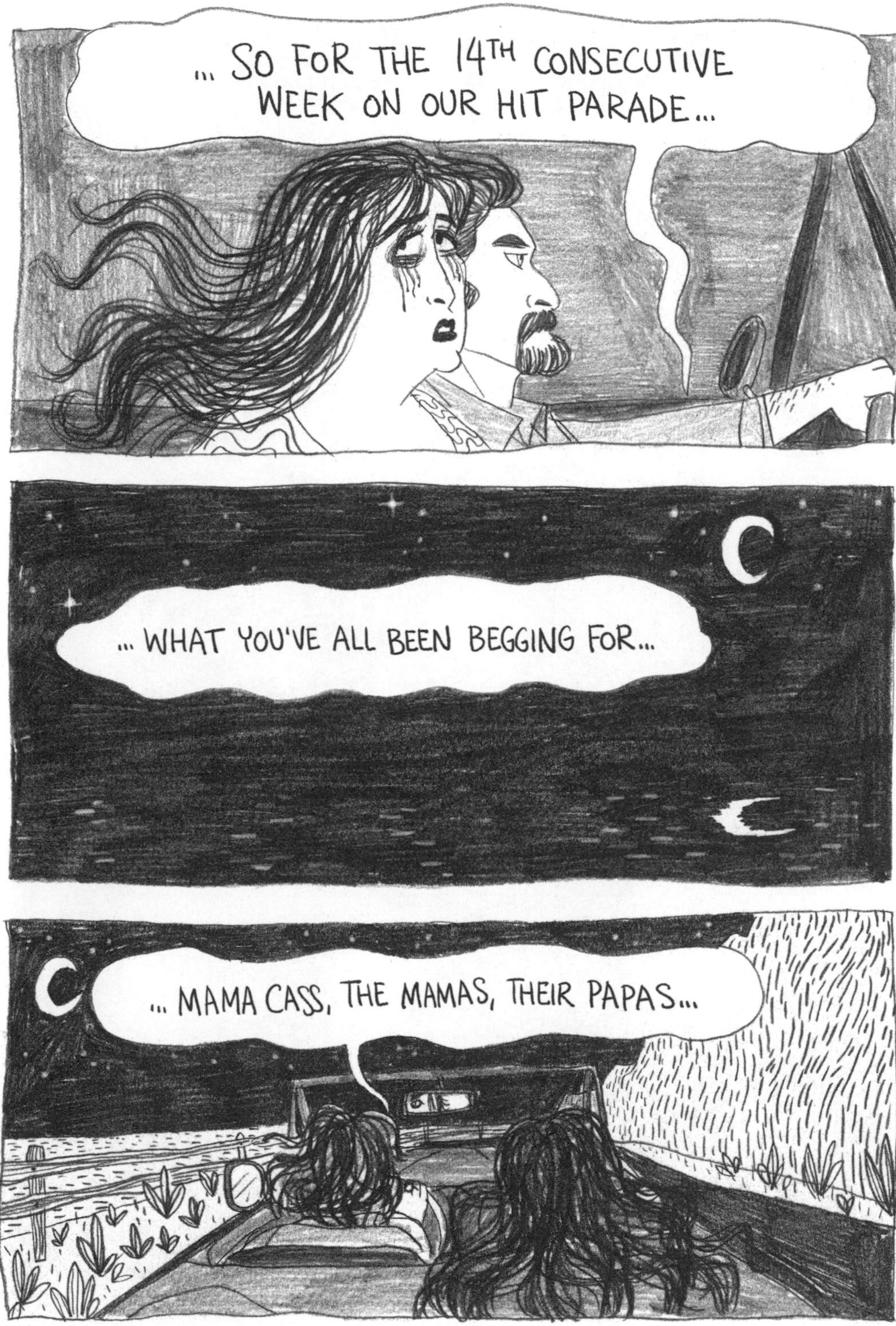
... SO FOR THE 14TH CONSECUTIVE WEEK ON OUR HIT PARADE...
... WHAT YOU'VE ALL BEEN BEGGING FOR...
... MAMA CASS, THE MAMAS, THEIR PAPAS...

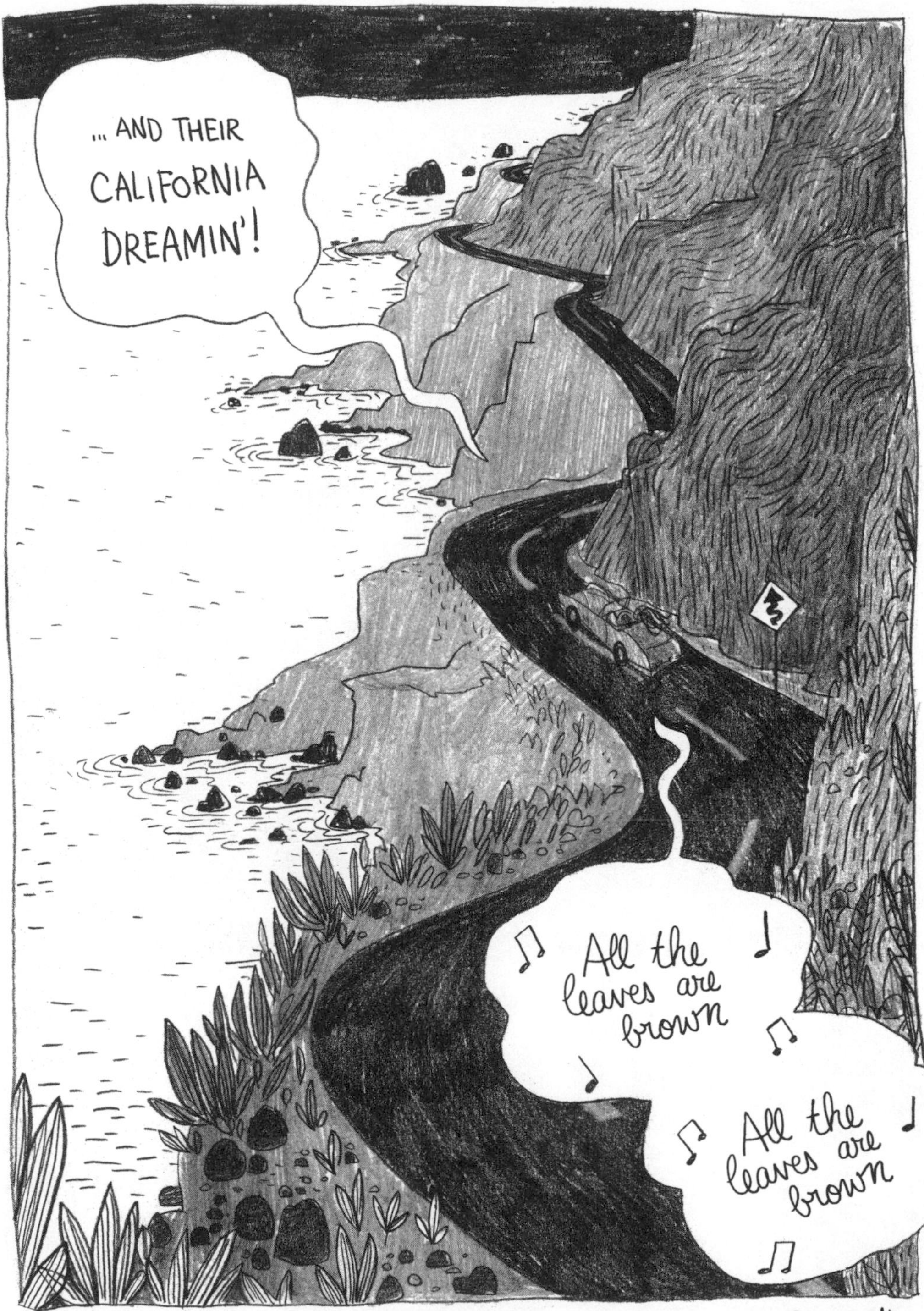
... AND THEIR CALIFORNIA DREAMIN'!
All the leaves are brown
All the leaves are brown

THE END

Main Bibliographical Sources

Fiegel, Eddi. *Dream a Little Dream of Me: The Life of "Mama" Cass Elliot.* London: Sidgwick & Jackson, 2005.

Greenwald, Matthew. *Go Where You Wanna Go: The Oral History of the Mamas and the Papas.* New York: Cooper Square Press, 2002.

Johnson, Jon. *Make Your Own Kind of Music: A Career Retrospective of Cass Elliot.* Los Angeles: Music Archives Press, 1987.

Phillips, Michelle. *California Dreamin'.* New York: Warner Books, 1986.

Playlist

Songs I like and that I recommend for discovering and appreciating the talents of Cass and The Mamas & The Papas.

California Dreamin': The melody and the arrangement are beautiful, but it's truly the second voice that makes all the difference. It's thanks to this effect that the song was such a phenomenal success and that it ranks among the "500 greatest songs of all time" according to *Rolling Stone*.

Do You Wanna Dance?: Released right after the much better known version by the Beach Boys, I think it overwhelmingly surpasses that one. It's probably the song in which the vocal alchemy between Cass and Denny is at its best: we really hear them answering each other, and the result is magnificent.

I Saw Her Again Last Night: The song where John had Denny sing, "I saw her again last night, and you know that I shouldn't," as if to atone for his mistake, during the period when Michelle had been completely excluded from the group in retaliation. (She subsequently returned.)

Dream a Little Dream of Me: This is the great classic of Cass's solo songs. A standard from the 1930s, she interprets it with a great deal of melancholy and gentleness. The song was released in 1968, at a point when the group was on the verge of exploding. So Dunhill Records decided to bet everything on Cass's popularity and to credit the record to "Mama Cass with the Mamas & the Papas" (to John Phillips's not-so-great joy).

Dedicated to the One I Love: The first song in which it was decided that Michelle would sing the main melody (which lets her voice be heard for once), even if Cass's chorus came in as reinforcement soon enough.

Dancing in the Streets: Yet another song that's been covered about a thousand times, from Bowie to the Kinks, but the version by The Mamas & The Papas, interpreted by Cass, really makes you want to dance in the street. At the end of the song, Cass and Denny talk to each other in the secret language they'd invented together.

Creeque Alley: The title refers to the street where The Mamas & The Papas lived in the Virgin Islands. The song is the short story of the group's journey: Cass dropping out of college, the trip to New York, The Mugwumps, their setbacks in the Islands, "California Dreamin'," and even Cass falling in love at first sight with Denny. And then, of course, the delightful phrase that's repeated at the end of each verse: "And no one's getting fat, except Mama Cass."

Midnight Voyage: For me, this is the song that offers the best insight into Cass's simultaneously strong but vulnerable voice, with all its nuances. She broke off at one point when she was reproached for starting in on the choruses too late, to which she replied that she was right, before asking mischievously, "You like that, Lou?" (to Lou Adler). And the song is worth listening to through to the end: It's the whole last part, which she sings with the most emotion, that gives me a lump in my throat every time.

Merci!

Once again, everyone at Gallimard:
Hedwige, Muriel, Nicolas, Olivier, Sandrine, and Thierry.

And Mark at First Second.

The first readers of this story, for their advice and encouragement:
Kader Aoun, Thierry Laroche, Christophe Ledannois, and Véronique Ovaldé.

Anne-Solange and Virginie for their invaluable authors' residence in Normandy.

Jérôme, who helped me discover Florence Foster Jenkins.

Oldelaf, who assured me that we don't say "la folk" in French,
but that in fact one says "le folk."

My family, my friends, and my studio for their support.

And more than anyone, even more than usual, thanks to Fred.

The facts related in this graphic novel come in great part from Eddi Fiegel's
book *Dream a Little Dream of Me: The Life of "Mama" Cass Elliot*, published
by Sidgwick & Jackson in 2005. The result of long investigation work, it is a
complete, meticulous, and captivating biography of Ellen Cohen.